BOOMS
AND BUSTS

An Encyclopedia of Economic History
from Tulipmania of the 1630s to the
Global Financial Crisis of the 21st Century

Volume 3

James Ciment, Editor

SHARPE REFERENCE
an imprint of M.E. Sharpe, Inc.

SHARPE REFERENCE

Sharpe Reference is an imprint of M.E. Sharpe, Inc.

M.E. Sharpe, Inc.
80 Business Park Drive
Armonk, NY 10504

Cover photos (background; left to right) provided by Getty Images and the following:
Mario Tama; Popperfoto; Yoshikazu Tsuno/AFP; Kean Collection/Hulton Archive; Melanie Einzig.

Library of Congress Cataloging-in-Publication Data

Booms and busts : an encyclopedia of economic history from Tulipmania of the 1630s to the
global financial crisis of the 21st century / James Ciment, editor.
   v. ; cm.
Includes bibliographical references and index.
ISBN 978-0-7656-8224-6 (hardcover : alk. paper)
1. Financial crises—Encyclopedias. 2. Finance—Encyclopedias. I. Ciment, James.

HB3722.B67 2010
330.03—dc22
   2010021272

Printed and bound in the United States

The paper used in this publication meets the minimum requirements of
American National Standard for Information Sciences—Permanence of
Paper for Printed Library Materials,
ANSI Z 39.48.1984.

CW (c) 10 9 8 7 6 5 4 3 2 1

Publisher: Myron E. Sharpe
Vice President and Director of New Product Development: Donna Sanzone
Vice President and Production Director: Carmen Chetti
Executive Development Editor: Jeff Hacker
Project Manager: Angela Piliouras
Program Coordinator: Cathleen Prisco
Assistant Editor: Alison Morretta
Text Design and Cover Design: Jesse Sanchez
Typesetter: Nancy Connick

Contents

BOOMS
AND BUSTS

Volume 3

Real Business Cycle Models

Real business cycle models, developed by Nobel Prize–winning economists Finn Kydland and Edward Prescott beginning in the early 1980s, suggest that fluctuations in economic activity are caused by changes in technology. These models focus on supply: as firms become more or less productive, economic activity rises or falls. The models are an outgrowth of the new classical business cycle models first developed by Robert E. Lucas, Jr., as an alternative to Keynesian models.

There are three important features in a real business cycle model. First, the term "business cycle" is redefined as a set of statistical regularities and not as the rise and fall of gross domestic product (GDP). Second, real business cycle models are equilibrium market clearing models. Both of these two features are common with the earlier new classical models. The distinguishing feature of real business cycle models is that fluctuations are caused by technological change. Since their inception, real business cycle models have become influential in professional macroeconomic research, although they have had limited impact on forecasting and policy discussions.

Defining the Cycle

Most people think of the business cycle as a recurring series of booms and recessions. In this view, the most important things to understand about the cycle are what causes a recession to begin and how to prevent the recession from lasting too long or becoming too deep. Recessions are typically viewed as a negative reaction of the economy to an adverse shock.

In real business cycle models, the focus changes away from the ups and downs of GDP movements. In the mid-1970s, Lucas argued that it was better to think about the business cycle as a set of empirical regularities. For example, Lucas identified the important features of the cycle as including regularities such as the fact that production of durable goods fluctuates more than production of nondurable goods, and both prices and short-term interest rates fluctuate in the same direction as output, but long-term interest rates do not fluctuate as much. The goal of a real business cycle model, like the goal of the new classical models that preceded them, is to explain these regularities. In particular, real business cycle models try to replicate the real world's changes in GDP, and the relationship between consumption, investment, and GDP, and other empirical regularities, such as changes in the number of hours worked. As a result, there is very little emphasis in research using real business cycle models on identifying what *caused* particular historical episodes to evolve the way they did. Instead, real business cycle models ask whether the model matches historical data.

Equilibrium Market Clearing Models

The second important feature of real business cycle models is that the economy is always in its long-run equilibrium. By contrast, in Keynesian business cycle theory the economy could be above or below the long-term potential, full-employment GDP. The role of Keynesian business cycle theory was to study GDP's fluctuations around this potential.

Real business cycle models seek to abolish the distinction between the long-run growth model and the business cycle model. Its proponents argue that there is no need for two separate theories to explain the features of the macroeconomy. The business cycle is perfectly well explained by simply assuming the economy is always on its long-run growth path. While there are no deviations from this path, the path itself is changing, sometimes rising faster than other times.

The importance of this feature shows up clearly in discussions about the labor market. Keynesian business cycle theory posited a natural level of unemployment. A recession is a time in which unemployment rises above its natural rate and large numbers of people are "involuntarily unemployed." Such people would like to work at the going wage rate, but are unable to find jobs at that wage. Yet, despite this large number of people who would like to work, the wage rate does not immediately fall to bring the economy back into equilibrium.

The new classical models in general, and real business cycle models in particular, abolish this notion of involuntary unemployment. In these models, the labor market is always in equilibrium; if there are people who do not have a job, it is because they have chosen not to work at the wage

rates that are offered to them. It is, after all, optimal not to take the first job available if you believe that by searching slightly longer you can find a job paying a higher wage rate. Employment will thus rise and fall over time, but at any given time, everyone who wants to work at the current wage will have a job, and anyone who does not want to work for that wage will not have a job. There will be fluctuations in this employment rate over time, but there is no reason to classify people who have chosen not to work as being either voluntarily or involuntarily unemployed.

Cycles: Real, Not Monetary

The feature that distinguishes the real business cycle models from the earlier new classical models is the cause of GDP fluctuations. Lucas's earlier models were monetary models in which changes in the money supply caused the cycle. *Real* business cycles are thus distinguished from *monetary* business cycles; the driving forces are real things and not nominal things.

Real business cycle models argue that fluctuations in the rate of technology innovation are the cause of business cycle phenomena. In effect, real business cycle models ask us to imagine that instead of technology growing at a steady 3 percent per year, there is some fluctuation in that growth rate. That fluctuating growth rate is sufficient to explain the fluctuations in the economy.

We can get a sense of how a real business cycle model works by thinking through an example. In the absence of a change in technology, workers must choose how much to work. Because they value not only their consumption but also their leisure time, working more results in more consumption but less leisure. Workers in the model optimally choose how much to work based on their preferences for consumption and leisure—a worker who enjoys leisure a great deal will work fewer hours (sacrificing consumption) than a worker who greatly enjoys consumption. If nothing changes, then the workers will settle down to a fixed work schedule.

If technological growth suddenly increases this year, what will happen? First, and most obviously, every worker will become more productive this year, and output will increase even if there is no change in labor input. However, labor input will not remain constant. Each worker is now faced with an additional trade-off: the worker can choose either to work a constant number of hours this month and next month, or, if paid by the piece, take advantage of the higher productivity this month by working more now and less next month when productivity will not be as high.

The other side of the same story occurs when there is a negative shock to technology. In this month a worker is less productive, and so the worker will optimally choose to work fewer hours, enjoying more leisure, and return to work when productivity rises again. This idea that workers are enjoying leisure when there is a negative technological shock strikes many as an oddity. Part of the oddity is resolved when we realize that leisure time can also be productive. Consider, for example, a worker faced with three options: working for pay at the going wage rate, working at home on projects around the house, or enjoying leisure. The pay rate for wage employment will vary over time as technology changes; the productivity of work at home is constant. So, at times when there is a negative technology shock, it becomes optimal for a worker to forgo the explicit wages of a paying job and instead engage in productive activity at home. Again, when the rate of technology improves, the worker will optimally choose to leave the productive activities at home and return to the labor force.

The effects of changing productivity are amplified in more complex real business cycle models by increasing the set of decisions facing people in the model. For example, if a positive shock to technology this year indicates a high probability that technology will also be relatively high next year, then firms will increase investment in order to have a larger productive capacity next year when productivity will still be unusually high. This investment effect will amplify the effect of both positive and negative changes in productivity. But, in the end, the root cause of economic fluctuations is exactly the same as the root cause of economic growth. Over time, economies become more productive, causing growth, but since the rate of productivity growth is not constant, in some years the economy will grow faster than in others.

Implications for Government Policy

Perhaps the most controversial conclusion from real business cycle theory is the implication for government policy. Traditional Keynesian models of the cycle have a large scope for governments to engage in activities to cure the problems of the cycle. In a real business cycle model, however, policy makers have no such role to play because there is nothing to cure.

Consider a situation conventionally labeled a "recession." In the Keynesian cycle, recessions are times when the economy is producing below its capacity and thus the government can do things to return the economy to potential output. But, in real business cycle theory, the economy is *always* producing at potential GDP. There is never a gap between the current state of the economy and some imaginary potential state of the economy. Given the level of productivity at the time, people in the economy are always optimally choosing how much to work, produce, and consume. Since the people in the economy have already made optimal choices, there is no scope for the government to improve upon the choices that people freely made.

This does not mean, however, that governments have no effect on the economy in a real business cycle model. Government policies have a large effect on economic performance though their effect on productivity. For example, a tax policy that provides disincentives to work will lower GDP. Governments should enact legislation that enhances rather than limits the growth in productivity. It is important to note, however, that this important role for government has absolutely nothing to do with the business cycle as conventionally defined. A tax policy with negative effects on productivity has the same undesirable effect when productivity levels are high as it does when they are low; thus an argument to alter such a tax policy has the same force no matter what the current state of the economy happens to be. The same holds true for government policies that encourage monopolies: governments should encourage competition and free trade to prevent the inherent inefficiencies of monopolies from having a detrimental effect on economic development.

As an example of the direction that real business cycle theory takes, consider the Great Depression. Output fell by almost one-third in the first few years of the Depression, and it took over a decade for output to return to the level of 1929. The story that emerges in real business cycle theory is that there was a dramatic fall in productivity starting around 1929, and then the amount of labor stayed low throughout the mid-1930s, making the recovery very slow. Seen in this light, there are two separate problems to investigate. Why did productivity fall? This question is still unanswered. Why did the amount of labor stay low? The New Deal programs effectively allowed firms and labor unions to restrict competition, with the result that firms and unions together agreed to hire fewer workers and pay them higher wages. In effect, the New Deal lowered the productive capacity of the country, resulting in a smaller labor force and thus lower levels of output. Note that in this explanation the economy is always at the best possible point, given the state of productivity. The government could have done nothing to offset a large drop in productivity in the early 1930s, but the New Deal policies were in effect a second, permanent negative shock to productivity.

Impact

Since its origin in 1982, real business cycle theory has been one of several competing theoretical frameworks to study the macroeconomy. Its impact was clearly demonstrated when Kydland and Prescott won the Nobel Prize in 2004. Much macroeconomic research since the early 1980s has been a response to the original Kydland and Prescott models, with the profession quite divided over whether the models are a useful way of thinking about the economy or fundamentally flawed. Critics have pointed to problems with many aspects of the model, from the definition of the cycle to the equilibrium market clearing assumption to the importance of technology and productivity shocks.

While the work has been quite important in the professional literature, it has had very little influence outside the confines of theoretical research. The major forecasting models still rely on fundamentally Keynesian explanations of the macroeconomy. And public debate on government policy in the midst of a recession is still framed in the same terms debates were in the 1960s and 1970s.

James E. Hartley

See also: Neoclassical Theories and Models; Technological Innovation.

Further Reading

Hartley, James E., Kevin D. Hoover, and Kevin D. Salyer, eds. *Real Business Cycles: A Reader.* London: Routledge, 1998.

Kehoe, Timothy J., and Edward C. Prescott, eds. *Great Depressions of the Twentieth Century.* Minneapolis, MN: Federal Reserve Bank of Minneapolis, 2007.

Miller, Preston J., ed. *The Rational Expectations Revolution: Readings from the Front Line.* Cambridge, MA: The MIT Press, 1994.

Parente, Stephen L., and Edward C. Prescott. *Barriers to Riches.* Cambridge, MA: The MIT Press, 2000.

Prescott, Edward C. "The Transformation of Macroeconomic Policy and Research." Nobel Prize lecture held 2004. Available at http://nobelprize.org/nobel_prizes/economics/laureates/2004/prescott-lecture.html. Accessed March 2010.

Snowden, Brian, and Howard R. Vane. *Modern Macroeconomics: Its Origins, Developments and Current State.* Cheltenham, UK: Edward Elgar, 2005.

Real-Estate Speculation

Real-estate appraisal, also called property valuation, is the estimation of the market value of a parcel of land, the buildings on it, and any other improvements. The market value is the price at which rational investors might (or do) buy or sell the property at a particular time. A rational buyer or seller is presumed to have access to all available information on the property and to be capable of comparing market alternatives. By basing their decision on full knowledge of the property, the marketplace, and broader economic conditions, buyers and sellers are assumed to make—or be able to make—a mutually acceptable deal for a fair price. That determines market value.

Speculation, in general, is a decision to buy, sell, or hold a given real or financial asset or commodity, such as real estate, stocks, bonds, and so forth, based on an assumption that the future value of the asset will increase and a profit will be made.

Speculation is based on the expectation of investors regarding the risk of losses versus the potential gains of a prospective investment. In other words, the speculator weighs the potential monetary penalty, and the odds of incurring it against the potential rewards, and the odds of realizing them. The decision is an educated guess based on perceived risk and necessarily incomplete information about the future (one can never know for certain what will happen next week, next month, or next year).

Risk and Reward

Real-estate speculation is based on the predicted value of a piece of property. The speculator buys, sells, or holds property consistent with a basic assumption about the future. That is, the speculator estimates the expected value of the property and compares it with the expect values of other real and financial assets, including the following types of financial instruments:

1. Securities representing the ownership of a transferable and negotiable monetary value. Securities take the form of debt securities (bonds, banknotes, and debentures, i.e., loan agreements) or equity securities (common stocks and equity shares of stocks, i.e., partnerships in corporations and common stocks);

2. Deposits, or the money put into a bank account;

3. Derivatives, or agreements such as forwards, futures, options, and swaps and securitizations. A forward is a written agreement or contract to buy or sell an asset on a particular date in the future at a price determined today. The value of a derivative contract originates from the worth of an underlying asset on which the contract is based. The underlying asset may be bonds, foreign exchange, commodities, stocks, or a pool of mortgages;

4. Goods or fungible commodities (such as wheat and currency);

5. Collectibles (precious items for particular collectors, such as art and antiques).

The rationale of real or financial speculations is not to use an asset for individual direct consumption or to make an income from it through rental, augmented dividend, or interest, but to profit from the variations in buying and selling prices. This is the fundamental distinction between speculation and investment. Investments are made to use them personally (or for the direct utilization of the firm if the buyer is a corporation) or to generate individual earnings (whether for a person or corporation). On the other hand, speculations are made to generate profits—usually in the short term and at a good profit margin—by realizing the difference between the price paid to obtain an asset (cost) and the sales price (revenue). Time is an important factor, as the speculator typically incurs special costs and higher risk in the expectation of a quick, hefty profit.

Real-estate speculators look for properties to buy and sell relatively quickly at a profit. In order to be successful, they must identify and take advantage of a disparity between the price the seller is asking and the price a prospective buyer will be willing to pay. This may not simply be a case of the seller misjudging the market value of a property. A real-estate developer, for example, might buy a property for a low price in a substandard area of a city knowing that the municipal government plans to redevelop the neighborhood. In a few years time, the developer could then sell the property at many times the price paid for it and realize a hefty profit.

In this respect, speculation can be compared to arbitrage in the financial world. In both cases, profits are earned by taking advantage of price differentials in the marketplace. At the same time, there are major dissimilarities between these two concepts. Arbitrage refers to profiteering from price differences in multiple markets, rather than buying an asset in one market and selling it in the same market for a higher price at a later date. In arbitrage, buying and selling occur almost simultaneously across markets and thus the arbitrageur makes a riskless profit by buying in the low-price market and reselling (instantaneously) in a high-price market. Thus, arbitrage is viable only with securities and financial assets, which—unlike real estate—can be traded electronically.

Basic on these characteristics, successful real-estate speculators generally adhere to the following criteria:

1. Buy a property to hold for a period of time—albeit brief for the real-estate market—and sell it later at a higher price;
2. Do not expect to earn a safe, steady income from speculation, as a long-term investor does;
3. Good timing is critical; buying and selling should not happen simultaneously, as in the case of arbitrage, but should occur at the lows and highs, respectively, of the marketplace;
4. The forecast of future prices should be fully informed, based on as much information as possible about the property, its perceived value in the marketplace, and the broader economic climate;
5. The reason for buying a property is purely to make a profit from fluctuations in (or misjudgments of) market value.

Market expectations play a critical role in real-estate speculation in a larger sense as well, beyond the future valuation of a particular property. Market expectations also help determine broader property cycles—recurring highs and lows in buying and selling. Such oscillations take the form of increases and declines in prices, vacancies, rentals, supply, and demand. For some speculators, the ongoing cycles of the marketplace provide a valuable tool for predicting future trends—a method called "adaptive expectation." In general, cycles in the commercial world affect the entire business cycle of a nation. The nature and direction of the commercial cycle also have a direct influence on property cycles.

Speculator Expectations

How people form expectations about market value is therefore important in understanding real-estate speculation. The academic literature describes several models. In the myopic (short-sighted) model, speculators lose clear vision in formulating their expectations, have no reliable sense of what the future may bring, and succeed or fail for reasons beyond their own doing. At the other end of the spectrum, the perfect-foresight model assumes that people have a clear, rational view of the future and make faultless predictions when it comes to their investments. The rational-expectations model assumes that people have access to and use all information necessary to make an optimal decision for the future. (Accordingly, the rational-expectations model is less optimistic than the perfect-foresight model.) Finally, according to the adaptive-expectations model, people look back to past events and patterns to predict upcoming events, as in the prediction on inflation based on historical data.

Speculative bubbles are caused in part by price expectations based on past increases, as investors tend to speculate that high prices will continue. In the real-estate market, such speculation often causes cycles without any actual changes or new trends in demand and supply. Thus, people's expectations—based on whatever criteria, with or without a rational basis, with whatever the financial outcome—may be a cause or symptom of property cycles.

Ulku Yuksel

See also: Florida Real-Estate Boom (1920s); Housing; Housing Booms and Busts; Mortgage-Backed Securities; Mortgage Lending Standards; Mortgage Markets and Mortgage Rates; Mortgage, Subprime; Recession and Financial Crisis (2007–).

Further Reading

Hardouvelis, G.A. "Evidence on Stock Market Speculative Bubbles: Japan, the United States, and Great Britain." *Federal Reserve Bank of New York Quarterly Review* 13:2 (1988): 4–16.

Kim, K.H., and S.H. Suh. "Speculation and House Price Bubbles in the Korean and Japanese Real Estate Markets." *Journal of Real Estate Finance and Economics* 6:1 (1993): 73–88.

Malpezzi, S., and S.M. Wachter. "The Role of Speculation in Real Estate Cycles." *Journal of Real Estate Literature* 13:2 (2005): 143–166.

Renaud, B. "The 1985–1994 Global Real Estate Cycle: An Overview." *Journal of Real Estate Literature* 5:1 (1997): 13–44.

Wheaton, W.C. "Real Estate 'Cycles': Some Fundamentals." *Real Estate Economics* 27:2 (1999): 209–230.

Recession and Financial Crisis (2007–)

The international financial meltdown that began in 2007 is considered one of the worst global economic crises since the Great Depression of the 1930s—if not the very worst. Like that earlier catastrophe, it was many years in the making.

In early October 2007, the Dow Jones Industrial Average (DJIA) reached an all-time high of over 14,000. By March 2009, it had fallen to under 7,000. Other stock market indices worldwide, from Western Europe to the high-growth economies of India and China, saw similar or greater drops. The triggering event was the collapse of the housing market in the United States, which saw nearly $6 trillion in home valuation disappear—a far greater amount than was lost in the U.S. stock market and a loss that affected a far larger cohort of Americans. The dramatic change in financial fortunes triggered a series of spectacular failures in the financial services and banking sectors, beginning with the March 2008 collapse of Bear Sterns, one of five major U.S. investment banks and a leader in subprime mortgage lending. The venerable financial institution was sold in a rescue merger with JPMorgan Chase engineered by the U.S. Federal Reserve; the final price was $10 per share of Bear Stearns stock, which had traded in excess of $170 per share a mere fourteen months earlier. The collapse and fire sale of Bear Stearns was followed in September by the failure of another major U.S. investment bank and leader in subprime mortgage financing, Lehman Brothers. This time, no federal bailout or emergency acquisition was arranged. The bankruptcy of Lehman Brothers was the largest in U.S. history, valued at over $600 billion.

Next came the September 2008 demise of Washington Mutual, the savings bank holding company, in what constituted the largest bank collapse in U.S. history. The federal government placed Washington Mutual into receivership under the Federal Deposit Insurance Corporation (FDIC), which in turn sold the company's banking subsidiaries to JPMorgan Chase for $1.9 billion. Then, during the rest of 2008 and into 2009, the federal government stepped in to rescue several of the nation's leading financial institutions with billions of dollars in loans and capital injections; among recipients were the insurance giant AIG, Citicorp, and Bank of America. European governments had to undertake similar actions.

Foundations: The Housing Bubble

Despite its global reach and historically severe impact, the meltdown of 2007–2008 reflects the characteristics of a classic boom-and-bust cycle, fed by excess credit. There was the development of a housing bubble beginning in 2003, its peak in August 2005, a steady decline in housing prices, and the inevitable collapse of the mortgage and housing markets in 2007 and 2008—all with dramatic economic and political consequences. Indeed, any reasonable analysis of the bubble in terms of classic boom-and-bust cycles should have raised early warnings about the housing market and its financial underpinnings. Yet even the few analysts and commentators who predicted the bursting of the housing bubble failed to predict the scope and scale of its financial and economic effects. The constriction of credit markets left financial institutions, major corporations, small companies, and private investors throughout the world unable borrow the funds necessary to conduct business, resulting in a deep global recession of indeterminate duration.

The root of the crisis thus lay in the securitized mortgage market and its role in the housing bubble. These processes took place in the context of the ongoing globalization movement and key changes in U.S. banking and security law—all of which came together in a kind of "perfect storm" with sudden, unexpected, and devastating force.

Structure and Evolution of the U.S. Mortgage Market

U.S. residential mortgages represent a multi-trillion-dollar market that expanded dramatically between 2002 and 2007. In June 2007, U.S. residential and nonprofit mortgages totaled $10.143 trillion, up from $5.833 trillion in September 2002 and $2.3 trillion in 1989. In other words, the market took thirteen years (1989–2002) to increase $2.5 trillion but only another five years (2002–2007) to increase by $4.3 trillion—nearly double again. (In both cases, the rate of increase far outstripped the growth of the general population.)

At the same time, the number of firms and organizations participating in the market also proliferated. Until the latter part of the twentieth century, home loans and mortgages in America typically were arranged between a bank or savings and loan (S&L) and a local borrower, with the bank or S&L holding the mortgage until maturity, the

sale of the home, or refinancing. But beginning in the 1980s and expanding in the 1990s and beyond, all that changed. Banks and S&Ls discovered the benefits of what is known as "securitization." Rather than holding loans in their portfolios as investments, banks and S&Ls began bundling individual mortgages into larger loan packages and selling them to outside investors. In addition to the sales proceeds, the banks and S&Ls obtained fees for helping service the loans. Because the banks and S&Ls no longer had to wait years or decades to be repaid for the loan, mortgage securitization meant that they could rapidly "turn over" their balance sheets; they were paid immediately by parties investing in the bundled loan packages. The process brought increased returns on capital and earnings per share, both for common stockholders and corporate officers with stock options.

Expansion of the System

The new system was tailor-made to expand nationally, and then internationally, as it both benefited lending institutions and facilitated homeownership. The securitization of mortgages created a circular and self-perpetuating flow of money from banks to global-securities investors to mortgage issuers of various kinds to families seeking to purchase a home. In the new system, banks began selling mortgage-backed securities to investors all over the world such as mutual funds, hedge funds, pension funds, corporate treasuries, insurance companies, and banks. The money invested in these securities ultimately flowed back to the banks, which originated more mortgages—and the process repeated itself. Meanwhile, because the banks themselves no longer relied on direct repayment from the mortgage holder for their returns, eligibility standards for prospective homeowners grew increasingly lax. Credit standards to qualify for a mortgage were lowered, and new financial instruments—such as the subprime, adjustable rate mortgage—were devised to expand the pool of borrowers, many of whom would not have qualified for a loan in the past.

A news ticker in London reports the September 2008 bankruptcy of U.S. investment bank Lehman Brothers, a major blow to the international financial system. *(Cate Gillon/ Getty Images)*

Moreover, as the market expanded, economies of scale in specialization emerged at different points in the mortgage financing and investment chain. To begin with, the development of the Internet created significant cost benefits in sourcing and processing mortgage applications and approvals online. Just as homebuyers could virtually tour several houses in an afternoon without leaving home, they could also compare mortgage rates from several sources. Lenders, for their part, could quickly scan the credit scores of prospective buyers. Similarly, advances in computing and telecommunications created economies of scale in servicing mortgages and investors. Under the new system, it became increasingly possible to sidestep restrictions imposed by government regulations, as it became easier to avoid doing business with a federally insured bank or S&L. Thus, for example, a mortgage broker (the intermediary between lender and borrower) could find a financial institution such as GMAC or GE Credit Services or Merrill Lynch instead of a traditional bank or S&L to grant the mortgage. These lenders would then bundle the mortgages they owned into "pools." In turn, either they or investment banks such as Bear Stearns or Lehman Brothers (the number one and two underwriters of mortgage-backed securities, respectively) would sell the bundles to other investors, specifically tailored to their individual requirements.

For example, long-term investors might want a commitment to final monthly payments, while shorter-term investors might want only the first three years of interest. No investor owned an entire mortgage, and none were involved in loan administration or handling security. Again, powerful computer systems serviced and supported the deals and structures in all their complexity. This gave an advantage to firms that could source and service in volume, spreading system costs over a large number of mortgages, customers, and investments.

The Bursting of the Bubble and Its Aftermath

The financial viability of the mortgage securitization process rested on two simple but essential requirements: (1) homeowners needed to continue making their monthly payments; and (2) homes needed to retain their market value. An increasing number of residential-housing loans, including subprime mortgages, were adjustable-rate mortgages (ARMs), in which interest rates rise after a specified period of time; how much they increase is based on a designated financial index. Any rise in interest rates pushes up monthly payments, sometimes beyond the means of low-income families or those who had taken out mortgages that were beyond their means. As long as home values continued to rise and credit remained loose, homeowners could refinance at lower rates. But with the collapse in home prices and the tightening of the credit markets, this was no longer possible, leading to a rush—then a flood—of foreclosures. With the peaking of the U.S. housing market in

August 2005, the second requirement (that homes needed to retain their market value) was cast into doubt. And with the increase in subprime lending during 2005 and 2006—including so-called NINJA loans (no declared income, job, or assets required)—the first requirement likewise was in jeopardy. Once problems started to emerge, the size of the mortgage-financing market, its rapid growth, and its increasing complexity combined to burst the bubble. Losses by financial institutions and investors quickly reached the tens of billions, then spread throughout the national and international financial system.

Financial calamity is typically followed by political finger-pointing, moral grandstanding, and criminal prosecution as the collapse exposes illegal schemes and unregulated practices that had gone unnoticed or simply ignored while all parties were making money. Individuals and institutions seek restitution of lost billions, policy makers discuss ways to prevent future abuses, and law-enforcement authorities seek to punish wrongdoers. Not surprisingly, litigation tends to focus on the handing off of loans by the bank or other lending institutions, such as mortgage brokers, to the mortgage providers. The reason is that these transactions entail the clearest documentation of warranties and responsibilities of the various parties.

These contractual obligations then become the basis for recovery. Even with such documentation, however, problems in achieving recovery have abounded. This is because the complexity of the system—and indeed the uncoordinated and disorderly way in which it was operated—made it unclear who was supposed to be in ownership and control of the loans, mortgages, and payment streams. Moreover, the system made it difficult either for the banks servicing the loans to renegotiate terms with borrowers or for the government to buy and restructure the various "toxic" assets.

The Boom-and-Bust Scenario

The pattern of the U.S. housing market followed the classic boom-and-bust model. Indeed, pre-

dicting the bust and its consequences might not have been as difficult as many have claimed. In his book *Subprime Mortgages* (2007), for example, former Federal Reserve Board governor Edward Gramlich did that exactly.

In the classic boom-and-bust scenario, every mania or bubble begins with a displacement or disruption to the economy that changes existing expectations, such as a major technical advance like the Internet or a large injection of government-printed cash into the economy. In the case of the global financial meltdown of 2007–2008, the disruption was a vast increase in liquidity and lower interest rates injected into the system by the Federal Reserve in the aftermath of the dot.com bust of 2001. The effects of that disruption, moreover, were compounded by two other factors: increasing government deregulation of the financial services industry and the proliferation of global telecommunications during the Internet boom. Government deregulation vastly increased the number of players in the mortgage-backed securities market, while the Internet boom created tremendous low-cost computing and communications power that facilitated and accelerated the credit expansion.

With these catalysts, financial activity and the value of assets grew in value according to the classic boom-and-bust model. The more money that was made, the greater the speculation and the more assets appreciated. Increasingly, investments were made—and profits earned—on the basis of greed rather than productivity or sound business. The bubble continued to expand until the leverage fueling it could no longer support the growth and expansion of the housing market. Mortgage-backed securities—themselves financial instruments without a sound foundation—finally collapsed under the pressure.

The Role of Banks and Subprime Mortgages

Overly aggressive bank lending was another critical element in the boom-and-bust cycle, as it fueled the expansion of the housing bubble in the early years of the decade, then accelerated the collapse of the market by restricting credit to the point of choking it off entirely. Exacerbating the situation was the advent of the largely unregulated market for credit default swaps (CDS). CDSs constitute a kind of insurance, or hedge, whereby investors speculate on whether an investment instrument—such as a mortgage-backed security—will go into default. If it does, the buyer receives a payoff. The premiums for such protection, of course, accrue to the seller. Devised in the 1990s as a hedge against default and to spread the risk around, CDSs came to constitute a windfall for major investment banks whose financial exposure was estimated in the hundreds of trillions of dollars by the mid-2000s.

With some investors leveraged at a ratio of more than 40 to 1 (i.e., homeowners and investors in mortgage-backed securities borrowing $40 for every dollar they actually had), any glitch in the housing market could set off a rapid downward spiral in sales and price—much as happened with stocks in 1929.

With housing prices already rising faster than people's incomes, lenders at first sought to continue expanding the pool of borrowers with low-interest "teaser" loans. In 2005, however, as the Federal Reserve began to tighten interest rates, adjustable mortgages had to be reset at the higher rates. Foreclosures began to increase as a result, and prospective new homebuyers began to be priced out of the market. These developments in turn prompted lenders and investors to reassess risk and to reduce new money, leading to a drop in residential real-estate values—one of the two key supports for the mortgage-backed securities market. Forced to reassess the value of their investments, heavily leveraged mortgage holders tried to convert to cash (sell), setting the stage for a wide-scale panic. The flood of mortgage-backed assets coming onto the market combined with increasing fear, decreasing demand, and lack of available credit to bring on the crash.

Historically, financial busts are often followed by a spate of litigation and revelations of scandal. The housing subprime mortgage meltdown of 2007–2008 was no exception. Indeed, evidence of mortgage fraud in the United States was on the rise during the boom phase of the cycle, as prospective borrowers were lured into commitments they simply could not keep. Between 1997 and 2005, suspicious activity reports related to mortgage fraud increased over 1,000 percent between 1997 and 2005. And the trend continued from 2002 to 2007, as pending mortgage-fraud investigations by the Federal Bureau of Investigation (FBI) rose from 436 to 1,210. The most common frauds involved "property flipping" and other schemes to gain proceeds from mortgages or property sales based on misleading appraisals or other false documentation.

Meanwhile, the U.S. Securities and Exchange Commission (SEC) was looking into insider trading at public companies with increasingly "toxic" assets associated with the mortgage crisis. And thousands of investors with Wall Street financier Bernard Madoff, a former chairman of the NASDAQ stock exchange, came to learn that they had squandered a collective $50 billion in Madoff's giant Ponzi scheme, said to be the single biggest financial fraud in U.S. history. Many regarded the Madoff case as symbol of the rampant fraud, lack of regulation, and sheer greed of the financial times. Madoff, at age 71, was sentenced to 150 years in prison after pleading guilty to multiple counts of defrauding clients.

Much as in other times of financial distress, political pressure began to mount for measures that would prevent future abuses. Such was the case after the stock market crash of 1929, with the formation of the SEC. In 1989, Congressional responses to the savings and loan crisis and the junk-bond scandal substantially increased the penalties for crimes affecting financial institutions and tightened capitalization standards for banks and S&Ls. These measures did not prevent or even moderate the 2007–2008 crisis and continuing recession, however, as the federal government was assigned a role many felt it did not carry out.

Under the 1989 legislation, the Federal Reserve was granted the authority to curb lending practices for home mortgages. Thus, the boom and bust of the housing market in the first decade of the twentieth century was regarded in many circles as a failure of federal regulatory control. Meanwhile, lawsuits have flown in the wake of the financial crisis and the growing revelations of misfeasance and even malfeasance by those institutions which marketed the debt-backed exotic securities. Most of these lawsuits involve charges that the issuers of the securities misled investors as to the risk of those securities; in some cases, plaintiffs are even demanding that the issuers buy back at least some of the tainted securities.

From Financial Crisis to Recession

The burst of the housing bubble and the subsequent crisis in the international financial system reverberated outward into the rest of the economy by late 2007, triggering what most analysts say is the worst downturn in the U.S. and global economy since the Great Depression.

Collapsing housing prices had a broad dampening effect on consumer demand, which generates roughly two-thirds of all economic activity in the industrialized economies of the West. During the housing boom from 2003 to 2006, many homeowners borrowed against the rising equity in their homes, either by refinancing their mortgages and taking out a percentage in cash or by obtaining low-interest home-equity loans. In addition, with interest rates on mortgages dropping, homeowners could reduce their monthly payments by refinancing, thereby freeing up a greater part of their income for discretionary spending. Rising home values also provided an indirect stimulus to consumer spending, as many homeowners came to regard their ever-increasing equity as a form of retirement savings, cut the amount of income they saved—the savings rate in the United States fell almost to zero at the height of the boom in 2006—and spent the rest on discretionary purchases. Thus, for example, the sale of new vehicles remained above $17 million annually from 2004 to 2006 (and fell to just over $13 million in 2008).

All of this reversed with the decline in housing values. Consumers cut back on spending and began saving more, both because they feared for their jobs and because they began to recognize that the equity in their homes might not see them through retirement. The savings rate in the United States climbed back into positive territory in 2009, to an annualized rate of 5.7 percent in April. With declining consumer demand came falling corporate revenues, expanding inventories of manufactured goods, and a slowdown in industrial output. The

The financial crisis of 2008–2009 became a global economic contagion, resulting in bank closures, stock market declines, business failures, and burgeoning unemployment. The recession proved deep, long, and widespread. *(Mark Ralston/AFP/Getty Images)*

national unemployment rate skyrocketed from the historically low 5.1 percent in 2005 to the historically high 10.2 percent in October 2009, which further depressed consumer demand.

In addition, the bursting of the housing bubble tightened credit markets across the board, not only in mortgages. Traditionally, banks tend to tighten credit as their own portfolios of outstanding loans—including home mortgages—show weakness. Thus, the growth of increasingly complex and exotic financial instruments such as mortgage-backed securities and credit default swaps heightened insecurity in the financial markets. So complex were these instruments, in fact, that nobody knew exactly what they were worth, especially as the security of the mortgages on which they were based became suspect.

Modern credit markets were already highly fluid, with banks constantly providing financing to each other in the interbank lending market. The 1999 repeal of that part of the 1933 Glass-Steagall Act that separated investment banks from commercial banks meant that major banks of all kinds now faced greater exposure to the collapse of the complex new financial instruments. Not knowing the value of assets on each others' books, banks all but stopped lending to each other in the late 2008. While a total freeze on interbank lending—which would have been catastrophic—was avoided by the injection of hundreds of billions of dollars by various central banks around the world, including the U.S. Federal Reserve, insecurity in the financial system led to a radical tightening of credit. The effects on business were devastating. Companies were forced to defer the hiring of new employees (or even fire existing ones), as well as the purchase of materials and equipment, which increased unemployment, depressed demand even further, and decreased production. Altogether, the recession had a major impact on the gross domestic products (GDP) of countries around the world—causing declines at an annualized rate of 15.2 percent in the first quarter of 2009 in Japan, of 9.8 percent in the United Kingdom, and of 5.5 percent in the United States.

To help economies escape this vicious recessionary cycle, governments around the world responded in a variety of ways. In the United States, the first major policy initiatives were the 2008 Temporary Asset Relief Program (TARP) and the American Recovery and Reinvestment Act of 2009, better known as the Economic Stimulus Package. TARP provided $700 billion of federal money to purchase or insure various mortgage-related securities of questionable value or security held by financial institutions, in the hope that this would create a greater sense of security in the credit markets and thereby facilitate lending. The stimulus package injected $787 billion directly into the economy in a number of ways—including tax credits and reductions, increases in unemployment compensation, money to state and local governments, increased federal government purchases, infrastructure development, and research—all with the Keynesian goal of increasing employment and, hence, consumer demand. At the same time, however, this spending raised the federal budget deficit and the national debt to a percentage of GDP not seen since the end of World War II.

Lessons

As for the subprime mortgage crisis that triggered the global financial meltdown and subsequent recession, experts began to recognize signs of the bubble's development as early as 2005. It was then, many analysts came to believe, that the Federal Reserve should have used its regulatory powers and authority as a bank examiner to impose stricter credit standards against such lending. If it had, it was suggested, market mania might have been avoided and its effects significantly moderated, including the collapse of global stock markets.

So what should be done to avoid future bubbles and the devastating consequences of their bursting? According to many economists, overreliance on laissez-faire (unregulated), market-based policies resulted in large asset bubbles in the late 1980s and in 2007–2008. Thus, analysts and policy makers assert, the Federal Reserve and U.S. Treasury need to develop regulations and policy responses to extreme asset inflation. The study of past booms and busts is essential to understanding when a rapid rise in asset prices is a bubble, when that bubble is likely to burst, and what to do in response.

William Rapp

See also: AIG; Asset-Price Bubble; Bear Stearns; Collateralized Debt Obligations; Collateralized Mortgage Obligations; Credit Default Swaps; Debt Instruments; Fannie Mae and Freddie Mac; Financial Markets; Housing Booms and Busts; Lehman Brothers; Mortgage-Backed Securities; Securitization; Stimulus Package, U.S. (2008); Stimulus Package, U.S. (2009); Systemic Financial Crises; "Too Big to Fail"; Troubled Asset Relief Program (2008–); Washington Mutual.

Further Reading

Barth, James R. *The Rise and Fall of the U.S. Mortgage and Credit Markets: A Comprehensive Analysis of the Market Meltdown.* Hoboken, NJ: John Wiley & Sons, 2009.

Fox, Justin. *The Myth of the Rational Market: A History of Risk, Reward, and Delusion on Wall Street.* New York: HarperBusiness, 2009.

Gramlich, Edward, *Subprime Mortgage Crisis.* Washington, DC: Urban Institute, 2007.

Kansas, Dave. *The Wall Street Journal Guide to the End of Wall Street as We Know It: What You Need to Know About the Greatest Financial Crisis of Our Time—and How to Survive It.* New York: HarperBusiness, 2009.

Kindleberger, Charles, and Robert Aliber. *Manias, Panics and Crashes,* Hoboken, NJ: John Wiley & Sons, 2005.

Krugman, Paul. *The Return of Depression Economics and the Crisis of 2008.* New York: W.W. Norton, 2009.

Posner, Richard A. *A Failure of Capitalism: The Crisis of '08 and the Descent into Depression.* Cambridge, MA: Harvard University Press, 2009.

Recession, Reagan (1981–1982)

The steepest economic recession since the Great Depression, the Reagan recession of 1981–1982—so designated because it occurred during the first term of President Ronald Reagan—produced America's highest unemployment rates since the Great Depression. While a number of factors contributed to the downturn, most econo-

mists cite a dramatic tightening of credit by the Federal Reserve, which was attempting to lower double-digit inflation, as the immediate cause. After bottoming out in the last quarter of 1982, the nation's economy began a slow recovery, aided by deficit spending and lower interest rates.

Troubled Economy of the 1970s

Although U.S. economic growth following World War II was sometimes slowed by recessions, far more serious downturns began during the 1970s and early 1980s. A number of factors contributed to the troubles, including increased competition from Western Europe and Japan, stagnating productivity, a destabilization of the global financial markets as the U.S. dollar was devalued, and, most importantly, shocks to world oil markets that sent crude prices from about $3 a barrel in 1972 to more than $40 a barrel in 1980 (from $14 to $100 a barrel in 2008 dollars). All of these factors produced an economic phenomenon that came to be called "stagflation"—a combination of stagnation and inflation—in which high unemployment and slow economic growth (or outright contraction) coincided with high inflation. Economists and the media also devised a new economic measure, the "misery index," to refer to the combined impact—and total percentages—of unemployment and inflation. By 1980, the misery index had reached 21.

The combination of stagnation and inflation baffled economic policy makers, who had relied on Keynesian countercyclical measures to maintain steady growth and to smooth out the business cycle for most of the postwar era. According to early-twentieth-century British economist John Maynard Keynes, governments could ease economies out of recession through a combination of monetary policies (lowering interest rates and/or increasing the money supply) and fiscal policies (tax cuts and/or government spending), thereby increasing aggregate demand. But such measures failed to lift the American economy out of the doldrums in the early 1980s, as tightening credit

The U.S. recession of 1981–1982 brought the nation's highest unemployment rate—10.8 percent in December 1982—since the Great Depression. GDP shrank by 2.9 percent for the period. *(Keystone/Stringer/Hulton Archive/Getty Images)*

threw the economy further into recession, while increased government spending and looser credit fueled inflation; the latter reached double digits in 1974 and the three years from 1979 to 1981.

Reaganomics

The economic woes of 1979 and 1980—along with foreign policy setbacks such as the Iranian hostage crisis and the Soviet invasion of Afghanistan—led to a dramatic realignment in American politics, as voters ousted moderate Democratic president Jimmy Carter in favor of conservative Republican Ronald Reagan. In Congress, Democrats saw their majority in the House shrink and their control of the Senate disappear. Reagan had based his successful campaign on a few simple messages: tax cuts, reducing government regulation and the growth in government spending, and a tougher foreign policy stance. Once in office, he immediately enacted his first plank, offering the largest tax cut in history (as a proportion of gross

domestic product, or GDP), equivalent to about 3 percent; much of it went to the upper-income brackets. He also moved on his third promise, dramatically increasing the defense budget and ratcheting up anti-communist rhetoric. Finally, in unilaterally firing and replacing striking air traffic controllers, he sent a strong message that he would rein in the power of unions and their ability to demand wage hikes.

The Reagan administration offered a number of explanations for these moves. First, it argued, giving tax cuts to the wealthy would spur investment and entrepreneurial activity that would benefit all workers with more jobs and higher wages, an argument that critics derided as "trickle-down economics." The administration further contended that lower taxes would actually increase government revenue, as the economic expansion they triggered would create more taxable income and capital gains. The increased revenue, it went on, would help pay for moderate growth in domestic spending as well as a dramatic increase in defense spending. (As for the latter, Reagan was determined to drive the Soviet Union into bankruptcy by forcing it to spend a far higher percentage of its smaller GDP to keep up with the United States on defense.) The entire plan was based on principles of "supply-side economics," a conservative school of thought which argued that the best way to achieve economic growth was by providing incentives— such as cuts in the marginal income tax rates and taxes on capital gains—for those supplying goods and services. This ran counter to long-standing Keynesian principles, which called for government measures to increase aggregate demand—through tax cuts for lower-income workers and increased spending on public works—as the key to economic growth in times of recession.

Monetarists and the Federal Reserve

Even as President Reagan was coming to power, conservative monetarists led by Nobel Prize laureate Milton Friedman of the University of Chicago were gaining the upper hand in policy-making circles. Monetarists, who believed in keeping the growth of the money supply roughly equal to overall economic expansion, argued that the crippling inflation of the late 1970s and early 1980s had resulted from excessively loose credit policies at the Federal Reserve (Fed). According to the monetarists, the Fed had pumped too much money into a system that was not producing enough goods and services to justify the increase, thereby fueling inflation. Indeed, they argued, inflation had wormed its way into the psyche of American workers and consumers. Workers were demanding wage hikes to keep up with rising prices, even though productivity did not justify them. Consumers were spending more of their money out of fear that prices would continue to rise, and that goods and services would cost more in the future. This built-in inflation, said some economists, was dragging down the American economy by distorting the natural workings of the marketplace, making it difficult for companies to invest—and consumers to spend—rationally. The only way to end the crippling cycle of inflation and slow growth, it was argued, was to contract the money supply dramatically. Fed chairman Paul Volcker, once a believer in Keynesian economics, had been converted to monetarist thinking as he witnessed the failure of Keynesian measures to lift the American economy out of the stagflation of the 1970s.

Upon taking office, Volcker raised the federal funds rate (the interest rate the Fed charges member banks to borrow money) from an already high 11.2 percent in 1979 to a peak 20 percent in June 1981. The increase did what it was intended to do, as banks raised the prime interest rate to a high of more than 21 percent. Interest rates at this level made it difficult for both businesses and consumers to borrow money, thereby reducing demand, investment, and employment. As workers began losing their jobs, demands for wage increases eased; and with less money chasing goods and services, prices increases slowed. Likewise, hikes in mortgage rates cooled an overheated housing market. All in all, between 1980 and 1983, the annual

inflation rate fell from 13.5 percent to just above 3 percent. Other than in 1990, it would never rise above 5 percent again; inflation had indeed been wrung out of the system.

The success came at a steep cost, however, as the Reagan recession brought some of the nation's worst economic data of the postwar era. In the first quarter of 1982, the U.S. economy shrunk at an annualized rate of nearly 7 percent, the most severe contraction since the Great Depression—and a figure not even matched by the financial crisis and recession of 2007–2009. The year 1982 witnessed a 2 percent decline in GDP. Late that year, the unemployment rate hit 10.8 percent, an all-time high for the post–World War II era.

Recovery

The U.S. economy was growing again by 1983, as Volcker and the Fed, convinced that inflation had been checked, lowered the federal funds rate to just over 8 percent, about where it would remain until being lowered to 3–6 percent during the much milder recession of the early 1990s. (By comparison, the Fed effectively lowered the rate to zero during the deep recession of 2007–2009.) But there were other factors behind the recovery. Keynesian economists cited the massive deficit spending of the Reagan years, as the president found it much easier to lower tax rates than he did to stop the growth in government spending. (His massive defense build-up did not help ease the deficit either.) Monetarists, on the other hand, argued that reining in inflation was critical because it made all economic players—from businesses to workers to consumers—act more rationally, ensuring that economic resources were allocated more efficiently. Entrepreneurially focused economists, such as those of the Austrian school, emphasized the introduction of new technologies that bolstered demand and improved productivity—most notably, the personal computer.

Still other economists argued that the recovery from the Reagan recession was not particularly robust by postwar standards. Whereas GDP grew by an average of 5 to 6 percent in the 1950s and 1960s, growth from the recovery year of 1983 until the beginning of the next recession in 1991 averaged only about 3 percent—not much better than during the nonrecession years of the 1970s. Nevertheless, Reagan was able to convince enough Americans that he had revived the country's economy to win reelection in a landslide in 1984 and to perpetuate the era of conservative economic hegemony.

James Ciment

See also: Monetary Policy; Recession, Stagflation (1970s); Volcker, Paul.

Further Reading

Heilbroner, Robert, and Peter Bernstein. *The Debt and the Deficit: False Alarms/Real Possibilities.* New York: W.W. Norton, 1989.

Hurewitz, J.C., ed. *Oil, the Arab-Israeli Dispute, and the Industrial World: Horizons of Crisis.* Boulder, CO: Westview, 1976.

Means, Gardner, ed. *The Roots of Inflation: The International Crisis.* New York: B. Franklin, 1975.

Mehtabdin, Khalid R. *Reaganomics: Successes and Failures.* Lewiston, ME: E. Mellen Press, 1986.

Niskanen, William A. *Reaganomics: An Insider's Account of the Policies and the People.* New York: Oxford University Press, 1988.

Sawyer, James E. *Why Reaganomics and Keynesian Economics Failed.* New York: St. Martin's, 1987.

Wilber, Charles K., and Kenneth P. Jameson. *Beyond Reaganomics: A Further Inquiry into the Poverty of Economics.* Notre Dame, IN: University of Notre Dame Press, 1990.

Recession, Roosevelt (1937–1939)

Often referred to as the Roosevelt recession—after Franklin Roosevelt, the president in office when it occurred—the sharp economic contraction from 1937 to 1939 prolonged the Great Depression and undermined support for the poverty-fighting, government interventionist New Deal economic agenda.

The Roosevelt recession can be understood only in the larger context of the Great Depression. Following the stock market crash of 1929, the U.S. economy was plunged into the worst downturn in its history. Bankruptcies soared, unemployment rose to 25 percent, and corporate profits declined by nearly 90 percent. All told, the gross national product (GNP) fell by one-third between 1929 and the depths of the Depression in early 1933. Herbert Hoover, the Republican president at the time, hewed to the economic orthodoxy of his day: cut back on government spending to keep it in line with the decline in government revenue. Federal deficits, it was believed, only prolonged economic contractions by absorbing capital that private enterprise needed for investment and job creation. Moreover, the semi-independent Federal Reserve tightened credit by cutting the money supply and raising interest rates, under the orthodox economic view that the crisis of the 1930s was one of too much industrial capacity rather than too little consumer demand. Raising interest rates would, by this reasoning, force businesses to cut production, thereby raising prices and profits.

Many later economists would cite these moves by both the Hoover administration and the Federal Reserve as grave mistakes, given the seriousness of the economic contraction. And at the time, emergent demand-oriented economists such as Britain's John Maynard Keynes insisted that, in the absence of private-enterprise initiative, the government must step in to bolster demand, either through monetary or fiscal policy—that is, either by increasing the money supply and lowering interest rates, or through tax cuts and public works projects that would pump money directly into the economy.

Ironically, in his first campaign for the presidency, against Hoover, Roosevelt stuck to economic orthodoxy, emphasizing the need for a balanced federal budget. Upon coming to office, however, Roosevelt abandoned his conservative economic beliefs to focus on three problems: fixing the financial system, which was on the verge of collapse; aiding the ailing agricultural sector; and reviving industry. He promptly sponsored legislation to guarantee bank deposits and thereby end the run on withdrawals (the Banking Act of 1933, which created the Federal Deposit Insurance Corporation, or FDIC); to subsidize farmers (Agricultural Adjustment Act); and to establish codes to regulate industrial output (National Recovery Act). (The latter two would be overturned by the Supreme Court in the mid-1930s.)

With the exception of the banking measure, these policies—collectively referred to as the First New Deal—were aimed at lowering production so as to bolster prices and profits. As for pumping money directly into the economy to increase employment and hence demand—as Keynes was coming to urge—Roosevelt was reluctant, insisting that direct government relief should always be the last option. Nevertheless, as the Depression persisted through the mid-1930s, and as the president faced increasing criticism from the political Left, Roosevelt expanded and federalized public works spending through the Works Progress Administration (WPA) as part of what came to be called the Second New Deal. Still, the wages offered on many of these projects were well below the subsistence level as determined by federal economists. In retrospect, however valuable for the bridges and artwork they created, these programs were far too limited in size to have a major impact on the national economy.

Roosevelt's efforts through his first term had mixed results. The immediate financial crisis had been fixed—depositor runs had largely come to an end, banking institutions were no longer failing in large numbers, and corporate profits were reviving. Overall, GNP had grown by a very healthy 10 percent annually—albeit from a depressed base—getting back to where it had been just before the stock market crash in 1929. Even the unemployment rate had fallen from its peak, if still at an abnormally high 14 percent. Nevertheless, many Americans, including Roosevelt and many members of Congress, were convinced the Depression was over.

Upon returning to office in 1937, Roosevelt reverted to his old conservative beliefs that fiscal deficits and massive relief programs hampered economic growth. In this he was not alone. Thus, as the president slashed the federal budget, Congress dramatically reduced funding for the WPA and the Federal Reserve, and, worried that the recovery might fuel inflation, raised interest rates. These moves, along with new Social Security withholding taxes, undermined investment and consumer demand, sending the economy into a steep recession. The stock market collapsed again, and 10 million new workers became unemployed.

Once again, Roosevelt changed direction and began pumping new expenditures into the economy. It was too late to avoid dramatic Democratic losses in the 1938 mid-term elections, and a more conservative Congress scaled back many of the Second New Deal programs of the mid-1930s. Still, in the end, Keynes's argument that massive government spending was the only way to revive an economy driven down by lack of aggregate demand—an idea that had slowly gained credence among Roosevelt's economic advisers—was put into action not long after the Roosevelt recession: the government began a program of massive defense spending leading up to America's entry into World War II at the end of 1941.

James Ciment

See also: Great Depression (1929–1933); New Deal.

Further Reading

Barber, William J. *Designs Within Disorder: Franklin Roosevelt, the Economists, and the Shaping of American Economic Policy, 1933–1945.* New York: Cambridge University Press, 1996.

Leuchtenburg, William. *Franklin Roosevelt and the New Deal.* New York: Harper & Row, 1963.

Rosen, Elliot A. *Roosevelt, the Great Depression, and the Economics of Recovery.* Charlottesville: University of Virginia Press, 2005.

Recession, Stagflation (1970s)

After a quarter-century of unprecedented growth and prosperity, the United States entered a period of economic uncertainty, stagnation, and contraction in the early 1970s, as a series of recessions slowed GDP growth and led to a virtual halt in per capita income increases. Marked by both high unemployment and inflation, the combination of which was dubbed "stagflation" by economists and the media, the economic slowdown of the 1970s baffled the Keynesian economic orthodoxy of the day and led to a reappraisal of the measures the government should take to lift the economy out of recession.

Post–World War II Boom

Along with most of the noncommunist industrialized world, the United States experienced sustained growth from the late 1940s through the early 1970s, fueled by enormous surges in aggregate demand, rapid population growth, dramatic improvements in productivity, increased exports, a lack of foreign competition in its huge domestic market, a stable global monetary system, cheap energy, and—say the Keynesian economists who advocated and orchestrated them—countercyclical fiscal and monetary economic policies that helped smooth the normal upturns and downturns in the economy. Between 1946 and 1970, the U.S. gross national product (GNP) nearly quadrupled, from about $200 billion to just under $1 trillion (in inflation-adjusted dollars). Per capita annual income also soared during that period, from about $1,500 to nearly $5,000. Unemployment remained in the 4–6 percent range, except during a few brief and mild recessions, such as those in 1957–1958 and 1969–1970. Inflation remained largely in check through the mid-1960s.

The 1960s marked the culmination of the postwar boom, with the U.S. economy boasting some of the fastest and greatest gains of the era. Indeed, some 60 percent of America's postwar GNP growth through 1970 occurred in that last decade alone. Yet much of the superheated growth was the result of deficit spending by the federal government. Rather than increase taxes to pay for these antipoverty programs and the war in Vietnam—and risk

undermining support for his domestic and military agenda—President Lyndon Johnson maintained the large tax cuts he had signed into law in early 1964. All of the additional money floating around the economy fueled inflation, which rose to nearly 6 percent in 1970. There were other negative economic factors in play as well, including increased competition from Western Europe and Japan, declining improvements in productivity, and instability in global financial markets. From the end of World War II through 1971, the U.S. dollar—the measuring stick for most other world currencies—had anchored those markets. But with rising U.S. inflation and a growing trade deficit, the dollar began losing ground, and made convertibility increasingly difficult to maintain. In August 1971, President Richard Nixon devalued the dollar, even as he declared a temporary freeze on wages and prices.

Oil Shocks

These efforts eased the twin crises of inflation and financial instability, but only temporarily. By February 1973, Nixon had again devalued the dollar, and then came an even greater shock to the U.S. economy—the energy crisis. The United States and the rest of the industrialized world had grown rich in the postwar era on cheap oil, much of it imported from the politically volatile Middle East. In response to the Arab-Israeli War of 1973, Arab oil exporters hiked crude prices and then imposed an embargo on the United States, resulting in shortages across the country. More long-lasting was the embargo's effect on prices, which quadrupled in just a few months from about $3 to $12 dollars a barrel (about $14 to $58 in 2008 dollars). As oil ran much of the American economy, the impact of the price hike reverberated through industry after industry and ultimately to consumer pocketbooks. By 1974, the rate of inflation had reached a crippling 11 percent. Rising oil prices also damaged the vital U.S. car industry, as buyers turned to more fuel-efficient foreign imports. This had a significant cumulative effect, as the automobile industry was among the largest purchasers of steel, rubber, glass, and tool-and-die products. Productivity increases throughout the U.S. economy also sagged, to roughly 1 percent in the early 1970s and near zero in the latter half of the decade. Stagnating productivity also meant stagnating wages and lost jobs. As the recession deepened in 1974 and 1975, the nation's unemployment rate climbed from 5 percent to nearly 8.5 percent.

Normally, stagnating wages and high unemployment reduce aggregate demand, which in turns brings inflation into check. But that was not the case this time. Rising oil prices, though critical, were not the only factor behind the phenomenon of stagflation. Conservatives blamed excessive government regulation, which they said stifled innovation and directly hurt the bottom lines of many businesses. Unionists blamed "unfair" foreign competition and demanded higher tariffs. Some economists blamed too much deficit spending by the federal government; others blamed excessive consumer spending, fueled by the mass introduction of credit cards and an inflationary cycle that prompted consumers to spend their money quickly so as to beat higher prices later. President Gerald Ford tried cajoling businesses, workers, and consumers to curb their inflationary habits voluntarily, but his Whip Inflation Now (WIN) program was largely ridiculed. More effective was the Federal Reserve's decision to raise interest rates for banks, tightening credit. While this helped lower inflation somewhat, it sent the economy deeper into recession.

Then came more blows on the energy front, as the Iranian Revolution of 1979 and the Iran-Iraq War, which began a year later, sent oil prices soaring again, to $40 a barrel by 1980 ($100 in 2008 dollars). (Iran and Iraq were the world's second- and third-largest oil exporters, respectively.) Stagflation returned. Economists, politicians, and the media began referring to the "discomfort" or "misery" index, which added together unemployment and inflation. The index, which had hit 17.5 percent at the depths of the 1974–1975 recession, climbed to nearly 21 percent in 1980. Political repercussions were inevitable, as voters replaced the

The oil shortage of 1973–1974 led to economic stagnation throughout the industrialized West, ending the post–World War II boom. In the United States, unemployment and inflation both soared, peaking at 9 and 11 percent, respectively, before mid-decade. *(Bill Pierce/Time & Life Pictures/Getty Images)*

incumbent Democratic president, Jimmy Carter, with Republican Ronald Reagan in the 1980 election, giving huge gains to Republicans in Congress as well. More importantly, the election brought to power a president and, to some degree, a Congress no longer enamored with the Keynesian countercyclical nostrums, whereby government dramatically increased spending and/or the money supply to overcome economic downturns. That ideology, the new Reagan administration contended, had led to stagflation by increasing the amount of money in circulation without improving productivity.

New Policies

Reagan had campaigned, among other things, on a vow to fix the economy by dramatically lowering taxes, reducing government spending, and eliminating unnecessary regulation. He was able to keep his first promise and, to some degree, the third, though deregulation took some time to affect economic growth. Reagan proved unsuccessful at reducing government spending, however, as his argument was that reducing taxes would spur enough growth so that tax revenues would actually increase. Things did not work out that way, and the Reagan administration, which spent heavily on defense, racked up the largest federal deficits in the nation's history. The budget deficits, along with other factors, helped produce a modestly growing economy through the middle and late 1980s.

Instead, what really ended the "stagflation" of the 1970s and early 1980s, according to most economists, were the policies of the Federal Reserve Board (Fed) under Chairman Paul Volcker. Increasingly influenced by monetary theorist Milton Friedman, Volcker—once a Keynesian—had come to the conclusion that lax monetary policy during the 1960s and 1970s was the major cause of the economic crises of the latter decade. To end the inflationary cycle, Volcker in 1981 rapidly raised the interest rates the Fed charged member banks, dramatically tightening credit. The result was the deepest recession and the highest unemployment

rate—peaking at 10.8 percent in late 1982—since the Great Depression. But the Fed's move, aided by falling oil prices, finally did squeeze inflation out of the system; the annualized rate fell from above 13.5 percent in 1980 to about 6 percent in 1982 and just above 3 percent in 1983. Stagflation had finally been put to rest.

James Ciment

See also: Inflation; Oil Shocks (1973–1974, 1979–1980); Recession, Reagan (1981–1982).

Further Reading

Barnet, Richard. *The Lean Years: Politics in the Age of Scarcity,* New York: Simon & Schuster, 1980.

Bluestone, Barry, and Bennett Harrison. *The Deindustrialization of America: Plant Closings, Community Abandonment, and the Dismantling of Basic Industry.* New York: Basic Books, 1982.

Heilbroner, Robert, and Peter Bernstein. *The Debt and the Deficit: False Alarms/Real Possibilities.* New York: W.W. Norton, 1989.

Hurewitz, J.C., ed. *Oil, the Arab-Israeli Dispute, and the Industrial World: Horizons of Crisis.* Boulder, CO: Westview, 1976.

Means, Gardner, ed. *The Roots of Inflation: The International Crisis.* New York: B. Franklin, 1975.

Niskanen, William A. *Reaganomics: An Insider's Account of the Policies and the People.* New York: Oxford University Press, 1988.

Refinancing

Refinancing is the process of renegotiating the terms and conditions of existing credit through new loan arrangements. Technically, then, it is the restructuring or refunding of a loan with a new debt or equity in which the contractual party renegotiates the sum or terms of the credit. In a vast number of cases, the client will require the bank (creditor) to grant new credit (most likely of higher value) to retire the existing credit debt, using the same or related collateral. Refinancing should leave the debtor in a more advantageous position, obtaining either better terms of credit or additional sums of money to invest in a profitable activity that will pay off the debt more quickly.

The latter option is known as cash-out refinancing, as the debtor will take some equity out of an asset. Refinancing operations usually are undertaken when interest rates are falling, as market conditions make it possible to negotiate a lower interest rate than the currently held loan has. The very decision as to whether or not one should consider refinancing—restructuring one's debt—thus should be based on a detailed deliberation of the time and savings involved.

In a refinancing transaction, the debtor usually requires the creditor to reconsider the sum owed (real refinancing) or the conditions of the credit without touching the approved sum (quasi-refinancing). In either situation, the debtor should be put in more favorable position, and the overall deal should be cheaper on a monthly/annual basis compared to the previous loan arrangements. However, the refinancing process itself may entail significant one-time fees, which the borrower should take into account as an initial, sunk cost of the renegotiated credit/loan.

Mortgage and Financial Market Refinancing

Refinancing is usually linked with mortgages, as debtors remain in constant search of better deals that are plentiful in highly competitive markets—-and most mortgages are made with no prepayment penalties to the borrower. Typically, debtors switch to another mortgage provider who offers a better rate or another type of mortgage, which, at least in the short term, lessens the burden of the mortgage repayment. Conventional wisdom in the developed mortgage market holds that a debtor should consider refinancing if the interest rate drops two points below the current mortgage rate, the debtor has paid at least two years of mortgage payments and plans to live in the property for more than two years in the future. If that is the case, refinancing should be available without much difficulty. However, during the easy-credit housing boom of 2003 to 2006, qualifications for mortgages were significantly relaxed

due to loose regulation and oversight. Thus, even in many cases where these conditions were not met, refinancing applications were approved.

In the case of refinancing of nonmortgage debt instruments such as bonds in financial markets, the issuer may decide to retire the existing issue of securities and offer new ones to the market, if the original instruments—that is, the market where basic factors, such as labor, capital or raw materials are bought and sold—allow the issuer to do so. The new securities may carry better terms or have lower interest rates. The total cash outlay needed to exercise the call provision includes payment to the holder of the security for any interest that has accrued to the date of the call and the call price, including the premium. The call premium compensates the bondholder for the risk of financial damage or disruption associated with recall.

It is also possible to build in the condition of deferred call, whereby the securities' issuer cannot exercise the call option until a stipulated period of time lapses (usually five or ten years). However, even if the deferral is built in, the issuer is always free to acquire the securities in the open market and annul them through market acquisition. Nevertheless, one should be fully aware that the securities markets (both government and commercial) are usually very thin, with only a small percentage of securities being traded. Thus, if the issuer is considering refinancing, it will most likely be necessary to resort to the call. The process of refinancing in the financial markets is also known as *re-funding*.

Refinancing in the financial markets requires an issuer to exercise the call option, which, as a rule, must be known from the outset. This provision gives the borrower the right to retire outstanding bonds at a stipulated price, most likely at a premium over face value, but never less than face value. A company may also opt for an open tendering procedure, which allows bidding for the securities, in order to acquire and retire them. While in the case of repurchase and call for retiring debt the price of the securities may be preset, in the case of tendering, the open competitive price will be achieved on the market, reflecting more or less successfully the quality of the market and market infrastructure.

Refinancing may also be used in the case of project and property (real-estate) financing, as the conditions of the existing credit are modified. The loan is usually extended for an additional period of time, to enable the developer to complete the project and realize a profit in the marketplace. In the case of companies as commercial issuers of debt, financial restructuring in the form of refinancing may be undertaken when the price of ordinary shares (i.e., common stock) is at the level that would cause the firm to replace its outstanding debt with equity (shares of stock).

Corporate and Government Refinancing

Corporate and/or government rescheduling of debt—loan restructuring or refinancing—attracts the attention of the general public, which would always like to give more consideration to the issues of government and large company private debt. When the decision to restructure debt is based on reliable risk-assessment procedures and input data, it is possible to gauge the impact of the restructuring on the overall business and future decisions regarding the corporate or government debt. In principle, the refinancing financial institution should conduct the necessary due diligence and ensure that the input data are accurate and in line with the annual report.

Although more rigorous refinancing criteria are often applied, common sense often prevails in banking allocation decisions, and many of the operations sanctioned by senior management are not in line with the proclaimed risk-management practices. In the late 1990s and early the following decade, especially in the United States and the United Kingdom, refinancing increased the overall risk in the system to a degree that few recognized, ultimately triggering the global financial crisis of 2008–2009.

Making a refinancing decision is particularly difficult for the refinancing agent (financial institution), which may base its approval or rejection on the past performance of an applicant (historical information) rather than on the applicant's current economic position and/or potential. As economic theory has amply documented, highly indebted customers are ready to accept virtually any interest rate and any condition in order to have their obligations rescheduled (the principle of moral hazard). Although systemic and regular refinancing may provide a boost to the financial system in the short run, it can accrue a dangerously high unsubstantiated debt over the long term and undermine the stability of the entire financial system—precisely what happened after the U.S. housing bubble began to burst in late 2006.

Thus, financial experts have maintained that it is necessary to regulate refinancing operations much more vigorously and for lending institutions to manage risk assessment for longer-term stability and growth rather than short-term profits (and the corporate bonuses that go with them).

Željko Šević

See also: Corporate Finance; Debt; Mortgage Equity; Mortgage Markets and Mortgage Rates.

Further Reading

Agarwal, S., J.C. Driscoll, and D.I. Laibson. *Optimal Mortgage Refinancing: A Closed Form Solution.* NBER Working Paper No. W13487 (October 2007). Boston: NBER.

Arsan, N., and E. Poindexter. "Revisiting the Economics of Mortgage Refinance." *Journal of Retail Banking* 15:4 (Winter 1993–1994): 45–48.

Caplin, A., C. Freeman, and J. Tracy. "Collateral Damage: Refinancing Constraints and Regional Recessions." *Journal of Money, Credit and Banking* 29:4 (1997): 496–516.

Regulation, Financial

The financial crisis of 2008–2009 brought the issue of financial regulation to the forefront of discussions involving business cycles and economic policy. In particular, the consensus among economists and business analysts was that the lack of such regulations—or at least their insufficiency—especially in the United States, was a primary reason for the worst economic crisis since the Great Depression.

Financial regulation is a form of governmental supervision relating to financial institutions and financial markets. Regulations are designed and implemented to ensure the integrity of financial systems and economies through the enforcement of laws and rules pertaining to financial organizations and instruments. Although there are several different types of regulations, involving different regulatory structures, financial regulations are usually seen as promoting the stability of financial systems through their ability to monitor and control excessive risk-taking behavior. Sound regulations ensure banking stability and promote fair practices to ensure an orderly functioning of financial markets.

Ensuring Financial Stability

There is no easy definition of financial stability. The literature, however, suggests that the conditions describing financial stability are not met when central banks remain the only institutions in which people put their confidence—in other words, when commercial banks and other credit institutions can no longer be relied on to avoid excessive risk taking. Such situations reveal a state of financial crisis—the very opposite of financial stability. Financial regulations are designed to prevent such crises from arising, as financial stability is closely related to banking stability.

At the beginning of the twenty-first century, the global economy is experiencing recurring financial disorders, ranging from financial crisis in emerging countries such as Turkey in 2000 and Argentina in 2001, to the bursting of the so-called dot.com and housing bubbles and the discovery of major accounting frauds at major corporations, such as Enron, Tyco International, and WorldCom. To prevent disorders of these kinds, financial regulations have been designed to enhance the quality of information, to develop reporting mechanisms, and to promote healthier banking structures. The Sarbanes-Oxley Act of 2002, one of the most notable recent efforts to regulate business practices—especially in the area of accounting—was passed after revelations of unethical behavior by U.S. corporations. Rules pertaining to asset allocation, deposit guarantees, and the maintenance of certain financial ratios help protect the well-being of investors by shielding banking institutions against inordinate or inappropriate risks.

Financial regulations can be issued by public or private bodies. One international regulatory institution, the Basel Committee on Banking Supervision, was created in 1974 by the central bank governors of the Group of Ten industrialized nations after two major international bank failures (Bankhaus Herstatt in West Germany and Franklin National Bank in the United States). The commission issues supervisory standards and statements of best practices in banking supervision to "enhance understanding of key supervisory issues and improve the quality of banking supervision worldwide" and to promote common international understanding and agreement about financial regulations. In 2004, the committee published an ambitious reform known as Basel II, whose purpose was to create international standards to regulate banking institutions through a set of principles known as pillars. The first pillar ensures that banks are well capitalized and that the risks they face are correctly qualified and identified. This pillar distinguishes three types of risks: credit risks, operational risks, and market risks. The second pillar provides another framework designed to help regulators to deal with residual risks (including, but not limited to, systemic risk, liquidity risk, legal risk, and reputation risk). The third pillar calls for more extensive and transparent disclosure regimes, allowing market participants to access information that alerts them to risks incurred when pricing or dealing with a given institution.

Regulatory Authorities

The idea of financial stability highlights the role played by regulatory bodies or authorities in governing financial institutions and markets. Every jurisdiction has its own authorities, and, despite efforts to homogenize regulations, the differences may be extensive. The three examples that follow reflect the different types of structures involved in financial regulation.

In the United Kingdom, basic forms of financial regulation can be found as far as back as the thirteenth century. The founding of the Bank of England, in 1694, provided an early model for central banks in other countries. Three objectives were assigned to the Bank of England: monetary control, the placement of government debt, and prudential control, the last being a key function to preventing financial crises. The Banking Act of 1979, amended in 1987, formalized the nation's system of financial regulation and supervision; it remains the prudential regulation to the present day. Paralleling the regulation of credit, lending, and deposit activities, banking supervision and investment-services regulation were merged into the Securities and Investment Board (SIB) in 1985, after a decision made by the chancellor of the exchequer. A series of scandals culminating in the 1995 collapse of the Barings Bank, the oldest merchant bank in the United Kingdom, led to the Financial Services and Markets Act of 2000, which defined the duties and responsibilities of the Financial Services Authority (FSA, formerly the SIB). Four statutory objectives were assigned to the FSA: "maintaining confidence in the financial system," "promoting public understanding of the financial system," "securing the appropriate degree of protection for consumers," and "reducing the extent to which it is possible for a business to be used for a purpose connected with financial crime."

In the United States, financial regulations are devised and enforced by several government bodies, of which the most important are the Federal Reserve (Fed) and the Securities and Exchange Commission (SEC). The Fed promotes the stability of the nation's financial system, and the SEC oversees market practices. The National Bank Act (1863) defined the duties and regulations applicable to national banks, federally chartered by the office of the comptroller of the currency. Fifty years later, in 1913, the Federal Reserve Act created a central bank to oversee the banking system, supplying liquidity in the event of crises like that of October 1907, when public panic threatened the existence of numerous banks and trust companies. As a consequence of the 1929 stock market crash, new regulations separating commercial banking from investment banking were issued, namely the Glass-Steagall Banking Act of 1933 and the Securities and Exchange Act of 1934. The latter led to the creation of the Securities and Exchange Commission, whose mission is to "protect investors, maintain fair, orderly and efficient markets, and facilitate capital formation."

In France, the Banking Commission (Commission Bancaire), created in 1800, is a regulatory body chaired by the governor of the French Central Bank (Banque de France). Its mission is to ensure that credit institutions and investment firms comply with laws and regulations; it has "the power to impose administrative penalties or financial sanctions to offenders," to "protect depositors," and "ensure the profitability and financial stability" of the French financial system. Authorizations to operate a financial company are guaranteed by a dedicated committee (Credit Institutions and Investment Firms Committee), while financial-market regulation and surveillance are enforced by the Autorité des Marchés Financiers. Insurance companies are, in turn, overseen by the Autorité de Contrôle des Assurances et des Mutuelles (ACAM).

Fair, Efficient, Transparent Markets

Regulatory bodies exist to promote financial stability; they also enforce market rules and ensure that financial practices do not operate outside the law. The underlying assumption governing the design, implementation, and deployment of financial regulations is that market competitiveness cannot be met without a common set of rules applicable to all participants. Without this, the exchange of financial instruments cannot occur in a stabilized environment where both buyers and sellers meet with equal knowledge about the financial instruments they are willing to exchange and the market within which such exchange takes place.

Financial transactions should be fair, efficient, and transparent—three conditions that provide the foundation of properly operating (i.e., competitive) markets. These principles were reaffirmed in 1998 by the International Organization of Securities Commissions (IOSCO), an international body created in 1983 that adopted a formal set of objectives and principles aimed at regulating activities relating to securities (revised in 2003). The document underlines the need for an effective regulation of practices in financial markets, protecting investors from "misleading, manipulative or fraudulent practices, including insider trading, front running or trading ahead of customers, and misuse of client assets." In addition, mechanisms of approval and accreditation, whether directed at market participants or market structures (exchange and trading systems), and the timely and widespread dissemination of relevant price information are promoted as part of IOSCO's effort toward market efficiency.

Once universal principles have been developed and announced, they need to be applied within organizations. To help the translation of principles into regulatory mechanisms, dedicated control functions undertaken by trained personnel within financial organizations have therefore been created. Consequently, financial institutions are now populated with risk managers, internal auditors, permanent controllers, anti–money laundering officers, and compliance officers, to name a few. These functions and the people in control of them ensure that appropriate controls are put in place, issues relating to conflicting areas are well addressed, and rules complied with. Beyond principles, codes of conduct, and standards of good

practice, compliance manuals, procedures, and routines are designed and applied.

The financial regulatory landscape is not static. Changes occur on a regular basis; each new financial crisis (the 1997–1998 Asian crisis, the dot.com bubble of 1998–2000, and the subprime mortgage crisis that began in 2006, for example) leads to shifts in regulatory models. Thus, the twenty-first century has seen the return of regulatory standards restricting the power of institutions to rule themselves after three decades of deregulation. And measures relating to best price and best execution rules, to the transparency of pre-trade and post-trade information, to disclosures about inducements (rebates, payments for order flow) have become mandatory for market intermediaries.

Financial regulations play an important role in the shaping of markets themselves. They have a great impact on the ways people transact business in financial markets. In times of crisis, regulations (or a lack thereof) are often cited as the cause of economic contraction. Not surprisingly, the financial crisis and global recession of 2008–2009 brought a hue and cry—and a substantive campaign—for renewed regulatory controls worldwide. Finally, it is important that there be global coordination of regulations among the major world economies. Regulations force institutions into behaviors that they would not engage in on their own and that reduce their profit. On their own, many institutions would take more risk, particularly in a world with deposit insurance or where there is thought to be a "lender of last resort" to bail out failed institutions. If regulations are not global—that is, if there is not a level playing field—then it is too easy for financial-market participants to move financial transactions to locales where regulation is less stringent.

Marc Lenglet

See also: Banks, Central; Federal Deposit Insurance Corporation; Federal Reserve System; Financial Markets; Glass-Steagall Act (1933); Liberalization, Financial; Securities and Exchange Commission.

Further Reading

Alexander, Kern, Rahul Dhumale, and John Eatwell. *Global Governance of Financial Systems: The International Regulation of Systemic Risk.* New York: Oxford University Press, 2006.

Basel Committee on Banking Supervision Web site: www.bis.org/bcbs.

Gray, Joanna, and Jenny Hamilton. *Implementing Financial Regulation: Theory and Practice.* Hoboken, NJ: John Wiley & Sons, 2006.

Heffernan, Shelagh. *Modern Banking in Theory and Practice.* Hoboken, NJ: John Wiley & Sons, 1996.

International Organization of Securities Commissions Web site: www.iosco.org.

May, Wilfried A. "Financial Regulation Abroad: The Contrasts with American Technique." *Journal of Political Economy* 47:4 (1939): 457–496.

Mitchener, Kris J. "Supervision, Regulation, and Financial Instability: The Political Economy of Banking During the Great Depression." *Journal of Economic History* 63:2 (2003): 525–532.

Mizruchi, Mark S., and Linda Brewer Stearns. "Money, Banking and Financial Markets." In *The Handbook of Economic Sociology*, ed. Neil J. Smelser and Richard Swedberg. Princeton, NJ: Princeton University Press, 1994.

Power, Michael. *Organized Uncertainty: Designing a World of Risk Management.* New York: Oxford University Press, 2007.

Singh, Dalvinder. *Banking Regulation of UK and US Financial Markets.* Farnham, UK: Ashgate, 2007.

Spencer, Peter D. *The Structure and Regulation of Financial Markets.* New York: Oxford University Press, 2000.

Resource Allocation

Every society must allocate its resources of land, labor, capital, and entrepreneurial ability to produce a chosen array of goods and services that satisfy the needs of the society. Economic systems organized according to capitalist principles allow markets and individual choices to determine the allocation of resources and the rewards from economic activities. Alternatively, in "command" economic systems, governments determine what is produced, how it is produced, and who gets what.

Most societies have evolved to embrace a mix of market and command features, such that governments play a significant direct role in certain economic sectors, like defense manufacturing and public transportation, as well as income redistribu-tion. The latter includes income support programs for the disabled and elderly, public education, and a variety of other public services, all financed through taxation.

Economic theory has evolved to explain the process of resource allocation and the concept of economic efficiency in resource allocation. The goal of economic activity regardless of the system or ideology of a particular society is to meet the needs of individuals and to match the additional benefits of various goods and services with the additional costs of providing them. At the outset, this process should embrace basic productive efficiency, so that goods and services are produced at minimum cost, and the broader concept of allocative efficiency, so that an efficient mix of goods and services is delivered to individuals.

Command Economies

Command economic systems would appear to offer significant advantages over capitalist systems to ensure allocative efficiency. From a central authority, production methods can be researched and applied in a controlled, integrated manner to ensure the most up-to-date production methods. Moreover, in a national emergency, the central planning authority can immediately assess the capacity of the economy to produce vital goods and services to meet specific national needs. At the same time, however, command systems are limited by the enormous information costs involved in centrally planned production and distribution. If a modern industrial society utilizes central planning and a command system in order to attain allocative efficiency, central planners need extensive, detailed information on consumer tastes and production methods for each region of the economy. A market economy leaves these decisions to market participants.

The eighteenth-century British economist Adam Smith was one of the first to observe that a capitalist system has built-in advantages to achieve allocative efficiency, although he did not use this term explicitly. Resources in a competitive market economy, he noted, are guided by an "invisible hand" that pushes the business community to produce products and services to serve consumer needs at the lowest possible cost. The self-interest of market participants—workers and business owners—to gain income acts in a way to maximize the return to society. Workers select lines of work in occupations of highest demand, and business owners are led by market forces to produce the products and services in highest demand at the lowest cost in order to maximize their own profit.

Economic theory has also identified the limitations of market systems, or the factors that lead a capitalist system away from allocative efficiency. But the most important aspect of the market system in achieving allocative efficiency is competition. With the discipline of competition, market agents acting in self-interest lead to efficiency-oriented behavior. Success, in terms of income, is measured by the degree to which the agent best meets the most important of society's needs at lowest cost. Without competition in products or services, the market serves self-interest rather than the needs of the society. A monopolist in the product or service market acts in a way that maximizes his own income at the expense of consumers by charging higher prices, limiting output, and producing inferior-quality goods.

Government acts in two primary ways to maintain competition. First, it monitors merger and acquisition activities of firms, disallowing monopolies or oligopolies (where a few large firms dominate an industry), which adversely affect competition. Second, governments take regulatory action in industries that are natural monopolies, such as a public water, natural gas, or electric utilities. Natural monopolies occur in situations where there are gains from size such that one large firm can produce the entire market quantity at a lower per-unit cost than if there are several firms. Regulatory action attempts to introduce competitive discipline by monitoring price levels, service quality, and profits to ensure that outcomes more closely resemble those of a competitive marketplace.

A monopolist in the factor market, called monopsony, has similar incentives in the absence of competition to reduce the quantity of the factor provided to increase resource return, and has incentives to restrict entry into the line of work. The factor market is where basic economic inputs—labor, capital, raw materials and so forth—are bought and sold. Examples of monopsonies include labor unions in labor markets, and OPEC nations in the market for crude oil.

Economic theory has also addressed other factors limiting the performance of market systems to achieve allocative efficiency. The technical nature of the provision of some goods and services—a notable example is the health care field—limits the ability of markets to perform efficiently. Some goods and services cannot be provided to the exclusion of any consumers; these are called public goods and services. Examples include fire protection, police protection, national defense, and the like. Consumers who may be excluded from the private market by not paying may hide their true preferences in the hope of having others pay for the goods on their behalf. The existence of "free riders" leads to underallocation of resources to the provision of such goods and services. Governments in these cases intervene to provide these goods and services, financing them through taxation.

Externalities

Market systems also do not perform efficiently in the presence of external effects in the production or consumption of goods and services. Perhaps the most familiar situation of external effects, also called externalities or spillovers, involves pollution. If a firm has access to natural resources as inputs or outputs in production, and degrades this resource through air and water pollution, for example, the process may adversely affect third parties who are not part of the production process and do not even purchase the goods. In this case, the market will over-allocate resources to the polluting industry, as it does not include all the resource costs within its production decision making. Simultaneously, market forces will underallocate resources to the industry adversely affected by pollution, since resource costs are increased by the amount of the pollution. Government action in these cases attempts to control the pollution either directly, through regulation, or through government-instituted market mechanisms such as effluent fees or tradable pollution permits that limit pollution to environmentally acceptable levels.

In some cases, the provision and consumption of goods and services can also involve positive externalities. The most frequently cited example is that of education. The benefits of education, for example, accrue to individuals and families as well to the community at large. The external benefits to the community include a more skilled, educated workforce, a more discerning electorate, and a more active, aware member of the community. Education tends to be underprovided in a market economy, however, as the total benefits are not captured by the individual or family unit. Thus, public funding of education through tax support is an attempt to create an optimum level of expenditure that reflects external benefits.

A lack of information, the cost of gathering information, or information imbalances among market participants pose obstacles to allocative efficiency. Most countries have legal systems that protect consumers, instituting laws and regulations to shield the public from hazardous products, unsafe food and medicine, and the like. In a completely unregulated environment, producers could develop products that are potentially harmful to users, the costs of which would not be included in the product cost. Consequently, the market system would overallocate resources to this activity.

Access to Information

On another level, the cost to an individual consumer of gathering essential information on products can be significant. If governments conduct such analysis, there would be an advantage in terms of economies of scale, and research results would allow consumers to make more informed product choices, which would enhance allocative efficiency.

Information problems also arise when information is withheld, manipulated, or gained through unethical means. Legislation related to fair trading and lending is intended to allow consumers to make more informed decisions, leading to an improvement in allocative efficiency. In financial markets, stringent rules on the gathering and use of information have been developed to ensure that all market participants have equal access to information. Individuals who have access to "inside information" on the future value of a financial security, and act on that information, can damage the credibility of the market for the general public, which does not have such special access. In the extreme, without securities laws to punish this behavior, the market cannot function and the potential for firms to raise funds and consumers to invest are eliminated.

The resource allocation process is central to any society in organizing the means of production and meeting the needs of the general populace. The two opposite means of carrying out this process are a command system in which there is planning by a central authority, and a decentralized system driven by markets. Most societies today are based on some variation, or combination, of the two extremes. The mixed economies of the Western world have evolved policies, laws, regulations, and public services to address social issues and directly intervene to address failures in resource allocation. The role of central planning in communist countries, meanwhile, has varied greatly. The Chinese model is based on rigid central control of social and political life, with the marketplace allowed to operate much more freely in the economic realm. In North Korea and Cuba, by contrast, strong central planning rules every aspect of life and society.

Derek Bjonback

See also: Classical Theories and Models; Financial Markets.

Further Reading

Blanchard, Olivier. *Macroeconomics.* 5th ed. Upper Saddle River NJ: Prentice Hall, 2009.

Blaug, Mark. *Economic Theory in Retrospect.* London: Cambridge University Press, 1978.

Samuelson, Paul A., and William D. Nordhaus. *Economics.* Boston: McGraw-Hill/Irwin, 2005.

Retail and Wholesale Trade

Retail and wholesale trade are two components of an economic process in which goods are transferred from manufacturers to consumers in exchange for money. The wholesale trade represents the intermediate step in which goods are sold by manufacturers to persons or companies that are retailers of various kinds, usually in large quantities and at below retail prices. In fact, there may be more than one step in wholesaling, as manufactured goods are often sold to distributors, who then sell them to retailers. Retailers, then, are the individuals and businesses that sell the goods to the ultimate consumers of those goods, be they individuals, businesses, or the government. In certain cases, the wholesaler and/or retailer may be bypassed as manufacturers sell directly to retailers and/or final consumers. Given that consumer demand is responsible for roughly two-thirds or more of all economic activity in industrialized countries, such as the United States, the retail and wholesale trades can both affect and be affected by the business cycle in a variety ways.

Wholesale Trade

Goods produced by manufactures need to be brought to market and made available for consumption. Wholesalers, such as the U.S. firm Sysco for food products, essentially move goods from producers to market. Wholesaling usually implies the purchase of goods from producers or other suppliers and their storage in warehouses, from which they are then made available for resale to companies that either intend to resell them directly to consumers or use them for their own operations. Wholesale trade usually includes establishments that sell products to retailers, contractors, and industrial, institutional, and other commercial users. Wholesalers, because of the intermediate position they occupy in the production-distribution chain, are able to compete with direct sales by manufacturers to retailers through economies of scale and scope in transport as well as in stock holding.

Generally speaking, two main categories of wholesalers can be distinguished: merchant wholesalers on the one hand, such as Michigan-based Apco for electronics or the Georgia-based S.P. Richards Company for furniture, and wholesale electronic markets, agents, and brokers, such as Washington state–based importers.com for a variety of industries on the other. The former purchase the merchandise they sell, taking full ownership of it. Within the general category of merchant wholesalers, a further distinction can be drawn between those that provide full service and those that provide only limited service. Full-service merchant wholesalers are differentiated by the larger volume of sales and the broader array of services they can offer. Limited-service wholesalers handle relatively smaller sales volumes and offer fewer services. Among the different kinds of limited-service merchant wholesalers are cash-and-carry wholesalers, jobbers (also known as truck wholesalers), and drop shippers, among others. Jobbers are wholesalers who transport and sell products, especially food, directly from their vehicles. Drop shippers are wholesalers who do not handle the merchandise they sell, but remit orders directly to producers. Their presence is common in bulk industries such as coal.

Unlike merchant wholesalers, wholesale electronic markets, agents, and brokers do not acquire ownership of the products they sell. Using the Internet or other electronic means, wholesale electronic markets put purchasers and sellers in touch with each other, usually for a commission. Brokers are marketing intermediaries common in certain sectors, such as food, insurance, and real estate. They often represent different producers of noncompeting goods and are paid on a commission basis. As for agents, three types can be differentiated: purchasing agents, manufacturers' agents, and sales agents. Purchasing agents generally perform the following functions: receipt, storage, and shipment of products to buyers. Manufacturers' agents are contractors who work on commission basis and handle the sale of products for two or more producers. In fact, manufacturers' agents frequently represent different companies that offer compatible but noncompeting goods. This system offers the practical advantage of limiting the costs of sale by spreading them across the different products. Manufacturers' agents are extensively employed by companies that lack the necessary financial resources to establish their own sales team. In general, manufacturers' agents can work quite independently, as they are not under the direct supervision of the manufacturer. Unlike manufacturers' agents, who do not handle the producer's entire output, sales agents have the contractual power to sell the entire output of a particular manufacturer. Working with relative autonomy, they can set prices and determine conditions of sale.

Wholesaling can also be conducted by producers themselves without hiring the services of independent wholesalers. This is made possible through manufacturers' sales branches.

Retail Trade

The direct sale of products to end users can be conducted by a wide variety of economic operators. Of the many kinds of retailers that make products available for consumption and handle the final sale, independent retailers are by far the largest group. They account for the most significant portion of the total volume of business done by retail stores. An independent retailer is different from other types of retailers, such as chain stores, in several key respects. Generally speaking, an independent retailer is a small enterprise owned and run by individual proprietors or smaller partnerships. If

not a family-run business, it tends to have the characteristics of one. Notable among these is the capacity to establish close relations with customers. In small shops, for instance, the owner knows many customers personally, remembers their tastes, and caters specifically to their needs. The close relationship between retailer and customers is a great competitive advantage against larger, more impersonal businesses. For many, in fact, it is crucial for the survival of the business at a time when local markets are increasingly dominated by a few large retailer companies. Independent retailers are often located in or close to residential areas. Being small-sized operators, they do not employ a specialized professional staff, with expertise in window display and advertising, for example. Owner-operators typically handle such functions themselves.

At the other end of the retail spectrum are chain stores, such as Target (general merchandise), Staples (office supplies), or Bed Bath & Beyond (housewares). A chain-store system is a group of at least four, but usually more, stores with common ownership and central management. The chain store is a comparatively recent form of retailing, emerging in the latter part of the nineteenth century and gaining prominence over the course of the twentieth century.

Retailing is also conducted through department stores. The department store is a retail establishment that sells a wide range of different products, such as clothes, furniture, kitchen and bath items, and appliances, among others. In the early part of the twentieth century, such establishments were located in big cities, often in the central downtown shopping area. In the decades following World War II, such stores were increasingly located in suburban shopping areas, especially malls.

In the next evolutionary phase in retail distribution, the shopping mall appeared in the post–World War II era as a confluence of social factors drew city dwellers to the suburbs. Shopping malls offer consumers the chance to shop for a large variety of different products in the same

With consumer sales down during times of recession, retailers find new ways to attract customers. Here, a woman shops at a grocery outlet—also referred to as a "surplus" or "salvage" grocer—where overstocked and out-of-date food is sold at a deep discount. *(William Thomas Cain/Stringer/Getty Images)*

place. In these establishments, in fact, there is a high concentration of stores that sell a wide range of goods. Shopping malls soon became a consumer mainstay and social attraction, opening in urban areas as well as the suburbs and exurbs.

Other common forms of retailing include discount stores (Costco), consumer cooperatives (often locally run, one-off establishments), and franchise organizations (best known in the food industry). Discount stores are establishments that sell merchandise at a discounted price, below the producer's list price, limiting their operating costs by offering fewer services and minimal customer assistance. Outlet malls, which have become increasingly popular in recent years, are home to several or many stores. By and large, they are located away from large cities and specialize in selling products—usually clothes and accessories—of well-known brands.

Consumer cooperatives (co-ops) are retail establishments created, owned, and operated by consumers for their own benefit. Membership is open and profits are shared among the members in the form of refunds for their purchases. Con-

sumer cooperatives offer a convenient alternative to consumers who are not fully satisfied with the prices and services offered by traditional retailers in the area where they live.

Franchise organizations have grown remarkably in recent decades and have become a common means of retail distribution. A franchise organization is based on a specific type of relationship between a producer (or wholesaler or service provider) and an independent entrepreneur, regulated by a special contract. Under the franchise agreement, the producer (franchiser) and the independent entrepreneur (franchisee) stipulate terms by which the latter purchases the right to own and run a number of units (retail outlets) in the franchise system. One of the defining characteristics of franchise organizations is that they handle a unique product or service.

Another way of retailing products to consumers is through merchandising conglomerates, which derive from the combination of different lines that share the same ownership. They have an integrated distribution and management system.

Since the 1980s, retailing has become one of

the fast-growing and most dynamic economic sectors in America, boosted in no small measure by the opening of new channels on the Internet. Many retailers, new and old, have successfully exploited the possibilities offered by electronic trade by operating Web sites where one can buy online the same products as in a "real" shop—generally for much lower prices because the seller carries no store overhead. The growth of electronic commerce and changes in the pattern of consumption in developed countries have made online shopping a new, appealing, and profitable way of retailing.

With consumer spending accounting for more than two of every three dollars of economic activity in the United States and other industrialized nations, the retail sector deeply affects the economic cycle. Retail and wholesale sales are affected by both season (retail sales spike before Christmas while wholesale numbers spike well in advance of the holidays) and by the business cycle and, in turn, have a major impact on the latter. During economic downturns—marked by declines in aggregate demand—retailers see sales drop off, leading them to cut orders to wholesalers and manufacturers. Drops in orders produce buildups in inventory, leading manufacturers to cut back on production in order to reduce those inventories. Drops in manufacturing activity lead to higher unemployment, less investment, and slower overall economic growth, or even decline. Such a slackening of economic growth further reduces demand; if demand falls off enough, a recession results. Ultimately, when inventories fall enough, businesses gear up production and hire workers, which stimulates demand and can lift the economy out of recession and back into growth.

At the same time, wholesale and retail sales represent a key indicator of economic growth or contraction. Retail and wholesale numbers are considered two of the most important economic indicators, and the monthly wholesale and retail trade reports put out by the U.S. Census Bureau are two of the sets of numbers most closely watched and analyzed by economists. If retail and wholesale numbers pick up, then it is likely that manufac-

turing will as well, as inventories diminish and manufacturers move to take advantage of increased consumer demand.

Financial Crisis and Recession of 2007–2009

The financial crisis and recession of 2007 to 2009 provides an example of how wholesale and retail sales are affected by the larger economy and, at the same time, drive larger economic trends. In January 2007—about eight months before the recession began in the United States—monthly retail sales stood at roughly $363 billion. (Note: U.S. Census Bureau data lumps together retail and food service numbers.) By January 2008, as the recession was just beginning to set in, the figure was $376 billion. While this represented a $13 billion increase in retail sales, the 3.6 percent increase pales in comparison to more prosperous years, such as January 2005 to January 2006, when the number climbed from roughly $330 billion to $358 billion, an 8.5 percent increase. By January 2009, at the tail end of the recession, the retail figures were well into negative territory. Between January 2008 and January 2009, retail sales had fallen from $376 billion to $340 billion, a 6.9 percent drop, slightly larger than the annualized gross domestic product contraction of 6.1 percent for the economy as a whole. By the second quarter of 2009, however, government analysts were declaring the recession over, despite very high unemployment numbers. One of the key factors behind this declaration was retail numbers. By January 2010, retail sales had climbed to $356 billion, an increase of 4.7 percent, though the figure was still below the number for January 2008.

While standard economic factors—such as slackening production and investment and rising unemployment—had an impact on retail sales, economists also point to the financial crisis and housing-price crash as critical in undermining retail demand. With house prices rising in the mid-2000s, many people began to spend more and save less. The rising equity in their homes convinced many that they needed to save less of that equity for retirement purposes. In addition, many people had taken out lines of credit against their rising home equity and used the cash to pay for home improvements—a key retail sector—and other consumer goods. Many were able to do this because interest rates were so low and lending standards had become lax. As housing prices began to fall, the financial industry began to tighten credit, making it more difficult for people to borrow and spend. Meanwhile, diminishing home equity forced many people to think again about their savings activity, sending savings up and retail spending numbers down. And, as noted above, slackening consumer demand reinforced weakening trends in the U.S. economy, helping to push the country into recession.

Antonella Viola and James Ciment

See also: Circuit City Stores; Consumption; Inventory Investment; Linens 'n Things.

Further Reading

Adcock, Dennis, Al Halborg, and Caroline Ross. *Marketing Principles and Practice.* Upper Saddle River, NJ: Pearson Education, 2001.

Alexander, Nicholas. *International Retailing.* New York: Oxford University Press, 2009.

Darnay, Arsen J., and Joyce Piwowarski, eds. *Wholesale and Retail Trade USA: Industry Analyses, Statistics, and Leading Organizations.* Detroit: Gale, 2000.

Rosenbloom, Bert, ed. *Wholesale Distribution Channels: New Insights and Perspectives.* New York: Haworth, 1993.

Sandhusen, Richard L. *Marketing.* New York: Barron's Educational Series, 2008.

Seth, Andrew, and Geoffrey Randall. *The Grocers: The Rise and Rise of the Supermarket Chains.* Dover, NH: Kogan Page, 1999.

Retirement Instruments

Between its inception in September 2007 and its low point in March 2009, the U.S. financial crisis cost an estimated $3.8 trillion in lost retirement savings for the American people, reducing the average retirement account by 43 percent. Although a portion of those losses was recouped in the market turnaround of succeeding months, the episode underscored the rising vulnerability of America's elderly in the current retirement system. Instead of providing economic security, changes in the nation's retirement and pension plans over time have increased the exposure of the older population to financial volatility. In addition, defined-benefit plans, in which employers guaranteed a specific monthly payment upon retirement, have been increasingly replaced in recent decades by defined-contribution plans, in which employers and employees put set amounts into retirement accounts each month. In other words, the retiree does not receive a fixed payment every month, but draws from a portfolio of investments that could be subject to market volatility if it consists of corporate securities and other volatile financial instruments.

Public Pensions and Defined Benefit Plans

Currently there are three major plans that provide retirement income in the United States: Social Security, employment-based plans (including defined-benefit and defined-contribution retirement plans), and non-employment-based savings and investments (including home equity, though the latter has been diminished somewhat by a slide in housing prices since 2007). Social Security was enacted in 1935 as part of President Franklin D. Roosevelt's New Deal policies to reverse and offset the effects of the Great Depression. Officially part of the Old-Age, Survivors, and Disability Insurance (OASDI) program, Social Security was expanded in the following decades to include the Medicare program and coverage for people with disabilities and their dependents. Its main purpose was to fight poverty among the elderly. It was, and still is, based on the principle of taking in contributions from active workers and paying out to those who are eligible to receive the retirement benefit. Since 1935, Social Security has been a major source of retirement income for the majority of Americans, constituting about 36 percent of the aggregate income of persons over the age of 65. In the early twenty-first century there has been an effort by some to change or privatize the Social Security system based on ideological opposition to public programs or the argument that the fund is not solvent. Others, however, claim that it is solvent and financially healthy enough to pay out to retirees until 2041 and to cover most payments beyond that date, as long as the Treasury Department pays back its debt to the Social Security program. The ideological (conservative versus liberal) controversy surrounding this issue continues into the second decade of the century.

Historically, employment-based retirement programs existed alongside the Social Security program. Until the late 1960s, defined-benefit pension plans were a prominent supplement to Social Security for many employees. Under these plans, the employer guaranteed a certain retirement income calculated using a formula based on years of service and a percentage of pay. The plans had to be fully funded even if the employee was not yet fully vested in the plan—that is, before the employee had worked long enough to be eligible to collect from the plan. In addition, the funds accumulated were not transferable—the employee could not take them along after changing jobs. In December 1963, the collapse of the automaker Studebaker left thousands of workers without a pension. The Studebaker event brought to public attention other episodes of poorly financed pension plans and complex requirements regarding vesting. In response to the public outrage, Congress drafted and passed the Employee Retirement Income Security Act (ERISA), which President Gerald Ford signed into law on September 2, 1974.

Defined Contribution Plans

ERISA established a set of regulations concerning the operation of pension plans. Through Keogh plans, it also expanded pension opportunities for the self-employed, who were not covered by Individual Retirement Accounts (IRAs). Although ERISA was proposed with good intentions, it took away some of the flexibility enjoyed by employers and employees in the pre-ERISA period. In addition, changes in tax codes regarding employee benefits raised new questions about the funding of defined-retirement benefits. Not surprisingly, in the 1970s defined-contribution plans started becoming more popular among employers, and they became a more common way for employees to fund their retirement.

Defined-contribution plans allocate the employer contribution to individual-employee retirement accounts according to a predetermined formula. There are a variety of such plans, each offering the benefit of tax deferment. That is, the contribution the employee makes is deducted from his or her gross income at the time the payment is made, with the tax paid upon retirement. The deferral of the tax payment is beneficial because it represents a smaller amount of money due to inflation. Upon retirement, the employer collects the account contributions and the returns to the account accumulated over time. In most cases the employer (called the sponsor) also contributes a percentage of the employee's salary to the retirement plan.

To expedite the management of the plans (and to distance itself from the entire retirement process) the sponsor chooses an administrator—for example, a mutual fund or insurance company, or a brokerage firm. The administrator offers a menu of assets the employee can choose from for investing. The menu consists of a diversified list of mutual funds, stocks, and bonds, options, money market securities, and so on. A mutual fund is a composite financial instrument where a large number of investors pool their contributions and invest in a mix of stocks, bonds, money market funds, and other securities. The value of the investment pool fluctuates in the market, and therefore there is no guaranteed return. A stock is a share of ownership in a company. If the company does well, the price of the share in the market rises; the reverse is true if it falls. A bond is a financial instrument that facilitates borrowing by companies with the promise that the principle and the predetermined interest will be paid at the end of a fixed term. Like stocks, bonds are traded and their price fluctuates. Money market securities are one of the more liquid and low-risk retirement instruments, and consequently have a relatively low return. They are IOUs issued by corporations, financial institutions, and government agencies with a short maturity.

The investment menu offered by mutual funds provides the opportunity to invest in equity funds, balanced funds, bond funds, and money market funds. Equity funds are invested in corporate stocks. If the stocks are of large corporations (large-cap), they have a relatively low risk. If the stocks are, on the other hand, of small and new companies (small-cap), the risk is higher. Some of the fund investments may be value investments in companies that are considered undervalued. Others may be growth investments in companies with a promise of future profit growth. The return on investment in equity funds depends on the income from stocks and bonds and on the growth of the value of stocks and bonds. A balanced fund is composed of stocks and bonds in variable proportions to appeal to investors with different risk preferences. They are relatively low-risk. Bond funds are low- to moderate-risk. The lowest-risk bonds are those backed by the federal government. Money market funds are also low-risk and offer only interest income. These funds invest predominantly in short-term securities, such as certificates of deposit (CDs) and U.S. Treasury bills.

Money-purchase pension plans are another financial retirement instrument in which the employer and employee make predetermined contributions based on a percentage of the employee's annual compensation. The sum is invested into mutual or other funds and is subject to vesting requirements. Returns are not guaranteed; they depend on market fluctuations.

Deferred profit-sharing plans are deferred plans (usually supplemental) whereby the employees get a share of the company's profits. These shares can be paid to the employees in the form of cash or stocks, or put into a deferred plan. The rules for these plans regarding tax treatment, vesting, employee eligibility, and funding are complex and are defined in ERISA in detail.

Employee stock ownership plans (ESOPs) are qualified defined-contribution retirement plans whereby the employee receives shares in company stock, either through a stock-option plan or a company 401(k) plan. As a result of stock ownership, the employee is vested in the company's success. Thus, it is sometimes argued, these kinds of plans have significant positive productivity effects. There are two kinds of stock-ownership plans. The leveraged-ownership plan allows the company to raise its capital by borrowing from bank and nonbank financial institutions to buy stocks. In the basic-ownership plan, on the other hand, the employer directly contributes tax-free cash or stock shares. ESOPs are more suitable for relatively large companies, and can be costly for smaller ones.

Stock-bonus plans are defined-contribution retirement plans under which the employer shares a portion of company profits with the employee in the form of stock options. Contributions are discretionary, so the employer may choose not to contribute in a given year. Employee performance is rewarded under such a plan, and giving employees a stake in the company can encourage efficiency and productivity. This plan is ideal for newer businesses with unstable profit patterns.

A simplified employee pension plan (SEP) is an easy way for an employer to help its employees begin saving for retirement. The employee establishes a SEP IRA into which tax-deductible contributions are made by the employer. The contribution limit is 25 percent of the participant's total compensation. This type of plan does not have the considerable amount of paperwork and compliance requirements of a regular retirement plan.

Individual retirement accounts (IRAs), as mentioned above, are tax-deferred retirement plans into which retirement contributions are made by those who are not covered by any other plan.

Shift to 401(k)s

In the course of recent decades, a number of large corporations (with the consent of the majority of employees) have replaced their defined pension plans with 401(k)s. In the 1990s especially, when the stock market was performing well, more and more defined-benefit plans were converted into defined-contribution plans. Since then, the 1978 Revenue Act has been amended numerous times to regulate diversification, maximum compensation, and defined and elective contribution limits, as well as to increase corporate responsibility and accountability (Sarbanes-Oxley Act of 2002). More recently, Roth 401(k)s have become increasingly popular among investors. Roth 401(k)s are different than other 401(k)s in that the contributions are taxed but the withdrawals are not, allowing the contributions to grow tax-free. Another difference between the two types is that the Roth 401(k) has no minimum withdrawal requirement at the age seventy-and-a-half. Since 401(k)s are tax-deferred, the Internal Revenue Service (IRS) requires that at, age seventy-and-a-half, a retiree starts withdrawing from the retirement savings according to a predetermined formula so that the IRS can start taxing the withdrawal and avoid the situation of not receiving any tax payments on deferred retirement savings.

Tax-deferred 403(b)s are plans for the employees of nonprofit organizations, such as churches and hospitals, and of public educational institutions. Similarly, 457s are for state and municipal employees, and thrift saving plans (TSPs) are for federal employees (including members of armed forces, public health service, and other government bodies).

IRAs, mentioned above, are available to individuals whose employers do not offer pension plans and whose adjusted gross income is below a specified level. They are tax-deferred plans until withdrawal, at which point proceeds are taxed as income. They also have contribution limits specified by law.

A different retirement instrument offered by insurance companies is the deferred annuity. Deferred annuities differ from aforementioned instruments in that they provide a guaranteed income stream in retirement (lump sum or incremental), the amount of which depends on the contributions one makes. Deferred annuities appeal to persons who prefer a guaranteed income in retirement as well as those who have reached their contribution limits to IRAs. Because of their high fees, however, they are expensive and carry restricted investment choices.

There are three major categories of annuities. Fixed annuities are relatively low-risk and have a minimum guaranteed return; they also carry a guarantee against losses by the insurance company that offers the annuity. In the case of variable annuity, contributions are not part of the insurance company's assets and there is no guaranteed return. The return and the risk of the annuity are determined by the market performance and composition of the securities in the fund. A third category is the so-called equity-index annuity, which bases returns on a specific market index, such as the Standard & Poor's 500, with a guaranteed minimum interest. Thus, one enjoys market gains but is protected against market losses.

In each of these deferred arrangements, the employer provides the employee with a list of different savings or "investment" options, usually in the form of mutual funds. In some cases, the employer also contributes a percentage of the employee's salary to the fund. The implicit assumption in this process is that each employee is a well-informed, rational decision maker regarding the maximization of the future retirement income stream. The employee is also expected to assess the potential risks and benefits associated with various investment opportunities, such as mutual funds based on different mixtures of domestic and international bonds, stocks, and money market securities. Even though the selection process is facilitated by the mutual fund companies with expert advice and retirement calculators, the wide variety of available funds presents a challenge for employees of different ages, risk preferences, retirement incomes, and retirement age goals. Nevertheless, as long as the markets perform well, defined-contribution plans are a rewarding source for retirement savings. Until 2007, they indeed provided a significantly higher return than traditional savings instruments such as CDs and bank savings accounts. As the markets started to melt down in mid-2007, however, people belatedly realized the extent of their exposure to market volatility. In fact, even before the crisis set in, in spite of the market gains in the 1990s and 2003–2006, the average American worker without a defined-benefit retirement plan had not accumulated enough savings to guarantee a decent retirement income. Half of the private-sector employees who contributed to a 401(k) had an average of only $25,000 in their account in 2006.

The complicated retirement financing system in the United States raises fundamental questions regarding effectiveness. Many people consider the system both insufficient and insecure. Consequently, a new initiative has been launched to create a mandatory, universal, secure retirement system, in addition to Social Security, under the auspices of the Economic Policy Institute (EPI) think tank and the Service Employees International Union (SEIU).

The recession and economic crisis of 2007–2009 highlighted the vulnerability of the retirement system in the United States. The decline in securities valuations caused significant declines in the retirement portfolios of millions of Americans. The impact was less severe for younger employees, who had smaller portfolios and a much longer time period in which to recoup their losses. But for retirees and those nearing retirement age, the losses can have a devastating effect, forcing many back to work—if they can find a job at all—to supplement depleted reserves and forcing those approaching retirement to put off the day on which they can stop working.

Mehmet Odekon

See also: Mortgage, Reverse; Savings and Investment; Tax Policy.

Further Reading

Center for Economic and Policy Research. *Slow-Motion Recession.* Washington, DC: CEPR, 2008.

Economic Policy Institute (EPI). 2009. *Principles for a New Retirement System.* Washington, DC: EPI, 2009.

Employee Benefit Research Institute. "How Much Have American Workers Saved For Retirement?" Fast Facts #19. Washington, DC: EBRI, 2009. Available at http://www.ebri.org. Accessed March 2010.

Service Employees International Union. "Coalition Partners Launch Retirement USA Initiative." Available at www.seiu.org/2009/03/seiu-coalition-partners-launch-retirement-usa-initiative.php. Accessed January 12, 2010.

United States Department of Labor. 2009. *What Is ERISA?* Available at www.dol.gov/index.htm. Accessed January 12, 2010.

Risk and Uncertainty

Risk is defined in economic terms as the possibility of suffering financial loss, and uncertainty as the state of not knowing whether one will experience gain or loss in the future. In economics, two general rules apply when it comes to risk—most people are risk averse; and the greater the risk, the greater the return. Much economic activity revolves around ways individuals and businesses seek to minimize risk for a given return, or maximize return for a given level of risk. In general, activities that reduce risk for a given return enhance general economic welfare.

Risk and uncertainty are, of course, inherent elements of life. We do not know, for example, what nature will send our way. In California, an earthquake can bring a homeowner's most important possession crashing to the ground; in Florida, an untimely frost can destroy an orange grower's carefully tended crop. In a sense, capitalist economics mimics nature, as market forces often resemble in their complexity and unpredictability the workings of geology or climate.

Risk Aversion

By nature, most people are risk averse. That is to say, gains and losses being equal, most people experience a greater degree of displeasure from loss than pleasure from gain. To take a simple example, say a person has $5,000 safely deposited in a federally insured bank account. The risk of keeping it there is virtually zero. But let's say someone comes along and offers that person the chance of doubling their $5,000 on the flip of a coin. Because there is an equal chance of doubling or losing one's money, economists say the bet has an "expected value" of zero. That being the case, such a bet can be considered fair. Nevertheless, most people would decline the offer. That is because the loss of the $5,000 could put the person in the street, unable to pay her rent, while the gain of $5,000 will just buy some luxuries or provide a degree of future security. Neither is as strongly positive as imminent homelessness is negative. In a sense, then, risk aversion is a subset of that bedrock principle of modern economic thought—the diminishing marginal utility of income. That is to say, the utility gained from the extra amount of money one gets from winning the coin toss is less than the utility lost from losing it.

While humans may be risk averse, they still have to live with risk and uncertainty. Thus, most people work hard to avoid or, at least, minimize risk. For instance, some people may choose career paths that have a higher probability of reward than those that do not, even though the latter may be more personally satisfying. And people tend to drive to work even though that is a riskier choice than walking. The marginal utility of driving is so much greater in terms of speed that most people are willing to accept the dangers to life, limb, and fortune of driving a car. Or at some point, most people will buy a home, even though they can never be sure if fire will destroy their investment or a downturn in the market will diminish its value.

Businesses, too, must exist in a world of uncertainty and risk, but with a difference. While individuals generally do not seek out economic risk, businesses must, if they expect to prosper or even survive. Retailers stock up for a busy Christ-mas season knowing full well that a retail slump could leave them with unsold inventory. A mining company invests huge amounts of capital in a new dig not knowing what the future holds. The mine may not bring in enough ore to pay back the investment, or demand for the metal may slump, or political instability in the host country may close down production.

Risk Minimization and Avoidance

There are two ways individuals and businesses can help to reduce or minimize risk for a given return. One is through information gathering and assimilation. Economic theory, of course, operates on the assumption that people and businesses act rationally on all available information. At the same time, risk and uncertainty imply that present information may be superseded by future, contradictory information.

Markets offer another way for people and businesses to avoid or minimize risk—risk sharing. The most common example of this is insurance. Most homeowners and businesses, for example, take out fire insurance. This works both for those taking out the policies and for those offering them. For the policyholder, it offers the peace of mind and certainty that the economic consequences of an unpredictable event—a fire or flood, for example—is minimized or eliminated. The marginal utility of protection from catastrophic loss outweighs the costs of monthly premium payments. But while fire or flooding is unpredictable for an individual or business, it is much more predictable for a given population. Thus, the insurance company can expect to make more money from the thousands of premiums than it does from paying the costs of dozens of fires or floods—that is, if it has the right information, in the form of actuarial tables, at its disposal.

On a larger scale, many governments work to reduce uncertainty and risk for individuals by insisting that their citizens buy into social insurance schemes. By forcing people to pay into a retirement plan, such as America's Social Security system, governments ensure that people will have some income when they are too old to work. On the other hand, if governments attempt to intercede to reduce market risks for businesses, they may in fact, through a phenomenon known as moral hazard, have the opposite effect. For example, critics of the U.S. government's 2008 bailout of major financial institutions argued that the payouts would induce riskier behavior in the future because the people making the investment decisions for those institutions may come to believe that they will not suffer the full economic consequences should those decisions in the future turn out to be bad ones.

Insurance, however, is only the most obvious market mechanism for risk minimization and avoidance. Speculation is another. At first glance, speculation appears to increase risk—one is buying something on the expectation that its value will go up, a highly uncertain and risky act. But speculation can also offer certainty. A farmer, for example, may sell his crop to a speculator for a particular price even before it is reaped, guaranteeing the farmer a predictable income against volatile market forces. Speculation, then, differs from gambling. While the latter offers no real social utility—other than the fleeting pleasure a gambler takes from the game—speculation does offer social utility.

Risk minimization can also be achieved through diversity of investment. As all financial advisers suggest, individuals and businesses should never place all of their capital in a single investment or even a single type of investment. By diversifying a portfolio with corporate securities, government bonds, real estate, money market accounts, and other investments, one minimizes the dangers of the boom-bust cycle, as many of these investments tend to perform differently in given market conditions. Moreover, each offers different levels of return, usually based on the level of risk. As noted earlier, with greater risk comes greater return.

The corporate structure and the joint venture provide other ways for individuals and businesses to share and, thus, minimize risk. Corporations offer risk minimization in two ways—one legal and one economic. The corporate form reduces the liability of the investor to the amount invested. Thus, if a corporation goes deeply into debt and becomes insolvent, the investor is not in danger of losing his or her personal fortune. Economically, corporations allow individuals and businesses to invest in a venture collectively, thereby spreading the risk. Similarly, joint ventures between businesses allow them to share the costs of large projects. Of course, the same relationship of risk and return applies in these cases as well. Two companies that choose to share the costs of a project on a fifty-fifty basis, thus reducing potential losses by 50 percent, also choose to forego 50 percent of the returns.

Recent Developments

While risk minimization is probably as old as economic activity itself, recent technological developments have allowed for innovation in risk sharing unknown to previous generations. Through sophisticated computer modeling and the communications revolution, financiers and financial institutions have been able develop and market a nearly endless array of instruments—from mortgage-backed securities to financial derivatives to hedge fund accounts—aimed at spreading risk and the returns that can derive from taking on risk. Such activities may have a social utility. Just as insurance spreads the costs of fire losses over a large population base, so securitization of debts spreads out the costs of default, making it possible for financial institutions to offer credit to more people at lower cost.

However, as the recent financial crisis of the first decade of the 2000s has made clear, risk sharing and minimization for the individual investor can increase risk to an economy as a whole. For example, by bundling mortgages into securities and then selling them, the initiators of the mortgages reduced their risk of default to the point where they minimized their own concern about the costs of those defaults, leading them to offer credit to those who really did not deserve it. When, inevitably, home valuations declined and the economy went into recession, those defaults piled up, diminishing the value of the mortgage-backed securities and increasing the risk attached to them. However, the bundling process made it difficult to assess the value of those securities. And because less information usually means greater risk, this inability to assess value greatly increased the risk of lending to institutions that held the securities, which led to the freezing up of the credit markets that helped plunge the world economy into the worst financial crisis and economic downturn since the Great Depression.

James Ciment

See also: Behavioral Economics; Classical Theories and Models; Financial Markets; Hedge Funds; Real-Estate Speculation.

Further Reading

Banks, Erik. *Risk and Financial Catastrophe.* New York: Palgrave Macmillan, 2009.

Rebonato, Riccardo. *Plight of the Fortune Tellers: Why We Need to Manage Financial Risk Differently.* Princeton, NJ: Princeton University Press, 2007.

van Gestel, Tony, and Bart Baesens. *Credit Risk Management. Basic Concepts: Financial Risk Components, Rating Analysis, Models, Economic and Regulatory Capital.* New York: Oxford University Press, 2009.

Von Neumann, John, and Oskar Morgenstern. *Theory of Games and Economic Behavior.* 3rd ed. Princeton, NJ: Princeton University Press, 1953.

Robbins, Lionel Charles (1898–1984)

British economist Lionel Charles Robbins was a prominent voice in British debates over macroeconomic policy and theory from the 1930s to his death in the 1980s. He helped integrate Austrian school economic theories into British economic thought, especially in relation to the business cycle. In addition, he was largely responsible for expanding the British university system.

Born on November 22, 1898, in Middlesex, England, Robbins was educated at Southall County School; University College, London; and the London School of Economics, from which he received his undergraduate degree in 1923. After lecturing for a year at New College, Oxford, he returned to the London School of Economics in 1925 as a lecturer. In 1929, he was named a professor of political economics, a position he held until 1961; he remained affiliated with the school on a part-time basis until 1980. During World War II, Robbins served as director of the economics section of the Offices of the War Cabinet, and was a member of the team that negotiated the 1945 Anglo-American Loan (from the United States to England to help the country get back on its feet following the war). He served as president of the Royal Economic Society from 1954 to 1955, and was made a life peer of Great Britain in 1959. From 1961 to 1970, he was chairman of the *Financial Times.* He also chaired, from 1961 to 1964, the committee on higher education, and in 1963 published the *Robbins Report,* which advocated the funding and expansion of higher education in Britain.

As a young economist, Robbins adopted the views of such Austrian school economists as Eugen von Böhm-Bawerk, Ludwig von Mises, and Friedrich von Hayek, rather than following the Marshallian and Keynesian tradition of British economics (associated with the work of Alfred Marshall and John Maynard Keynes). His best-known book, *An Essay on the Nature and Significance of Economic Science* (1932), remains an extremely influential text, regarded by some as one of most important works of twentieth-century economics. In it, Robbins defines economics as "the science which studies human behaviour as a relationship between given ends and scarce means which have alternative uses." He posits that there is a clear separation between economics and such disciplines as psychology and sociology, and he seeks to distinguish value (or subjective) judgments from those aspects of economics that he believed were objective and "scientific" (hence his use of the term *economic science*).

Robbins was an exponent of the Austrian theory of the trade cycle, using it to interpret the Great

Depression of the 1930s. The central feature of the Austrian theory was the belief that depressions are an inevitable consequence of earlier expansions in a country's money supply and an overexpansion of production capacity. Robbins believed that the impact of World War I and subsequent economic problems in the early 1920s had led to the overexpansion and overdevelopment of industries that produced capital goods. When banks were forced to halt credit expansion, consumer expenditures declined and half-completed investment projects were abandoned.

Robbins's views countered those of Keynes, who believed that the government should infuse a depressed economy with money to encourage easier borrowing. Robbins thought that easy credit was among the factors that had caused economic instability in the first place. He published his views in *The Great Depression* (1934), but later, in his *Autobiography of an Economist* (1971), he confessed to being unhappy with his earlier work and said he would rather see it forgotten. The change of attitude stemmed from Robbins's contention that his ideas about correcting economic depressions had been swayed by the elegance of the Austrian model. In other words, he believed that he had become a hostage to a theoretical construction that was not appropriate to the economic situation of the 1920s and 1930s.

Robbins came to regard his earlier rejection of Keynes as the greatest mistake of his professional career. In fact, during the 1940s, his views on macroeconomic policy were similar to Keynes's. Robbins spent his later years writing about the history of economics, lecturing, and supporting education and the arts. He died in London on May 15, 1984.

Christopher Godden

See also: Austrian School; Hayek, Friedrich August von; Mises, Ludwig von.

Further Reading

Howson, Susan. "The Origins of Lionel Robbins's Essay on the Nature and Significance of Economic Science." *History of Political Economy* 36:3 (2004): 413–443.

Robbins, Lionel. *An Essay on the Nature and Significance of Economic Science.* London: Macmillan, 1932.
———. *Autobiography of an Economist.* London: Macmillan, 1971.
———. *The Great Depression.* London: Macmillan, 1934.

Robertson, Dennis Holme (1890–1963)

Dennis Holme Robertson was a British economist who made important contributions to the study of money supply and business cycles in the early part of the twentieth century. His work on business cycles, which emphasized the role of technological innovation, is regarded by modern economists as being ahead of its time.

Robertson was born on May 23, 1890, in Lowestoft, England. He was educated at Eton and at Trinity College, Cambridge, where he was elected a fellow in 1914. During World War I, he served as a transport officer and was awarded the military cross for gallantry. He taught at Cambridge from 1930 to 1938, at which time he joined the faculty of the University of London as the Sir Ernest Cassel professor of money and banking. After working in the British Treasury during World War II, Robertson returned to Cambridge in 1944, where he taught political economy until his retirement in 1957. He was knighted in 1953.

In his first major work, *A Study of Industrial Fluctuation* (1915), Robertson uses historical evidence to support his argument that fluctuations in economic activity do not arise from psychological or monetary forces, but rather from the impact on the economy of technological innovations and inventions. In this respect, Robertson viewed business cycles as a consequence of the process of economic growth resulting from the introduction of new technology. He suggests that innovations create upswings in the business cycle, leading to massive overinvestment as entrepreneurs take economic advantage of the new technology.

However, Robertson argues, because investments are generally made without taking into account true economic conditions, such as actual demand, overinvestment will eventually lead to a downturn of the cycle or even an economic contraction. Robertson's ideas about the role of innovations in business cycles and economic development had much in common with those of the Austrian economist Joseph Schumpeter.

In his next major work, *Banking Policy and the Price Level* (1926), Robertson considers the impact of the monetary system on the course of the business cycle. He distinguishes between "appropriate" or "justifiable" changes in output on the one hand, and "inappropriate" or "actual" changes in output on the other hand. Within a money-using economy, he argues, inappropriate fluctuations are likely to exceed appropriate fluctuations. And, he maintains, inappropriate fluctuations can be minimized if monetary authorities regulate saving and investment through control of the money supply, through such measures as adjusting interest rates. Although it was a highly innovative work at the time, *Banking Policy and the Price Level* was considered one of the most difficult books in the whole of economic literature, owing in part to Robertson's use of rather complex language.

Throughout the 1920s, Robertson had a close working relationship with Cambridge economist John Maynard Keynes, who had been one of his teachers before World War I. The relationship became strained in the 1930s because of their opposing interpretations of the nature of saving, investment, and the rate of interest, and the publication in 1936 of Keynes's major work, the *General Theory of Employment, Interest and Money*. Although Keynes died in 1946, his work continued to be influential at Cambridge. Robertson, who became an increasingly isolated figure within the Cambridge economic community, died there on April 21, 1963. His was reappraised in later years, and came to be regarded as one of Britain's foremost economists of the early twentieth century.

Christopher Godden

See also: Keynes, John Maynard; Keynesian Business Model; Schumpeter, Joseph.

Further Reading

Fletcher, Gordon. *Dennis Robertson.* Basingstoke, UK: Palgrave Macmillan, 2008.

———. *Dennis Robertson: Essays on His Life and Work.* Basingstoke, UK: Palgrave Macmillan, 2007.

Laider, David. *Fabricating the Keynesian Revolution: Studies of the Inter-war Literature on Money, the Cycle, and Unemployment.* Cambridge, UK: Cambridge University Press, 1999.

Robertson, Dennis H. *Banking Policy and the Price Level: An Essay in the Theory of the Trade Cycle.* London: P.S. King, 1926.

———. *A Study of Industrial Fluctuations: An Enquiry into the Character and Causes of the So-Called Cyclical Movements of Trade.* London: P.S. King, 1915.

Robinson, Joan (1903–1983)

Associated for most of her career with Cambridge University, British economist Joan Robinson expounded on the theories of John Maynard Keynes, particularly with regard to government involvement in a nation's economy. As a member of the Cambridge school (also known as the Cambridge Circus), Robinson became known for her contributions in the 1930s to the Keynesian explanation for the rises and falls in the business cycle.

She was born Joan Violet Maurice on October 31, 1903, in Surrey, England. She attended Girton College, Cambridge University, as an undergraduate student in economics, receiving a bachelor's degree in 1925; that same year she married economist Adam Robinson. She remained at Cambridge, taking positions at Newnham College, where she was elected a fellow in 1962; Girton College, where she became a full professor and was named a fellow in 1965; and King's College, where she was named the first female fellow in 1979. The main focus of her work was in the area of full employment and how and when it can occur in the business cycle, as envisioned by Keynes. It was a topic she would further develop in subsequent years, importantly in *The Accumulation of Capital* (1956). Robinson, along with economist Nicholas Kaldor, also expanded on discussions of international trade and the growth of economic development in what was called the Cambridge growth theory. In this work, she wrestled with such aspects of economic theory as the role of imperfect competition in business cycles when monopolies or large firms control markets. Robinson proposed the Keynesian approach, according to which imperfect competition is an important part of a real-world economy and must be incorporated into growth models.

In the early 1960s, Robinson and Peiro Sraffa entered into a debate with economists Robert Solow and Paul Samuelson in which Robinson and Sraffa contended that corporate profits grow from—and are determined by—tensions among different societal classes. Solow and Samuelson argued that profits are nothing more or less than economic benefits earned by the companies that most efficiently use their means of production. In other words, the debate questioned whether profits occur because of purely economic factors or because of political (that is, class) differences. The debate, conducted through written articles, continued for several years, with Robinson ultimately claiming victory. Since that time, most commentators have generally agreed the result was a draw, although some believe that, as a school of thought, neoclassical economics—which argues for pure competition and no government regulation—suffered greatly as a result of the debate.

While Robinson described herself as a "philosophical Marxist," economists have questioned whether she was truly that. Either way, there is little doubt that the theories of Karl Marx had a significant influence on her and informed much of her work. Although she frequently criticized Marxist economics, she was consistently critical of capitalism. She acknowledged that the capitalist system appeared to be successful in the United States but viewed it as a "very cruel system." She also argued that the capitalist system—marked by imperfect competition arising from its lack of planning and its acquisitiveness—leads to economic instability and downturns in the business cycle, and results in great hardship for the working class, as occurred during the Great Depression of the 1930s. Robinson died on August 5, 1983, in Cambridge, England.

Robert N. Stacy

See also: Kaldor, Nicholas; Keynes, John Maynard; Samuelson, Paul; Sraffa, Piero.

Further Reading

Asimakopulos, A. *Investment, Employment and Income Distribution.* Boulder, CO: Westview, 1988.

Feiwel, George R., ed. *Joan Robinson and Modern Economic Theory.* Hampshire, UK: Macmillan, 1989.

Marcuzzo, Maria Cristina, Luigi L. Pasinetti, and Alessandro Roncaglia, eds. *The Economics of Joan Robinson.* London: Routledge, 1996.

Rima, Ingrid H., ed. *The Joan Robinson Legacy.* Armonk, NY: M.E. Sharpe, 1991.

Robinson, Joan. *Collected Economic Papers.* Oxford, UK: Blackwell, 1980.

———. *Further Contributions to Modern Economics.* Oxford, UK: Blackwell, 1980.

Romer, Christina (1958–)

Christina Romer is an American economist and economic historian whose area of specialty is the study of recessions and depressions, especially the Great Depression of the 1930s. In addition to her academic career, she has applied her study of business cycles to the formulation of public policy. In November 2008, Romer was named head of the Council of Economic Advisers by newly elected President Barack Obama. Her primary initial task in that position was to draft the administration's recovery plan for the recession it inherited upon taking office in early 2008.

Christina Duckworth Romer was born December 25, 1958, in Alton, Illinois, and received her bachelor's degree from the College of William and Mary (1981) and a Ph.D. in economics from the Massachusetts Institute of Technology (1985). After beginning her academic career as an assistant professor at Princeton University, Romer moved to the University of California at Berkeley in 1988, where she became the Garff B. Wilson professor of

A respected scholar and experienced economic policy maker, Cristina Romer advised candidate Barack Obama during the 2008 presidential campaign. Upon taking office, Obama named her chair of the Council of Economic Advisers. *(Bloomberg/Getty Images)*

economics. She became known as a leading expert on government intervention in the economy, especially on matters of monetary policy, the impact of tax cuts and increases, and the effects of all these factors on inflation.

Romer's focus on the relationships among various economic data has led her to take occasionally contrarian and controversial positions. In the 1980s, for example, she argued that government economic estimates—based on agriculture and manufacturing exclusively—exaggerated unemployment rates and the overall economic volatility of the U.S. economy during the depression of the 1930s. Had the service sector been properly factored in, she maintained, economic data for the period would have painted a somewhat better picture of the economy and contributed to a greater sense of optimism. Romer's conclusions questioned the conventional wisdom that it was Keynesian-inspired government stimulative measures that finally stabilized the economy. In fact, she insisted, the nation's economy leading up to and during the Great Depression had never been as unstable as historians have maintained.

In addition to her teaching, research, writing, and other academic pursuits—including a vice-presidency of the American Economic Association—Romer has compiled an impressive record as an economic policy adviser and strategist. She served as co-director of the Program in Monetary Economics at the National Bureau of Economic Research and, until her appointment to the Obama administration, served on the bureau's Business Cycle Dating Committee (which determines whether or not the economy is in a recession).

While serving in these positions, Romer went on record commending the Federal Reserve for its efforts to stabilize the U.S. financial system by purchasing equity stakes in major financial institutions and agreeing to insure hundreds of billions of their troubled assets in late 2008, all part of a program known as the Troubled Assets Relief Program (TARP). Based on her own previous research and the work of monetary theorist Milton Friedman, Romer opined that had the Federal Reserve taken similar moves during the financial crisis of the early 1930s, the Great Depression would not have been as deep or as lasting as it was.

President Obama's decision to appoint Romer as head of the White House Council of Economic Advisers was not unexpected, as she had advised candidate Obama through much of the 2008 campaign. The appointment was widely hailed by fellow economists, who cited her work on government policy during the Great Depression and its relevance to the current-day economic crisis. After taking office, Romer argued forcefully for selective tax cuts, particularly for the middle class. President Herbert Hoover's tax hikes of the early 1930s, imposed to help balance the federal budget, had been a disastrous mistake, she maintained. Romer also remained a strong advocate of TARP, holding that continued government infusions of capital in major financial institutions are critical to the restoration of properly functioning credit markets, both at home and abroad.

Robert N. Stacy and James Ciment

See also: Council of Economic Advisers, U.S.; Keynesian Business Model; National Bureau of Economic Research; Troubled Asset Relief Program (2008–).

Further Reading

Romer, Christina D. *Changes in Business Cycles: Evidence and Explanations.* Cambridge, MA: National Bureau of Economic Research, 1999.

———. "The Great Crash and the Onset of the Great Depression." *Quarterly Journal of Economics* 105:3 (August 1990): 597–624.

———. *Monetary Policy and the Well-Being of the Poor.* Cambridge, MA: National Bureau of Economic Research, 1998.

Röpke, Wilhelm (1899–1966)

A German economist known for his strong support of free-market economics, Wilhelm Röpke was admired for his humane views and strong beliefs in social and economic justice, which were founded on his religious beliefs and conservative social values. Considered a member of the Austrian free-market school, Röpke was opposed to left-wing socialism, communism, and any form of state-run economics.

Born on October 10, 1899, in Hannover, Germany, Röpke served in the German army during World War I, which moved him to become profoundly antiwar and actively supportive of individual human rights. After the war, he studied economics at the University of Marburg and received his doctorate in 1921. He went on to teach economics in Jena, Graz, Marburg, and, having fled the Nazis in 1933, the University of Istanbul in Turkey and then the Institute of International Studies in Geneva, Switzerland, where he remained until his death in 1966.

Röpke's first attempt to shape government policy occurred in the early 1930s, when he proposed that Germany's Weimar government abandon its inflationary policies to combat the results of the economic collapse and instead adopt the kinds of policies articulated by John Maynard Keynes in 1936. Later, sharply critical of the economics of Benito Mussolini's fascist Italy as well as the proposed economic policies of the Nazi Party, Röpke claimed that fascism lacked intellectual freight and, as in the case of Italy, was more of a slogan than a well-thought-out political philosophy.

Although he did not see the state as an appropriate authority to run a system as complex as an economy, he did see a role for it. Here he broke with the Austrian school, for he believed that the state should make and enforce rules that guaranteed fairness—particularly in competition, by means of antitrust legislation, for example—and justice. He thought the state should support small businesses and provide temporary aid and assistance to people whose livelihoods were disrupted by economic downturns and downtrends in the business cycle. Röpke drew a line, however, at the creation of a welfare state, believing it would have too much influence over its citizens and lead to social decay.

In his analysis of the causes of business cycles, Röpke noted the important role played by technology. He observed that innovations such as railroads, steel manufacturing, automobiles, and electricity create spikes in investment that, in turn, cause sudden rises in all economic forces reacting to the stimulus. Such disturbances can only be overcome by a resulting depression. In linking the business cycle with technological developments, his ideas clearly influenced the great economist Joseph Schumpeter and were the precursor to the latter's theory of the role of "creative destruction" in the business cycle.

Following World War II, Röpke served as an economic adviser to the West German government. He was opposed to the Marshall Plan, believing foreign aid would not bring about the needed economic recovery. After the war, the German zones occupied by Great Britain, France, and the United States retained aspects of Nazi economic policy, such as wage-and-price controls and inflation, resulting in a halt to production and shortages of many goods. In this environment, the black market thrived. The result was an economy in shambles.

Röpke recommended the abolishment of all controls, a halt to the printing of money, and the institution of a solid currency. The immediate result was a great deal of hardship, but eventually the German economy recovered.

Robert N. Stacy

See also: Austrian School; Hayek, Friedrich August von; Mises, Ludwig von.

Further Reading

Boarman, P.T. "Wilhelm Röpke." *German Economic Review* 4 (1966): 149–152.

Hudson, M. "German Economists and the Great Depression, 1929–33." *History of Political Economy* 17:1 (1985): 35–50.

Röpke, Wilhelm. *The Crisis of European Economic Integration.* Zurich: Swiss Credit Bank, 1963.

———. *Economics of the Free Society,* trans. Patrick M. Boarman. Chicago: H. Regnery, 1963.

———. *A Humane Economy: The Social Framework of the Free Market.* Chicago: H. Regnery, 1960.

———. *Welfare, Freedom, and Inflation.* Tuscaloosa: University of Alabama Press, 1964.

Zmirak, John. *Wilhelm Röpke: Swiss Localist, Global Economist.* Wilmington, DE: ISI Books, 2001.

Rostow, Walt Whitman (1916–2003)

American economist Walt Whitman Rostow was an academic, political theorist, and high-ranking government adviser best remembered for his role in advocating U.S. involvement in the Vietnam War. As an economic historian, he first attracted notice for his writings on economic growth in developing nations from a democratic and capitalist (anti-Marxist) perspective.

Rostow was born on October 7, 1916, in New York City. After receiving undergraduate and graduate degrees from Yale University, he went on to teach briefly at Columbia University, then Cambridge University, and later at the Massachusetts Institute of Technology (MIT). He served in the Office of Special Services (OSS, predecessor to the Central Intelligence Agency) during World

Best known as an architect of the Vietnam War in the Kennedy and Johnson administrations, Walt Whitman Rostow earned his reputation as an economist with the 1960 book *Stages of Economic Growth*, which posited a five-stage process based on the human life cycle. (*The Granger Collection, New York*)

War II, then joined the State Department as an administrator for the Marshall Plan (designed to help an economically devastated Europe). This experience likely contributed to his strong opposition to communism. Later he worked for the United Nations Economic Commission for Europe under Swedish economist Gunnar Myrdal.

During his years at MIT (1950–1961), Rostow continued U.S. government service, first as a speechwriter for President Dwight Eisenhower and later as a deputy assistant for national security in the John F. Kennedy administration. Following President Kennedy's assassination, he served in the Johnson administration until 1968.

In 1959 Rostow published an article titled "The Stages of Economic Growth" in the *Economic History Review*, followed the next year by a book of the same title, which was to be his best-known published work. In it, Rostow described a model of economic growth (referred to as the Rostovian take-off model) centered on what he called a biological view—similar to the human life cycle. This five-stage process begins with what Rostow defined as "traditional society" and progresses to preconditions for economic take-off, followed by take-off, drive to maturity, and, finally, mass consumption. Rostow's model was seen as important to understanding the "take-off" of the industrial revolution in the nineteenth century, first in England and then in the United States.

In his model, Rostow describes a point in an economy, called "beyond consumption," at which people's lives would no longer be dominated by the pursuit of food, shelter, clothing, and durable goods. Instead, with these needs satisfied, political considerations would come to dominate. Because of his ideological bent—and because it was the cold war era—Rostow talked of these political factors in terms of capitalism versus communism. He rigorously reinforced this point in a controversial book titled *The Stages of Economic Growth: A Non-Communist Manifesto* (1960), in which he reinterpreted his earlier ideas on the stages of economic growth from as much a political perspective as an economic one.

Some economists criticized the book, pointing to methodological problems with Rostow's analysis. Others claimed that Rostow's ideas seemed to be firmly rooted in a nineteenth-century point of view, which took progress for granted and assumed that all actors perform rationally according to self-interest. By the middle of the twentieth century, following two world wars and political and intellectual revolutions, such assumptions were deemed no longer valid. Critics also noted Rostow's occasional inconsistencies, his predominantly Western perspective, and examples said to be exceptional rather than typical.

In 1968, Rostow left government service and moved with his wife Elspeth to the University of Texas at Austin, where he had a long career as an academic. He died on February 13, 2003.

Robert N. Stacy

See also: Growth, Economic; Myrdal, Gunnar.

Further Reading

Milne, David. *America's Rasputin: Walt Rostow and the Vietnam War.* New York: Hill and Wang, 2008.

Rostow, W.W. *Concept and Controversy: Sixty Years of Taking Ideas to Market.* Austin: University of Texas Press, 2003.

———. *The Economics of Take-Off into Sustained Growth.* London: Macmillan, 1963.

———. *The Process of Economic Growth.* New York: W.W. Norton, 1952.

———. *The Stages of Economic Growth: A Non-Communist Manifesto.* Cambridge, UK: Cambridge University Press, 1960.

Rubin, Robert (1938–)

Financier and business executive Robert Rubin served as secretary of the treasury from 1995 to 1999 under President Bill Clinton, who hailed him as the greatest treasury secretary since Alexander Hamilton. However, Rubin's enthusiasm for market deregulation later was seen by many as a contributing factor to the crisis in the U.S. economy that began in the late 2000s.

Robert Edward Rubin was born on August 29, 1938, in New York City. His family relocated to Florida, and he attended public high school in Miami. He received a bachelor's degree in economics from Harvard University in 1960, and then briefly attended Harvard Law School and the London School of Economics. After earning a juris doctorate from Yale Law School in 1964, Rubin joined the law firm of Cleary, Gottlieb, Steen & Hamilton before taking a position at the investment firm Goldman Sachs. There, in 1971, he was named a general partner; in 1980, a member of the management committee; and in 1987, vice chair and a chief operating officer, a position he held until 1990, when he became a chair and a senior partner.

Following Clinton's election to the presidency, Rubin was named director of the National Economic Council, which was established by the administration to coordinate all agency and departmental activities affecting the economy.

A former Goldman Sachs executive, Robert Rubin served as Treasury secretary during the Bill Clinton administration. Rubin was lionized for his role in the economic boom of the 1990s but later criticized for lax oversight of the financial community. *(Tim Sloan/Stringer/AFP/Getty Images)*

During Rubin's tenure as director, the North American Free Trade Agreement was signed. Two years later, Rubin was sworn in as secretary of the treasury. Considered highly effective in that position, Rubin—along with Lawrence Summers, deputy secretary of the treasury, and Alan Greenspan, chair of the Board of Governors of the Federal Reserve System—led efforts to stabilize developing financial crises in Mexico, Russia, Korea, Indonesia, Thailand, and Latin America. Rubin's conservative approach, particularly with regard to deficit reduction, garnered support for Clinton from the business and financial sectors, and earned praise from Republicans and Democrats alike. By the time Rubin stepped down from his post in 1999, the U.S. unemployment rate was at 4.3 percent and the government had a budget surplus of $79 billion.

As head of the treasury, Rubin, an advocate of free-market economics, often supported deregulation. He successfully lobbied for congressional repeal of the Glass-Steagall Act, legislation passed in 1933 that had made it easier for banks to borrow from the Federal Reserve, separated investment banking from commercial banking and insurance underwriting, and had given increased power to the Federal Reserve. Following deregulation, Citicorp (a bank for which Rubin later would work) merged with Travelers Group (insurance underwriters) in a deal valued at about $70 billion. With Greenspan's support, Rubin successfully urged Congress to oppose the regulation of trading in the credit derivatives of mortgage-backed securities. Regulation had been supported by, among others, Brooksley Born, head of the Commodity Futures Trading Commission. Much later, large holdings by financial institutions of these so-called toxic securities would lead to the demise of several prominent investment firms, including AIG (American International Group), Bear Stearns, and Lehman Brothers, and contribute to the financial meltdown of 2007–2008.

After leaving the Treasury Department, Rubin accepted a position on the board of a community development organization. He joined Citigroup as a member of the board of directors and an executive officer—overlapping and potentially conflicting roles that raised concerns outside the company as well as among shareholders. In 2001, he urged the Treasury Department not to downgrade the rating of the (later notorious) Enron Corporation because it was a creditor to Citigroup. The request was refused, and the episode was investigated by a congressional committee, which cleared Rubin of any wrongdoing. In 2007, Rubin served temporarily as chair of the board of directors of Citigroup. But, facing increasing criticism as a result of mounting shareholder losses, as well as a 2008 shareholder lawsuit that accused Rubin and other firm executives of steering the company toward financial ruin, Rubin announced his resignation from Citigroup in January 2009, where his earnings are estimated to have been anywhere from tens to hundreds of millions of dollars.

In January 2009, a MarketWatch article named Rubin as one of the "10 Most Unethical People in Business," claiming that he was among those whose "flubs have tarnished the financial world." Nevertheless, a number of key figures who served under Rubin were appointed to positions in the administration of President Barack Obama, including Treasury Secretary Timothy P. Geithner, Senior White House Economic Adviser Lawrence Summers, and Budget Director Peter R. Orszag.

Robert N. Stacy

See also: Citigroup; Treasury, Department of the.

Further Reading

Rubin, Robert E., and Jacob Weisberg. *In an Uncertain World: Tough Choices from Wall Street to Washington.* New York: Random House, 2004.

U.S. Senate Committee on Governmental Affairs, Permanent Subcommittee on Investigations. *The Role of the Financial Institutions in Enron's Collapse: Hearing Before the Permanent Subcommittee of {sic} Investigations of the Committee on Governmental Affairs, United States Senate, One Hundred Seventh Congress, Second Session, July 23 and 30, 2002.* Washington, DC: U.S. Government Printing Office, 2002.

Russia and the Soviet Union

A geographically vast nation of approximately 140 million people, Russia stretches across the northern half of the Eurasian landmass from Eastern Europe in the west to the Pacific Ocean in the east. While the country has a major heavy industrial infrastructure, most of its exports consist of raw materials, especially oil and gas.

Ruled until the early twentieth century by absolute monarchs known as czars, Russia lagged economically behind the rest of Europe, its modernization stunted by a repressive social structure in which the peasantry had little freedom. Rapid industrialization began in the late nineteenth and early twentieth centuries, a process contributing to the social unrest that brought down the czarist state and replaced it with a communist one.

Under successive regimes, the renamed Union of Soviet Socialist Republics, or Soviet Union, made great industrial strides between the 1920s and the 1960s, though its collectivized agriculture produced perennial food shortages.

Centralized planning and a repressive political environment also stunted economic innovation, however, leading to stagnation from the 1970s on, and ultimately the collapse of the Communist regime and the Soviet state itself in the early 1990s. Russia, which inherited most of the territory and population of the former Soviet Union, experienced great economic dislocation through the 1990s, leading to near collapse in 1998.

Since then, the Russian economy has recovered somewhat as market forces, a more efficient bureaucracy, and high market prices for natural resources led to substantial growth in the early years of the twenty-first century. The wealth generated has been unevenly distributed, with well-connected elites, often former Communist Party officials, reaping the lion's share of income. The period of growth came to an end with the fall in energy prices and the global financial crisis of 2008–2009.

Economic History Before the Communist Era

Modern Russia dates back to the creation by Viking invaders of the Kievan Rus in the ninth century CE, which, within a few centuries, emerged as the most prosperous state in Europe. With trade networks that linked it to the Black Sea, Scandinavia, and other parts of northern Europe, and with its capital in what is now the Ukrainian capital of Kiev, Kievan Rus was more of a trading alliance than a unified state. It eventually succumbed to repeated invasions by Turkic peoples and Mongols in the twelfth and thirteenth centuries.

By the fourteenth century, a new center of Russian power had emerged around Moscow, with an ever more powerful czar controlling territories that by the end of the sixteenth century had come to incorporate much of what is now western Russia and western Siberia. During the reign of Ivan IV, also known as Ivan the Terrible, in the mid-sixteenth century, the social and economic order of the next several centuries of czarist Russian history was established. Through violent means, Ivan reduced the power of the aristocrats and established serfdom in the countryside, whereby peasants were turned into quasi-slaves of landholders who owed their elite status to the czar in Moscow. These serfs were legally tied to the land, with almost all facets of their lives dictated by their landholding masters.

Ivan established a similarly authoritarian order over towns, where artisans and traders were bound to their occupations and localities so that they could be more efficiently taxed. Property rights, even of wealthy merchants, were granted at the pleasure of the czar as well. After Ivan's death in 1584, a period of anarchy ensued in Russia, gradually giving way to new czarist authority in the early seventeenth century.

Under Peter the Great, who ruled Russia from 1682 to 1725, Russia built up the largest standing army in Europe and proceeded to conquer new territories around the Baltic Sea. Peter established even more authority in the central state, raising taxes and arbitrarily assigning serfs to work in emerging factories and mines. But he was also a reformer, encouraging education, importing Western economic ideas, and building the port of St. Petersburg on the Baltic, giving the country its "door" to Europe and the transatlantic world. Under Peter, Russia became a major exporter of grains, furs, timber, and minerals to Europe.

Still, Russia remained a largely agricultural state and a relatively poor one, compared to Western Europe, through the early nineteenth century. Russia's loss to France and England in the Crimean War during the 1850s forced it to begin an economic and social modernization process, starting with the abolition of serfdom in the 1860s. But the collectivist agriculture that replaced the old order proved inefficient, and the farming sector continued to underperform. More successful was

the government's effort to expand the vast country's transportation network. Between 1860 and 1900, the railroad network expanded from about 1,250 miles of track (2,000 kilometers) to more than 15,000 miles (24,000 kilometers).

The new railroad network increased exports, bringing in the capital Russia needed to spur its belated industrialization. By the turn of the twentieth century, numerous new factories had emerged around St. Petersburg, Moscow, and other western Russian cities, along with a new urban proletariat.

Communist Economics

Among the new working class, radical economic ideas of both the anarchist and communist varieties took hold. This led to the revolution of 1905, which established a nominal constitutional monarchy, and then the Bolshevik Revolution of 1917, spurred by the sufferings of the Russian people in World War I. Under Vladimir Lenin, the last of the czars was murdered, and the Bolsheviks fought off counterrevolutionary forces in a brutal civil war that lasted into the early 1920s.

The conflict left the country in ruins, with agricultural output off more than 50 percent from its pre–World War I peaks and heavy industrial production down by as much as 95 percent. Initial efforts to collectivize agriculture and light industry were abandoned, in favor of limited market freedoms for farmers, petty traders, and small manufacturers; heavy industry remained nationalized. By the mid-1920s, the New Economic Policy (NEP) had helped revive agricultural and industrial output to near or above prewar levels.

But with the emergence of dictator Joseph Stalin in the late 1920s, the NEP was abandoned in favor of more centralized planning and control. In 1927, the Soviet government launched the first of its five-year plans, with the emphasis on collectivized agriculture and state-directed heavy industrial development. Resistance among land-owning peasants, known as Kulaks, was ruthlessly crushed, though the state reluctantly allowed them to grow their own crops for sale on tiny plots.

To pay for the industrialization, Stalin imposed large, indirect taxes on peasants and workers, millions of whom died in the effort to collectivize agriculture and rapidly build a heavy industry infrastructure. Such human costs aside, the results were remarkable, as steel, coal, and other heavy industry output soared, even while consumer-goods production lagged.

World War II struck a heavy blow to Soviet economic development as invading German armies and the struggle to oust them decimated western Russia, the heartland of the country's modern industrial economy, though efforts were made to relocate some factories to east of the Ural Mountains. Victorious Soviet armies occupied much of Eastern Europe after the war, helping to dismantle some of East Germany's factories and move them to the Soviet Union as compensation for the damage inflicted by Germany during the war. With Stalin's death in 1953, the country underwent a period of limited political liberalization, though Stalinist centralized planning and development continued to be the hallmark of the Soviet economy. For a time, such planning worked, providing an ever-rising standard of living for the Soviet people and a growing, albeit still limited, array of consumer goods.

Still, compared to the economic "miracle" in Western Europe, the Soviet Union continued to fall behind, even as it maintained one of the most powerful military systems in the world. But, as many Western economists pointed out, centralized planning simply could not keep up with modern consumer demands in the same way that free-market economies could. By the 1970s, the country's economy was stagnating, with consumers unable to obtain the products they desired or else forced to wait in long lines to buy them. Meanwhile, a thriving black market in goods and services emerged, despite being officially frowned upon by the state. Collectivized agriculture also proved a disappointment, as the country was forced to turn to the West to fill its larders.

By the 1980s, the limitations of Soviet economic planning had become apparent even to the Communist Party leadership, who appointed reformer Mikhail Gorbachev to run the country in 1985. Gorbachev immediately initiated twin policies aimed at shaking up the sclerotic and repressive Soviet system. Glasnost, or openness, was intended to allow competing and critical voices to emerge in media, government, and civil society. Perestroika, or restructuring, permitted more market forces in the setting of prices, increased independence of industrial managers from centralized planning, and the legalization of profit-seeking private cooperatives in the service sector.

Gorbachev hoped to reform and modernize the country's socialist economics and politics, but his efforts had unintended consequences. By ending Soviet control over Eastern Europe, Gorbachev helped catalyze a series of largely nonviolent revolutions in that region, leading to the end of Communist rule there and the breakaway of the three Baltic republics from the Soviet Union in 1989 and 1990. Following an unsuccessful coup by hardliners in the Communist Party and military, the Soviet Union itself broke apart in 1991 as Communist Party rule gave way to a limited multi-party democracy.

Post-Soviet Economic Chaos

After the breakup of the Union of Soviet Socialist Republics in 1991, Russia attempted to transition from a government-owned economy to a market economy with enterprises in the hands of private owners. To achieve this, a massive privatization program was launched: factories, plants, stores, and offices were given out to people virtually for free.

But in a country with no history of democratic institutions and no knowledge of how a market economy worked, former government assets became concentrated in the hands of just a few federal and local elites. The new owners had no entrepreneurial experience, often did not even believe in the market economy, and were not interested in restructuring their new properties into effective enterprises. Instead, so-called stripping of assets became prevalent. No investments were made in growing new businesses; rather, the machinery, tools, technology, and even bricks from the building walls were sold for cash. The enterprises were falling apart as their owners became richer. The new owners also often removed money from the economy by transferring it abroad—opening bank accounts, purchasing real estate, or acquiring business in Western Europe and the United States. Thus, privatization largely failed, as it did not create efficient owners who would (or could) grow their businesses.

With domestic production virtually nonexistent, so too were manufacturing jobs. This situation led most of the population to seek employment in commerce, both domestic and foreign. Most of the consumer goods and food items purchased by the people were imported, often going through a long chain of traders before reaching the end consumer. Imports of foreign products effectively substituted for domestic production. However, enormous assets inherited from the former Soviet Union allowed the country to exist quite well by simply selling them and purchasing what the country needed from abroad. In addition, Russia had large natural reserves of oil, gas, metals, and minerals. As long as oil prices remained high, the country was able to continue its somewhat stable economic existence.

Meanwhile, the immediate post-Soviet problem of inflation eased as the government shifted to treasury bills to pay for its debt. Russia did not have a balanced budget because it continuously spent more than it earned. To finance the deficit, the government, following the instructions of International Monetary Fund (IMF), issued short-term federal-debt obligations, known as GKOs—zero-coupon treasury bills issued by the Russian Finance Ministry. With the real economy not growing, GKOs became a Ponzi scheme: the payments for matured obligations were financed by the issuance of new obligations. The Russian government had to offer high return on this debt to compensate for the risk; in the wake of the crisis, some government-issued bonds produced yields

of almost 200 percent. The debt was becoming unsustainable.

The ruble exchange rate was stable because of an artificially fixed currency exchange rate. Attracted by large returns, foreign investors began entering the Russian market. Deficits continued to grow even as stores were full of goods from all over the world and at reasonable prices (thanks to an artificial exchange rate). International brands started advertising in Russia as consumers there developed capitalist-style consumption habits. The Russian economy seemed to be booming despite the fact that its deficits were growing and its gross domestic product (GDP) was decreasing annually.

Crisis of 1998

World oil prices, however, started declining in 1998, falling to below $10 per barrel from over $20 per barrel just a year before. And the prices of many other natural resources were also falling significantly. Because much of the Russian economy was based on exporting these natural resources, the result was a sharp decline in revenues for the country. In turn, this made it difficult to pay for the import of foreign products.

With the lack of revenues, the Russian government had to sell dollars from its reserves in order to support the fixed ruble/dollar exchange rate. In an economy where debt was growing and pressures on the ruble were increasing, the government had to sell more and more dollars. Because the dollar reserves were not unlimited, they were eventually depleted.

By spring 1998, the Russian economy was in trouble, and Russian president Boris Yeltsin attempted to take control of the situation. That March, he dismissed the entire government, including Prime Minister Viktor Chernomyrdin. Yeltsin appointed Sergei Kiriyenko, a young liberal, as the acting prime minister, but the State Duma, or parliament, twice rejected his appointment. Only on the third attempt, on April 24, 1998, facing the threat of new parliamentary elections, was Kiriyenko approved.

Oil exports, the mainstay of the Russian economy, brought good times in the mid-1990s and mid-2000s, when oil prices were high, and hard times in the latter part of both decades, when prices dropped. An aging pipeline system poses a long-term challenge. *(AFP/Stringer/Getty Images)*

As prime minister, Kiriyenko focused on negotiations with the IMF in attempts to secure additional loans to pay off the country's internal and external debt. Finally, in July, a new loan in the amount of over $22 billion was approved. The new loan, however, was not able to cover all of the outstanding obligations. The government owed over $12 billion in unpaid salaries to state employees alone. Kiriyenko also developed a comprehensive anticrisis plan, but the State Duma rejected it. By the end of July, the situation was out of control.

On July 29, 1998, President Yeltsin interrupted his vacation to return to Moscow. Realizing that the economy could not be saved, the money from the IMF loan was removed from the government's accounts and disappeared. Even today, it is unclear what happened to those funds. Despite expectations of another change of government and prime minister, President Yeltsin made only one change—appointing as the head of the Federal Securities Services an obscure public official,

Vladimir Putin, who had completed his graduate degree less than a year earlier.

On August 17, 1998—a day Russians would come to call Black Monday—the Russian economy collapsed because of the decline in economic production, uncontrolled budget deficit, the plummeting prices of oil and other natural resources, an artificial currency exchange rate, and the resulting undermining of investor confidence. Russia defaulted on its debt obligations. The government and the central bank issued a statement saying that they were suspending trading of GKOs, and they introduced compulsory restructuring of GKOs and other short-term debt obligations into new long-term securities on very unfavorable terms for investors. Russian banks, which had invested heavily in GKOs, lost almost half of their assets. Many of them went bankrupt and had to close down. Russia also imposed a ninety-day moratorium on payments on the loans issued by nonresident lenders.

The fixed currency exchange rate was abandoned and the ruble was devalued by more than two-thirds. Inflation started growing again. The cost of living increased substantially as Russia relied heavily on imported goods to make up for the lack of its own production. Many foreign products became too expensive, quadrupling in price, and imports declined. In anticipation of a complete collapse of the economy, people cleaned off the shelves of stores in an attempt to stockpile basic goods. As stores stood empty, the shortage of even basic necessities became inevitable. The Russian people took to the streets. The economic collapse was threatening political turmoil.

Kiriyenko and his cabinet were dismissed. The new cabinet, appointed in violation of the Russian constitution, was rejected by the Duma. President Yeltsin had to back down and appoint a prime minister who would be acceptable. On September 11, 1998, Yevgeny Primakov became the new prime minister of the Russian Federation and the Duma began working on President Yeltsin's impeachment hearings.

Post-1998 Economy and the Crisis of 2008–2009

For the remainder of 1998, the economy began to show signs of improvement. The impeachment of Yeltsin never materialized, and political stability was restored. The conservative government of Yevgeny Primakov introduced a more balanced budget and started working on improving fiscal policies in Russia. The devaluation of the ruble made imported goods unattainable for the general public, which provided a stimulus to production of Russian goods and services. For the first time since the end of the Soviet Union, Russian goods became available in stores around the country.

The growth of domestic production also led to increased tax revenues and greater investment in domestic production. Infusions of money into the economy allowed companies and government to start paying off arrears in salaries to their workers, who in turn increased their consumption, creating

the need for more domestic production. The Russian Federation was also helped by the stabilization of oil prices.

Indeed, rising oil and commodity prices helped buoy the Russian economy in the early and middle 2000s, even as President Vladimir Putin, in office since 2000, enhanced the powers of the government and continue paying out pension, as well as salaries, that had been in arrears for years under Yeltsin. The new revenues allowed Russia to service its foreign debt more effectively, repay international loans, and build up a surplus of foreign reserves in the central bank, with part of the surplus going into a stabilization fund to help tide Russia over during future drops in oil and natural gas prices.

As the country's fiscal house was being put in order, its economy was also reviving. GDP growth rates between 2000 and 2008 averaged between 7 and 8 percent annually in most years, and industrial output increased by 75 percent. By 2008, the per capita GDP was about $11,000, measured in purchasing power parity. (That statistic helps compensate for variations in currency values, putting Russia at the higher end of middle-income countries.) Meanwhile, the more stable political environment and increasing consumer demand spurred domestic and foreign investment, which, together, rose 125 percent in these years. Still, all of these gains were largely catch-up, as it was only in 2008 that the country's GDP surpassed the level it had reached in 1990, the last full year of the Soviet Union's existence. In other words, the impressive growth of the 2000s served only to recoup the losses incurred in the economically disastrous 1990s.

A combination of factors in 2008 and 2009—including war with Georgia, which quelled foreign investment, falling energy prices in the late 2008, and the global financial crisis and recession—ended the period of growth, creating yet another economic crisis in Russia, though one not nearly as catastrophic as that of 1998. Russian securities prices plummeted in late 2008 as foreign investors pulled out their assets, the ruble plunged in value, interest rates skyrocketed, and bankruptcies spread through the financial system.

Unlike 1998, this time the Russian government had large capital reserves at its command to respond to the crisis. Pledging he would do whatever was necessary to keep the financial system functioning, President Dmitry Medvedev, a Putin protégé in power since 2008, injected nearly $200 billion dollars into the country's struggling financial institutions even as he offered some $50 billion in loans to major corporations suffering from the rapid withdrawal of foreign capital in the wake of the global financial crisis. Over the longer term, the government attempted to revive business by dropping corporate tax rates and lifting tariffs on imported capital goods needed by business and industry.

Despite the various bailout and stimulus measures, which amounted to some 13 percent of GDP, the country's bonds continued to be downgraded by foreign rating services, unemployment rose to roughly 12 percent in 2009, and growth was expected to go into negative territory for the first time since the crisis of 1998. By mid-2009, however, many economists had come to believe that Russia, like quite a few other emerging economies, was poised to recover ahead of many Western countries.

James Ciment and Alexander V. Laskin

See also: BRIC (Brazil, Russia, India, China); Eastern Europe; Emerging Markets; Marx, Karl; Transition Economies.

Further Reading

Buchs, T.D. "Financial Crisis in the Russian Federation: Are the Russians Learning to Tango?" *Economics of Transition* 7:3 (2003): 687–715.

Longworth, Philip. *Russia: The Once and Future Empire from Pre-History to Putin.* New York: St. Martin's, 2006.

Malleret, T., N. Orlova, and V. Romanov. "What Loaded and Triggered the Russian Crisis?" *Post-Soviet Affairs* 15:2 (1999): 107–129.

Popov, A. "Lessons of the Currency Crisis in Russia and in Other Countries." *Problems of Economic Transition* 43:1 (2000): 45–73.

Service, Robert. *A History of Modern Russia: From Tsarism to the Twenty-first Century.* Cambridge, MA: Harvard University Press, 2009.

S&P 500

The S&P 500 is a stock market index that measures the prices of 500 representative large companies and has served as an important index of stock prices in the United States since 1957. It is also one of the most important indicators of business cycle expansions and contractions. The Dow Jones Industrial Average (DJIA), another popular index, contains only thirty companies and so is considered less representative of the U.S. market than the S&P 500. The S&P 500 is among the best known of many indices and is owned and maintained by Standard & Poor's, a financial research firm whose parent company is McGraw-Hill.

S&P 500 refers not only to the index but also to the 500 companies that have their common stock included in the index. The ticker symbol for the S&P 500 Index varies. Some examples of the symbol are ^GSPC, .INX, and $SPX. The stocks included in the S&P 500 Index are also part of the broader S&P 1500 and S&P Global 1200 stock market indices. Other popular Standard & Poor's indices include the S&P 600, an index of small companies with a market capitalization between $300 million and $2 billion, and the S&P 400, an index of midsize companies with market capitalization of $2 billion to $10 billion.

The S&P 500 indexes the prices of 500 American common stocks for large publicly held companies that trade on either of the two largest American stock markets—the New York Stock Exchange (NYSE) and the National Association of Securities Dealers Automated Quotations (NASDAQ). The companies are chosen from leading industries within the U.S. economy, including utilities, construction, energy, health care, industrials, materials, information technology, and telecom services. The index does include a handful of non-U.S. companies for various reasons.

The S&P 500 is widely employed in the financial services industry as a measure of the general level of stock prices because it includes both growth stocks and the generally less volatile value stocks. The index is one of the most commonly used benchmarks for the overall U.S. stock market and is considered by many to be the very definition of the market. It is included in the Index of Leading Economic Indicators (LEI), which predicts future economic activity. The S&P 500 is often used as a baseline for comparisons in stock performance calculations and charts. A chart will show the S&P 500 Index in addition to the price of the target stock.

The S&P 500 is maintained by the S&P Index Committee, a team of Standard & Poor's economists and index analysts who meet on a regular basis. The Index Committee's goal is to ensure that the S&P 500 remains a leading indicator of U.S. equities, accurately reflecting the risk and return characteristics of the U.S. market as a whole on an ongoing basis. The Index Committee follows a set of established guidelines (available at standardandpoors.com) that provide transparency and fairness needed to enable investors to replicate the index and achieve the same performance as the S&P 500.

Standard & Poor's introduced its first index in 1923 as the S&P 90, an index based on ninety stocks. By linking this index to the S&P 500 Index, the latter can be extended back for comparison purposes to 1918. In 2000, the index reached an all-time same-day high of 1,552.87 and then lost approximately half of its value in a two-year bear market, reaching a low of 768.63 in 2002. In 2007, the S&P 500 closed at 1,530.23 to set its first all-time closing high in more than seven years and a new same-day record of 1,555.10. In late 2007, difficulties stemming from subprime mortgage lending began to spread to the wider financial sector, resulting in the second bear market of the twenty-first century. The resulting crisis became acute in September 2008, commencing a period of unusual volatility and a significant downturn. The index bottomed out in early March 2009, closing at 735.09—its lowest close since late 1996. The loss in 2008 was the greatest since 1931. Beginning in March 2009, the index began to recover, reaching 1,045.41 on November 3, 2009—still far below its previous peak in October 2007.

Maria Nathan

See also: Dow Jones Industrial Average; Nasdaq; New York Stock Exchange.

Further Reading

Sommer, Jeff. "A Friday Rally Can't Save the Week." *New York Times*, November 23, 2008.

Standard & Poor's. "Indices." Available at www.indices.standardandpoors.com. Accessed April 2009.

———. "Standard & Poor's 500 Fact Sheet." Available at www.indices.standardandpoors.com. Accessed April 2009.

———. *Standard & Poor's 500 Guide.* New York: McGraw-Hill, 2007.

Standard & Poor's Web site: www.standardandpoors.com.

Samuelson, Paul (1915–2009)

One of the towering figures in twentieth-century economics, the Nobel Prize laureate and neo-Keynesian Paul Samuelson pioneered the study and application of international trade theory, business cycle analysis, and equilibrium theory.

Paul Anthony Samuelson was born on May 15, 1915, in Gary, Indiana. He received his undergraduate degree from the University of Chicago in 1935 and earned master's and doctorate degrees from Harvard in 1936 and 1941, respectively. At Harvard, Samuelson studied with such Keynesian luminaries as Alvin Hansen and Joseph Schumpeter, both of whom were involved in the study of business cycles. Samuelson's own work went beyond Keynesianism, combining principles from that school with others from neoclassical economics to form what became known as the neoclassical synthesis. In awarding him the Nobel Prize for Economics in 1970, the Nobel committee declared, "He has shown the fundamental unity . . . in economics, by a systematic application of the methodology of maximization for a broad set of problems." Indeed, Samuelson's career has been characterized by the broad reach and influence of his work, which encompasses many different subfields of the science. Specifically, the Nobel was awarded "for the scientific work through which he has developed static and dynamic economic theory and actively contributed to raising the level of analysis in economic science."

In 1940, Samuelson joined the faculty at the Massachusetts Institute of Technology (MIT) as an assistant professor of economics; he became an associate professor in 1944 and a full professor in 1947. During his tenure at MIT, Samuelson also served as professor of international economic relations at the Fletcher School of Law and Diplomacy at Tufts University; as a consultant to the Rand Corporation, a nonprofit think tank; and as an economics adviser to the U.S. government. Beginning in 1966, he was an institute professor emeritus at MIT. In addition to the Nobel Prize, Samuelson was awarded the John Bates Clark Medal by the American Economics Association in 1947.

Samuelson's first major work, *Foundations of Economic Analysis* (1947), grew out of his doctoral dissertation of the same title. Its publication led to a renewed interest in neoclassical economics, exploring the theories underlying such critical areas of study as equilibrium systems, maximizing behavior of agents, comparative statistics, cost and production, consumer behavior, elasticities, cardinal utility, welfare economics, linear and nonlinear systems, and dynamics—such as those associated with the business cycle. In *Foundations*, Samuelson emphasizes the mathematical underpinnings of economics and the formal similarity of analyses regardless of the subject. He draws a number of comparisons between economics and the mathematics of other sciences such as biology and physics, particularly thermodynamics. Even his focus on equilibrium is the result of taking the mathematical models from the field of physical thermodynamics and generalizing them for use in economics.

In 1948, Samuelson published *Economics: An Introductory Analysis*, which became the best-selling textbook in the United States—in any subject—for nearly thirty years. Published in over forty languages and twenty English-language editions, the text remains in wide use into the twenty-first century. (The twelfth edition, published in 1985, and subsequent editions were written with Yale economist William D. Nordhaus.)

More than a synthesizer, popularizer, and teacher, Samuelson was also an economic theorist of the first order. Among the concepts for which he is known is the Samuelson condition, introduced in a 1954 article titled "The Theory of Public Expen-

A longtime MIT professor and government adviser, economist Paul A. Samuelson won the 1970 Nobel Prize and wrote the best-selling college textbook in the field. He was cited by the Nobel committee for "raising the level of analysis in economic science." *(Yale Joel/Time & Life Pictures/Getty Images)*

diture." The construct and its underlying theory help explain why social utility will decrease if a certain quantity of private good is substituted for public good. Another of his theories, the Balassa-Samuelson hypothesis, is the causal model used to explain the Penn effect, a theory developed by economists at the University of Pennsylvania. Specifically, the Balassa-Samuelson hypothesis predicts that consumer prices will be higher in wealthy countries than in poor ones because productivity varies most in the traded-goods sector. The Stolper-Samuelson theorem, originally derived by Samuelson and Harvard economist Wolfgang Stolper from the Heckscher-Ohlin model of international trade, predicts that a rise in the relative price of goods will lead to a rise in the return to the most-used factor in the production of those goods—a theory later derived using other models.

Samuelson continued to write and edit works on economics into his nineties. With William A. Barnett, he edited *Inside the Economist's Mind:*

Conversations with Eminent Economists (2007). During the financial crisis and economic recession of 2007–2009, he remained an active media commentator on public policy and prospects for recovery. Samuelson died on December 6, 2009, at his home in Belmont, Massachusetts.

Bill Kte'pi

See also: Friedman, Milton; Hansen, Alvin Harvey; Keynes, John Maynard; Neoclassical Theories and Models; Schumpeter, Joseph.

Further Reading

Samuelson, Paul. *Foundations of Economic Analysis.* Enlarged ed. Cambridge, MA: Harvard University Press, 1983.

———. "The Pure Theory of Public Expenditure." *Review of Economics and Statistics* 36 (1954): 386–389.

Soloki, E. Cary, and Robert M. Brown. *Paul Samuelson and Modern Economic Theory.* New York: McGraw-Hill, 1983.

Szenberg, Michael, Lall Ramrattan, and Aron A. Gottesman, eds. *Samuelsonian Economics and the Twenty-First Century.* New York: Oxford University Press, 2006.

Wong, Stanley. *Foundations of Paul Samuelson's Revealed Preference Theory.* New York: Routledge, 2009.

Savings and Investment

In economics, "savings" is defined as the income that is not spent on consumption. "Investment" most often refers to business investment—expenditures by businesses on capital goods such as equipment and tools, factories, warehouses, and offices necessary to operate the business. "Total investment" also includes expenditures for new housing construction. All of these investments contribute to gross domestic product (GDP) because new goods are produced. "Financial investment" refers to something closer to the everyday use of the term "investment" and includes the purchase of paper instruments such as stocks and bonds, which are not counted in GDP because they produce no new goods or services. The interaction of savings and investment—and the decisions economic players make concerning that interaction—is at the core of significant aspects of economic theory.

Classical, Stockholm School, and Keynesian Views

Adam Smith, in *The Wealth of Nations* (1776), linked savings and investment in a theory of national economic growth. According to Smith, economic growth took place as a result of the parsimonious behavior of entrepreneurs (business owners) who saved out of their business profits to invest back into the businesses they owned.

However, as the market system evolved, it became clear that this picture of the process of capital accumulation was too simplistic. Questions arose about the process by which savings of individuals and institutions neatly flowed into business investment. Classical economists Lord Lauderdale, Thomas Malthus, and Jean Charles Léonard Sismondi asked, what would happen if savings and investment were not exactly in balance with one another? In this framework, would the interest rate move so as to adjust savings and investment into a balance, or equilibrium? Suppose there were a greater amount of investment than there were savings to facilitate it? Then interest rates would be increased due to the demand for investment funds. As interest rates began to go up, savers would be attracted to the higher interest rates that could be earned on savings. On the other hand, if there were a surplus of savings compared to investment, interest rates would decrease. As a consequence of lower interest rates, more investment would be undertaken, and at lower interest rates savers would not save as much. The change in the level of interest rates would cause an adjustment, bringing savings and investment into equilibrium with one another.

This analysis was eventually labeled the loanable funds approach to savings and investment equilibrium. At the start of the twentieth century, the founder of the Stockholm school, Knut Wicksell, raised a major theoretical objection to the theory that the interest rate always brought savings and investment into balance. Wicksell's approach pointed out that investment by business firms was financed not just by savings but by bank credit extended through loans to business. It is possible that credit will expand to finance investment beyond the level of savings in the economy.

John Maynard Keynes built on the possibility of disengagement between investment and savings to explain the depression of the 1930s and cyclical movement of economics in general. Keynes's theory of the business cycle is based on the inherent instability of investment decisions in the private business sector due to the uncertainty and risk in investment expectations. The critical theoretical element in the Keynesian approach was that planned or anticipated investment and savings would not necessarily be in balance with each other. Decisions about business investment, said Keynes, are made by business owners or managers and are based on expectations about future profits that depend on a set of rational calculations about individual business investment as well as the mood of the business community. This mood could be affected by optimistic or pessimistic conditions in the stock market, so that a major downturn in the stock market, or some other financial market, could create a mood of pessimism in the business community, which might influence, or even offset, the rational calculations about expenditures on business investment. On the other hand, households make savings decisions based on the level of income and the propensity to save or to consume. Therefore, there is no particular reason why the consequences of these two sets of decisions would coincide.

Keynes and others pointed out that after the fact, savings and investment would eventually adjust to a balance, or equilibrium. However, this equilibrium could be at a level of national income or national output less than the full employment of labor. The Great Depression of the 1930s was a clear example of a decade-long national income equilibrium at less than full employment.

Savings and Investment in a Globalized Economy

In the modern global economy, analysis of aggregate savings or aggregate investment is much less constrained by national political or economic boundaries. In particular, there is now a much freer flow of savings and financial investment across national boundaries through international financial markets. Therefore, the analyses of savings and investment must be understood as looking at flows of global savings or global investment. For example, in the middle of the first decade of the twenty-first century, the U.S. financial markets depended upon savings from the rest of the world, especially Asia. Historically, this reliance on global factors has been true in earlier periods; a good deal of the industrial expansion in the United States was financed by European savings, but now investments move much more easily and much faster across national boundaries. The newly available global flow of savings became a source for bubbles in global financial markets when the search for investment opportunities led to overinvestment in speculative securities.

The flow of savings from those economies with high levels of aggregate savings is usually directed at relatively safe financial markets. This is particularly true when there is a diversity of financial investment opportunities with high rates of return. The U.S. economy provided these opportunities, and continues to do so, in what is considered the safest and one of the most innovative financial markets. One of the innovations in the last quarter-century was the creation of derivatives from bonds. These were new securities based on characteristics of bonds, such as interest-only or principal-only derivatives. It was the creation of derivatives connected to home mortgage that stimulated interest early in the twenty-first century. The derivatives were bundles of mortgages divided up into high-, middle-, and low-risk categories that were then rated by private sector bond-rating agencies. Savings from the United States and outside the United States flowed through a variety of financial institutions into these derivatives at the start of the twenty-first century. This was the foundation of the financial bubble that burst in 2007–2008. The bursting of this bubble happened as a result of underlying weaknesses in the mortgage market and the level of speculation in these derivatives. As a consequence, a worldwide financial panic ensued, and the U.S. and global economies moved into the Great Recession of 2007–2009.

William Ganley

See also: Banks, Commercial; Banks, Investment; Consumption; Interest Rates; Investment, Financial; Retirement Instruments.

Further Reading
Akerlof, George A., and Robert J. Schiller. *Animal Spirits.* Princeton, NJ: Princeton University Press, 2009.
Cooper, George. *The Origins of Financial Crises: Central Banks, Credit Bubbles and the Efficient Market Fallacy.* New York: Vintage, 2008.
Fox, Justin. *The Myth of the Rational Markets: A History of Risk, Reward, and Delusion on Wall Street.* New York: HarperBusiness, 2009.
Hunt, E.K. *History of Economic Thought.* Updated 2nd ed. Armonk, NY: M.E. Sharpe, 2002.
Kates, Steven. *Say's Law and the Keynesian Revolution.* Cheltenham, UK: Edward Elgar, 1998.
Keynes, John M. *The General Theory of Employment, Interest and Money.* New York: Macmillan, 1936.
Minsky, Hyman. *Can "It" Happen Again?* Armonk, NY: M.E. Sharpe, 1982.
Roncaglia, Alessandro. *The Wealth of Ideas.* New York: Cambridge University Press, 2005.
Skidelsky, Robert. *Keynes: The Return of the Master.* New York: Public Affairs, 2009.
Snowdon, Brian, and Howard R. Vane. *Modern Macroeconomics.* Cheltenham, UK: Edward Elgar, 2005.
Stiglitz, Joseph. *Free Fall: America, Free Markets and the Sinking of the World Economy.* New York: W.W. Norton, 2010.
Tily, Geoff. *Keynes's General Theory, the Rate of Interest and 'Keynesian' Economics.* New York: Palgrave Macmillan, 2007.
Zamagni, Stefano, and Ernesto Screpanti. *An Outline of the History of Economic Thought.* New York: Oxford University Press, 1993.

Savings and Loan Crises (1980s–1990s)

Beginning in the mid-1980s and continuing into the early 1990s, the U.S. savings and loan industry experienced a wave of bankruptcies that produced tens of billions of dollars in losses. Triggered by deregulation and excessive real-estate speculation, the crises prompted a massive federal government bail-out program in the late 1980s and early 1990s. Some economists have argued that the bailout program prompted the much greater speculative real-estate financing of the early and middle 2000s—a major cause of the financial crisis of the late 2000s—as the financial community came to believe that, should such speculation lead to major losses, it would once again be rescued by Washington.

History of S&Ls

Savings and loan associations—also known as S&Ls or thrifts—emerged out of the mutual aid societies established by working people and small business owners in the early and middle years of the nineteenth century. These were cooperatives in which people pooled their money and then lent it to each other, at relatively low interest, usually for extraordinary expenses, such as funerals, or to establish or expand businesses.

From the beginning, S&Ls differed from banks in a number of ways. They were smaller and not-for-profit; they emphasized long-term savings accounts over short-term checking accounts; and their owners (the depositors) and management identified not with the financial industry but with the various reform movements of the day. In other words, the primary aim of S&Ls was to provide services and financial help to depositors rather than profits for shareholders. Because they had no profits and offered limited services, S&Ls could often pay more in interest, thereby attracting more depositors.

S&Ls also differed in the kinds of home mortgages they offered. While banks and insurance companies—a major source of home financing through the early twentieth century—offered short-term mortgages (in which borrowers paid interest for a few years before having to make a balloon payment to cover the principle at the end of the mortgage), thrifts pioneered the amortizing mortgage (in which borrowers paid both principle and interest over a longer term, with no balloon payment at the end). By the late 1920s, S&Ls had become an attractive alternative for homebuyers, financing about one in five mortgages in America.

Being more conservative than banks in the kinds of investments they made, thrifts suffered less from the Great Depression of the 1930s, though many struggled as foreclosures mounted. In the early part of that decade, the federal government initiated several programs to aid the S&L industry, including the Federal Home Loan Bank to offer loans to struggling thrifts; federal charters; and the Federal Savings and Loan Insurance Corporation (FSLIC), which protected S&L depositors in the same way the Federal Deposit Insurance Corporation (FDIC) did bank depositors.

During the post–World War II boom of the late 1940s through the early 1970s, the S&L industry thrived, now highly regulated by the states and the federal government. Millions of suburbanizing Americans deposited their money in S&Ls and bought homes with S&L-offered mortgages. By 1974, there were more than 5,000 S&Ls nationally, holding assets worth nearly $300 billion.

Deregulation and Crisis

High interest rates and slow growth in the recession-wracked middle and late 1970s hit the S&L industry hard. Tightly regulated regarding the interest rates they could charge, S&Ls saw depositors pull out their money in increasing volume and place it with financial institutions that could pay higher returns. Meanwhile, those same high interest rates were cooling the housing market, cutting off the major source of income—mortgage interest—that S&Ls needed in order to survive.

In the more conservative political climate of the early 1980s, the industry's pleas for regulatory relief fell on receptive ears, with Congress passing two laws allowing thrifts to offer different kinds of savings accounts and to expand the kinds of loans they offered. The laws also increased the maximum amount of depositors' money insured by the FSLIC to $100,000 per account and eliminated restrictions on the minimum number of S&L stockholders; the latter law concentrated decision-making power in a smaller number of people.

Collectively, these changes led S&Ls to en-

The 1989 failure of California-based Lincoln Savings and Loan, part of a wave of S&L bankruptcies, cost taxpayers $2 billion. Financial contributions to five senators by Lincoln owner Charles Keating touched off a political scandal. *(Patrick Tehan/Time & Life Pictures/Getty Images)*

gage in more lucrative but riskier lending practices. While continuing to offer mortgages on single-family homes, many S&Ls branched out into financing commercial properties, including shopping centers, resorts, and condominium complexes. To obtain the funds for these loans, the S&Ls began to offer much higher interest rates, paid for by the returns on commercial property loans. Despite the higher risks associated with this kind of speculative financing, depositors continued to put their money in S&L accounts. With the new $100,000 limit on FSLIC protection, making deposits felt safer for those who could afford it, knowing that the federal government would bail them out should the institution fail.

While such practices were perfectly legal in the new deregulated S&L industry, some thrift owners took their lending practices beyond the law. Among these was Charles Keating, Jr., a real-estate developer and financier who had purchased Lincoln Savings and Loan of California in 1984.

When federal regulators began to look into Lincoln's lending practices, Keating turned to five U.S. senators—to whom he had made substantive campaign contributions—to put pressure on the investigators to call off their probe. Ultimately, Lincoln failed, costing taxpayers $2 billion, and the senators were either criticized or reprimanded by a Senate investigatory committee for their participation in the scandal.

By the late 1980s, so many S&Ls were going into bankruptcy that the industry itself was becoming tainted. Many depositors pulled their money out of any thrifts even remotely suspected of being in trouble and thereby triggered more failures. Not only was the number of S&Ls going bankrupt increasing, but so was the size of the institutions. Indeed, by 1987, the FSLIC had become insolvent. Congress authorized more money, but it waived rules on closing technically insolvent S&Ls in the hopes that they could get back on their feet and save the FSLIC money. However, this only delayed and increased the size of the insolvencies in future years. Meanwhile, the rate of S&L failures soared, from about 60 annually in the mid-1980s to 205 in 1988 and 327 in 1989; in 1989, the total insured assets of failed S&Ls amounted to $135 billion.

Government Response and Legacy

In response to the crisis, Congress passed the Financial Institutions Reform Recovery and Enforcement Act (FIRREA) in 1989, which provided tens of billions of dollars in bailout money to S&Ls and created a new Office of Thrift Supervision (OTS) to impose tighter regulations. Among these was a requirement that the thrifts maintain higher asset-to-loan ratios. FIRREA also created another government-authorized institution, the Resolution Trust Corporation, to dispose of the assets of the failed S&Ls in order to recoup some of the bailout money.

By the early 1990s, the federal initiatives seemed to be working, as the number of S&L failures returned to historic norms. But $600 billion in lost assets in the period between the deregulation of the early 1980s and the end of the crisis in the early 1990s represented the costliest financial collapse in the history of any nation to that time. In the end, the S&L debacle cost America taxpayers some $500 billion, also setting a record as the greatest financial bailout in history to that time.

While the newly regulated S&L industry largely avoided investments in the exotic, lucrative, and highly risky derivatives markets of the early 2000s, the bailouts of the 1980s–1990s era encouraged other financial institutions to abandon more cautious lending practices. Those bailouts may have led many in the financial services industry to believe that the government would bail them out in the event of any failures. Meanwhile, the OTS, which oversaw regulation of many of the mortgage-backed securities at the heart of the late 2000s financial crisis, had become so lax in its oversight that the Barack Obama administration called for its abolition, with its duties consolidated into a new national bank supervisory agency as part of its 2009 reform package for the financial services industry.

James Ciment and Bill Kte'pi

See also: Community Reinvestment Act (1977); Depository Institutions; Mortgage, Commercial/Industrial; Mortgage Markets and Mortgage Rates; Real-Estate Speculation; Regulation, Financial.

Further Reading

Black, William K. *The Best Way to Rob a Bank Is to Own One.* Austin: University of Texas Press, 2005.

Lowy, Michael. *High Rollers: Inside the Savings and Loan Debacle.* New York: Praeger, 1991.

Mayer, Martin. *The Greatest-Ever Bank Robbery: The Collapse of the Savings and Loan Industry.* New York: Scribner, 1992.

Pizzo, Steven, Mary Fricker, and Paul Muolo. *Inside Job: The Looting of America's Savings and Loans.* New York: McGraw-Hill, 1989.

Robinson, Michael A. *Overdrawn: The Bailout of American Savings.* New York: Dutton, 1990.

White, Lawrence J. *The S&L Debacle: Public Policy Lessons for Bank and Thrift Regulation.* New York: Oxford University Press, 1991.

Schumpeter, Joseph (1883–1950)

Best known for his work on the relationship between technology, entrepreneurialism, and long-term economic development—as well as for popularizing the phrase "creative destruction" to describe technological innovation's transformative effect on capitalist economies—Joseph Alois Schumpeter was a Czech-born, Austrian-educated economist whose most important work dates from the first half of the twentieth century. Among his most influential books are *Business Cycles* (1939), which examined the relationship between short-term and long-term economic cycles, and *Capitalism, Socialism, and Democracy* (1942), in which he posited, in a variation on Karl Marx's ideas, that capitalism sowed the seeds of its own destruction and would be supplanted, albeit in evolutionary rather than revolutionary fashion, by socialism.

Born on February 8, 1883, into a well-off textile manufacturing family in what was then the Austro-Hungarian Empire, Schumpeter studied law and economics at the University of Vienna, receiving his PhD in the latter, in 1906. After a short time abroad, where, among other things, he served as financial manager to an Egyptian princess, Schumpeter returned to the empire. For the next eleven years, he alternated between positions in academia and government. Shortly after World War I, he served as minister of finance. In 1920, he left to become president of the Biedermann Bank, until its collapse—a result of excessive speculation—and his own personal bankruptcy forced him to return to teaching. From 1925 to 1932, he served as a professor of economics at the University of Bonn, Germany, until the rise of the Nazis forced him to emigrate. Moving to the United States, he took a teaching position at Harvard University, where he remained until a year before his death in 1950.

Schumpeter's first significant foray into the relationship between entrepreneurialism, technology, and economic growth came in his 1911 book, *Theory of Economic Development*, in which he outlined what would become his signature idea—that entrepreneurs are the major agents of economic change. He began the book by reexamining late-nineteenth- and early-twentieth-century neoclassical economist Léon Walras's general equilibrium theory in which, simply put, supply and demand roughly balance one another, producing economic stasis or gradual incremental growth. Schumpeter argued that entrepreneurs periodically upset this equilibrium. By introducing new technologies and/or new business methods, they became the prime agents of economic change and development. As for innovation itself, Schumpeter saw it as a creative activity, an act of genius that eludes economic understanding and analysis. He

Austrian-American economist Joseph Schumpeter maintained that fluctuations in the business cycle are consequences of the growth process, which is driven by innovation, "creative destruction," and new innovation in products and production processes. *(Imagno/Hulton Archive/Getty Images)*

also accorded a prominent role in this process to the financial sector, which provides the credit necessary for the entrepreneur to realize his or her vision.

At the same time, Schumpeter identified a downside to this process. As more entrepreneurs seek to exploit technological innovations, profit margins shrink and eventually disappear, leading to widespread bankruptcy, the drying up of bank credit, unemployment, and ultimately, economic recession or depression. This contraction, Schumpeter said, is a necessary evil, as it eliminates less efficient, less innovative business firms from the system. Once that shaking-out process takes place, the cleverest entrepreneurs can again obtain the capital they need to exploit new innovations, renewing the dynamic character of capitalism. Schumpeter would later borrow and popularize the term "creative destruction"—originally coined by German economist Werner Sombart in 1913—to describe this process.

Given his interest in innovation and economic change, it is no surprise that Schumpeter also had an interest in the economics, econometrics, and historical properties of business cycles, a subject he turned to in earnest with his 1939 book *Business Cycles.* In this work, Schumpeter attempted to bring together cycles, or waves, of three different lengths—each named after the economist who first described them—in a synthesis that would explain the basic ebb and flow of capitalist economic growth, stagnation, and contraction: the Kitchin cycle (3-to-4-year cycles revolving around the accumulation and reduction of business inventories, usually involving consumer goods); the Juglar cycle (concerning business investment and capital equipment, lasting 8 to 11 years); and Kondratieff cycles (long-term cycles of between 45 and 60 years, in which the adoption of major technological innovation plays a key role).

In his last decade, Schumpeter broadened his perspective, incorporating a wider social, political, and historical context to his economic analysis. In his widely read *Capitalism, Socialism, and Democracy* (1942), he moved beyond the study of business

cycles, combining sociology, politics, and economics to examine the future of capitalism itself. Like Marx, he concluded that capitalism contains the seeds of its own destruction and will eventually evolve into socialism—not because of its failures but because of its successes. Rather than being destroyed by the social unrest of the exploited working class, the transformation would come about because of capitalism's efficiencies and enormous capacity for wealth creation. First, through the process of "creative destruction" inherent within the business cycle, larger risk-averse firms with their heavy managerial bureaucracy would come to replace innovative and risk-taking smaller firms. Second, the increased income generated by capitalism would, he argued, swell the ranks of the educated middle class—a cohort that tended to be highly critical of laissez-faire capitalism and that favored more government bureaucracy and regulation of the economy. Both forces, then, would restrict the capacity of entrepreneurs to guide capitalism's future, leading to economic stasis and eventually to socialism.

Also occupying the last years of his life was Schumpeter's study of the history of economic thought, published in two well-received posthumous publications—*Ten Great Economists* (1951) and the magisterial, if unfinished, *History of Economic Analysis* (1954).

In the years following his death, Schumpeter came to be recognized as one of the most influential, if somewhat iconoclastic, figures in the history of economics. Indeed, scholars cite him as the originator of an entirely independent school of economic thought—alongside the classical, Keynesian, and neoclassical schools—which gives primacy to technological, institutional, organization, and social innovation in determining economic trends and cycles and how capitalism itself operates. As the enormous forces of technological change, financial innovation, and economic restructuring have continued to propel and buffet the economy in the late twentieth and early twenty-first centuries, Schumpeter's shadow has only grown longer. As Lawrence Summers, director of the National Economic Council under President Obama, suggested in the early 2000s, "the economy of the future is likely to be 'Schumpeterian.'"

Christopher Godden and James Ciment

See also: Austrian School; Creative Destruction; Technological Innovation.

Further Reading

Allen, Robert Loring. *Opening Doors: The Life and Work of Joseph Schumpeter.* 2 vols. New Brunswick, NJ: Transaction, 1991.

Heertje, Arnold. *Schumpeter on the Economics of Innovation and the Development of Capitalism.* Cheltenham, UK: Edward Elgar, 2006.

McCraw, Thomas K. *Prophet of Innovation: Joseph Schumpeter and Creative Destruction.* Cambridge, MA: Harvard University Press, 2007.

Schumpeter, Joseph. *Business Cycles: A Theoretical, Historical and Statistical Analysis of the Capitalist Process.* 2 vols. New York: McGraw-Hill, 1939.

————. *Capitalism, Socialism and Democracy.* New York: Harper, 1942.

————. *History of Economic Analysis.* London: George Allen & Unwin, 1954.

Swedberg, Richard. *Schumpeter: A Biography.* Princeton, NJ: Princeton University Press, 1991.

Monetary policy expert Anna Schwartz, a six-decade member of the National Bureau of Economic Research who co-wrote several books with monetarist Milton Friedman, opposed the stimulus measures and bank bailouts of the Bush and Obama administrations. *(Bloomberg/Getty Images)*

Schwartz, Anna (1915–)

An economist at the National Bureau of Economic Research (NBER) since 1941, Anna Jacobson Schwartz has had a long and remarkable career as a monetary theorist. In 1963, she cowrote, with economist Milton Friedman, *A Monetary History of the United States, 1867–1960,* which remains one of the most important works in economic history and in the grand debate between Keynesians and monetarists on macroeconomics. A carefully researched study of the role of monetary institutions in booms and busts in the U.S. economy, it is as relevant as ever in the twenty-first century.

Anna Jacobson was born on November 11, 1915, in New York City, to Hillel and Pauline Shainmark Jacobson. She earned a bachelor's degree in 1934 from Barnard College and a mas-

ter's degree in 1935 from Columbia University, where, in 1964, she also was awarded a doctorate in economics. In 1936, she married Isaac Schwartz, whom she had met at a high school Hebrew camp; they would have four children.

After a brief stint at Columbia University's Social Science Research Council, Schwartz began her lifelong career at the NBER in 1941. In addition to her position at the bureau, she has been an adjunct faculty member at both the City University of New York and New York University since 1964 and has served on the editorial boards of such prominent journals as the *American Economic Review,* the *Journal of Money, Credit, and Banking,* and the *Journal of Monetary Economics.*

During her distinguished career, Schwartz has authored or coauthored several books and dozens of articles in leading economics journals. In addition to *A Monetary History,* her most important contributions to economics include two collaborative projects with Friedman—*Monetary Statistics of the United States* (1970), and *Monetary Trends in the United States and the United Kingdom: Their Relation to Income, Prices, and Interest Rates, 1867–1975* (1982)—as well as *Growth and Fluctuations in the British Economy, 1790–1850: An Historical, Statistical, and Theoretical Study of Britain's Economic Development* (1953), which she cowrote with Arthur Gayer and Walt Whitman Rostow. Together these works demonstrate Schwartz's skill as an economic historian and empiricist. Her collaborations with Friedman were groundbreaking in their use and presentation of data to combat Keynesianism.

While Schwartz is best remembered for her work with Friedman, she also has made important contributions to financial market regulations, monetary policy debates, and business-cycle theory. Her research, largely historical in nature, led to a shift in monetary policy. Thanks to Schwartz and Friedman, monetary policy makers began to concentrate more on price stability and less on the management of other macroeconomic variables.

Schwartz's influence in the field of economics continues in the 2000s. *A Monetary History* is required reading in many graduate macroeconomics and money and banking courses, and her writings on price stability and financial institutions have influenced policy makers in the United States and around the world. During the financial meltdown of 2007–2008, Schwartz took Federal Reserve (Fed) leaders—Chair Ben Bernanke, in particular—to task for not doing their jobs to alleviate the crisis. In a 2008 *Wall Street Journal* article, she asserted that the "credit market disturbance" was not the result of a lack of money to lend but rather a lack of "faith in the ability of borrowers to repay their debts." She faulted the Fed and the U.S. Treasury Department for "recapitalizing firms that should be shut down," asserting that "firms that made wrong decisions should fail." In a *New York Times* op-ed piece a year later, she urged President Barack Obama to choose an economist

other than Bernanke as Federal Reserve chair, accusing Bernanke of having "committed serious sins of commission and omission" in his failure to convince the faltering markets that the Fed had a plan to help turn the ailing economy around.

Scott Beaulier and Joshua Hall

See also: Friedman, Milton; Monetary Policy; Monetary Stability; Monetary Theories and Models.

Further Reading

Carney, Brian M. "Bernanke Is Fighting the Last War." *Wall Street Journal,* October 18, 2008.

Feldstein, Martin. "Anna Schwartz at the National Bureau of Economic Research." *Journal of Financial Services Research* 18:2/3 (2000): 115–117.

Friedman, Milton, and Anna Jacobson Schwartz. *A Monetary History of the United States, 1867–1960.* Princeton, NJ: Princeton University Press, 1963.

———. *Monetary Statistics of the United States.* New York: Columbia University Press, 1970.

———. *Monetary Trends in the United States and the United Kingdom: Their Relation to Income, Prices, and Interest Rates, 1867–1975.* Chicago: University of Chicago Press, 1982.

Schwartz, Anna Jacobson. "Man Without a Plan." *New York Times,* July 25, 2009.

Seasonal Cycles

Seasonal cycles are short-term business cycles that occur within the course of a year and are determined by such factors as weather, social phenomena, and cultural events. Weather affects annual swings in agricultural activities, with peak levels of activity occurring at planting in the spring and harvesting in the fall. In certain parts of the United States where favorable climate and availability of irrigation are the norm, including California and the Southwest, agricultural cycles can be repeated a number of times during the year. Weather also has a major impact on construction cycles in most regions of the country. Winter is a slow time when low temperatures prevent the application and curing of concrete, and precipitation makes it difficult or impossible to undertake many outdoor tasks involved in the erection of residential and commercial structures and in the construction of roads and bridges. Weather is critical to outdoor recreation activities and their associated economic activities, such as the accommodation and restaurant industries. Favorable winter weather (adequate snow pack for skiing) or sunny, warm days of summer are important to the economic vitality of firms in these industries.

Social and cultural activities also drive seasonal production cycles. Christmas has a major effect on retail sales and the vacation travel industry. Bookstores, for example, make the majority of their annual sales in November and December. Thanksgiving creates a surge in retail sales related to the preparation of food to celebrate the event. Super Bowl Sunday is a major boost to the food and beverage industries. Memorial Day weekend is a big travel time for families to visit friends and relatives. All that traveling creates a surge in gasoline consumption, accommodations, and restaurant activities.

Economic Implications

Seasonal cycles matter a great deal to the economy for a variety of reasons. First, marketing and sales plans must consider expected seasonal patterns in consumer purchases, and must be able to forecast these trends. State and local governments need to understand the ebb and flow of seasonal cycles in order to plan for government services such as police and emergency services, scheduling of highway maintenance, and forecasting government revenues and expenditures, such as provision for unemployment insurance claims. The federal government and the Federal Reserve Board have a keen interest in monitoring national economic trends during the year in terms of overall employment growth or decline, and changes in price levels. These national agencies must be able to distinguish between trends in employment and prices that are driven by seasonal factors, and the shifts in longer-term fundamentals that indicate

the economy is moving into a period of recession, with impending dangers of excessive unemployment or inflation.

Seasonal cycles have an impact on levels of employment, sales, prices, and the costs of doing business. The seasonal cycle in agriculture drives prices down at harvest time, while those prices rise as inventories are depleted during the rest of the year. The farm community may also experience a shortage of workers that will increase wages during harvest time. There may be a temporary, seasonal reduction in the wages of construction workers, as well as the prices of building materials, as the weather deteriorates and the demand for workers declines. But as good weather returns, wages and materials prices may increase as construction firms respond to an increased demand for their services. Employment and wages in a region may decline due to purely seasonal factors. For example, a region that has a vibrant tourist trade in the summertime might always experience a decline in economic activity in the fall.

Information on how to understand the seasonal impacts on employment, sales, prices, and the costs of doing business are important to decision making in the private and public sectors. Business and governments are aware of the seasonal cycles, but there is still a critical need to distinguish between seasonal effects and longer-term fundamental trends. Is there a longer-term trend affecting the prices of crops produced by the farm community in a region, or are there changes in labor market conditions (such as changes in immigration) that would attenuate or diminish the effects of the seasonal cycle? This could have implications for crop planning and future production decisions. Construction activity always improves in the spring, but the question for a contractor is, are the improvements in the springtime over the past few years trending in a particular direction? A county government in a summertime tourist region may have an ongoing concern for lower levels of employment and wages in the fall and winter months, but the issue is whether this decline is getting less serious or more serious over time.

Measuring the Impact of Seasonal Cycles

Many of the important measures of economic activity reported on a monthly or quarterly basis are presented on a seasonally adjusted basis. The national unemployment rate, compiled by the U.S. Bureau of Labor Statistics (BLS), is calculated on a seasonally adjusted basis; that is, the influence of seasonal effects is removed. For example, the BLS's press release indicated that the seasonally adjusted unemployment rate for February 2010 was 9.7 percent. The nonseasonally adjusted measured unemployment rate is actually 10.4 percent, the difference being the expected seasonally higher unemployment rate for February, on average. Other important monthly and quarterly statistical series released by the BLS on a seasonal basis include the consumer and producer price indexes and the employment cost index. The U.S. Department of Commerce's Bureau of Economic Analysis (BEA) is responsible for reporting data on the national income and product accounts. Monthly and quarterly data are provided on a seasonally adjusted basis for personal consumption expenditures (which constitutes about 65 percent of national product), personal income, government receipts and expenditures, business inventories, and residential and nonresidential construction.

These national economic indicators, which are seasonally adjusted, are a great help to private- and public-sector planning. However, seasonal adjustment of time-series data is not available for all industry sectors or for all regions. Seasonally adjusted series for unemployment are provided at the national, state, and major metropolitan levels only, and are not available for localities such as nonmetropolitan counties. To meet their planning needs, businesses and governments may decide to develop seasonal adjustments to important time-series data. That information is now unavailable from government sources.

In short, seasonal cycles and data about seasonal cycles play an important, continuing role in economic performance. The process of adjusting actual time-series data during the year to compensate for expected seasonal swings can provide important information. This information is important for planning purposes to distinguish between seasonal swings in economic data from more fundamental trends and events that affect the economy.

Derek Bjonback

See also: Agriculture; Jevons, William Stanley; Sunspot Theories.

Further Reading

Hanke, John E., and Dean Wichern. *Business Forecasting.* 9th ed. Upper Saddle River, NJ: Pearson Prentice-Hall, 2005.

Hooshmand, A. Reza. *Business Forecasting: A Practical Approach.* 2nd ed. New York: Routledge, 2009.

Securities and Exchange Commission

The economic crisis of 2008–2009 has put the U.S. Securities and Exchange Commission (SEC) in an unfavorable light due to the general consensus that the SEC was negligent as a supervisory agency just when it was needed the most. The crisis thus underscores the role that the SEC is supposed to play in helping to prevent, or at least mitigate, financial disasters that stem from fraudulent behavior on the part of public corporations and those active in the trading of public securities.

The SEC is a U.S. government agency. On its Web site, the SEC states that its main mission is "to protect investors, maintain fair, orderly, and efficient markets, and facilitate capital formation." To achieve these goals, the SEC oversees the federal securities laws, maintains the disclosure of financial information by publicly traded companies, and brings enforcement actions against violators of the securities law. The SEC works in close cooperation with several other U.S. government agencies, such as the Federal Reserve and the Treasury Department.

Prior to 1933, the United States did not have comprehensive regulation of the securities markets on the federal level. Instead, individual states were left to enact their own laws to protect their citizens against investment fraud. These state laws were enacted in response to a growing number of fraudulent speculative schemes targeted at the general population. The schemes were not backed up by any assets or reasonable business plans; such fraudulent claims were thus said to have come "out of the blue sky." Thus, these con artists were referred to as blue-sky merchants, and the state laws protecting against these schemes came to be known as blue-sky laws.

Nevertheless, in the early 1930s, it became apparent that state laws alone could not combat securities fraud. The development of communication and transportation networks made interstate securities trading easily accessible to both the general public and con artists. State laws were virtually powerless and, in fact, did not even have legal standing against interstate fraud. It soon became clear that the federal government needed to step in, and Congress did so by passing the Securities Act of 1933, which required any original interstate sale or offer of securities to be registered and to meet certain disclosure requirements. Subsequently, Congress passed the Securities Exchange Act of 1934, aimed at regulating secondary market trading of securities. As part of these federal regulations, the SEC was created.

Structure of the SEC

The SEC is headed by five commissioners, who are appointed by the president of the United States for five-year terms. The SEC must be a bipartisan body. To achieve this, no more than three commissioners can belong to the same political party. One of the commissioners is designated by the president to be the chair of the commission.

Today the SEC employs nearly 3,500 people. The commission's organizational chart consists of four divisions and nineteen offices. The Division of Corporate Finance is directly charged with overseeing corporate disclosure practices and making sure that all investors, from Wall Street financial analysts to retiring teachers in rural Iowa, have equal access to corporate financial information. The division reviews required disclosure documents filed by companies planning to sell their securities to the general public, as well as periodic disclosures by publicly traded corporations. It encourages corporations to provide extensive and timely information, both positive and negative, about the company's business to ensure that investors can make an educated decision as to whether to buy, hold, or sell securities of the company.

The Division of Trading and Markets provides oversight of securities trading. It controls the work of stock exchanges, brokers, dealers, transfer agents, clearing agencies, credit rating agencies, and others. The goal of this division is to ensure reliable and efficient operations of the securities trading markets.

The Division of Investment Management is in charge of mutual and pension funds operating in the United States. A large portion of the money in these funds is collected from private investors who are saving for retirement, college, a new house, or another purpose. Professional fund managers pool together money from millions of such individuals and manage it on their behalf. This division ensures that fund managers act in the best interests of all individual investors and provide full disclosure of fund activities to them.

The Division of Enforcement investigates securities law violations, obtains evidence of unlawful activities, and prosecutes civil actions in court. It also collects complaints from private and professional investors and monitors market activities daily to ensure the legality of all operations.

The nineteen offices of the commission ensure that the SEC can fulfill its functions in accordance with its mission. For example, the Office of Compliance Inspections and Examinations makes sure that companies follow all the compliance regulations. The Office of Investor Education and Advocacy helps individual investors with their problems and concerns, promotes the issues important to such investors, and carries out educational efforts. The role of the Office of Risk Assessment is to predict potential threats to the investment markets and to identify fraudulent or illegal activities.

In addition, several offices serve to advise the commission on various issues. Among them, the Office of Economic Analysis advises the SEC on the economic issues, the Office of the Chief Accountant on the accounting issues, and the Office of the General Counsel on the legal issues.

The SEC also has eleven regional offices, in Atlanta, Boston, Chicago, Denver, Fort Worth, Los Angeles, Miami, New York, Philadelphia, Salt Lake City, and San Francisco.

Data Gathering and Distribution

The SEC also maintains the Electronic Data Gathering, Analysis and Retrieval (EDGAR) system. All publicly traded companies are required to submit their financial information to EDGAR, and that information becomes available to anybody who has a computer with Internet connection. EDGAR, however, is a noninteractive system—the information is presented simply as text. In early 2009, the SEC introduced new regulations stating that, starting from a fiscal period ending on or after June 15, 2009, all large companies must use the new system—Interactive Data Electronic Application (IDEA). IDEA relies on the new interactive data format—extensible business reporting language (XBRL). All other companies will start using IDEA by June 2011.

XBRL makes financial data not simply readily available to investors, but it also allows investors to download these data directly into spreadsheets and perform data analysis. The data reporting will be standardized across companies; thus, investors will be able to compare companies side by side. Finally, XBRL allows automated searching within data. The key to XBRL is tagging—every variable coded in XBRL has a unique tag that identifies the category the number belongs to. Thus, for example, if the tag for net profit is entered, the system will show net profit for each company.

As the financial debacle of 2008–2009 grew, some economists and other experts blamed the SEC for contributing to the crisis in three ways: (1) for failing to stay current with the ever-increasing complexity of the financial markets and the variety of new instruments traded on these markets by many players; (2) for its laissez-faire approach to regulations when it allowed the markets to basically regulate themselves and avoided interventions as much as possible; and (3) for following the markets rather than leading them—in other words, for investigating fraud once it happened and attempting to establish who was to blame for the fraud rather than trying to anticipate and prevent the fraud from happening in the first place through changes in legislation and enhanced monitoring. Probably the most notorious example of SEC failure to prevent fraud despite several warnings was that of Bernard Madoff, who committed the largest investment fraud ever by a single person. Madoff had been under SEC investigation sixteen times in the years while the fraud was being committed. Another high-profile case involves a prominent financier from Texas, Robert Allen Stanford, who, as a CEO of Stanford Financial Group, misappropriated billions of investors' money.

Today the SEC joins other government agencies in dealing with the current financial crisis. On its Web site, the SEC created a page dedicated to actions the agency is taking to mitigate the effects of the credit crisis. Among these actions, the SEC lists aggressive fraud investigation, especially fraud connected with the subprime mortgages, investigations of false rumors in the market, investigation of accounting fraud, and investigations of illegal trading practices. The SEC also took actions to modify the regulations of the market by requiring disclosure of hedge-fund positions in certain securities and updating regulations for banks and credit default swaps. Finally, the SEC requested all companies to provide enhanced and full disclosure to supply investors with more relevant and reliable information in a timely manner.

Alexander V. Laskin

See also: Consumer and Investor Protection; Glass-Steagall Act (1933); New Deal; Regulation, Financial; Stock Market Crash (1929).

Further Reading

Alvares, R.I., and M.J. Astarita. "Introduction to the Blue Sky Laws." Available at www.seclaw.com/bluesky.htm. Accessed April 2009.

"Part III: Securities and Exchange Commission." *Federal Register* 74:26 (February 2009).

Securities and Exchange Commission Web site: www.sec.gov.

Securitization

Securitization is the process that financial institutions use to create financial securities from pools of financial instruments. The securities created by this process are called either asset-backed securities (ABSs) or mortgage-backed securities (MBSs). The classification of ABS or MBS depends on the financial instrument that backs, or collateralizes, the security. If the financial instrument is a mortgage loan issued to finance residential real estate, the securitization of a pool of these mortgage loans results in the issue of an MBS. If the mortgage loans are used to finance commercial real estate, their securitization creates a commercial mortgage-backed security. Any asset with a cash flow can be securitized if the cash flows are pooled together and sold off to investors. When the financial instruments that are securitized are loans to fund the purchase of automobiles from dealers, then the special purpose vehicle (SPV) issues ABSs backed by auto loans. Automobile dealers borrow to finance their inventories of cars and trucks. These loans are called dealer floor-plan loans and are frequently securitized. In this case, the SPV issues ABSs backed by dealer floor-plan loans. Other cash flows from financial instruments that have been securitized include credit card balances, small business loans, student loans, aircraft and railroad car leases, other equipment leases, home-equity lines of credit, retail automobile leases, accounts receivable, and loans to finance manufactured housing.

The securitization process gained worldwide attention during the financial crisis of 2008–2009 because it allowed credit to flow unsecured across many sectors of the global economy. This set the stage for the severe economic contraction that occurred globally.

Process

The process of securitization works basically as follows: (1) a financial institution originates loans; (2) the originator finances the loans until the pool of loans on its balance sheet is large enough to securitize; (3) the originator sells the loans to an SPV; (4) the SPV issues mortgage- or asset-backed securities to raise the funds to pay for the financial assets it has purchased from the originator; (5) the funds obtained or raised from the securitization of the original pool of mortgages are used by the originator to make new loans—which may lead to another securitization transaction. In short, securitization effectively cycles funds from the broader capital and money markets back to borrowers via the banking system. Securitization is a form of direct finance where the ultimate lender (purchaser of the security) has a direct claim on the cash flow from the pool of assets rather than an indirect claim on a financial intermediary.

Commercial banks, savings banks, and finance companies originate and securitize financial assets. While the loans are on the balance sheet of the originator, they must be financed. Because bankers expect to finance the loans only while the pool is being accumulated, perhaps over a few months or less, only short-term financing is arranged. An SPV is set up to act as the purchaser and financier of the pool of loans. It is called an SPV because, unlike a financial institution that can use its balance sheet to finance a broad array of ever-changing assets, the SPV is constrained to buy and finance a specific pool of financial assets. Some financial assets are revolving loans; so the amount financed by the SPV may change as the loan balances change.

The SPV cannot engage in any other activities except those that are directly related to financing the pool of assets it buys from the originator. The SPV may issue multiple classes of ABS/MBSs or a single class. An example of a single class would be an MBS that is structured as mortgage pass-through security. In most securitizations other than those that issue mortgage pass-through securities, multiple classes of securities are issued by the SPV. Each class of securities will have rights to a different stream of the cash flows that are generated by the securitized asset pool. Some securities will be subordinate to others with respect to credit risk. Some securities will have the same credit risk but different rights with respect to the timing of principal repayments. The ability to reallocate the payments from a pool of assets has enabled MBS and ABS to be designed for a very broad spectrum of investors all over the world. Some investors are more willing to take risks than others. For these investors, risky securities are created. Because the total risk of a pool of assets cannot be changed, if a risky security is created, it means that a safer security is also created. It is possible to create short-, medium-, and long-term securities by issuing ABS/MBSs that amortize classes sequentially. Sequential amortization means that one class must be paid off before the second class of investors begins to receive principal payments. Depending on how many securities are in the sequence, the SPV may issue very short–, short-, medium-, and long-term securities to finance a single pool of financial assets.

Subordinate securities are designed to finance a disproportionate level of losses caused by borrower defaults. For example, a $1 million pool of auto loans is securitized. One subordinate class of securities is issued (class B) having a principal value of $100,000 (10 percent of the pool value), and one senior class (class A) is issued with a principal value of $900,000. Class B is structured to absorb all losses of the asset pool before class A. MBS and ABS are generally rated by at least one rating agency. The ratings assigned to a security, including the various classes of ABS and MBS, are an indication of how likely investors are to receive timely payment of all promised interest and principal payments. A triple-A rating is the highest a security can receive and indicates very strong credit.

Financial assets must be serviced whether they are securitized or financed on the originator's balance sheet. If the assets are securitized, the servicing function must be explicitly paid for out of the cash flows generated by the assets. Typically, one-quarter to one-half of a percentage of the outstanding asset balance is the servicing fee per year. Servicing may be retained by the originator or sold to another financial institution. The role of the servicer is to collect payments from borrowers and to funnel the collections into the appropriate bank accounts, where they will be used by the paying agent to pay investors. The servicer can advance funds when borrowers are delinquent, with the servicer receiving compensation for making the advance. The servicer is also responsible for organizing collection efforts and foreclosure proceedings if borrowers are delinquent or have defaulted.

Separation of Loan Origination, Financing, and Servicing

Prior to the widespread adoption of securitization, banks and finance companies traditionally originated, financed, and serviced financial assets such as mortgages, consumer loans, car loans, equipment leases, and business loans. Origination, financing, and servicing were bundled together and could not be effectively separated.

Securitization enables bankers to separate the three formally connected banking activities—the origination, servicing, and financing of financial assets. A bank can originate mortgage loans and securitize the loans. Even though securitization involves selling the loans, the bank will earn a fee for the origination of the mortgage as well as fees for servicing the mortgage. The risk to ABS/MBS investors is that the asset pool will perform worse than expected or that guarantees of the performance of the ABS/MBS cannot fulfill their obligations.

A financial receivable is short-term extension of credit. It is an asset of the company that has extended the credit. For example, if a manufacturer of television sets allows Wal-Mart to have sixty days to pay for televisions once they are delivered, the supplier has extended credit to Wal-Mart. The supplier of the televisions now has what is called an account receivable on its balance sheet.

Because securitization is a dominant form of financing for financial institutions, it is a vital conduit for funds and must operate effectively if credit is going to flow smoothly among the universe of borrowers. However, the securitization process played a pivotal role in the financial meltdown of 2007–2008, in part because it was the instrument by which highly risky (or even insufficiently collateralized) mortgages became integrally linked to a vast network of unsecured financing throughout the U.S. and world economics. Many of the mortgage-backed securities that were subprime, and consequently had low credit ratings, were packaged together into instruments that received top credit ratings and were sold into the global marketplace. Consequently, when the less-than-investment-grade mortgages failed, the top-rated securities were compromised, and the U.S. and global financial structure shattered. The default rates on credit card receivables, automobile loans, home-equity loans, and mortgages were much higher than investors in ABSs and MBSs had expected when they purchased these securities. The high default rates severely depressed prices of MBSs and ABSs and constrained new issues of the securities.

Charles A. Stone

See also: Collateralized Debt Obligations; Collateralized Mortgage Obligations; Credit Default Swaps; Debt Instruments; Innovation, Financial; Liberalization, Financial.

Further Reading

Fabozzi, Frank J., ed. *Accessing Capital Markets Through Securitization.* Hoboken, NJ: John Wiley & Sons, 2001.

Fabozzi, Frank J., and Vinod Kothari. *Introduction to Securitization.* Hoboken, NJ: John Wiley & Sons, 2008.

Kendall, Leon T., and Michael J. Fishman, eds. *A Primer on Securitization.* Cambridge, MA: MIT Press, 2000.

Obay, Lamia. *Financial Innovation in the Banking Industry: The Case of Asset Securitization.* London: Taylor & Francis, 2001.

Tavakoli, Janet M. *Structured Finance and Collateralized Debt Obligations: New Developments in Cash and Synthetic Securitization.* Hoboken, NJ: John Wiley & Sons, 2008.

Shackle, George (1903–1992)

Economist and professor George Shackle is remembered for his work on uncertainty, specifically regarding crucial choices whose outcomes may define, for better or worse, the chooser's future possibilities. His work frequently is cited by economists and management theorists in the areas of uncertainty, information asymmetry, game theory, competitive options, and knowledge management.

George Lennox Sharman Shackle was born on July 14, 1903, in Cambridge, England. He attended the Perse School and then worked his way through undergraduate school as a bank clerk and a teacher; he earned a bachelor's degree in 1931 from the University of London. He obtained his doctorate from the London School of Economics in 1937; his dissertation on business-cycle theory was based on John Maynard Keynes's *General Theory of Employment, Interest and Money* (1936). Shackle's focus was on expectations and uncertainty in the analysis of economic behavior, and the related theme of the question of time. The work was published in 1938 under the title *Expectations, Investment and Income*. In 1939, Shackle served in British Prime Minister Winston Churchill's office as an economist. After World War II, he held posts in the Cabinet Office and at the University of Leeds. He became a professor of economics at the University of Liverpool in 1951, where he remained until his retirement in 1969.

Most of Shackle's academic writings expanded

on the topic of his dissertation, in particular, the influence of entrepreneurs' and consumers' expectations on the business cycle and, hence, on the rate of employment. In 1958, he published *Time in Economics;* in 1961, *Decision, Order and Time in Human Affairs;* and in 1965, *A Scheme of Economic Theory.*

The study of expectations in the area of macroeconomics led to new discoveries about the causes of business cycles. One study focused on the effects of the changing nature of human expectations (in particular, those of entrepreneurs), which impart the dynamic impulses to the economic system that generate cycles. The second study focused on the distinction between initial planning expectations and the assessment of final outcomes, both of which are captured in what are known as ex ante and ex post (before and after) multiplier effects, respectively. A multiplier effect expands or intensifies as an activity is repeated or spreads from person to person, rippling throughout the economy. For example, the multiplier effect of an initial increase in the aggregate flow of a net investment in facilities will be unexpected by the investor; it will improve the profit outlook and lead to a further acceleration in investment and a further multiplier effect. Eventually, such multiplier effects will be expected, at which stage net investment flow will have reached its maximum, as there will be no more unexpected increases in aggregate income to further stimulate investment. The failure of net investment to accelerate further will deprive investors of the multiplier effect, which they have come to expect. Investors will be disappointed by the anticipated but unachieved "growth," and as a result, they will reduce their rate of investment. The cycle's downswing and reversal are mirror images of its upswing and subsequent downswing. Thus, the entire cycle is a result of changing expectations, which are continuously influenced by the effects of previous changes.

Shackle considered his greatest work to be "A Student's Pilgrimage" (1983), in which he addressed the difference between uncertainty and risk. By uncertainty, he was referring to the inability to predict with certainty what is going to happen in the future (e.g., with interest rates, prices, political situations). In such cases, probability cannot be scientifically or mathematically calculated and applied—thus, the decision maker, when choosing a particular course of action, is faced with uncertainty and can only anticipate a range of outcomes.

In addition to writing about his own theories, Shackle wrote classic texts on the history of economic thought, including *The Years of High Theory: Invention and Tradition in Economic Thought, 1926–1939* (1967) and *Epistemics and Economics* (1972). He died on March 3, 1992.

Carol M. Connell

See also: Risk and Uncertainty.

Further Reading

Ford, J.L. *G.L.S. Shackle: The Dissenting Economist's Economist.* Northampton, MA: Edward Elgar, 1994.

———. "G.L.S. Shackle, 1903–1992: A Life with Uncertainty." *Economic Journal* 103:418 (1993): 683–697.

Shackle, George L.S. *Epistemics and Economics: A Critique of Economic Doctrines.* Cambridge, UK: Cambridge University Press, 1972.

———. *Expectations, Investment and Income.* Oxford, UK: Oxford University Press, 1938.

———. *Keynesian Kaleidics: The Evolution of a General Political Economy.* Edinburgh, UK: Edinburgh University Press, 1974.

———. "A Student's Pilgrimage." *Banca Nazionale del Lavoro Quarterly Review* 145 (1983): 107–116.

Shadow Banking System

The shadow banking system is an umbrella name for a range of highly leveraged financial intermediaries such as hedge funds, private equity funds, money market mutual funds, monoline insurers, conduits, structured investment vehicles (SIVs), special-purpose vehicles (SPVs), and other off-balance-sheet vehicles that are centered around the credit markets. The shadow banking system has come to play a key role in financial intermediation both in the United States and in other developed nations as businesses and consumers have increasingly shifted away from commercial banks to the markets for their borrowing and lending needs.

Lack of Regulation

The institutions that populate the shadow banking system effectively function as commercial banks in supplying credit and even accepting deposits. Unlike commercial banks, however, they are not granted access to the lender of last resort (the central bank) or to the institution that insures bank deposits (the Federal Deposit Insurance Corporation—FDIC—in the United States). Due to the lack of access to the lender of last resort and deposit insurance, they are not subject to regulations, such as effective capital requirements, leverage limits, and other restrictions imposed on commercial banks. Nor do they come under the supervision of the central bank.

The only type of regulation, if any, that these institutions are subject to in the United States is capital market regulation provided by the Securities and Exchange Commission (SEC), which is designed to provide full disclosure to potential investors in the securities but not to provide prudential regulation nor to function as a lender of last resort. Unlike regulated and protected commercial banks, many shadow banking institutions, such as SIVs, have few or no reporting obligations or governance standards (again, those registered with the SEC do). In the past, even when regulations did exist, they were often suspended; for example, collateralized SPVs were granted registration and reporting exemptions, and SIVs were granted reporting consolidation exemptions.

In sum, despite the fact that some of these institutions are regulated by the SEC and function as banks, they are not subject to prudential regulations, which are basically aimed at insuring the liquidity of assets. Rather, they are regulated as capital market institutions, the aim of which is to ensure that the mark-to-market value of assets of the entity will be sufficient to liquidate assets at all times. This absence of proper regulation for these financial intermediaries has allowed the shadow banks to employ a high degree of leverage, the expansive use of which was one of the main causes of the global financial crisis that started in 2007.

Traditionally, commercial banks have been the main suppliers of credit in economies, but in the past three decades, market-based institutions have taken over a large part of this business. A commercial bank creates liquidity by ensuring that its liabilities—largely, its deposits—have a higher liquidity premium than its assets, mostly its loans outstanding. It issues short-term highly liquid deposits, which can always be easily converted into the currency and are the closest substitutes for cash that there is.

The asset side of bank balance sheets was traditionally dominated by commercial and industrial loans supported by income flows they helped generate, although in the past couple of decades most large banks shifted out of shorter-term industrial loans and into longer-term mortgages. Even though the possibility always exists that banks might not have enough liquidity at any point in time to meet redemptions of their liabilities, the lender of last resort and the deposit insurer are put in place to increase confidence in the banking system and to mitigate the liquidity problems a solvent bank might face.

Money market mutual funds are very similar to banks in their liability structure and in the manner in which they create liquidity. They issue short-term liabilities similar to bank deposits with a promised equivalent redemption value, and use the funds to buy short-term, highly liquid credit market instruments, such as commercial paper, essentially funding corporate borrowing. Investment banks, for instance, create liquidity by acting as broker-dealers in the securities market and hence facilitating the transformation of longer-term illiquid higher-risk assets into shorter-term liquid lower-risk assets.

Role in Housing Bubble

Despite the existence of capital market–based institutions functioning as banks, it was not until the mass securitization drive of the past decade that the U.S. shadow banking system exploded in size, overtaking the commercial banking sector in terms of asset size. In the second quarter of 2007, near the peak of the housing bubble, market-based institutions (such as government-sponsored enterprises, or GSEs, GSE pools, asset-backed security issuers, broker dealers, and finance companies) involved in securitization had assets valued at $16 trillion, equal to 120 percent of assets of depository institutions (commercial banks, savings and loans, and credit unions). This rising importance of the shadow banks was especially pronounced in the mortgage market, with market-based institutions holding about two-thirds of the $11 trillion dollars of home mortgages.

In the case of securitization, liquidity is created by transforming longer-term, higher-risk illiquid assets into short-term, low-risk, and highly liquid assets through the balance sheet of an SPV. The SPV set up by banks and other financial institutions issues asset-backed commercial paper (that is, rolled over or redeemed at par) to finance its position in a securitized asset, thus transforming illiquid mortgage loans into highly liquid short-term credit market instruments. The next step forward in the innovative world of shadow banks involved structured securitizations such as auction rate notes and collateralized debt obligations, which also create liquidity, albeit in a different manner. The liquidity of these depends on the proper functioning of the securities market, and they have no explicit price guarantees except for insurance of principal provided by credit default swaps or other credit enhancement products sold by third-party monoline insurers.

The funding of shadow banking institutions is short term and usually comes in the form of secured or unsecured borrowing in the commercial paper market, as well as reverse repo transactions. Although some shadow banking institutions, such as SPVs sponsored by commercial banks, can be backed by credit lines from the sponsoring bank (and hence have indirect access to the lender of last resort), most of them depend on the normal functioning of short-term funding markets. Once these dry up, the shadow banks have no lender of last resort to turn to.

The lack of regulation and the employment of high leverage and risk distribution through securitization have allowed the shadow banks to meet borrowers' needs for financial intermediation more cost-effectively, resulting in an explosive increase of their share in the financial sector assets. While the main source of income for traditional banks was the interest rate spread between long-term assets and short-term liabilities, the majority of shadow bank income came from loan origination and servicing fees. Due to regulatory arbitrage and lack of supervision, the shadow banking system took over the main function of commercial banks, facilitating borrowing and lending, including maturity intermediation. Positions in longer-term, higher-risk, lower-liquidity assets were financed by issuing shorter-term, lower-risk, and higher-liquidity assets. In this scenario, the only way for commercial banks to maintain their profitability was by setting up off-balance-sheet entities and acquiring affiliates that were a part of the shadow banking system to be able to utilize high leverage and participate in the activities that commercial banks were forbidden to engage in.

Since the shadow banks were major participants in the liquidity creation that fueled the historic U.S. housing bubble of 2003–2007, it is not surprising that the bursting of the bubble and the financial crisis essentially began with a run on the shadow banks—that is, withdrawal of short-term financing from the securitization market due to declining asset-backed security prices. As investors became concerned about the state of the housing market, short-term funding markets dried up, cutting short the life support of these institutions. The life span of the shadow banking system was limited to the willingness of institutional investors to invest in short-term credit market instruments.

The public safety nets put in place to safeguard against a run on the commercial banking system were useless for preventing a run on the shadow banks, hence all the extraordinary measures taken by the Federal Reserve to prevent a total collapse of the system. Once an asset is securitized through an off-balance-sheet entity, the loan disappears from the bank's balance sheet and so do government guarantees (some institutions did have recursive arrangements with their sponsors, mostly commercial banks, and so got indirect support from the government). Under current institutional arrangements, when these securities go bad, the government does not stand ready (or is not supposed to) to rescue the holders of their liabilities, unlike the case of commercial banks.

The shadow banking system was a major contributor to the global financial fiasco. If these institutions are to engage in financial intermediation, advocates of more government oversight say, they need to be as tightly regulated and supervised as commercial banks are, and government guarantees available to the latter need to be extended to them as well. This will eliminate the cost advantage of shadow banks relative to commercial banks, and will effectively limit the size of the shadow banking system, preventing another financial debacle, for now.

Yeva Nersisyan

See also: Countrywide Financial; Luminent Mortgage Capital; Money Store, The; Regulation, Financial; Venture Capital.

Further Reading

Adrian, T., and H.S. Shin. "The Shadow Banking System: Implications for Financial Regulation." *Staff Report no. 382*, Federal Reserve Bank of New York Staff Reports, July 2009.

Kregel, J. "No Going Back: Why We Cannot Restore Glass-Steagall's Segregation of Banking and Finance." *Public Policy Brief no. 107*. Levy Economics Institute, 2010.

Shock-Based Theories

Single-shock theories of the business cycle combine the concept of a business cycle with that of general equilibrium theory, treating the events of the cycle as a "shock" that disrupts the equilibrium of the economy.

General Equilibrium Theory

Equilibrium is a persistent and self-sustaining state of balance and stability. Examples in the physical world are easy to identify and useful for basic understanding. The planets' orbiting around the sun represents equilibrium in that their movement through space—which should propel them away from the sun—is balanced by the gravitational force of the sun. They will remain in their elliptical orbits until an exogenous force, such as the gravity of another star, or an endogenous one, the sun's eventual collapse, upsets the equilibrium. Moreover, as this example shows, a state of equilibrium does not imply lack of motion. An economic market in which prices and profits remain the same, without excess supply or unmet demand, is another example of equilibrium.

In economics, equilibrium theory is generally microeconomic in focus. That is, it is concerned with prices, supply and demand, and consumer decisions rather than with the inflation, unemployment, and economic policy decisions studied in macroeconomics. The equilibrium price of a good is the one that will satisfy supply and demand without surpluses or shortages. It is often viewed as the price achieved naturally after some transitional volatility, bouncing back and forth like a tennis ball in response to corrective forces (overproduction, underproduction, and the like). Thus, for example, if one were to introduce a new type of automobile into a market, one could expect to sell more automobiles in the first year than in subsequent years. Once everyone owns the car, new customers will be created slowly (as children grow up and reach driving age, or individuals' incomes increase to enable them to afford a car), and most sales will be replacement vehicles rather than first-time purchases. Equilibrium is achieved when the number of cars sold each year becomes stable and predictable.

This example represents a case of partial equilibrium analysis—it considers only one good and assumes that all other prices remain constant or irrelevant. Modern economists focus on the problem of general equilibrium, a model that takes everything into account. General equilibrium is implicitly macroeconomic in scope in that it attempts to postulate and model a state of equilibrium for the entire economy.

Sudden and General Disturbances

Although general equilibrium became a special concern of economists beginning in the 1920s, it had been the subject of previous study. In the late nineteenth century, the French neoclassical economist Léon Walras was the first to attempt to model equilibrium prices for a whole economy. His *Elements of Pure Economics*, published in 1874, describes the effects of what we now call the business cycle: "Just as a lake is at times stirred to its very depths by a storm, so also the market is sometimes thrown into violent confusion by crises, which are sudden and general disturbances of equilibrium." However, Walras and the economists who followed him were unable to adequately explain these disturbances. They could only describe a model of equilibrium that would persist for as long as such disturbances could be avoided.

After the banking panics of the late nineteenth and early twentieth centuries and the Great Depression, as economists delved deeper into the phenomenon of booms and busts, the business cycle came to be seen as less and less compatible with general equilibrium theory. In the 1930s, however, Norwegian economist Ragnar Frisch and Ukrainian economist Eugen Slutsky were the first to overcome this view. Frisch and Slutsky both argued in favor of analyzing the effects of "sudden and general disturbances"—or economic shocks—without worrying about their cause. Or, to extend Walras's lake analogy, one does not need to know whether a rock or a tennis ball has been thrown into the lake in order to know how the water will be affected. Shocks to the equilibrium of the economy are common, even if individual types of shocks are rare, and they are randomly but normally distributed. By extension, a roughly equal number of shocks are positive (booms) and negative (busts), and most of them are small. A single large shock to the equilibrium accounts for a major economic downswing, such as that experienced during the Great Depression.

The Frisch-Slutsky marriage of equilibrium theory with the business cycle paints the cycle as a series of random variations to the trend of general equilibrium. The business cycle, in this view, is a series of shocks—those that arise from the interaction between predictable, nonrandom phenomena and random phenomena. However, the shocks—and the mechanics of the equilibrium—are not so simple that a negative shock can be corrected by a positive shock of equal value. For example, there may be no government policy that will simply flip one switch back on when a shock to the equilibrium switches it off. The forces of stability are strong enough that there is a lag time, the effect of which is that further shocks can prolong the negative effect rather than cancel it out. By way of analogy, consider the difficulty of trying to cancel out the ripples in Walras's lake caused by a thrown stone. What can one throw into the water to reverse the ripples? In short, this approach to business cycles denies their cyclicality. The shocks occur not with a periodicity that can be described, but stochastically (randomly).

Other Shock Theories

The Polish economist Michal Kalecki incorporated the concept of exogenous shocks (those that originate outside the system, such as a rock thrown into the lake) in his 1954 book *Theory of Economic Dynamics: An Essay on Cyclical and Long-Run Changes in Capitalist Economy.* According to this model, continual shocks to the economy are responsible for oscillations in the business cycle.

The Frisch-Slutsky theory of shocks was revived in the 1980s and incorporated into "real business cycle" or "stochastic growth" theory, which blends neoclassical models of production, spending levels, and consumer preference with Frisch-Slutsky-type shocks.

The implications of the real business cycle theories are profound for economic policy makers. If, as argue some economists, booms and busts are a natural process as the market economy efficiently responds to endogenously triggered increases and falls in demand, then governments should not attempt to respond to shocks with short-term fiscal and monetary policies. In particular, governments should not attempt to bolster employment and demand during times of recession. Instead, they should focus on long-term policy, both structural and monetary, creating the infrastructure needed by a growing economy. In addition, they should not adjust monetary policy to meet the short-term ups and downs of the economy but instead emphasize stable growth of the money supply to keep up with overall economic growth.

On the other hand, some economists respond that exogenous shocks are critical to the economic cycle, and markets cannot necessarily adjust to them on their own. Consequently, the government does have a role in implementing short-term fiscal and monetary policy to respond to the shocks. The recent financial crisis has bolstered the position of those who argue that governments do have a role to play in adjusting to shocks to the economy.

Bill Kte'pi

See also: Catastrophe Theory; Frisch, Ragnar; Kalecki, Michal.

Further Reading

Schumpeter, Joseph A. *History of Economic Analysis.* New York: Oxford University Press, 1996.

Strøm, Steinar. *Econometrics and Economic Theory in the 20th Century: The Ragnar Frisch Centennial Symposium.* New York: Cambridge University Press, 1999.

Tangian, Adranik, and Josef Gruber, eds. *Constructing and Applying Objective Functions: Proceedings of the Fourth International Conference on Econometric Decision Models.* New York: Springer, 2001.

Van Overtveldt, Johan. *The Chicago School: How the University of Chicago Assembled the Thinkers Who Revolutionized Economics and Business.* Chicago: Agate, 2007.

Slow-Growth Recovery

As the name implies, a slow-growth recovery is a postrecession economic rebound characterized by anemic economic growth and persistent high levels of unemployment. Given the importance of the latter to the overall health of the economy, a newly popular term for the phenomenon has arisen—"jobless recovery." What constitutes a slow recovery is debated by economists, but most agree it is marked by growth rates of between 1 and 2 percent rather than the 4 or 5 percent needed to make a dent in high unemployment levels.

In addition, most economists agree that the U.S. economy has experienced a slow-growth recovery since the official end of the "Great Recession" of 2007–2009, though there was debate as the country emerged from the downturn as to whether the rebound would become more robust, remain slow, or fail altogether, leading to what is known as a "double dip recession"—that is, two recessions separated by a brief period of modest growth.

The U.S. economy emerged very slowly from the Great Depression of the 1930s, with gross domestic product (GDP) reaching only its precrash levels of 1929—as measured in inflation-adjusted dollars—in 1936. Meanwhile, unemployment remained quite high. After peaking at over 25 percent in 1933, the rate remained in the double digits until at least 1941, even though the economy was growing from 1933 onward, aside from a brief but sharp recession in 1937–1938.

In the post–World War II era, however, recoveries have tended to be more rapid. While the U.S. economy was buffeted by several recessions in the 1970s and early 1980s, business activity rebounded robustly after each of them, and employers quickly began rehiring. Indeed, some economists even came to argue that the sharp recoveries were structured into the U.S. economy of the postwar period.

The recession of 2007–2009, however, was different. First, of course, it was of much greater duration and severity than any other economic downturn of the post–World War II era. Between the fourth quarter of 2007, when the recession officially began, and its conclusion in the second quarter of 2009, the U.S. economy shed roughly 8.3 million jobs, with the unemployment rate peaking at 10.1 percent in the third quarter of 2009. Meanwhile, overall GDP contracted between 6 and 8 percent, depending on how it is measured, over this same time period.

At first glance, the U.S. economy appeared to be recovering nicely after the end of the recession. The annualized growth rate for the fourth quarter of 2009 was a robust 5.9 percent, more than adequate, if sustained, to invigorate the kind of hiring necessary to make up for those 8 million-plus lost jobs. Meanwhile, the Dow Jones Industrial Average of major corporate securities rose more than 60 percent from its low point of around 6,500 in March 2009.

But by other measurements, the rebound was occurring slowly and painfully. Consumer confidence remained low, aggregate demand was weak, and unemployment remained stubbornly high, at 9.7 percent into January and February 2010, with the economy still shedding jobs, though at a much reduced rate.

Economists—at least, those who insist this recovery will be much more anemic than other postwar ones—cite a wide variety of explanations for why the U.S. economy is experiencing a slow-growth recovery following the great recession of 2007–2009. High levels of accumulated debt and a depressed housing market are causing consumers to save more and spend less, driving down demand. High unemployment rates are driving down consumer confidence, which is further undermining demand. Fearful that demand will remain weak, businesses are less willing to expand and hire.

Perhaps the most widely cited reason behind the slow-growth recovery of 2009–2010 is the credit crisis. After relaxing their lending standards for years—particularly in the mortgage sector—lenders in the financial sector experienced unprecedented losses, as many of the loans they made proved to be bad ones, with mortgagors defaulting on their loans in record numbers. To shore up their balance sheets and avoid further losses, banks and other lenders raised credit standards and tightened the amount of money they were willing to loan.

Tightening credit standards mean that businesses cannot get the loans they need to invest and expand, thus reducing the amount of new hiring they can do. Without access to capital, businesses tend to make do with what they have, even as demand rises, which usually translates into more productivity per hour worked.

Meanwhile, homebuyers find it much more difficult to obtain mortgages, which continues to keep the housing market depressed. With home equity having fallen by a historic degree and remaining far below where it was at the peak of the housing boom in 2006, homeowners—even those with jobs—feel poorer and are less likely to engage in discretionary spending. This means that the economy is unlikely to get a boost from consumer spending and, as this spending accounts for roughly 70 percent of all economic activity, the tightening credit market contributes to very weak overall demand.

In short, say many economists, earlier recessions that were caused either by weakening demand—such as those of the 1990s—or by the Federal Reserve hiking interest rates—as was the case with the recession of the early 1980s—tend to produce sharp recoveries. But those recessions that are caused by credit contractions, such as that of the early 1990s and that of 2007–2009, are followed by very slow and weak recoveries.

James Ciment

See also: Employment and Unemployment; Great Depression (1929–1933); Growth, Economic; Recession and Financial Crisis (2007–).

Further Reading

Aronowitz, Stanley. *Just Around the Corner: The Paradox of the Jobless Recovery.* Philadelphia: Temple University Press, 2005.

Reddy, Sudeep. "The Economic Recovery: Fast, Slow or Neither?" *Wall Street Journal*, August 18, 2009. Available at http://online.wsj.com/article/SB125055148430738445.html. Accessed March 2010.

Roubini, Nouriel. "A 'Jobless' and 'Wageless' Recovery?" *Forbes.com*, August 13, 2009. Available at www.forbes.com/2009/08/12/payroll-losses-jobless-recession-consumer-opinions-columnists-nouriel-roubini.html. Accessed March 2010.

Smith, Adam (1723–1790)

One of the most influential economic thinkers in history, Adam Smith was one of the architects of classical economics and is generally considered the father of modern economics. His 1776 work, *The Wealth of Nations*, laid out the basic principles of the field, even as it helped persuade British policy makers, albeit decades later, to gradually move their country toward a laissez-faire, free trade economy.

Born in Kirkcaldy, Scotland, in 1723, Smith was raised by his mother; his father died several months before his birth. A child prodigy, Smith entered the University of Glasgow at the age of fourteen and then studied for a time at Oxford University, though he did not receive a degree, being forced to leave when his scholarship ran out. In 1751, he became a professor of moral philosophy at Glasgow University, where he taught logic, ethics, rhetoric, law, and economics. In 1778, he was appointed a commissioner of customs, a post that provided him with a secure source of income but also required him to crack down on smuggling even though his own writings had justified such clandestine activities in the face of "unnatural" legislation that tried to restrict trade.

Smith began his intellectual career as a philosopher, and his first book, *The Theory of Moral Sentiments* (1759), reflects his interests, being an examination of the influence of social relationships on individual conscience. In it, Smith argues that selflessness and sympathy for others has a positive effect on the individual, making him or her more moral and more self-aware.

The book stands in stark contrast to his most celebrated work, *The Wealth of Nations*, which makes the argument that the collective self-interest of individuals affects social and economic progress. Recent scholarship on Smith, however, has tried to reconcile the two contradictory messages, saying that Smith's two major works illustrate how people must and do act differently in their various roles in life.

Widely regarded as the foundational text of classical economics, *An Inquiry Into the Nature and Causes of the Wealth of Nations*, as its full title reads, was in fact a five-book series that attempted to decipher the causes and nature of a nation's prosperity. Using the now-famous example of pin makers, Smith argued that increasing labor specialization was the key to economic growth. That is, he wrote, "ten workers could produce 48,000 pins per day if each of eighteen specialized tasks was assigned to particular workers. Average productivity: 4,800 pins per worker per day. But absent the division of labor, a worker would be lucky to produce even one pin per day."

More broadly, Smith compared and contrasted the political and economic systems of Britain and France to reach his conclusions about what made nations prosperous. In doing so, he offered three basic arguments. First, he said, prices for goods were not arbitrary but reflected underlying value, largely the labor that went into making them. He then argued that society and political systems could influence the kinds of goods being manufactured and that certain policies can ensure that the right kinds of goods are being made and in the most economically efficient manner. Finally, he put forth the basics of supply-and-demand theory, arguing that high prices are a "self-curing disease," since an increase in price will ensure an increase in production, thereby lowering costs.

Smith offered up his timeless "invisible hand" metaphor to illustrate how collective self-interest promotes social good. "By directing that industry

Scottish-born political philosopher and economist Adam Smith argued in one work that selflessness makes a person moral and self-aware. In *Wealth of Nations,* he used the term "invisible hand" to explain how collective self-interest promotes social good. *(The Granger Collection, New York)*

in such a manner as its produce may be of greatest value," Smith wrote in *The Wealth of Nations*, "he [the individual economic actor] intends only his own gain, and he is in this, as in many other cases, led by an invisible hand to promote an end which was no part of his intention."

Although the "invisible hand" is referred to only once in *The Wealth of Nations*, it is Smith's best-remembered metaphor for the smooth operation of the free market. Smith declared that consumers choose a product or service for the lowest price and that entrepreneurs choose to sell said good or service for the highest rate of profit. He asserted that by thus making their choices or needs (demand) known through market prices, consumers "directed" entrepreneurs' investment money to the most profitable industry. For example, if an entrepreneur is making a large profit by selling a particular product, other entrepreneurs will enter the market because profit opportunities are available.

Typically, he went on, when additional entrepreneurs enter a market, the price offered to purchase the product is lower, so the new entrepreneurs can attract customers. This undercutting process forces established entrepreneurs to find ways to become more efficient and/or less expensive so that they, in turn, can charge less for the same product. Entrepreneurs will continue to enter the market until a barrier to entry is created or profits for that product are no longer attainable. When goods are highly valued by consumers, profits increase; profits attract competition, and so the general economic well-being of both the individual and the nation increase.

Because of his emphasis on free markets, economic conservatives (economic "liberals" in British and European political parlance) have long embraced Smith to bolster their argument that the government has a minimal role to play in directing the economy and that when it does interfere, the effects are usually deleterious in that they distort the natural workings of the "invisible hand." But, say many Smith scholars, this oversimplifies and misunderstands the economist's thinking. Not only did Smith argue that governments should enforce contracts and issue patents and copyrights to encourage invention—positions that even most modern conservatives embrace—he also contended that governments should actively prevent collusion and price-fixing by businesses and that governments should invest in useful public works projects that private interests would not and could not undertake because said projects might not produce direct and immediate profit. Nor was Smith a pure free trade theorist, contending that retaliatory tariffs were a legitimate weapon of economic policy makers.

Unsatisfied with his later writings, Smith asked friends to burn nearly all of his work after *The Wealth of Nations*, though a series of essays on physics, metaphysics, and astronomy was published after his death in 1790.

Michael Rawdan

See also: Classical Theories and Models; Law, John; Marx, Karl; Mill, John Stuart.

Further Reading

Coase, R.H. "Adam Smith's View of Man." *Journal of Law and Economics* 19:3 (1976): 529–546.

Ross, Ian Simpson. *The Life of Adam Smith.* New York: Oxford University Press, 1995.

Smith, Adam. *An Inquiry Into the Nature and Causes of the Wealth of Nations.* Chicago: University of Chicago Press, 1977.

————. *The Theory of Moral Sentiments*, ed. Knud Haakonssen. Cambridge, UK: Cambridge University Press, 2002.

Souk al-Manakh (Kuwait) Stock Market Crash (1982)

The largest financial crisis to emerge out of the oil price boom of the 1970s and early 1980s, the Souk al-Manakh stock market crash of 1982 involved a dramatic collapse in share prices on an over-the-counter, or direct trader-to-trader, exchange established in Kuwait in the early 1980s. The crash, which led to the closing down of the exchange, also contributed to the economic downturn that afflicted the oil-rich Persian Gulf nations through the 1980s.

The origins of the Souk al-Manakh crash date back to the Arab oil embargo of the early 1970s and the run-up in crude oil prices that followed it. From 1973 to 1974, oil prices roughly quadrupled, from about $3 to $12 a barrel (about $14 to $58 in 2008 dollars). The price hikes flooded oil exporting countries with cash—none more so than Kuwait, with about 10 percent of the world's proven petroleum reserves. With the nation pumping approximately 2 million barrels per day, its oil revenues jumped from $6 million per day to $24 million per day, or from about $2.2 billion to $8.7 billion annually—this with a population of less than 1 million people. The dizzying increase in revenues brought legitimate investment in the nation's infrastructure as well as conspicuous consumption and speculative financing on the official Kuwait Stock Exchange (KSE). In 1977, the KSE crashed, though not nearly on the scale that the Souk would five years later. The government responded to the 1977 decline in two ways: first,

it imposed much stricter regulation on the KSE, making it difficult to speculate in securities traded there; second, it bailed out investors hit hard by the drop in prices.

The two responses would do much to encourage the development of the highly speculative Souk in the early 1980s. Tighter regulation made the KSE a more staid venue, focused on the sale of large blocs of stock to a handful of very wealthy and interconnected families. This left few opportunities for other investors. And because prices moved relatively slowly on the KSE, those who were interested in riskier investments had to find another forum for their activities.

By 1981, there were plenty of such investors. Encouraged to overlook risk by recalling the government's bailout of investors in 1977, Kuwaiti investors were once again flush with oil money, as the Iranian Revolution of 1979 and the onset of the Iran-Iraq War a year later had pumped up prices to $40 a barrel (about $100 in 2008 dollars). Although the war drove down Kuwaiti oil exports to about 1.5 million barrels per day, revenues were still about $22 billion annually—this for a country that, despite high birth rates, still had a population of only 1.4 million.

With all that cash in circulation, with so many investors believing that risks were minimal, and with an official stock exchange allowing no real outlet for investments, it was all but inevitable that a new, more speculative forum for investment would emerge. (U.S. and European stock exchanges offered little opportunity at the time, as both were suffering severe downturns amid the deepest economic recession since the Great Depression.) Housed in an air-conditioned parking garage in Kuwait City, the unregulated, highly speculative, over-the-counter stock market known as the Souk al-Manakh fit the bill perfectly. And the money poured in. At one point, in the summer of 1982, the Souk had the third-highest market capitalization in the world, after the New York Stock Exchange and the Nikkei Index of Japan. Brokers and bankers added to the investment fervor by accepting postdated checks for the purchase of shares, flooding the market with additional credit.

It was a classic financial bubble, drawing investors from around the oil-rich Persian Gulf, and it burst as soon as confidence in the system was compromised. Investor checks began to bounce in August 1982, and the exchange collapsed within a month. The Kuwaiti Ministry of Finance insisted that all postdated checks be cleared by banks and officially shut down the exchange. The government established a clearinghouse company that tried to untangle the commitments of investors and brokers and set up an arbitration panel to settle disputes between traders or to enforce deals made voluntarily by the affected traders themselves. In addition, the government set up a $1.7 billion trust fund to compensate some of the less speculative investors. This was actually far less generous than the compensation package that followed the 1977 collapse, as an official investigation found that some 6,000 investors had passed nearly $100 billion in bad checks at the height of the 1980s boom.

In the end, the Souk al-Manakh collapse triggered a major crisis in the Kuwaiti economy and, to a lesser extent, the economies of other Persian Gulf countries. As in much of the Arab world, Kuwait's economy was based less on individuals than on families, many of which were financially crippled by the actions of a single member who used family credit to fund speculation. Meanwhile, all the unpaid debts drove every Kuwaiti bank into insolvency except for the very largest, the National Bank of Kuwait. By weakening the national economy and ruining the finances of many Kuwait families, the Souk al-Manakh crash left the country even more vulnerable to the dramatic decline in oil prices later in the 1980s—a drop that pushed much of the Persian Gulf region into recession.

James Ciment and Marie Gould

See also: Asset-Price Bubble; Middle East and North Africa; Oil Shocks (1973–1974, 1979–1980); Stock Markets, Global.

Further Reading

Al-Yahya, Mohammed A. *Kuwait: Fall and Rebirth.* New York: Kegan Paul International, 1993.

Dawiche, Fida. *The Gulf Stock Exchange Crash: The Rise and Fall of the Souq Al-Manakh.* Dover, NH: Croom Helm, 1986.

South Africa

Situated at the southern tip of the African continent, the Republic of South Africa is an ethnically diverse country with a population of nearly 49 million. It has the largest and most developed economy on the continent, anchored by commercial agriculture, manufacturing, tourism, and most important, mining. Still, the country faces daunting economic challenges—partly a legacy of its racist past—including widespread poverty, high levels of unemployment, and some of the most egregious income and wealth inequalities in the world. With its macroeconomic fundamentals in good shape, South Africa seemed well positioned to avoid the worst of the financial crisis of 2008–2009, but the subsequent recession undermined demand and prices for key commodity exports, leading to a nearly 2 percent contraction in gross domestic product (GDP) in 2009.

Economic History to the Apartheid Era

Archaeological finds indicate that South Africa has been inhabited by protohumans and modern humans longer than any other part of the world, barring East Africa. Around the middle of the first millennium CE, the native hunters and gatherers of the region were joined by farming Bantu peoples from the north, who soon displaced many of the former to deserts and other outlying regions.

South Africa's strategic location and the resources under its soil played a key role in introducing the region to the larger world economy in the modern era. Situated on the key shipping route between Europe and the East Indies, South Africa's second-largest city, Cape Town, was first settled by the Dutch in the mid-seventeenth century, serving as a provisioning port. Gradually spreading out into the hinterlands, the Dutch were joined by British settlers in the eighteenth century, and the colony fell into Great Britain's permanent possession in the early nineteenth. Angered by Britain's decision to ban slavery and to promote more equal treatment of native Africans, the descendants of the Dutch settlers, known as Afrikaners or Boers, moved further inland beginning in the 1830s, meeting stiff resistance from the native peoples, particularly the Xhosa and the Zulu.

When first diamonds, in the 1860s, and then gold, in the 1880s, were discovered in the interior of the country, the finds set off a rush of prospectors and businesses that further antagonized relations between the Afrikaners and the British. This provoked two hard-fought wars, the second of which, from 1899 to 1902, was particularly brutal and led to a half century of subjugation of the Boers. In 1910, the British gave South Africa limited independence as a dominion within the empire, with English-speaking whites in control of the government.

Meanwhile, the diamond mines of Kimberley and the gold mines of the Transvaal, around the boomtown of Johannesburg, South Africa's largest city, drew hundreds of thousands of people, both immigrants and indentured servants from overseas and native Africans from rural areas. The influx of capital into the region helped the country establish a manufacturing base and a large commercial agriculture sector. At the same time, the country's urbanization—which inevitably led to racial mixing—prompted authorities to implement segregation measures, which triggered the beginning of an African nationalist movement and the founding of the South African Native National Congress in 1912 (known as the African National Congress, or ANC, from 1923 on).

With its economy highly dependent on extractive industries and the export of commodities such as minerals and agricultural goods, the country was hard hit by the global depression of the 1930s,

though exports to war-torn Britain and Europe led to renewed prosperity—at least for the minority white population—in the 1940s.

Apartheid Era

With the triumph of the Afrikaner-led National Party in the election of 1948—a poll largely restricted to white voters—the South African government introduced its policy of apartheid, or strict separation of the four main ethnic groups in the country. These were, in descending order of official status, (1) persons of European descent; (2) persons of Asian descent, largely Indians brought into the country by the British as indentured servants to work mines and plantations in the nineteenth century; (3) "colored" or mixed-race persons, largely situated in Cape Town and the environs; and (4) native Africans, who made up the vast majority of the country's population. The last group was divided further into ten Bantu nations, or Bantustans, each of which was assigned a rural homeland. Today the country is roughly divided along the following lines: black African (79 percent), white (9.6), "colored" (8.9), and Asian (2.5).

The apartheid system was about more than simple separation of the races; it also was about economic power. The most lucrative occupations were reserved for whites, as was the best agricultural land, forcing rural native Africans to either scratch out a living in the overcrowded Bantustans or migrate to the cities and mines in search of work. Strict laws regulated their movement, so many had to leave their families behind. In urban areas, they were relegated to overcrowded and underserviced townships on the peripheries of the cities. Meanwhile, Indians and "colored" persons also were relegated to low-paying occupations and specific neighborhoods, though many of the former became petty merchants. Public investments in infrastructure, health, and education were skewed to favor the white population.

Meanwhile, these measures were deeply opposed by a growing antiapartheid movement among blacks, "coloreds," and Asians. They also were condemned by the international community, especially after a protest in the Johannesburg-area township of Sharpeville led to the massacre of sixty-nine unarmed demonstrators by security forces.

Despite the political troubles, the South African economy prospered in the 1950s and 1960s, its mineral exports much in demand by a booming global economy. South Africa's finance sector became the wealthiest and most sophisticated in Africa, while domestic and foreign capital helped lay the foundation for large manufacturing and commercial agricultural sectors, the most highly developed in Africa and comparable, if smaller in scale, to those in the developed world. A modern and extensive transportation and communications infrastructure also was developed.

After a relatively quiescent decade, the anti-apartheid movement was revived by street protests in the 1970s, leading to crackdowns at home and calls abroad for economic sanctions against the country. At first, foreign corporations maintained their presence in South Africa—it was too lucrative a market to disinvest, and foreign executives argued that they were the only economic entities in the country offering opportunities to blacks—but a growing solidarity movement in the West eventually forced most companies to leave by the 1980s.

South African authorities remained defiant, viciously cracking down on protests, declaring Bantustans independent states (technically making most native Africans living in urban areas foreigners in their own country, a move that was disregarded by the international community), embarking on an aggressive actions against pro-ANC regimes in neighboring black-run states, and developing an autarkic, or self-reliant, economy so as not to be subject to international pressures.

But the costs were too high. South Africa, especially its prosperous white community, was simply too small to provide a sufficient market for the country's manufactured goods. Without access to foreign expertise and capital, domestic industry became uncompetitive. Meanwhile, the costs of maintaining a major defense and security system resulted in crippling deficits and high interest rates. The sagging economy and the country's growing isolation internationally, combined with mass protests at home, finally convinced the country's Afrikaner leadership that it must abandon apartheid and white minority rule.

Dramatic reforms ensued over the course of the late 1980s and early 1990s, as apartheid laws were eased and finally ended. ANC officials—including the revered leader Nelson Mandela—were released from prison, and full democracy was restored. In 1994, an election was held in which all adult South Africans participated. That election brought the ANC to power and Mandela to the presidency. The end of apartheid and the onset of majority rule provided an immediate fillip to the economy, as governments around the world lifted their embargoes on South Africa, foreign investors began to put their money into the economy, and international corporations began to do business again in South Africa.

Postapartheid Era

While the ANC long had been affiliated with the South African Communist Party and its leaders had espoused leftist economic rhetoric, the Mandela government—and those of presidents Thabo Mbeki and Jacob Zuma to follow—generally have pursued free-market policies and maintained what economists call solid macroeconomic fundamentals, keeping government spending in line with revenues, pursuing conservative monetary policies, and upholding private property rights. At the same time, the government has tried to undo the gross inequities that were created by apartheid and more than 100 years of white domination of the economy. The ANC has embarked on an ambitious plan to provide decent housing, more utilities, better health care, and higher-quality education to black Africans, who constitute roughly 80 percent of the country's population.

Most economists give high marks to successive ANC governments on both counts—maintaining solid economic growth and providing more basic services to poorer South Africans. On the first front, the country has enjoyed impressive GDP growth in the years since the ANC's triumph in 1994, while bringing inflation down from its double-digit highs near the end of the apartheid era. By the middle of the 2000s, many were speaking of South Africa as one of the economic leaders of the developing world—a smaller version of China, India, or Brazil.

Still, the country faced major problems: unemployment, particularly among the black majority, remained stubbornly high; income and wealth inequality—not just between blacks and whites, but now also between a minority of successful blacks and the vast majority of still impoverished blacks—remained at some of the highest levels in the world; and crime exploded, with the country's urban areas suffering from some of the highest rates of violent crime in the world.

Still, with its solid GDP growth and well-maintained macroeconomic fundamentals—along with the fact that South Africa's relatively conservative financial sector largely had avoided investing in the exotic debt-backed securities that crippled financial institutions in the United States and some European countries—many economists expected the country to weather the financial crisis and global recession of the late 2000s. But much of South Africa's solid, postapartheid economic performance relied—as that performance always had—on commodity exports. This had served the country well in the years between 1995 and 2007, as a boom in demand—fueled in part by burgeoning economies in Asia—had led to sustained high prices for the minerals and agricultural products the country produced in abundance. But the global recession hurt demand and caused a dramatic fall in prices, leading to a growing government deficit and a 2 percent contraction of GDP in 2009.

However, with demand expected to revive—driven by reviving Asian economies in 2010—many say that South Africa will see growth again

soon. The long-term problem, say experts, remains what it has been throughout the postapartheid era—how to maintain the solid macroeconomic fundamentals that assure foreign investment and steady growth while addressing the overwhelming problems of poverty and inequality from the country's racist past.

James Ciment

See also: Africa, Sub-Saharan; Emerging Markets; Transition Economies.

Further Reading

Allen, Michael H. *Globalization, Negotiation, and the Failure of Transformation in South Africa: Revolution at a Bargain?* New York: Palgrave Macmillan, 2006.

Aron, Janine, Brian Kahn, and Geeta Kingdon, eds. *South African Economic Policy Under Democracy.* New York: Oxford University Press, 2009.

Feinstein, Charles H. *An Economic History of South Africa: Conquest, Discrimination, and Development.* New York: Cambridge University Press, 2005.

Hamilton, Carolyn, Bernard Mbenga, and Robert Ross, eds. *The Cambridge History of South Africa.* New York: Cambridge University Press, 2009.

Jones, Stuart, ed. *The Decline of the South African Economy.* Northampton, MA: Edward Elgar, 2002.

South Sea Bubble (1720)

The best known example of speculative excess in the emerging capitalist marketplaces of early modern Europe, the South Sea Bubble of 1720 occurred when investors rushed to put their money in the South Sea Company, which had been granted a British royal monopoly on trade with Latin America in exchange for assuming a large national debt incurred by the British government during the War of the Spanish Succession.

The origins of the bubble go back nearly a decade earlier, to the decision of the British government to grant a monopoly on trade with Latin America to Robert Harley, a well-connected politician of the day who served as Lord Treasurer in the early 1710s. (In those days, all the waters surrounding Latin America were referred to as

A period engraving satirizes the South Sea Bubble of 1720 with symbols of greed and suffering, including clergymen gambling (bottom left) and investors being taken for a ride—literally—on a merry-go-round. *(Hulton Archive/ Getty Images)*

the "South Seas.") The granting of the charter was part of a complex deal Harley and the government had come up with to retire about £10 million in short-term debt it had incurred fighting the War of the Spanish Succession, a conflict that had begun in 1701 to prevent the merger of the French and Spanish crowns, and thereby upset the balance of power in Europe.

Harley was looking to develop a means to sell the debt, or government bonds, through private channels. Setting up a joint-stock bank was the most straightforward means to this end. The bank, whose shares would be owned by private investors, would then invest in the government bonds. Under British law, however, the Bank of England was the only joint-stock bank permitted to do business in the country.

So Harley came up with a scheme. He would create a company whose official mandate was trade but would, in fact, really function as a bank. (Underlining the secondary role of trade in the company's bottom line, the Treaty of Utrecht, which ended the War of the Spanish Succession in 1713, granted the company the right to send just two ships a year to Spanish colonies in Latin America, one of them a slave ship.) To get investors to buy into the firm, the government offered the South Sea

Company a perpetual annuity. In other words, the bank would own the £10 million in debt forever, with a guaranteed return of 6 percent, or a total payment of over £500,000 each year.

In 1717 and 1719, the company took on even more debt. Indeed, in the latter year it assumed roughly half the British national debt, or about £31 million, with guarantees of slightly lower returns of 5 percent through 1727 and 4 percent thereafter. The idea was that the government would convert high-interest debt to low-interest debt, thereby saving it money, while investors would be offered a guaranteed return forever.

The returns were solid but not spectacular and failed to attract many investors. In 1719, the company changed its marketing strategy, playing up the trading possibilities of its monopoly with Latin America, even though such possibilities were meager. The strategy worked, producing a frenzy of investment. By the early eighteenth century, the British economy had emerged as the most powerful and expansive in Europe, having displaced the Dutch as the continent's great trading nation. Many of the merchants and others who had done well by this trade had excess capital to invest.

Shares in the company took off in value, from

£128 in January 1720 to more than £500 by May, an increase of more than 300 percent. To maintain government support for the scheme, politicians were essentially loaned shares and then allowed to sell them when the price went up, thereby pocketing profits on money they had never actually invested. The company then used the names of these prestigious individuals to sell more shares in the company to less well connected investors.

Meanwhile, other financiers tried to jump on the bandwagon by developing similar joint-stock trading companies in Britain, as well as in France and the Netherlands. To stop such activity, at least in Britain, the government then passed the Royal Exchange and London Assurance Corporation Act in June 1720, requiring all joint-stock companies to get a royal charter. This stipulation effectively ended any competition to the South Sea Company, which had a charter, sending its shares even higher to about £1,000 at the peak of the bubble in August 1720.

By this point, thousands of ordinary people were buying shares or partial shares in the company, often with loans given to them by the company expressly to make the purchases. By August, however, some of the loans were coming due. When investors could not come up with the money to pay them back, they began unloading shares. These sales exerted downward pressure on prices, which brought share values back to roughly £150 by September. Contributing to the downward push were the simultaneous collapses of other joint-stock schemes elsewhere in Europe, most notably, France's Compagnie des Indes, or Company of the Indies. Indeed, some historians refer to 1720 as the "bubble year."

The collapse in the value of South Sea Company shares reverberated through the British financial system as banks that had accepted stock in the company or had made loans against those stocks began to fail. Thousands of individual investors also failed financially, including some of the most illustrious names in Britain.

Responding to widespread outrage, Parliament soon launched an investigation that not only un-covered fraudulent activities among the company's directors but corruption and bribery that went to the highest level of government, including members of the cabinet, some of whom were impeached. Led by Robert Walpole, the newly appointed lord treasurer, Parliament confiscated the estates of the company's directors and used the proceeds to partially compensate defrauded investors. Meanwhile, remaining stock in the company—essentially the national debt it held—was turned over to the Bank of England and the East India Company.

James Ciment

See also: Asset-Price Bubble; Mississippi Bubble (1717–1720); Tulipmania (1636–1637); United Kingdom.

Further Reading

Balen, Malcolm. *The King, the Crook, and the Gambler: The True Story of the South Sea Bubble and the Greatest Financial Scandal in History.* New York: Fourth Estate, 2004.

Dale, Richard. *The First Crash: Lessons from the South Sea Bubble.* Princeton, NJ: Princeton University Press, 2004.

Garber, Peter M. *Famous First Bubbles: The Fundamentals of Early Manias.* Cambridge, MA: MIT Press, 2000.

Southeast Asia

Southeast Asia, a region bounded by India to the west and China to the north, consists of twelve nations with very different demographics, histories, and economies. These include Brunei, Cambodia, Indonesia, Laos, Malaysia, Myanmar (Burma), Papua New Guinea, Philippines, Singapore, Thailand, Timor-Leste (East Timor), and Vietnam. Demographically, the region is dominated by giant Indonesia, Philippines, Vietnam, Thailand, and Myanmar. Altogether, the region has a population of roughly 600 million.

The culture of the region has long represented a cross of indigenous, Indian, and Chinese influences. The major religions of the region are Islam (Brunei, Indonesia, and Malaysia), Buddhism (Cambodia, Laos, Myanmar, Singapore, Thailand, and Vietnam), Hinduism (parts of Indonesia),

Christianity (Philippines and many Vietnamese), and animist faiths (Papua New Guinea).

Home to some of the most vibrant civilizations in Asian history prior to the sixteenth century CE, much of the region—aside from Thailand—fell under the sway of European colonizers between the sixteenth century and the first half of the twentieth. After being occupied by the Japanese during World War II, most of the countries in the region won their independence peacefully, though Indonesia and Vietnam were forced to fight protracted wars of independence in the 1940s and 1950s. In the years since, three of the countries—Cambodia, Laos, and Vietnam—became communist states, though all three now combine a communist-dominated political system with a transitional market economy. For the most part, the countries in the region are democracies—with the significant exceptions of Vietnam and Myanmar—though most have been under authoritarian regimes in the recent past.

Economically, the region offers dramatic contrasts. Tiny Cambodia, still recovering from the genocide of the 1970s, and Myanmar, ruled by a brutal junta since the early 1960s, are among the poorest nations in Asia, while oil-rich Brunei and the city-state of Singapore are among the richest.

Economies and Population of Southeast Asian Countries, 2009 (estimate)

Country	Population (in millions)	GDP (in millions of dollars)	GDP per capita (in dollars)
Brunei	0.4	14,700	36,700
Cambodia	14.8	10,900	800
Indonesia	240.3	514,900	2,200
Laos	6.3	5,721	900
Malaysia	28.3	191,400	6,800
Myanmar (Burma)	50.0	26,820	500
Papua New Guinea	6.7	8,200	1,200
Philippines	92.0	158,700	1,700
Singapore	5.0	177,100	35,500
Thailand	67.8	263,500	3,900
Timor-Leste (East Timor)	1.1	599	500
Vietnam	88.1	97,120	1,100
Total	600.8	1,470,060	2,447

Source: CIA World Factbook.

Many of the countries in the region have seen significant export-driven economic expansion in recent decades, despite the major setback of the Asian financial crisis of 1997–1998. This has especially been the case in the middle-income countries of Indonesia, Malaysia, and Thailand, along with Vietnam.

History Through Independence

Even before European penetration of the region, Southeast Asia was a major center of regional trade, offering spices and tropical goods, such as exotic animals and rare hardwoods, to China. Situated at the crossroads between the great civilizations of the Indian subcontinent and East Asia, it was populated—particularly the regions that would become Malaysia and Indonesia—by merchants from both, who also brought their culture with them. Next came Arab merchants from across the Indian Ocean beginning in the eighth century CE. As with the Europeans who would follow, the Arabs came in search of spices, which were used in their own territories or traded to Europe. And as with the Indians and Chinese before them, Arabs helped culturally influence the ever more cosmopolitan littoral of the region, bringing advances in the sciences, along with the Islamic faith.

The first Europeans to arrive in the region were the Spanish and the Portuguese in the sixteenth century, the former conquering parts of the Philippine archipelago and the latter ousting Arab traders from strategic ports in what are now Indonesia and Malaysia. The Portuguese, in particular, developed a lucrative trade, offering silver mined in the Americas, along with European manufactured goods, for the spices grown in the region, which included nutmeg, cinnamon, cloves, and, most important, pepper.

But the Portuguese were soon pushed from the region by the more entrepreneurial and better-armed merchants of the Dutch East India Company in the early seventeenth century. The Dutch would eventually establish settlements on Java and other parts of Indonesia, which, as the Dutch East Indies, would remain part of the overseas empire of the Netherlands into the middle of the twentieth century. The Spanish established colonial settlements in the Philippines, but their economic exploitation of the archipelago was not as extensive as that of the Dutch in the East Indies. However, they did eventually convert much of the country to Catholicism, and the Philippines became the only Christian-majority country in Asia.

For the most part, mainland Southeast Asia remained independent of European colonizers into the nineteenth century. Between the 1850s and the 1880s, however, the French military extended its sway over Indochina—present-day Cambodia, Laos, and Vietnam. The British, meanwhile, began to occupy the Malay Peninsula in the late eighteenth century and established the critical trading port of Singapore in the early nineteenth. Myanmar (then Burma) also came under British control in the nineteenth century. Only Thailand remained as an independent kingdom, serving as a buffer territory between French Indochina and British possessions in Burma and the Malay Peninsula.

The French and British more effectively exploited the region economically than had earlier Dutch, Spanish, and Portuguese colonizers. Rather than merely trading for spices and other indigenous commodities and manufactured goods, both the French and British established large plantations and developed extensive mining concerns. The British, for example, established a near hegemony over the world rubber trade by the early twentieth century, and French Indochina became a major supplier of tin.

European economic and political control of the region was finally broken not by indigenous independence movements but by another outside force, the Japanese in the 1940s. Having adopted European technology, Japan became militarily powerful and imperialistic in the first half of the twentieth century. In 1941, it launched a multipronged invasion of Southeast Asia that overwhelmed the small European garrisons in the region. The Japanese also conquered the Philippines, which had become an American colony as a result of the Spanish-American War of 1898.

The Japanese talked of "Asia for the Asians" and incorporated Southeast Asia into their Greater Asian Co-Prosperity Sphere. However, the sphere was really an empire by another name. The region was meant to serve as a supplier of raw materials, including crucial petroleum, which had been drilled for in Indonesia by the Royal Dutch Shell Company since the early twentieth century, and a captive market for Japanese manufactured goods. Never popular, the Japanese faced tough resistance from local independence movements, which were aided by the Americans and the British. At the end of World War II, the Japanese were driven from the region.

Early Independence Era from the 1940s Through the 1970s

While the Japanese occupation was brief, it had far-reaching consequences for Southeast Asia, as independence movements became more emboldened in militarily confronting European colonizers. The Dutch were challenged in Indonesia, which they surrendered in 1949; the British faced armed resistance in Malaysia, eventually pulling out in 1957. The toughest fighting, however, occurred in Vietnam, where the French attempted to set up a puppet regime under their control until being defeated, after a brutal independence war, in 1954.

While each was different in its own way, all of these nationalist struggles were inspired by a mixture of nationalism and left-wing economics and politics. Each country went its own way after independence. In Indonesia, a socialist regime headed by independence leader Sukarno (Indonesians often go by a single name) was overthrown in a bloody coup in the 1960s, leading to years of dictatorial corruption and economic stagnation under Suharto. Ethnically mixed Malaysia went a more capitalist route, but with a government policy of economically favoring the native Malay population over the more entrepreneurial Chinese and Indian populations.

Vietnam split into two warring halves, a communist north and a capitalist south, eventually drawing in American forces in the 1960s and finally being reunited under communist rule in 1975. That struggle would be mirrored by similar civil wars between pro-Western governments and communist-inspired guerrilla movements in Cambodia and Laos before both fell to the latter in the mid-1970s. Cambodia's fate proved catastrophic as the new Khmer Rouge regime attempted to return the country to what it called "year zero," a kind of precapitalist utopia, murdering millions of people in the process.

Chinese-dominated Singapore broke from Malaysia in 1965 and soon established itself as a critical trading and financial hub, becoming the second richest nation in the region, after oil-rich Brunei. The Philippines, the most economically advanced country in the region upon winning its independence from the United States in 1946, also

fell under a corrupt dictatorship, that of Ferdinand Marcos, and stagnated economically. Thailand, always independent, also went a more pro-Western, capitalist route.

Era of Rapid Development and Crisis Since the 1980s

The economic and political history of the various countries in Southeast Asia began to converge again in the 1980s and 1990s. To varying degrees, all of the larger countries in the region—with the notable exception of authoritarian Myanmar—began to industrialize rapidly, first developing low-tech manufacturing, such as textiles and shoes, and then moving on to more value-added products, such as electronics. In many cases, much of the foreign capital came from abroad, with American, European, and Japanese companies establishing branch plants in the region to take advantage of lower labor costs.

This general economic convergence was

Still a relatively poor country, Vietnam has enjoyed one of the world's fastest-growing economies since the early 1990s on the strength of market reforms. A billboard advertises private villas in the city of Da Nang, site of a major airbase during the Vietnam War. *(Hoang Dinh Nam/AFP/Getty Images)*

evidenced institutionally in the growth of the regional policy coordination organization, the Association of Southeast Asian Nations (ASEAN). First founded by Indonesia, Malaysia, the Philippines, Singapore, and Thailand in 1967, ASEAN had expanded to include all the countries of the region—even isolationist Myanmar—by the mid-1990s. It had also become more of a coherent organization, with member countries—along with important outsiders such as China—using the frequent summits to coordinate economic, security, and environmental policies, among other things.

During this same period, two of the largest countries in the region—Indonesia and the Philippines—made the transition from dictatorship to democracy, while Malaysia, Thailand, and Singapore saw a more modest transition to semi-democratic rule. In Myanmar, the military junta continued its authoritarian rule, while Vietnam, following the path pioneered by China, combined one-party communist political rule with an emerging free-market economy.

Southeast Asia's emergence as an economic powerhouse did not come without its setbacks. Its reliance on large infusions of foreign investment for rapid growth led to speculation in local securities and real estate in the 1980s and 1990s. In addition, many of the countries in the region failed to modernize their financial sectors, with governments providing little regulatory oversight of banks. The result was financial bubbles that eventually popped, as foreign investors began to pull capital out of these markets, first in Thailand in 1997 and then across much of the region. The Asian financial crisis of 1997–1998 set back the growth of much of the region through the early years of the twenty-first century, though the impact varied between hard-hit Thailand and the less-affected Vietnam.

A booming China and a growing world economy from 2002 to 2007 helped revived the fortunes of the region, as virtually all of the countries experienced strong growth rates. When an even greater financial crisis rocked much of the industrialized world in 2008, many experts expected the region to be badly hit, as foreign investors pulled out and exports to recessionary Europe and the United States shrank. However, while growth rates in the major Southeast Asian economies did slow—and even shrank slightly in Malaysia and the Philippines in 2009—overall the region's economy proved more resilient, buoyed by strong internal demand and pulled along by a still surging Chinese economy. Economists even began to speak of Southeast Asia—as well as other rapidly developing regions of the world—becoming "decoupled" from the more advanced but sluggish Western and Japanese economies.

James Ciment

See also: Asian Financial Crisis (1997); China; India; Indonesia; Philippines.

Further Reading

Association of Southeast Asian Nations (ASEAN) Web site: www.aseansec.org.

Borthwick, Mark. *Pacific Century: The Emergence of Modern Pacific Asia.* 3rd ed. Boulder, CO: Westview, 2007.

McGregor, Andrew. *Southeast Asian Development.* New York: Routledge, 2008.

McLeod, Ross, and Ross Garnaut, eds. *East Asia in Crisis: From Being a Miracle to Needing One?* London: Routledge, 1998.

Owen, Norman G., ed. *The Emergence of Modern Southeast Asia: A New History.* Honolulu: University of Hawai'i Press, 2005.

Rigg, Jonathan. *Southeast Asia: The Human Landscape of Modernization and Development.* 2nd ed. New York: Routledge, 2003.

SarDesai, D.R. *Southeast Asia: Past and Present.* 6th ed. Boulder, CO: Westview, 2010.

Stiglitz, Joseph E., and Shahid Yusef, eds. *Rethinking the East Asian Miracle.* New York: Oxford University Press, 2001.

Spain

A medium-sized country of about 47 million people located on the Iberian Peninsula in southwestern Europe, Spain has a long and varied economic and political history. Inhabited since at least 35,000 BCE, Spain is home to several distinct ethnic groups, including the dominant Castilian speakers of the middle and southern parts of the country, the Basques of the north, the Galicians of the northwest, and the Catalans in the northeast. Spain has been populated by Celts and Iberian peoples since the third century BCE, when it was conquered by Rome. By the early eighth century, some 300 years after the fall of the Roman Empire, much of the country was occupied by Moorish invaders.

For the next 700 years, the Christian kingdoms of the north fought a successful battle to drive the Moors out. That goal finally was achieved in 1492, the same year Christopher Columbus, an Italian explorer in the employ of the Spanish monarchy, sailed to the Americas. The voyage inaugurated a period of conquest during which Spain seized much of the Americas and other overseas possessions. During the fifteenth and sixteenth centuries, Spain was the dominant power in Europe, before falling behind Great Britain and France. It languished economically and politically through much of eighteenth, nineteenth, and twentieth centuries, emerging as a dictatorship following a civil war in the 1930s.

Since the fall of the dictatorship in the 1970s, Spain has emerged as an economically and politically vibrant democracy, joining the European Community (later the European Union) in 1986. Several decades of high growth came to an abrupt end, however, with the financial crisis of 2008–2009, when a housing bubble and construction boom that had buoyed the economy burst. As a result, the country i

Economic History Through the Conquest of the Americas

Home to the caves of Altamira, with paintings dating to roughly 15,000 BCE, Spain was inhabited by Celts, Iberians, and Basques at the beginning of the second millennium BCE. The region was incorporated into various Phoenician and Greek trading networks by the early part of the first millennium, becoming an important source of gold and silver. Both established trading colonies along the country's Mediterranean coast, with the Carthaginians, the North African–based heirs of the Phoenicians, taking control of the region around 300 BCE.

Rome seized Spain from the Carthaginians during the Punic Wars of the third century BCE. Under the Romans, the culture of much of Spain was Latinized, and local leaders became part of the Roman aristocracy. The province of Hispania, as it was called, was incorporated into the Roman economy, exporting gold, silver, mercury, olive oil, and wine.

With the fall of the Roman Empire in the fifth century C.E., Spain came under the rule of various Christianized Visigoth leaders, until much of the Iberian Peninsula was conquered by invading Muslim armies in the early eighth century. For the next 700 years, the country was divided between an ever-expanding northern Christian section and a slowly contracting Moorish Muslim south.

Despite sporadic warfare with the north, Moorish Spain flourished in the Middle Ages as a center of learning, commerce, and art. Not only a source of great scientific, literary, artistic, and philosophical achievements, Moorish Spain also served as a conduit through which the learning of the ancient and Islamic worlds was passed on to Christian Europe, helping to bring about the Renaissance. The cities of Moorish Spain also were major centers of trade, with a large merchant class that exported the region's products to both the Islamic and Christian worlds. The north prospered as well, gradually being integrated into the Mediterranean economy of Christian Europe, with pilgrims traveling to the shrine of Compostela providing a major source of foreign capital.

The 700-year *reconquista,* or reconquest, of the Iberian Peninsula created a militarized state in the north, in which successful conquistadores, or conquering warriors, were rewarded with extensive land grants that they often turned into large-scale wool-producing sheep and cattle ranches. The pattern of giving huge land grants and feudal control over local peasants would be replicated when Spain conquered much of the Americas in the sixteenth century.

In 1469, the crowns of Aragon and Castile, the two main Christian kingdoms of the Iberian Peninsula, were united, leading to the conquest of Granada, in Andalusia, the last Moorish outpost in western Europe, in 1492. That year proved momentous in Spanish history. Not only did it mark Spain's first encounter with the Americas, but it also saw the government issue an order expelling the Jews, who, as merchants, traders, and artisans, had been integral to the commercial success of Moorish Spain.

The conquest of the Americas, with its Aztec and Inca riches and lucrative silver and gold mines, brought a flood of money into the country. However, this newfound wealth proved to be a mixed blessing for the Spanish economy. The influx of precious metal devalued the currency, creating runaway inflation and making Spanish-made goods less competitive in foreign markets. In addition, the newly enriched Hapsburg monarchy in Spain used its wealth to launch a series of wars, both to expand its holdings in Europe and to fight the wars of the Counter-Reformation in an effort to halt and roll back the Protestant revolution in northern Europe.

Wars, Economic Decline, and Dictatorship: 1600s Through 1975

Together, the ongoing wars, the loss of much of the merchant class through the expulsion of the Jews and Moors, and the inflation set off by the influx of American gold and silver eventually undermined the Spanish economy and power in Europe, leading to a long-term decline during the seventeenth and early eighteenth centuries. Spain lost most of its European possessions in the aftermath of the long-term independence struggle of the Netherlands in the late sixteenth and early seventeenth centuries and the War of the Spanish Succession in the early eighteenth century.

The War of the Spanish Succession put into power a new dynasty, the French Bourbons, who moved to establish a more centralized government, ending the loose alliance of provinces. Under the Bourbons, the Spanish government adopted administrative reforms to make its tax collection more efficient and imposed tighter controls over trade with its possessions in the Americas, both of which led to some economic improvement.

The Napoleonic Wars of the early nineteenth century undid much of that progress as armies battled across Spain, wrecking the economy. Unable to control Atlantic sea routes, Spain could not stop an independence movement that saw much of mainland South and Central America fall from its grip by the 1820s. Throughout the rest of the nineteenth century, Spain remained one of the most economically backward countries in western Europe, predominantly agricultural—and inefficient agriculture at that—and a stunted manufacturing center. Outside the Basque and Catalan regions of the north, where metalworking and textile industries emerged, the country largely was bypassed by the economic dynamism of the industrial revolution that swept much of northern Europe in this period.

The decline culminated in what Spaniards call the "disaster of '98," the country's abject defeat at the hands of the rising economic and military power of the United States in the Spanish-American War of 1898. The United States either seized Spain's colonies in the Americas and the Philippines for itself or, in the case of Cuba, granted it independence.

Well into the early twentieth century, Spain lacked effective irrigation to make its lands more productive; its land tenure system did not encourage agricultural innovation; its banking sector offered little credit for businesses and industry; and road building, education, and other state services remained well behind those in much of the rest of western Europe. Napoleon's famous quip that Europe ended at the Pyrenees, the mountains separating Spain from France, still seemed to hold true.

Modest reforms to help manufacturing in the 1920s, including state planning and tariffs, largely were undone by the Great Depression and a catastrophic three-year-long civil war in the late 1930s, which left much of the country destroyed, wiped out the country's gold and foreign currency holdings, and brought to power the fascist dictatorship of Francisco Franco, who would rule the country until his death in 1975. Not until the 1950s would manufacturing and agricultural output reach their pre–civil war levels.

Under Franco, Spain was saddled with a large and unresponsive bureaucracy, which led to cronyism, corruption, and stagnant growth through the early 1960s, when free-market reforms were imposed. The government also introduced measures at the time to bring its own fiscal house in order and to reduce inflation. Together, these reforms, along with an increasing tourist sector and remittances from Spanish workers who were drawn to the booming economies of western Europe, led to substantive growth in the 1960s and early 1970s. Spain benefited from the economic boom in the rest of western Europe and built a transportation and industrial infrastructure, even as it modernized its agricultural sector, which became a major source of citrus and other subtropical products for the rest of Europe.

Economic History After Franco

The death of Franco ushered in a democratic government in the mid-1970s, but the oil shocks of that period undermined growth, as they did in much of the industrialized world. The stagnant economy and desire for change led to the victory of the Socialist Party in the early 1980s, less than a decade after the end of a regime that essentially had outlawed socialist politics. But the Spanish socialists were no economic radicals. They applied fiscal discipline to the government, closed inefficient state enterprises, and improved labor market flexibility. Between the late 1980s and mid-2000s, Spain—which in 1986 joined the European Community, the predecessor of the European Union—had one of the fastest-growing economies in Europe, though it continued to be plagued by one of the continent's highest unemployment rates. The country's rapid growth was the result of several factors: relatively low wages, compared to much of the rest of the European Union, which made it competitive; successive governments that maintained solid macroeconomic fundamentals to keep inflation in check; and large subsidies from the European Union.

Never before had the Spanish economy seen such a long period of continued high growth. For the twelve years from 1995 to 2007, gross domestic product (GDP) grew at an average annual rate of 3.5 percent. This impressive performance was fueled mainly by a construction boom that was unparalleled in western Europe. Half of all new houses in Europe during this time were built in Spain and sold in advance to both investors and ordinary citizens mainly from European countries (United Kingdom, Germany, and, of course, Spain).

However, the construction boom began to run out of steam by the middle of 2007 and was dampened further by the financial crisis that dried up most of the international funding that financed the country's huge infrastructure investments in 2008. In turn, this sparked higher unemployment—more than 14 percent by early 2009—and dragged down investment and consumer spending. Fortunately, Spain avoided excessive exposure to the subprime mortgage crisis that wreaked havoc in the United States because of the Bank of Spain's strict regulations on commercial banks.

Spain suffers from a particularly specific economic crisis, with causes different from those of the international financial crisis of the 2000s. It was not simply a construction boom that went wrong in the country. Rather, the economy was overheated beyond capacity, causing a severe current account deficit, as imports were sucked in to satisfy the voracious demand fueled by the jump in construction activity and the wealth effect of steadily rising property prices. Apart from this, it became clear by the mid- to late 2000s that Spain's economy was derailing, a situation made worse by the external debt accumulated by the inflow of foreign funds and the large number of migrant workers who were sucked into the boom. As of late 2009, there were 5 million immigrants working in Spain, making up about 12 percent of the population—the highest proportion of first-generation immigrants in the European Union. In an effort to free up more jobs for Spaniards, the government offered legal immigrants a monetary incentive for returning to their home countries. For those who agreed to leave Spain for at least three years, the government paid the unemployment benefit they were entitled to receive in a lump sum—40 percent upon leaving and 60 percent upon arrival back home—with average payments running approximately $14,000.

All the ingredients were in place for the country's downturn during the global economic collapse of 2008–2009. Spain's property market dropped fast, declining as much as 60 percent in some places. Up to 1.5 million unsold new homes stood empty in 2009, equivalent to five years of sales at the depressed rates. The prices of existing homes fell by 10 percent or more well into 2009, and more than 1,000 Spanish property and building firms filed for bankruptcy in 2008. The same number followed suit in 2009 as they struggled to repay more than €447 billion ($625 billion) in debt. Meanwhile, the collapse of Spain's decade-long housing boom, according to economists, increased nonperforming loans from 4 percent in 2009 to some 9 percent by early 2010, threatening the solvency of savings banks, which hold more than half of all property debt.

In an effort to bolster the ailing economy, the Spanish government in November 2008 instituted a €38 billion ($52 billion) stimulus package of spending and tax measures, which received a mixed reception from economists and business groups. One of the plan's chief measures, cash handouts to households totaling around €20 billion ($28 billion), did little to support the economy. In addition to the controversial cash benefits, the supplementary budget allocated €10 billion ($14 billion) to revitalizing local economies and supporting small companies. Bills linked to the supplementary bud-

get also included a measure to raise the limit on injecting public funds into ailing banks.

Although the new plan intended to boost investment in public infrastructure by €25 billion ($35 billion), channeled through regional and local governments, Spain's budget deficit remained below the European Union threshold of 3 percent of GDP in 2009. At the end of the year, the public deficit stood at 8 percent, and the International Monetary Fund predicted that it would reach double that amount in 2010.

Under Prime Minister José Luis Rodríguez Zapatero, the Spanish government remained steps behind other European countries in the global economic crisis. The nation's 19 percent unemployment rate ranked second only to Latvia's in the European Union. The government's series of emergency welfare measures aimed at saving jobs, increasing consumption, and reviving the stagnant housing market did little to bolster Spain's economy, and economists predicted that the country would experience a level of economic decline unprecedented in the last half century of its history.

As a result of the collapse in construction and the housing market, along with the global economic slowdown, Spain saw GDP growth slow to just 0.9 percent in 2008 and shrink by 3.9 percent in 2009, one of the poorest performances in western Europe. Moreover, by early 2010, in the aftermath of financial difficulties in Greece, there were fears in international financial markets that Spain's large public debt—estimated at 11.4 percent of GDP, well above the European Union limit of 3 percent—threatened to send foreign investors in Spanish government securities fleeing, making it harder and costlier for the country to borrow to finance its debt.

James Ciment and Jesus M. Zaratiegui

See also: Greece; Ireland; Portugal.

Further Reading
Barton, Simon. *A History of Spain.* New York: Palgrave Macmillan, 2003.
Carr, Raymond. *Spain: A History.* New York: Oxford University Press, 2000.

"Europe: Unsustainable; Spain's Economic Troubles." *The Economist,* November 28, 2009.

Harrison, Joseph, and David Corkill. *Spain: A Modern European Economy.* Burlington, VT: Ashgate, 2004.

"Spain's Happy-Go-Lucky Government: When Good Politics Is Bad Economics." *The Economist,* July 30, 2009.

"Spanish Banks: The Mess in La Mancha." *The Economist,* April 2, 2009.

Spiethoff, Arthur (1873–1957)

Arthur Spiethoff was a member of the German historical school of economics. His research on business cycles, on which he had his greatest impact, was based on Mikhail Tugan-Baranovsky's overinvestment theory. The impulse to overinvest, he suggested, was sparked by such innovations as technological inventions and by the discovery of new markets.

Arthur August Kaspar Spiethoff was born on May 13, 1873, in Dusseldorf, Germany. He became a leading economist of the "younger generation" of the German historical school, which disagreed with many of the central constructs of the Austrian school of economics, such as the nature of business cycles and the methodology of economics in general.

Spiethoff was heavily influenced by the economist Gustav Schmoller and later by the works of Ukrainian economist Mikhail Tugan-Baranovsky, who themselves had influenced the work of Nikolai Kondratieff, a major figure in business-cycle theory. In general, these economists believed that overinvestment—which occurred for any number of reasons, including a misreading of the available market—was the cause of downturns in the business cycle. They argued that overinvestment led to overproduction, which resulted in a surplus of a particular good, thus forcing down its price. When this became widespread, it would lead to a recession. Spiethoff first outlined this idea in "Preamble to the Theory of Overproduction," published in 1902.

As the influence of the Austrian school's economic theories about business cycles grew, Spiethoff became one of the school's most vigorous opponents. Whereas Spiethoff and the economists of the German historical school focused on endogenous (internal) economic forces—especially investment patterns—to explain business cycles, the Austrian school pointed to exogenous (external) psychological factors, or the role of the individual and individual choice in economic processes. Spiethoff—one of the few German school economists to make much headway against the Austrian school and the economic mainstream it represented—rejected theory in favor of empirical research. Using empirical data to illustrate historical patterns in the numerous booms and busts of nineteenth-century Europe, he argued that before the mid-1800s, most economic downturns and periods of great prosperity had correlated to periods of war, and good or bad harvests. He pointed out that in the nineteenth century, this changed, as countries' economies became more and more closely linked, especially on the European continent, where large-scale mass production was taking place. According to Spiethoff's theory of business cycles, published in 1923, companies during periods of continuous boom initially use their profits to pay shareholders and owners. Next, companies begin to invest in new factories that can produce more goods to satisfy increasing demand. Companies pay for much of this expansion with borrowed money. As a result, during economic downturns, the economy is hit twice—first with a credit shortage, rising interest rates, and growing debt when companies cannot repay their loans, and again when consumers' wages diminish (or are expected to diminish), and they buy less.

Ironically, Spiethoff, an empiricist and anti-theorist, devoted much of his later research and writing to examining the relationship between empirical and theoretical economics. After World War II, his major works included "The Historical Character of Economic Theories," published in the *Journal of Economic History* (1952); and "Pure Theory and Economic Gestalt Theory," published in *Enterprise and Secular Change* (1953). Spiethoff died on April 4, 1957, in Tübingen, Germany.

Justin Corfield

See also: German Historical School.

Further Reading

Blaug, Mark. *Great Economists Before Keynes. An Introduction to the Lives and Works of One Hundred Great Economists of the Past.* Atlantic Highlands, NJ: Humanities, 1986.

Spiethoff, A. "Crises." *International Economic Papers* 3 ([1925] 1953): 75–171.

Spillover Effect

Spillovers are the exchange of ideas among individuals or groups, especially when businesses expand into new locations and begin operations. Once operations have gotten under way and firms have conducted business for a period of time, spillover begins to occur. Since the nineteenth century, knowledge and technology spillovers are believed to have been major drivers of productivity growth and economic expansion in regional and national economies throughout the Western world. As such, knowledge and technology spillovers are important factors in the expansion phase of business cycles.

In this context, there are two types of spillovers: knowledge spillovers and technology spillovers. (Technically speaking, there are other, less positive types of spillovers, or externalities, as economists sometimes call them. Examples include the noise produced by an airport or carbon released into the atmosphere by utilities companies. This article, however, focuses on the narrower definition and more salutary understanding outlined above.) Knowledge spillovers can be defined as the exchange of information developed and shared from within the same industry or between industries. For example, a green company develops new technology to produce solar cells that will save energy and reduce emissions—an innovative product that requires unique materials and inputs. Unless the company is entirely vertically integrated, it will need to buy materials from outside businesses in order to build the solar cells. Thus, very quickly, some of the knowledge and expertise to produce the new solar cells will be shared outside the company. Moreover, employees of the green company may get hired by a vendor or competing firm. The institutional knowledge and expertise required to produce the new solar cells is thereby transferred to outside interests and is no longer secret. This can be considered knowledge spillover, as the essential know-how from the original firm has spilled over to other firms. Often in a market economy, the external company will use its newfound knowledge to compete with the originating firm. Also, once an industry gets to a certain size in an area, local community colleges might start training programs to supply workers with the skills needed in the industry. When the industry is small, no such programs would be started.

Knowledge spillovers generally occur within the same industry, but they can also occur between companies in unrelated or marginally related industries or sectors. Spillover between directly competing companies is exemplified by the following hypothetical: Hewlett-Packard (HP) develops a new computer code that requires less hardware and saves significant energy. One of the HP engineers who helped develop the code then decides to leave the company and work for Dell, a competing computer manufacturer. The engineer then transfers the knowledge developed at HP to his new employer, and knowledge spillover has taken place simply by virtue of the employee job change. Depending on the extent and nature of the information, the knowledge spillover may have a significant impact on marketplace competition.

Spillovers also occur within companies belonging to unrelated industries. In the same hypothetical situation, HP develops a new computer code. The engineer who helped develop it leaves the company and goes to work for a solar cell manufacturer. If this manufacturer is able to use the computer code to help improve one of its own programs or processes, a true knowledge spillover has occurred between industries. In today's world, firms are increasingly relying on contract hires as opposed to full-time permanent employees because of cost benefits and the lack of long-term commitments to regular employees. Contract hires are brought on board for specific projects and move much more easily from one employer to the next. In such a world, the spillover of knowledge from firm to firm and industry to industry is enhanced.

The intangible nature of knowledge spillover and the lack of empirical evidence regarding its effects—or even its specific occurrence—have given rise to considerable debate within the economics community. According to Nobel Prize–winning economist Paul Krugman, "Knowledge flows are invisible; they leave no paper trail by which they may be measured." In other words, when any type of spillover occurs, it is difficult, if not impossible, to quantify the amount of spillover or its effects.

Technology spillovers are similar in definition and pattern to knowledge spillovers but entail the transfer of tangible goods. In other words, technology spillovers are the exchange, development, and improvement of technologies among individuals or groups. Like knowledge spillovers, they can occur both within and between industries.

As early as the mid-nineteenth century, knowledge and technology spillovers have been closely associated with the spread of industry and advanced technology. New England gave rise to the textile and machine-tool clusters along the rivers of Massachusetts and Connecticut; upper New York State spawned the Niagara-region cluster based on cheap hydroelectric power; and more recently, the Silicon Valley in northern California became a national center of computer and electronics development. In all of these instances, knowledge and technology spillovers played a vital role in establishing and expanding highly competitive but closely interlinked business communities—all of which were focal points of national economic growth during expansive periods in the business cycle. By the same token, the close intellectual and economic relationships formed by knowledge and technology spillovers between companies in a creative cluster can also have a damaging domino effect, with the failure of one company damaging another company during times of economic retraction. This phenomenon was much in evidence in the Silicon Valley during the economic crisis of 2007–2009.

Michael Rawdan

See also: Technological Innovation.

Further Reading

Carlino, Gerald A. "Knowledge Spillovers: Cities' Role in the New Economy." *Business Review, Federal Reserve Bank of Philadelphia* (4th quarter, 2001): 17.

Kokko, A. "Technology, Market Characteristics, and Spillovers." *Journal of Development Economics* 43:2 (1994): 279–293.

Krugman, Paul. *Geography and Trade.* Cambridge, MA: MIT Press, 1991.

Sprague, Oliver (1873–1953)

Oliver Mitchell Wentworth Sprague was a Harvard economist and an adviser to the U.S. government and other nations in the years prior to World War II. An expert on banking and banking crises, he believed that increased taxation, price regulation, and competition were necessary to minimize the impact of economic crises, such as the Great Depression.

Sprague was born on April 22, 1873, in Somerville, Massachusetts. He attended St. Johnsbury Academy, in Vermont, and Harvard University, from which he received a bachelor's degree in 1894, a master's in 1895, and a doctorate in economics in 1897; he then joined the faculty as an assistant professor in economics. From 1905 to 1908, on sabbatical from Harvard, Sprague taught economics at the Imperial University in Tokyo, Japan. Upon his return to Harvard, he helped establish the university's Graduate School of Business Administration, where he became an assistant professor in banking and finance before being named Edmund Cogswell Converse professor of banking and finance in 1913. Sprague's first major work, *History of Crises Under the National Banking System*, was published in 1910; *Banking Reform in the United States* appeared the following year. Sprague held the Edmund Cogswell Converse chair at Harvard until his retirement in 1941.

In addition to his academic responsibilities, Sprague worked as an adviser to the U.S. government from the late 1910s to the early 1930s. In this capacity, he was able to apply his economic research to the formulation of public policy at the federal and international levels. During World War I, he recommended funding the escalating war expenditures through increased taxation rather than through government borrowing. This fundamentally conservative view put him at odds with many politicians who believed it was easier to borrow money in order to keep the government and the banking system "healthy"—a view Sprague roundly criticized in his third major work, *Theory and History of Banking* (1929).

With the onset of the Great Depression, Sprague went to London at the behest of the British government, serving as an adviser to the Bank of England from 1930 to 1933. Soon his expertise was being sought—and received—by governments and financial institutions around the world, including Germany's Reichsbank, the Bank of France, the Bank for International Settlements, and the League of Nations.

In 1933, Sprague returned to the United States to participate in the establishment of the New Deal by the new Franklin D. Roosevelt administration. Sprague's work as a financial and executive assistant to Secretary of the Treasury Henry Morgenthau led to his highly controversial 1934 booklet *Recovery and Common Sense*, which caused a major split within the administration over the best way to achieve economic recovery. Sprague recommended raising taxes to pay for New Deal projects, arguing that lower prices and increased competition would stimulate demand for consumer goods as well as for capital.

Resigning from government service in 1933 over Roosevelt's decision to end the gold standard and devalue the dollar, Sprague devoted more time to academic research, receiving a doctor of letters degree from Columbia University in 1938. After his retirement from Harvard in 1941, he served on the board of directors of the National Shawmut Bank of Boston, on the advisory board of the Massachusetts Investors Trust, and as an adviser on foreign exchange issues for the General Motors Corporation. Sprague died in Boston on May 24, 1953.

Justin Corfield

See also: Great Depression (1929–1933); New Deal; Regulation, Financial.

Further Reading

Cole, A.H., R.L. Masson, and J.H. Williams. "Memorial O.M.W. Sprague, 1873–1953." *American Economic Review* 44 (1954): 131–132.

Schlesinger, Arthur M. *The Coming of the New Deal*. London: Heinemann, 1960.

Sprague, O.M.W. *History of Crises Under the National Banking System*. Washington, DC: Government Printing Office, 1910.

———. *Theory and History of Banking*. New York: Putnam, 1929.

Sraffa, Piero (1898–1983)

Italian economist Piero Sraffa is regarded as one of the twentieth-century giants in the field. His book *Production of Commodities by Means of Commodities: Prelude to a Critique of Economic Theory* (1960) is credited with starting the neo-Ricardian school of economic thought, which combined the fundamental ideas of early-nineteenth-century economics with twentieth-century mathematical and theoretical advances.

Sraffa was born on August 5, 1898, in Turin, Italy, to Angelo and Irma Sraffa. He attended schools in Parma and Milan and graduated from the University of Turin. After serving in the Italian army during World War I, he returned to Turin and earned a doctorate in 1920; his thesis was titled "Inflation in Italy During and After the War." From 1921 to 1922, he studied at the London School of Economics. Back in Italy, he served as director of the provincial labor department in Milan and then as a professor of political economy at universities in Perugia and Sardinia.

Sraffa's experience in World War I made him a lifetime pacifist, and he strongly opposed the rise to power in Italy of fascist Benito Mussolini. His doctoral thesis had earned him a reputation as a "monetarist" interested in the role of the money supply in economic systems. This, in addition to his friendship with Italian Communist Party leader Antonio Gramsci, led him into conflict with Mussolini's government. The situation worsened following the publication of several articles in the *Economic Journal* and the *Manchester Guardian* in which Sraffa exposed the problems that had led to Italy's banking crisis.

British economist John Maynard Keynes came to Sraffa's rescue, inviting him to the University of Cambridge. There, Sraffa and Keynes—both book collectors as well as economists—became close friends. In 1925, Sraffa translated into Italian Keynes's *A Tract on Monetary Reform*, and both men argued against the Austrian school's theory of the business cycle as a product of overproduction and deficient demand. Sraffa also opposed Alfred Marshall's neoclassical economic theories, which stressed—and indeed relied on—the belief that, when making economic decisions, people behave completely rationally in order to optimize their material well-being. With Keynes's help, Sraffa was appointed a lecturer in the faculty of economics at the University of Cambridge. Keynes's ideas were greatly influenced by Sraffa, and the two argued publicly against the neoclassical economists regarding the forces behind business cycles.

Painfully shy, Sraffa despised lecturing. He resigned his post at Cambridge in 1930 and, with Keynes's support, was appointed Marshall librarian at King's College, Cambridge, before being named assistant director of research there. In 1931 Sraffa started on a monumental, twenty-year project editing the complete writings of nineteenth-century economist David Ricardo, whom he greatly admired. Published between 1951 and 1971, the eleven-volume *Works and Correspondence of David Ricardo* was noted for its clear interpretation of classical and neoclassical economic theory, particularly surplus theory, the labor theory of value, and the basis of Karl Marx's critical analysis of capitalist production.

Sraffa was named a fellow of Trinity College, Cambridge, in 1939 and a reader in economics in 1963. In 1961, he was awarded the prize of the Stockholm Academy of Science, the highest award for economics at the time. (The Nobel Prize for Economics was not awarded until 1969). After editing Ricardo's works, Sraffa's major theoretical work, *Production of Commodities by Means of Commodities* (1960), reinterpreted Ricardo's theory for the twentieth century and led to the founding of the so-called neo-Ricardian school and the classical revival at Cambridge. Sraffa's work influenced not only Keynes but also, among others, philosopher Ludwig Wittgenstein. Following Sraffa's death on September 3, 1983, economist Paul Samuelson remarked that he doubted whether any scholar who had written so little had contributed so much to economic science.

Justin Corfield

See also: Keynes, John Maynard.

Further Reading

Schefold, B. "Piero Sraffa 1898–1983." *Economic Journal* 106: 438 (1996): 1314–1325.

Sraffa, Piero. *Production of Commodities by Means of Commodities: Prelude to a Critique of Economic Theory.* New York and Cambridge, UK: Cambridge University Press, 1960.

Stability and Stabilization, Economic

A stable economy is one in which there is sustained growth along with low inflation and low unemployment. It is an economy in which there is general equilibrium between aggregate supply and aggregate demand. Another sign of stability is that the economy is neither experiencing an unsustainable boom or bubble, which is often accompanied by high inflation, nor is it experiencing little or negative growth, which is usually accompanied by high unemployment. Stability, then, is not the same as stasis. An economy that is not growing and changing is, in fact, an economy that is malfunctioning.

Since economic stability is a desirable condition, governments employ two basic kinds of policies to achieve, recover, or maintain it: fiscal policies (taxing and spending) and monetary policies (adjusting the money supply). Usually, governments employ some of both to affect economic stability, although sometimes the policies work against one another. For example, expansionary fiscal policy may be accompanied by contractionary monetary policy, and vice versa. Collectively, such efforts are known as economic stabilization policies. For the most part, these policies focus on the demand side of the equation.

Fiscal and Monetary Policy

When an economy begins to slow or contract—that is, when it is entering or already in a recessionary period—economic output begins to fall significantly below the economy's potential, leaving both workers and capital equipment idle. To lift aggregate demand, the government can employ fiscal policy—that is, taxing and spending policies—attempting to spur investment by lowering taxes on businesses and to spur consumption by lowering taxes on households. Alternatively, or at the same time, the government can increase spending on infrastructure, stimulating demand for goods from the private sector and giving jobs to idle workers, or it can increase transfer payments that are then spent on consumption, which increases demand and employment. Similarly, governments can impose higher taxes or cut spending to cool an economy if it is overheating and threatening to trigger inflation. Of course, by spending money or cutting taxes during recessionary periods, which usually coincide with low-

ered revenues, governments run budget deficits, which can have negative effects on future growth and inflation if they became too large.

To stabilize an economy, a government can also use monetary policy, essentially altering interest rates and the growth rate of the money supply. To do so, the government, through its central bank, has several tools at its disposal. In the United States, the Federal Reserve Bank can raise or lower the interest rate it charges member banks for loans, thereby forcing commercial banks to raise or lower their interest rates to businesses and households. Making money more expensive leads to less borrowing and thus shrinks, or slows, the growth of money in circulation. This essentially makes money more expensive, thereby cooling inflation. By lowering interest rates, central banks make it cheaper to borrow, thereby increasing the money in circulation and helping to stimulate demand and employment. The central bank can also purchase or sell government securities. Purchasing securities puts more money in circulation; selling them shrinks the money in circulation. Finally, a central bank such as the Federal Reserve can increase or lower liquidity requirements for commercial banks. By increasing these—that is, by requiring banks to hold more money against their outstanding loans—they in effect lower the amount of money in circulation. Conversely, by decreasing liquidity requirements, they increase the amount of money available for borrowing by businesses and households, thereby increasing aggregate demand. The preponderance of economic stabilization by the Federal Reserve is done through the second of the above-noted methods—that is, the buying and selling of government securities to pump loanable funds into the economy or to pull them out.

Bureaucracy and Politics

Theoretically, both fiscal and monetary policy can be effectively used to alter aggregate demand and therefore achieve economic stability. The real world, however, presents more complexities. In democratic countries such as the United States, fiscal policy is initiated by elected representatives. This immediately presents two problems in its goal to achieve economic stability. The first concerns timeliness. Legislatures often find it difficult to move quickly in response to rapidly changing economic situations. For example, while the recession of the late 2000s began in the fourth quarter of 2007, it took the U.S. Congress until after the November 2008 elections to pass a major stimulus package. In addition, legislators naturally find it easier to cut taxes than to raise them. In other words, it is politically easier to stimulate aggregate demand to fight a sluggish economy than it is to slow it down.

Finally, fiscal policy often fails to work even when employed in a timely fashion. There are several reasons for this. First, most people view changes in the tax code as temporary and fail to adjust their spending patterns in response. In addition, even when businesses and consumers respond to a tax cut or rebate, the effect lasts only as long as the tax cut and rebate are in effect. Thus, for example, the 2009 Cash for Clunkers program, in which the federal government offered a rebate to consumers exchanging an old car for a new, fuel-efficient one, produced a flurry of demand in the automobile business but only for a short time period and not enough, according to most economists, to lift demand for that troubled sector over the long term. Also, a long time line is often required in order for a spending increase to work its way through the economy. For example, it could take a year or two for the government to get an infrastructure project going. By that time, the economy may have turned on its own, and the impact of the stimulus might hit just at the time when the economy needs to slow down.

By contrast, monetary policy is much more indirect. Rather than injecting money directly into the economy, it tends to pull the strings behind the economy, triggering the private financial sector to change its lending patterns and hence stimulate or curb demand. Moreover, monetary policy in most democracies is under the control of nonelected

central bankers. In the United States, the chairman and governors of the Federal Reserve are appointed by the president with approval of the Senate to fourteen-year terms, somewhat insulating them from political pressure. These officials are not entirely insulated from the will of the people, but they nevertheless enjoy great independence from the political process. This ensures that monetary policy is not unduly influenced by the election cycle, which otherwise could hamper economic stability. Elected central bankers might well choose to stimulate the economy to create an illusion of prosperity before an election even if the state of the real economy does not call for such stimulus. This is more critical since inflation, which is the cost of any overly stimulative policy, occurs with a lag and might not begin until after the election. Moreover, as institutions, central banks are less unwieldy than legislatures, allowing them to respond more quickly to changes in the economy.

Shift from Fiscal to Monetary Policy

Because of all of these factors, both economists and policy makers have shifted the emphasis in their thinking and activities over the course of the late twentieth and early twenty-first centuries from fiscal to monetary policy as the most effective means of altering demand and achieving economic stability. They have tended to utilize the former only during times of especial economic distress, such as the "stagflation" period of the 1970s and early 1980s (where the response was the 1981 Reagan tax cuts) and the recession of the late 2000s (responding with the economic stimulus package of 2009).

Yet while most economists agree that monetary policy is more effective than fiscal policy in responding to changes in the economy and securing economic stability, the debate remains heated over how much impact such policies have and over what time period. Studies have found that increasing the money supply through the various means at the disposal of central banks tends to more effectively stimulate output in the short term, in the first one to three years. Wages and prices, however, tend to respond more sluggishly, with most of the inflation caused by increasing the money supply felt three to five years out. After roughly five years or so, most of the effect of the increase in the money supply comes in the form of higher prices and wages. This fact must be accounted for in the decision making of monetary authorities if they are not to trigger too much inflation as a result of their efforts to lift aggregate demand.

Still, while monetary policy is considered more effective in lifting overall demand, fiscal policy can be used to great effect by shifting the composition of economic output. As the Cash for Clunkers program made clear, tax policy can be used to stimulate a specific economic sector. More generally, it can be used to increase investment over savings during times of recession and savings over investment during periods of inflation. In addition, fiscal policies can alter the effectiveness of monetary policies, and vice versa. Thus, most policy makers recognize the importance of coordinating the two policies in their efforts to achieve economic stability. In the real world, this often has not happened, as large government deficits limit the increase of deficits in recessions and put the onus on the Federal Reserve to fight inflation in situations where politicians do not want to either increase taxes or cut government spending.

Finally, there is an international dimension to economic stabilization policies. Monetary policy in particular has to be considered in the light of international capital flows, especially for countries that are highly dependent on them for their growth, such as many of those in the developing world. For example, expanding the money supply by lowering interest rates may stimulate growth, but it can also trigger capital flight, as international investors seek better returns on their capital elsewhere, thereby curbing investment and undermining any increase in aggregate demand triggered by the initial effort to increase the money supply. Thus, in the pursuit of economic stability, a government can trigger the opposite.

James Ciment

See also: Employment and Unemployment; Fiscal Policy; Growth, Economic; Inflation; Monetary Policy; Tax Policy.

Further Reading

Lewis, William W. *The Power of Productivity: Wealth, Poverty, and the Threat to Global Stability.* Chicago: University of Chicago Press, 2004.

Nardini, Franco. *Technical Progress and Economic Growth: Business Cycles and Stabilization.* New York: Springer, 2001.

Norton, Hugh S. *The Quest for Economic Stability: Roosevelt to Bush.* 2nd ed. Columbia: University of South Carolina Press, 1991.

Perkins, Martin Y., ed. *TARP and the Restoration of U.S. Financial Stability.* Hauppauge, NY: Nova Science, 2009.

Røste, Ole Bjørn. *Monetary Policy and Macroeconomic Stabilization: The Roles of Optimum Currency Areas, Sacrifice Ratios, and Labor Market Adjustment.* New Brunswick, NJ: Transaction, 2008.

Wray, L. Randall. *Understanding Modern Money: The Key to Full Employment and Price Stability.* Northampton, MA: Edward Elgar, 2003.

Steindl, Josef (1912–1993)

Although he was trained in the Austrian school of economics, Josef Steindl developed his theories primarily in England and was especially influenced by the Polish economist Michal Kalecki. Steindl's books *Small and Big Business: Economic Problems of the Size of Firms* (1945) and *Maturity and Stagnation in American Capitals* (1952) are considered classics of the postwar economics literature.

Born in Vienna, Austria, on April 14, 1912, Steindl was educated at the Hochschule für Welthandel (now the Vienna University of Economics and Business Administration) in that city. He received his doctorate in 1935, after which he worked for three years at the Austrian Institute of Economic Research, founded by Ludwig von Mises, where he was introduced to the work of John Maynard Keynes. When the Nazis occupied Austria in 1938, Steindl lost his job and was forced to flee the country. With the help of Friedrich von Hayek, von Mises, and Gottfried von Haberler, he received a post at Balliol College, Oxford, and then at the Oxford Institute of Statistics, which had become home to a group of European intellectuals fleeing fascism.

At the institute, Steindl met Kalecki, whom he later acknowledged was his greatest intellectual influence. Kalecki's emphasis on imperfect competition and his denial of neoclassical labor theory (or the marginal productivity of labor demand theory) formed the basis of Steindl's own economic theory. The denial of perfect competition—along with Keynesian theory on the policy side and a Marxist historical perspective—combined with Steindl's formidable mathematical talent to give his thinking a unique heterodox shape.

Steindl's first book, *Small and Big Businesses: Economic Problems of the Firm*, was a microeconomic investigation into the effects of business size on profitability, cost structures, investment decisions, and capacity. Steindl contended that the economy has a tendency toward large-scale production, owing to the fact that, as a result of economics of scale, cost factors favor large enterprises. Although not denying the existence of small enterprises, Steindl believed that the representative firm is the oligopolistic firm. Thus, any investigation into general economic developments must use this as a starting point for contemplation of the larger macroeconomic problems of unemployment, slow growth, and unused (both capital and labor) capacity. This refutation of Alfred Marshall's idea of the cyclical rebirth of small firms through a perfectly competitive environment endogenized the elements that were said to lead to economic instability.

Maturity and Stagnation in American Capitalism was a macroeconomic continuation of the microeconomic study in *Small and Big Business.* Written at the institute in Oxford, the book is an investigation of the Great Depression. While the Depression was difficult to explain in terms of orthodox economic doctrine, Steindl's thesis states that the crisis had its roots in the growing monopolization of industrial economies. He maintains that when output in specific industries becomes concentrated in the hands of a few firms, competition fails, and with it, investment.

In a perfectly competitive model, the interaction of profits, prices, investment, and capacity utilization combine to maintain a macroeconomic equilibrium (through the entry and exit of small firms). In an oligopolistic market, however, there are no small firms to eliminate, and therefore, excess capacity cannot be reduced through competition. In the standard model, any temporary economic contraction gives way to expansion; but in an oligopolistic economy, declining investments continue undetected and lead to stagnation.

Steindl's thesis placed the origins of the Great Depression in the growing concentration of industry, which was itself a result of competition. Competition led to revenues, and winners accumulated business earnings that needed to be invested. In Steindl's model, the investment was entered in the market for smaller firms, thus squaring the circle: competition led to concentration, which led to the Depression, and the result was endogenous capitalist development.

Unfortunately for Steindl, the publication of *Maturity and Stagnation,* which coincided with the economic boom of the 1950s, received little attention. The economic stagnation of the 1970s brought renewed interest in the book, however, and Steindl, continuing to work on his theories, adding to his original model the increased role of government and trade liberalization.

In 1950, Steindl returned to Austria and joined the Austrian Institute, where he continued to explore the problems that occupied his intellectual mentors, Kalecki, Keynes, and Marx. There, he published works on saving, investment, income distribution, stagnation, and growth. Steindl was made an honorary professor at Vienna University of Economics and Business Administration in 1970 and was a visiting professor at Stanford University in California in 1974–1975. When he died on March 7, 1993, he left behind a body of work that was a testament to a mind searching for an economic view originating with theory and moving into issues of economic policy and social justice.

Robert Koehn

See also: Austrian School; Great Depression (1929–1933); Kalecki, Michal; Keynes, John Maynard.

Further Reading

Shapiro, N. "Market Structure and Economic Growth: Steindl's Contribution." *Social Concept* 4 (1988): 72–83.

Steindl, Josef. "Capitalist Enterprise and Risk." *Oxford Economic Papers*, no. 7 (1945): 21–45.

———. *Economic Papers, 1941–88*. London: Macmillan, 1990.

———. *Maturity and Stagnation in American Capitalism*. Oxford, UK: Basil Blackwell, 1952.

———. *Random Processes and the Growth of Firms*. London: Hafner, 1965.

———. *Small and Big Business: Economic Problems of the Size of Firms*. Oxford, UK: Basil Blackwell, 1945.

———. "Stagnation: Theory and Policy." *Cambridge Journal of Economics* 3 (1980): 1–14.

———. "Technical Progress and Evolution." In *Research, Development and Technological Innovation*, ed. Devendra Sahal. Lanham, MD: Lexington, 1982.

Stimulus Package, U.S. (2008)

The Emergency Economic Stabilization Act of 2008, popularly known as the fiscal stimulus package of 2008, was a $170 billion federal program aimed at easing the effects of a recession that had begun in the last quarter of the previous year. Heavy on tax cuts and rebates, the package failed to prevent a deepening of the economic downturn, leading Congress and the new Barack Obama administration to pass an even costlier and more far-reaching stimulus package in 2009.

Deepening Recession

By late 2007, there were a host of signs that the U.S. economy was entering a period of slow or negative growth. Beginning in late summer 2006 came a decline in home prices across much of the country. For some five years prior to that, U.S. home prices had undergone unprecedented increases, a result not so much of overall prosperity but of government policies—most notably efforts by the Federal Reserve Board (Fed) to lower interest rates, reducing the rates paid by homebuyers for mortgages—and the financial industry's development of new types of more affordable mortgages. As home equity values rose and mortgage rates fell, homeowners came to believe they could spend more on general consumer purchases, thereby creating greater economic activity and growth.

The fact that many of the new mortgages were based on adjustable rates created a dire situation when rates rose. Many homeowners were forced to sell their homes or go into foreclosure, which contributed to a rapid decline in home prices. As existing homeowners saw their equity continue to shrink, in many cases owing more than the value of the property, they cut back significantly on overall spending. Retailers began to see the change during the Christmas season of 2007, as sales dropped off sharply from the previous year. Meanwhile, the consumer confidence index had declined steadily through much of 2007, even as unemployment rate remained relatively low. The jobless rate remained below 5 percent in February 2008—when President George W. Bush signed the stimulus package into law—but many policy makers, looking ahead to the 2008 elections nine months away, feared it would rise as economic activity slowed.

The collapse in the housing market created problems in the financial industry as well. Many banks and other financial institutions found themselves highly exposed to nonperforming mortgages, particularly of the subprime variety that allowed people with low income or bad credit to obtain mortgages, usually of the adjustable-rate variety. Many of these mortgages had been packaged into securities and sold to other financial institutions, increasing their exposure to the continuing decline in housing prices. Further destabilizing the financial industry were collateralized debt obligations, securitized assets that amounted to a kind of insurance policy taken out by financial institutions against mortgage-backed securities. In short, rising foreclosure rates were creating a ripple effect throughout the financial industry, both in the United States and abroad.

As recession loomed in early 2008 (in fact, later numbers would show that it had begun in the fourth quarter of 2007), both President Bush and Congress decided to take action. Congress was urged on by Fed chairman Ben Bernanke's testimony that prompt, strong measures were needed to prevent an economic downturn. In January 2008, Bush proposed a stimulus package of just under $150 billion, almost all of it devoted to tax cuts and rebates. While there was a consensus in Congress that a federal stimulus was needed to prevent a recession, the exact form the stimulus should take was hotly debated.

What Kind of Package?

Governments generally have three options for stimulating an economy: tax cuts or rebates, increased spending, or a combination of the two. In general, Democrats tend to favor more government spending, either in the form of increased payments for unemployment, aid to states, and food stamps or in infrastructure projects. When they do push for tax cuts or rebates, they tend to want them targeted at lower- and middle-income taxpayers. More often, Democrats argue, increased federal benefits pump more money into the economy in the short term than do tax cuts. Tax refunds are often saved rather than spent, and tax cuts may take a while to show up in consumer and business spending patterns. While the economic impact of infrastructure projects may also take time to be felt, they provide a more permanent stimulus. Nevertheless, in the debate over the 2008 stimulus package, Democrats also called for special tax incentives to support investment in green technologies.

Republicans, to the contrary, tend to prefer tax cuts and rebates for all income groups and businesses. An exception to this trend is the earned income tax credit, a refundable credit aimed at lower-income workers, which is more typically supported by Democrats and opposed by Republicans. The reasons they give are both pragmatic and ideological. First, Republicans argue that it is more in keeping with American values to allow taxpayers to keep more of their own money and let them choose how they want to use it. Second, they argue, putting more money in the hands of consumers and businesses allows more efficient market forces to determine how that money will be spent. In addition, they say, tax rebates put money into the economy much more quickly than infrastructure projects. In the debate over the 2008 stimulus package, Republican legislators also pushed for an accelerated depreciation allowance for small businesses. (Depreciation is the amount of money a business can write off against an asset as it loses value over time, such as a computer that becomes increasingly outdated; accelerating the allowance offers a more immediate tax break for businesses, thereby encouraging capital equipment purchases.)

Despite the extent and nature of the debate, seasoned congressional observers were impressed at the alacrity with which Congress moved to pass a stimulus package. Historically, Congress has acted to stimulate the economy only when a consensus develops that market forces—usually taking the form of lower prices and wages, which stimulate demand and hiring—will take too long to reduce unemployment or increase production. By early 2008, such a consensus had emerged.

The package proposed by President Bush in January 2008 totaled $145 billion, but by the time the bill wended its way through Congress, the projected cost of the program was nearly $170 billion. In late January and early February, the House passed its version of the stimulus by a margin of 385–35 (with 11 congressmen present but not voting), and the Senate voted 81–16 in favor of a slightly different bill (with 3 present but not voting). The House immediately approved the Senate bill, which Bush signed into law on February 13.

Even though Democrats had seized control of Congress in the 2006 midterm elections, the stimulus package as approved by legislators and signed by the president emphasized tax cuts over

With congressional leaders and cabinet members looking on, President George W. Bush signs the Emergency Economic Stabilization Act of 2008. The measure granted tax rebates of $300 to $1,200 to American households, totaling $170 billion. *(Alex Wong/Getty Images)*

federal spending. Holding slim majorities in both houses of Congress and facing a conservative Republican in the White House, the Democrats felt it was necessary to take the traditional GOP approach to stimulus in order to avert congressional filibuster or presidential veto.

Under the stimulus plan, married couples with a taxable income of under $150,000 who filed joint returns in the spring of 2008 received $1,200 in rebates, plus an additional $300 per child. Individual taxpayers with a taxable income of less than $75,000 received a rebate of $600, plus $300 per child. Those with incomes of more than $150,000 were ineligible. In addition, the package included an accelerating depreciation allowance for newly purchased equipment costing up to $800,000 and an increase in the size of mortgages that could be backed by government-sponsored enterprises, such as Fannie Mae and Freddie Mac, thereby lowering interest payments.

Effects of the Package

As the recession continued to deepen through 2008 and 2009—becoming America's worst economic downturn since the Great Depression—most economists came to the conclusion that the stimulus act of 2008 had failed to turn the economy around. They cited several reasons for the lack of effect, most of them associated with the observation that the tax rebates did little to encourage long-term changes in consumer behavior.

Foremost, critics pointed out that the stimulus was simply too small for an economy facing such a severe economic crisis. In addition, the stimulus lagged because of a well-known factor economists call the "irreversibility effect," a phenomenon first theorized by the French-born physicist-turned-economist Claude Henry, based on the work of English economist John Maynard Keynes in the 1930s. In times of economic uncertainty, Henry noted, people are reluctant to spend money or to lend money to someone else so that *they* can spend because the purchase of durable goods (such as a car or appliance) or a long-term loan to a borrower represents a serious commitment that may be difficult to back out of when earnings fall. Decisions taken today about the purchases of durable goods, especially when financed through credit, may be hard to reverse at a later date. In short, these decisions are "irreversible." Moreover, in times of economic distress, it is naturally better to wait for conditions to improve before making a major expenditure. While consumers collectively might recognize that the economy would be better off if everyone continued to borrow, lend, and spend at previous levels, self-interest dictates that individual consumers will wait to see what happens with the economy. It was precisely this strong relationship between effective demand and the irreversibility effect, according to many economists, that limited the effectiveness of the 2008 stimulus package.

According to a survey by the National Retail Federation (NRF) in May 2008, just as the first rebate checks were being mailed out, fewer than 40 percent of consumers planned to spend their rebate money—a figure seconded by a Congressional Budget Office (CBO) analysis; the rest would save the money in case of future financial setbacks, such as a job layoff. Indeed, later estimates indicated that the NRF survey and CBO analysis were overly optimistic and that only 20 percent of tax refunds were put into the economy (spent) within six months.

As for the accelerated depreciation allowance, evidence has emerged that it may have cost the government up to four times the amount in lost revenue that it generated in new business spending. This is because purchases of new equipment and other forms of business investment may have been perceived as inopportune, despite the tax advantages, for a variety of reasons—such as lack of confidence in future economic growth, heavy inventory, and idle capacity.

Overall, assessing the impact of the 2008 stimulus package was complicated by the fact that, between May and July 2008, as the rebate checks were distributed, real-estate credit became tighter, gasoline prices rose sharply, and consumer confidence fell still further below the already low levels of late 2007. All three of these factors countered the expansionary effect of tax cuts. In addition, after falling dramatically between October 2007 and June 2008, investment spending in the third quarter of 2008 increased by only 0.4 percent over the second quarter of that year and then dropped 12.3 percent in the fourth quarter. The difficulties faced by private and federally supported financial businesses, such as Fannie Mae and Freddie Mac, especially since the global financial crisis of late 2008, all contributed to lower consumer confidence, depressed investment spending, and increasing unemployment.

With the general consensus among economists and policy makers that the 2008 stimulus package had failed to halt a skidding economy, the candidates in the presidential campaign of that year began to debate the possibility of a second stimulus. Some argued that the Bush stimulus was too small; others contended that it overemphasized tax cuts and rebates and underemphasized govern-ment spending. Fiscal conservatives insisted that the failure of the package to boost the economy indicated that no further stimulus measures should be taken.

By early 2009, with Democrat Barack Obama in the White House and a much larger Democratic majority in Congress, the impetus for a new and much larger stimulus package—one emphasizing government spending rather than tax cuts—gained momentum, ultimately leading to passage of the $787 billion American Recovery and Reinvestment Act of 2009, popularly known as the economic stimulus package of 2009.

James Ciment

See also: Fiscal Policy; Recession and Financial Crisis (2007–); Stimulus Package, U.S. (2008); Tax Policy; Troubled Asset Relief Program (2008–).

Further Reading

Bernanke, Benjamin. "Irreversibility, Uncertainty, and Cyclical Investment." *Quarterly Journal of Economics* 98:1 (February 1983): 85–106.

Broda, Christian, and Jonathan A. Parker "The Impact of the 2008 Rebate." Available at www.voxeu.org/index .php?q=node/1541. Accessed February 2009.

Congressional Budget Office. "Did the 2008 Tax Rebates Stimulate Short-Term Growth?" *Economic and Budget Issue Brief,* June 10, 2009.

Keynes, John Maynard. *The General Theory of Employment, Interest and Money.* New York: Harcourt, Brace, and World, 1964.

Rivlin, Alice. "The Need for a Stimulus Package Now." Testimony to House Budget Committee, January 29, 2008. Available at www.brookings.edu/testimony/2008/0129_ fiscalstimulus_rivlin.aspx. Accessed October 2009.

Zandi, Mark M. Written Testimony Before the House Committee on Small Business, Hearing on "Economic Stimulus For Small Business: A Look Back and Assessing Need For Additional Relief." July 24, 2008.

Stimulus Package, U.S. (2009)

The U.S. financial crisis of 2008–2009, which resulted from the collapse of the nation's housing bubble and followed the declaration of bankruptcy by the investment banking firm Lehman Brothers in September 2008, sent stock prices tumbling, unemployment soaring, and banks into a deep freeze during which they were lending no money. Without lending by banks, firms could not borrow and remain in business, and consumers could not borrow money to purchase goods such as homes and cars and faced reduced credit card limits.

As John Maynard Keynes and others explained during the Great Depression, two policy actions are needed to deal with this kind of situation. First, the central bank must lower interest rates. In 2008, heeding that advice, the Federal Reserve pushed its interest rates down toward zero. This move was replicated by many central banks around the world, as the financial crisis and recession that resulted from the burst housing bubble in the United States spread to other countries. Second, said Keynes, the government must cut taxes and increase its spending, using fiscal policy to get the economy growing again. Because the George W. Bush administration was in its last months, with presidential and congressional elections scheduled for November, the United States was at loss for major fiscal policy changes in late 2008. It would have to await the next administration.

A Brief History

Upon his election in November 2008, Barack Obama with his economic advisers began devising an economic stimulus package. Their original plan was for a large spending program with a few tax cuts thrown in. Over time, in order to appeal to Republicans and conservative Democrats, the emphasis was more on tax cuts and less on government spending. To appease those in Congress concerned about the deficit, the cost of the bill was reduced from $1 trillion to less than $800 billion.

On January 26, 2009, David Obey (D-WI) introduced the American Recovery and Reinvestment Act of 2009 in the House of Representatives; the bill passed two days later. The Senate approved a similar measure on February 10. Once the few differences were reconciled, the House

passed a new bill on February 12 followed by the Senate on February 13, with votes essentially following party lines. No Republicans in the House voted for the measure, and only three Republican senators voted for it—Susan Collins and Olympia Snowe from Maine, and Arlen Specter of Pennsylvania, who soon thereafter changed his party affiliation.

With much fanfare, President Obama signed the law on February 17, 2009, at an economic forum he was hosting in Denver. Christina Romer and Jared Bernstein, the chief economic advisers to President Obama and Vice President Joe Biden, respectively, estimated that the stimulus bill would create or save 3.5 million jobs over two years, with more than 90 percent of them in the private sector. Its main features were tax cuts, an expansion of unemployment insurance and other social programs to aid those hurt by the recession, and increased government spending for education, health care, and infrastructure.

The Congressional Budget Office, an independent arm of Congress, estimated that the bill would cost $787 billion. This figure included the interest costs of having to borrow money to provide fiscal stimulus to the economy and subtracted the increased taxes and lower government spending resulting from the positive economic impact of the stimulus.

Main Provisions

A bit more than one-third of the stimulus package, or $286 billion, was devoted to tax cuts. The other $501 billion involved additional government spending, including the future interest costs of borrowing money to stimulate the economy.

Tax Breaks

Most of the tax breaks in the stimulus bill went to individuals—roughly $116 billion of the total $288 billion in the bill—with the rest going to businesses. A payroll tax credit of $400 per worker and $800 per couple added $13 per week in 2009 to the average paycheck and $7.70 per week in 2010. Since this credit was refundable, people owing no income tax also received it. The credit was phased out for individuals earning more than $75,000 and couples making more than $150,000. The payroll tax credit for individuals cost a total of $116 billion.

The second-largest tax break dealt with the alternative minimum tax (AMT). Enacted in 1969 to keep wealthy individuals from escaping taxation through large deductions, the AMT over time has applied to more and more taxpayers because it was not indexed to inflation. Every year Congress has provided a temporary fix so the tax would not hit middle-class households, but it has refused to make permanent changes, which would acknowledge greater budget deficits in the future. The ATM patch for 2009 and 2010 cost $70 billion. This provision offered no real stimulus, since it would have taken place anyway and did not give people more money to spend.

There were a number of smaller tax breaks for individuals as well. Some received little public attention, others a great deal of publicity. In the former category were $4.7 billion to expand the Earned Income Tax Credit and $4.3 billion in tax credits to homeowners who made their homes more energy efficient by installing new energy-efficient windows, doors, and air conditioners. In addition, at a cost of $5 billion, the first $2,400 of unemployment insurance was made exempt from taxation, and college students or their parents received a tax credit of up to $2,500 for tuition and related expenses in 2009 and 2010 (cost, $14 billion).

Better publicized was the $8,000 tax credit for new homebuyers on properties purchased by November 1, 2009; the total estimated cost of this benefit was $14 billion. Its effects were noticeable in the summer and fall of 2009, when median U.S. home prices rose by a small percentage for the first time since 2006 and home sales stabilized after falling sharply for several years. The program was so successful that Congress expanded eligibility to June 30, 2010, to include existing homeowners who buy a new house.

To help the auto industry, persons buying new cars, trucks, and SUVs (costing up to $49,500) between February 18 and December 31, 2009, could deduct all sales taxes from their federal income tax. Taxpayers who do not itemize their deductions were eligible for this benefit, but not wealthy taxpayers. The initial cost of the program was $2 billion. When this program failed to spur auto sales, the government provided additional aid in June 2009 with its Cash for Clunkers program, which granted vouchers of $3,500 to $4,500 for purchasing a new fuel-efficient car.

Numerous tax breaks, estimated to cost $51 billion, were directed at business firms. Firms could use current losses to offset profits for the previous five years ($15 billion); they were given credits for renewable energy production ($13 billion), and they were allowed to depreciate equipment such as computers more quickly for tax purposes ($5 billion).

Government Spending

The stimulus bill included two forms of government spending: funds spent directly by the federal government and funds spent through aid to state and local governments. Unlike the federal government, which can incur an ongoing deficit by increasing the money supply or borrowing from foreigners, state and local governments must balance their annual budgets except for capital projects, such as building new schools. This becomes a problem during times of recession, when tax revenues fall and state governments must spend more on programs to support the needy (such as unemployment insurance and Medicaid). To keep their budgets in balance, state and local governments must therefore raise taxes, cut spending, or both. These actions counter any stimulus from the federal government, resulting in a smaller total impact from government actions.

One way around this problem is for the federal government to provide revenue assistance to state and local governments. For this reason, the federal government increased its contributions to state Medicaid spending by $87 billion and to state spending on education (public schools plus public colleges and universities) by $67 billion, increased unemployment insurance benefits ($36 billion), gave additional benefits to the hungry and poor ($21 billion), and increased funds for teaching children with special needs ($12 billion). The federal government also spent $4 billion so that state and local governments could hire additional police officers and expand programs to prevent drug-related crimes, violence against women, and Internet crimes against children.

Most economists regard these provisions as the most effective part of the stimulus bill; they helped some state and local governments avoid or limit tax increases and the laying off of public employees, which would have significantly worsened the recession. Another success was government aid so that people could keep their health insurance after being laid off. At a cost of $25 billion, the federal government subsidized nearly two-thirds of health insurance premiums for the newly unemployed for a period of up to nine months.

Initially, the Obama administration stressed direct spending on "shovel-ready" projects, where spending could take place immediately and jobs be created quickly. But this was just a small part of the final bill that Congress passed. The stimulus package allocated $30.5 billion for building and repairing bridges and highways, improving public lands and parks, and developing high-speed rail lines between major cities. A total of $11 billion went to make the energy grid more efficient, and $6 billion went to water treatment projects. Several billion dollars went to other infrastructure projects, such as dam repair and flood control, increasing energy efficiency in public buildings and military facilities, and expanding broadband access in rural areas. In practice, it proved difficult to start these projects quickly. As a result, few additional jobs were created in 2009 from infrastructure spending.

Finally, the stimulus bill gave a great deal of money directly to people. Interest expenses on the stimulus were estimated at about $50 billion. The

President Barack Obama seeks public support for his economic stimulus plan in February 2009. The $787-billion package, passed by Congress later that month, included tax cuts, job-creation incentives, and social welfare benefits in the face of the ongoing recession. (Getty Images)

maximum Pell Grant to college students increased by $500 (to $5,350), a total cost of $15.6 billion. A one-time payment of $250 was made to all Social Security and Supplemental Security Income (SSI) recipients, plus everyone who was receiving veteran's benefits. The cost of this provision was $14.4 billion.

An Assessment

From the moment it was proposed, the stimulus package generated a great deal of controversy. A full-page ad in the *New York Times* funded by the Cato Institute, a right-wing think tank, criticized the large amounts of government spending and feared the consequences of the large deficits. Among the 200 economists who endorsed the ad with their signatures were Nobel laureates James Buchanan, Robert Lucas, and Vernon Smith.

Another petition signed by nearly 200 economists and sponsored by the Center for American Progress, a middle-of-the-road think tank, supported the stimulus package as essential for dealing with the nation's rising unemployment rate. This petition was also signed by several Nobel Prize–winning economists, including Kenneth Arrow, Lawrence Klein, Paul Samuelson, and Robert Solow.

From the left of the political spectrum, Nobel laureate Paul Krugman criticized the stimulus package as insufficient to deal with the economic problems facing the United States. He called for a larger stimulus, focused more on government spending and less on tax cuts, and argued that it would be hard politically for President Obama to ask Congress for more spending after the first stimulus proved ineffective.

Other critics complained that $134 billion of the stimulus would not be spent until fiscal year 2011, and another $90 billion not until fiscal years 2012 through 2015. This, they maintained, would do nothing to help the economy until the end of 2010 and thereafter, when the economic crisis would likely be history and a stimulus unnecessary. Moreover, several provisions of the stimulus bill, such as $18 billion to support scientific research and development, would have positive long-term benefits but would not create many new jobs.

By late 2009, some economists were claiming "the proof is in the pudding." Alan Blinder, for one, maintained that the stimulus package, while hardly perfect, had basically done what was necessary and what Keynes had prescribed. It provided large tax cuts to households and business firms and sharply increased government spending. As such, it kept the U.S. economy from falling into another Great Depression, which many had seen as a very real possibility only months earlier.

Steven Pressman

See also: Fiscal Policy; Recession and Financial Crisis (2007–); Stimulus Package, U.S. (2008); Tax Policy; Troubled Asset Relief Program (2008–).

Further Reading

Blinder, Alan. "Comedy Aside, an Obama Report Card." *New York Times*, October 18, 2009.

Burtless, Gary. "The 'Great Recession' and Redistribution: Federal Antipoverty Policies." *Fast Focus*, December 2009.

Krugman, Paul. *The Return of Depression Economics and the Crisis of 2008.* New York: W.W. Norton, 2009.

Pressman, Steven. *Fifty Major Economists.* 2nd ed. New York: Routledge, 2006.

Stochastic Models

Stochastic business cycle models are mathematical representations that attempt to make predictions about the economy's ups and downs. Unlike traditional or deterministic macroeconomic models, stochastic business cycle models incorporate the fact that the state of the economy in a country can be affected by random, unexpected shocks. In the case of the 2007–2009 recession in the United States, for example, the random shock was the unanticipated collapse of the financial market and economic system as a result of shock waves caused by excessive subprime lending, liquidity issues in banking institutions, foreclosures, Ponzi schemes, declines in investor and consumer confidence, regulatory failure, and a record high unemployment rate.

Nature of Business Cycles

Business cycles, also referred to as trade or economic cycles, are time periods with identifiable patterns of fluctuation in business and economic activity measured primarily by national income or real gross domestic product (GDP). In the United States, these indicators are determined by the National Bureau of Economic Research (NBER). Identification of a recession by the NBER is based on a notable decline in economic activity across most industries lasting for two quarters in succession. The stage of the cycle is measured by the condition of the country's industrial productivity, employment status, consumption, and other key economic indicators. The highest point in the expansion period is called the peak, and the lowest point in the contraction period is called the trough. A full business cycle period includes an expansion period or boom (upward pattern from a trough to peak) and a contraction period or bust (downward pattern from a peak to trough).

Although a typical cycle lasts about five years, it can vary from as little as a year to as long as a decade. In between the expansion and contraction phases are progressive periods called growth and recession. The amplitude of a business cycle—the difference between the extreme points of the cycle, from peak to trough—also can vary significantly. Governments attempt to mitigate the amplitudes by implementing fiscal (tax-and-spend) policies or monetary (changes in money supply) policies to ease volatility.

Stochastic Process and Outcomes

The stochastic model attempts to describe the business cycle by including random or varied behavior due to incomplete information and uncertain or unpredictable input variables as part of the independent or exogenous factors. These stochastic processes usually involve time-related data series, subject to unpredictable random variations. They are described by a probability distribution, that is, they are measured by the likelihood of an event occurring. For example, suppose there is a 50 percent chance the market will begin to recover or grow again in two years. Often the stochastic processes will have similar functions or mathematical ranges or have strong correlations with each other, thereby making them more easily represented in the model.

Time and Geographic Effects

Stochastic models are especially relevant and indispensable as new random factors are taken into consideration in a fast-changing, volatile, and global economic environment. One example is a comparison of the 1930s and 2008–2009 financial crises. By looking at the different government policies and remedial rescue efforts in a stochastic business cycle model theory, it is possible to better understand what caused each crisis and what worked or could have worked to resolve them.

Another application of stochastic business cycle models is the examination of distinctive regional variations in economic cycles. For example, the economic impact of the subprime mortgage crisis was more acutely felt in markets, such as Florida and the West, where the housing bubble had inflated the most, even though these regions followed general regulatory guidelines similar to the rest of the country's. The stochastic model can help us understand the different outcomes in business cycle stage between states that were triggered by varied levels of real-estate business, the economic conditions prior to the burst of the bubble, and regions' varying responses to the problem.

Contributing Factors

Research using stochastic models reaches a variety of findings. According to studies by economists Chang-Jin Kim and Jeremy Piger, shifts in stochastic trends in an economy have permanent effects on the level of output, though findings in a study by Whelan Karl suggest that shocks such as changes in technology are not dominant forces driving the business cycle. In the international market context, studies have found that world real interest rate shocks (adjusted for inflation) can explain up to one-third of the output fluctuations and more than half of the fluctuations in net exports (a component of a nation's GDP). The world real interest rate therefore can be an important transmission mechanism in driving the business cycle phases in a small open economy.

In addition, stochastic models show that the prices of a nation's exports and imports are an important source of business fluctuations, or cycles, in a small and developing open economy. For instance, if the terms of trade (the relative prices of exports and imports) deteriorates, the country may experience a downward business cycles.

Moreover, Stephen DeLoach and Robert Rasche find that, even for a large economy such as that of the United States, permanent changes in exchange rates adjusted for inflation can have a large impact on business cycles. Finally, M. Ayhan Kose has found that world commodity price shocks have a significant role in driving business cycles in the developing economy.

Beryl Y. Chang

See also: Shock-Based Theories.

Further Reading

Canova, Fabio, and Angel Ubide. "International Business Cycles, Financial Markets and Household Production." *Journal of Economic Dynamics and Control* 22:4 (1998): 545–572.

DeLoach, Stephen B., and Robert H. Rasche. "Stochastic Trends and Economic Fluctuations in a Large Open Economy." *Journal of International Money and Finance* 17:4 (1998): 565–596.

Kim, Chang-Jin, and Jeremy Piger. "Common Stochastic Trends, Common Cycles, and Asymmetry in Economic Fluctuations." *Journal of Monetary Economics* 49:6 (2002): 1189–1211.

Kose, M. Ayhan. "Explaining Business Cycles in Small Open Economies: 'How Much Do World Prices Matter?'" *Journal of International Economics* 56:2 (2002): 299–327.

Mullineux, A.W. *The Business Cycle After Keynes: A Contemporary Analysis.* Brighton, UK: Wheatsheaf, 1984.

Stock and Bond Capitalization

In microeconomics, stock and bond capitalization represents the ways that a business enterprise can commence, continue, or grow its operations. The way a company gets the funds needed to operate is called its means of capitalization. These means fall into three general categories: self-financing, debt financing, and equity financing.

As the name implies, self-financing means that the firm's proprietor or proprietors provide all of the financing themselves. Typical with start-up companies—which are small, require little capital, and lack a business record that would allow them to secure financing from other individuals and institutions—self-financing has the advantage of giving the proprietor complete control of the firm's management and operations. The disadvantages come in the relatively limited supply of capital available and the great risk to the proprietor of being solely responsible for the company's financial success. Self-financing means that the proprietor must finance the company with his or her own funds or through the profits the enterprise makes.

A proprietor who seeks to expand operations but still retain full control of the company can use debt financing, which can take two forms. One way is simply to borrow money from a financial institution, such as a bank or credit union. In the case of sole proprietorship, the individual doing the borrowing is then liable for the debt; thus, even a proprietor's personal assets can be taken by the lender in the case of the company's bankruptcy. For that reason, many proprietors incorporate. This makes the corporation alone liable for the debts, leaving the personal assets of the corporation's owner or owners protected. In most cases, small corporations retain all of their shares internally—that is, the shares are owned by the proprietor or proprietors. However, in most cases, even when the firm is incorporated, banks require personal guarantees from the owners to lend funds to the firm. Incorporation does prevent the owner's personal assets from being at risk from a lawsuit against the firm.

A company may also secure capitalization through the issuance of bonds. In essence, a bond is a financial instrument that requires the issuer to pay back the principal of the bond, plus interest, over a given period of time. The terms of the bond, the record of the company, and the guarantees for paying back the bond determine the interest rate. In general, a bond's interest rate goes up with the perception of risk of nonrepayment attached to it. Bonds tend to vary in their rates more than bank loans, where government regulations and bank policy determine rates.

A third means of capitalization is equity financing. Rather than borrowing money from a bank or through the issuance of bonds, equity financing involves selling partial or full ownership rights—in the form of stock shares—to outsiders. Selling shares in a company turns it into a publicly owned firm. This dilutes the authority of the proprietor, who must answer to the shareholders. Moreover, publicly owned corporations must abide by government regulations and laws that require them to operate in a more transparent fashion than is the case with a sole proprietorship, which only requires the owner to divulge financial information to tax authorities and to holders of company debt.

In general, both financing through bonds and equity sales involve large enterprises and are usually conducted through institutions that specialize in the business of capitalization, such as investment banks. Not only do investment banks market the bonds and shares and provide expertise in the tax and legal complexities of bond and equity financing, but they often underwrite the sale as well, by directly purchasing the newly issued stocks and bonds and then marketing them. In this respect, the underwriter bears the risk that the instruments will not sell for as high a price as expected.

Most large companies finance their operations in various ways simultaneously—equity and bond sales, and loans. A company that does so is said to have both debt and equity capitalization. The relative amount of debt and equity capitalization is known as the debt-to-equity ratio, which often determines the financial viability of the company. An inordinately low debt-to-equity ratio may mean that the company is not adequately leveraging its assets and could be underperforming, which can affect its share value. An extremely high ratio can put a strain on a company's capital flow, meaning that too much of its revenue is obligated to servicing its debts.

In the case of very large corporations, management and ownership are separated. The owners of the company hire managers or executives who run the day-to-day operations and even conduct long-term strategy, though the latter is usually conducted in coordination with the owners, who have the ultimate decision-making power. (Of course, managers themselves may own shares, making them partial owners.) Moreover, in large corporations, ownership may be so dispersed that the shareholders elect a board of directors to work with management in fashioning long-term company strategy.

Such structures of ownership and management allow for the smooth operation of vast enterprises with widely dispersed ownership, as is the case with most large corporations. During periods of economic expansion, there is usually little tension between shareholders, boards of directors, and management. Executives receive bonuses—often in the form of shares or share options, which allow them to buy shares in the future at a specified price—while both the boards of directors and shareholders receive positive returns on their investment. When a company starts to perform poorly, tensions can arise as shareholders, who are losing money on their equity stakes, begin to chafe at the bonuses earned by managers—bonuses that are often agreed upon by boards of directors in consultation with the managers themselves.

James Ciment

See also: Capital Market; Corporate Finance; Debt; Savings and Investment.

Further Reading

Baskin, Jonathan Barron. *A History of Corporate Finance.* New York: Cambridge University Press, 1997.

Haas, Jeffrey J. *Corporate Finance in a Nutshell.* St. Paul, MN: Thomson/West, 2004.

Stock Market Crash (1929)

The largest decline in publicly traded securities prices in modern history, the stock market crash of late 1929 wiped out billions of dollars in paper fortunes before triggering a larger economic downturn that would plunge the United States and much of the industrialized world into the worst depression of the twentieth century. The crash followed an unprecedented run-up in stock valuation in the late 1920s—valuation that ran far ahead of the underlying worth of the securities being traded. Economic historians cite this securities bubble, fueled by loose credit, as the major cause of the crash. At the same, experts argue that it was deeper problems in the economy that translated a downturn in securities prices into a major economic collapse. While the U.S. economy would gradually recover through New Deal stimulus spending, the massive defense expenditures of World War II, and pent-up demand after the war, the Dow Jones Industrial Average (DJIA), a key index of thirty major industrial stocks, did not reach its pre-1929 crash level until 1954.

1920s Economic Growth

By many but not all measures, the U.S. economy in the 1920s was strong and stable. Significant gains in productivity—a result of breakthroughs in communication, electrification, and transportation—were coupled with strong consumer demand, as Americans bought a host of newly available, mass-produced items such as radios and automobiles. This combination of circumstances produced an economy marked by low unemployment and inflation but solid growth. However, there were still significant weaknesses in the U.S. economy, mainly in agriculture and declining industrial sectors such as coal (hit by competition from petroleum) and railroads (facing competition from automobiles, buses, and trucks). The greatest weakness, according to some economists, was the growing disparity in income and wealth. Much of the economic gain of the decade accrued to the top 10 percent of the population, with the lion's share going to the wealthiest 1 percent. The latter saw its share of national income climb from 12 to 34 percent between 1919 and 1929, the fastest gain in American history. And even as their income increased, their taxes went down. Thus, by 1929, the top 1 percent of the population owned more than 44 percent of nation's financial wealth, while the bottom 87 percent owned just 8 percent.

The wealth accruing to the top income earners had to go somewhere. A portion of it went toward conspicuous consumption, contributing to the ebullient culture of the Roaring Twenties. But most of it was invested, much of it in speculative pursuits. Through the early years of the decade, a significant portion of this money went into real estate, driving up land, housing, and commercial building values to record highs. Suburbs blossomed across the country as the automobile-owning middle class sought refuge from cities overcrowded with immigrants. In certain areas of the country, such as Southern California and South Florida, the real-estate boom led to bubble economies that, in the case of Florida, came crashing down by the middle years of the decade. However, even in less expansive regions of the country, real-estate values began to stagnate and even decline after 1927.

Contributing to the real-estate boom were the monetary policies of the U.S. Federal Reserve (Fed). To help purge the economy of post–World War I inflation, the Fed dramatically hiked the interest rate it charged on loans to member banks, helping to trigger a deep recession in 1921–1922. As the economy came out of that recession, however, economists noted that solid growth was not accompanied by inflation, permitting the Fed to drop interest rates, thus making credit cheaper and more available to real-estate buyers and speculators. After real-estate gains stalled in the mid-1920s, the Fed loosened the spigots even more, dropping interest rates further.

Stock Market Bubble

Virtually all economists agree that the low-interest, expansive money policies of the Fed helped fuel the dramatic run-up in securities prices in the late 1920s. The solid economic growth of the general economy contributed as well. The gains in productivity and a wave of corporate mergers helped push the Dow Jones Industrial Average (DJIA), an indicator measuring the collective performance of thirty major stocks traded on the an unprecedented number to that time, had done exactly that.

Making things easier for these investors was the spread of the stock market ticker, which allowed for the instantaneous transmission of stock data throughout the country and the practice of margin buying. With interest rates low and credit easy to come by, brokerage houses began to allow customers to buy stocks with a down payment rather than the full price, sometimes as low as 10 percent. To make up the other 90 percent of the purchase price, the brokers lent money, which they themselves had borrowed from banks, to stock purchasers, who secured the loans using the collateral in the rising equity of the stocks themselves. These practices are illegal now—many made so by regulations and laws passed in response to the 1929 crash—but it was not illegal in the 1920s. Indeed, there was almost no regulation of the securities industry; even commercial banks were allowed to invest assets—that is, depositors' money—in securities, even of the riskiest sort. Among the most popular of these stocks were high-profile "blue chips," which were perceived as being on the economic edge. RCA, the highest flying of the stocks, saw its share price rise from $20 in 1927 to nearly $120 on the eve of the great crash in October 1929.

Downturn and Crash

It all worked smoothly as long as share prices continued to rise. By 1929, however, share valuations for many companies were far in excess of underlying worth, as measured by price-to-earnings (P/E) figures, the most widely used measure of the ratio between the stock price and corporate net income, or profit. While the historical average for the S&P 500, a much broader index than the DJIA, was about 16:1 for the years 1925–1975, the P/E ratio stood at 32:1 at the height of the 1929 boom. Not only were investors paying too much for share prices in 1929, they were also ignoring underlying problems in the economy.

By 1927, economic growth was beginning to

TAIL HOLT

Pulitzer Prize–winning cartoonist Rollin Kirby was one of the few to perceive that the stock market was out of control in 1929. His depiction of a runaway bear pulling along a helpless investor was prescient. The cartoon appeared three weeks before the crash. *(The Granger Collection, New York)*

New York Stock Exchange, dramatically upward, as it doubled from a low of just above 60 at the tail end of the 1921–1922 recession to a high of about 125 at the beginning of 1925, surpassing the previous high of nearly 120 in 1920. By the beginning of 1927, the Dow had climbed to about 160, a rise of 33 percent in two years. Nevertheless, these gains would pale in comparison to what happened over the following two years and eight months, as the DJIA climbed to 200 by the end of 1927, 300 by the end of 1928, and 381.17 at its peak close on September 3, 1929.

Fueling the run-up was a boom in stock trading, as middle- and even working-class investors tried to get their share of rising returns on securities, especially as the press began to play up stories about the huge profits being made on Wall Street and offering advice on how average citizens could make their own fortunes. By the height of the boom in 1929, about 1 million Americans, slow, as consumers began to spend less, bogged down by increasing debt, stagnant income, and a dearth of new products to capture their interest. As demand slackened, retail and wholesale inventories grew, reducing manufacturers' orders, sending unemployment creeping higher, further depressing demand. Already saddled with a number of sagging sectors, the economy became further burdened by a slowdown in construction, a major engine of growth in the early and middle 1920s.

By early September 1929, these weaknesses were beginning to be felt on Wall Street, as the DJIA stalled and then began to fall. After a slight recovery in early October, stock prices began to go down again, with the biggest losses hitting what had been the highest-flying stocks—General Electric, Westinghouse, and Montgomery Ward among them. The media, always looking for a new angle, began to play up the new "bear market," contributing to the growing panic among investors. Then came the crash. Over a series of "black" days in late October, the DJIA began to plunge by dozens of points. On October 23 alone, known as Black Wednesday, the DJIA lost 7.5 percent of its value, falling from 415 to 384 in one trading session. In October, total U.S. stock market valuation plummeted from $87 billion to $55 billion (or about $1.8 trillion to $685 billion in 2008 dollars). Since rising stock equity was the key to margin buying, the loss of equity sent investors and brokers scrambling to get loans paid back, forcing people to dump stocks as fast as they could, sending prices down even faster and pushing many brokers and even some banks into insolvency.

The largest investment banks made efforts to shore up stock prices with highly publicized block purchases, but the bear market was too fierce. Subsequent months did bring rallies as investors thought the worst was over—one in early 1930 sent the DJIA from just under 200 back to near 300—but the gains inevitably were undermined by growing investor pessimism. Moreover, by this point, the underlying weaknesses in the economy were beginning to be felt. Bankruptcies increased rapidly, as did unemployment. By the depths of

the Great Depression in early 1933, the DJIA had plunged nearly 90 percent, from just over 381 to just over 41. By that time, U.S. stock valuation had plunged to less than $10 billion. Not until November 23, 1954, more than a quarter-century later, would the DJIA climb above where it had closed at its peak in September 1929.

The more than 22 percent drop in the DJIA on Black Monday, October 19, 1987, was nearly twice the biggest one-day loss during the 1929 crash—that of October 28, when the index fell by just under 13 points—but nothing in the history of Wall Street would ever again equal the cumulative losses of the great crash of 1929 and the early 1930s. Nor would the impact of subsequent crashes on Wall Street ever have such a wide and long-lasting impact on the general economy of the United States and the world.

James Ciment

See also: Asset-Price Bubble; Boom, Economic (1920s); Great Depression (1929–1933); New York Stock Exchange.

Further Reading

Galbraith, John Kenneth. *The Great Crash, 1929*. Boston: Houghton Mifflin, 1997.

Klein, Maury. *Rainbow's End: The Crash of 1929*. New York: Oxford University Press, 2001.

Klingaman, William K. *1929: The Year of the Great Crash*. New York: Harper & Row, 1989.

Thomas, Gordon, and Max Morgan-Witts. *The Day the Bubble Burst: A Social History of the Wall Street Crash of 1929*. New York: Penguin, 1980.

Wigmore, Barrie A. *The Crash and Its Aftermath: A History of Securities Markets in the United States, 1929–1933*. Westport, CT: Greenwood, 1985.

Stock Market Crash (1987)

On Monday, October 19, 1987, the Dow Jones Industrial Average (DJIA), a leading index of U.S. stock market prices, fell by 508 points and lost 22.6 percent of its total value. It was the largest one-day percentage drop in U.S. stock market history. The events of "Black Monday," as it came to be called, caused panic on Wall Street and in stock markets around the world as images of the Great Depression of the 1930s were played up by the media, leading to greater fear of investing in stocks. The market crash precipitated major declines in foreign markets. By the end of October, stock markets in Hong Kong had fallen 45.8 percent, Australia 41.8 percent, the United Kingdom 26.4 percent, and Canada 22.5 percent. In the United States, the overall net loss in market capitalization of all stocks has been estimated at half a trillion dollars.

Economists define a market crash as an event whereby the stock market experiences a sudden, rapid, and significant decline in stock prices. It can be caused by a number of factors, including major national or international crises, lack of accurate market information, or irrational or uninformed actions of investors or speculators who distort the true value of stocks and send panic throughout the financial community. When investors react to negative news or fears of an economic or financial crisis, selling activity increases, and the overall market suffers through a loss in overall value.

The Black Monday Crisis

Before trading began in New York on October 19, stock markets in Tokyo and Europe declined when, for reasons still being debated among economists and financial analysts, U.S. investors began selling prior to the opening of the market in New York. However, the high level of stock market volatility and the unprecedented magnitude of the 508-point drop in the Dow on Black Monday were generally unexpected.

During the crisis of October 19, 1987, the New York Stock Exchange (NYSE) considered taking the unusual step of halting trading but determined that such an action could increase investor panic and produce greater selling activity. The severity of the crisis was revealed later that day when stocks stopped trading because of the overwhelming amount of sell orders. The halt in trading occurred because certain specialist firms

on the exchange—which, because of their great liquidity, generally can maintain orderly markets by buying and selling in specific stocks during volatile conditions even when there is no other market for a given stock—were now simply overwhelmed and found themselves without adequate capital resources to continue to maintain a market. Stock options and futures trading also deteriorated as the underlying securities tied to the options and futures had ceased to trade.

On Tuesday, October 20, the NYSE opened in hopes that the panic would subside, but the trading crisis continued. By noon, many stocks had stopped trading due to a lack of buy orders. The drop in the price of stocks caused banks to stop extending credit to securities dealers. Unlike the 1929 crash, however, some stability took hold later in the afternoon, and buying outweighed selling for the remainder of the session. By the end of the day, even though some indices still were down, the DJIA closed up an impressive 102 points (5.88 percent) and posted a gain of 186 points on Thursday, October 22.

Government Intervention

To avoid continued losses and any further disintegration of the stock market, the Federal Reserve Bank of New York (the leading branch of the U.S. central bank) took steps to provide credit and liquidity to the securities dealers through an infusion of cash. This was accomplished by taking the necessary actions to lower short-term interest rates on government securities. As a result, cheaper credit became available to securities dealers, easing their concerns about the market and helping to spur increased buying activity. This, in turn, boosted the Dow Jones Industrial Index and, in effect, saved the world's financial markets from further disaster.

Causes of the Crash

In late October 1987, Nicholas Brady, a former Wall Street investment banker and New Jersey senator, was appointed chair of the Presidential

The stock market crash of Monday, October 19, 1987, was a global event, starting in Hong Kong and spreading like a seismic wave through Europe to North America. The Dow Jones Industrial Average lost nearly a quarter of its value that day—a record. *(Hulton Archive/Getty Images)*

Task Force on Market Mechanisms, an investigative commission formed to examine and report on the causes of the crash and suggest regulatory safeguards as necessary. The Brady Commission report of January 1988 concluded that the chief cause of Black Monday was the poor performance of financial specialists. Some brokers on the Big Board had helped fuel the crash by not having accurate, up-to-date information on the state of the market. Their picture of market conditions, which was far worse than was actually the case, caused them to erroneously sell more stock than they bought.

Specifically, the Brady report faulted two groups of Wall Street specialists, portfolio insurers and speculators, who acted at cross-purposes and in ways that accelerated the crash. Portfolio insurers protect the prices of specified stocks when prices fall below a certain point by selling them as futures to speculators. Speculators buy those stocks as futures in the hope that their price will rebound and they can then sell them back at a profit. Portfolio

insurers, by facilitating this process, can help stabilize the price of stocks—unless they sell off too many stock futures in a short amount of time.

The Brady Commission concluded that "a few portfolio insurers" sold futures equivalent to just under $400 million in stocks in the first half hour of futures trading on Black Monday. The unprecedented intensity of futures activity generated fear in the market and led to widespread sell-off of many stocks, which, in turn, caused stock prices to decline precipitously.

Finally, the report also faulted the lack of safeguards in place for new trading technologies, including computer-driven, automatic trading. Many larger investment institutions had created computer programs designed to sell off stock in large batches automatically when certain marketplace conditions, such as those on Black Monday, are in place. Much of the supposed emotional "panic selling" of the stock market crash was in fact done by cold, calculating machines.

Not all economists and investors subscribed

to the Brady report or at least not completely. These skeptics cited longer-term causes, putting the origins of the crash at the beginning of the 1980s bull market, when the Dow rose from 776 points in August 1982 to a high of 2,722 points in August 1987. The stock market was overvalued and has been described by some analysts as having been an accident waiting to happen.

In response to the crash, the New York Stock Exchange undertook a number of reforms, such as banning esoteric trading strategies and instituting careful monitoring of electronic trading. Under the new rules, if the DJIA fell by more than 250 points in a day, program trading was prohibited for a time, thus allowing brokers time to contact each other, regroup, and reevaluate the market. In the wake of Black Monday, many computer programs added built-in stopping points. Limits to program trading were removed on November 2, 2007. However, circuit breakers that halted all market trading remained in force. Circuit breakers were originally triggered by a given point fall in the DJIA. As the DJIA increased dramatically, a given point reduction was recognized as sufficient because such a reduction, to be meaningful, was dependent on the overall level of the market. After several iterations of the system, a percentage decline process was adopted under which circuit-breaker halts in trading would be established. Currently, there are circuit breakers in place that halt all market trading on any day under the following circumstances: if the DJIA falls 10 percent, trading on the NYSE is halted for one hour; if the DJIA falls 20 percent, trading is halted for two hours; and if the DJIA falls 30 percent, trading is halted for the rest of the day. The actual point drops are revised every quarter based upon the DJIA.

Although many economists feared the crash would trigger a recession, the fallout from the crash was relatively small, in part due to the efforts of the Federal Reserve. It took only two years for the Dow to recover completely, and by September 1989 the market had regained all of the value it had lost in the 1987 crash. This is in stark contrast to how the crisis in mortgage and mortgage-backed securities and collateralized debt obligations spread to the global economy in 2008 and 2009 to cause the severest downturn in economic activity since the Great Depression.

Teresa A. Koncick

See also: Automated Trading Systems; New York Stock Exchange.

Further Reading

Brady, Nicholas F., James C. Cotting, Robert G. Kirby, John R. Opel, and Howard M. Stein. *Report of the Presidential Task Force on Market Mechanisms.* Washington, DC: GPO, January 1988.

Carlson, Mark. *A Brief History of the 1987 Stock Market Crash with a Discussion of the Federal Reserve Response.* Washington, DC: Board of Governors of the Federal Reserve, 2006.

Metz, Tim. *Black Monday: The Stock Market Catastrophe of October 19, 1987.* Washington, DC: Beard Books, 1988.

Stewart, James B., and Daniel Hertzberg. "Terrible Tuesday." *Wall Street Journal,* November 20, 1987.

United States Securities and Exchange Commission (Division of Market Regulation). *The October 1987 Market Break.* Washington, DC: GPO, February 1988.

Stock Markets, Global

Global stock markets are organized exchanges that facilitate the trading of equity shares in corporations globally. Equity shares, or stocks, represent claims to profits of corporations. Shares of stock in corporations also represent voting rights concerning corporate leadership. Global stock markets therefore play a central role in coordinating international production and capital investment.

Capital investment funds the purchase of machinery or other equipment used to make consumer goods. The task of planning global capital investment requires some institutional means of coordinating industrial development among nations. There are two difficult problems with planning industrial development in the modern global economy. First, capital must be divided between nations. Second, the use of capital must be organized or planned within each nation.

These two problems are interrelated because investment plans within nations make sense only in the context of rational division of capital between nations. For example, nations such as the United States and Japan have invested heavily in steel production. The specific plans for investment in the United States and Japanese steel industries make economic sense only if other countries are unable to produce steel more efficiently than the United States or Japan.

Increasing Integration

There has been a trend toward the integration of global stock trading. Perhaps the single most important event in the globalization of stock markets was the fall of the Soviet Union in December 1991. That event allowed for the development of Eastern and Central European stock markets. There has been greater development of stock markets outside of the former Soviet bloc nations as well. The older, more traditional stock exchanges in Western Europe, the United States, and Japan have extended trading beyond their borders. Established stock exchanges often list foreign companies and sell stock to foreign investors.

Also, stock exchanges themselves are becoming more integrated. The NASDAQ exchange (the National Association of Securities Dealers Automated Quotations) and the American Stock Exchange (AMEX) merged in 1998. This merger was undone in 2004. In recent years the Frankfurt Stock Exchange (owned by Deutsche Börse) and NASDAQ both attempted to acquire the London Stock Exchange. While the NASDAQ and Frankfurt mergers failed, the New York Stock Exchange did manage to merge with the Paris-based Euronext exchange in 2006. Modern technology has also made it easier for global investors to buy and sell globally in stock exchanges. While stock exchanges are nowhere near full integration, international financial markets have grown and spread to reach into all but the most remote corners of the world.

Role of Stock Markets

The globalization of investment has been important to economic development. Stock markets play an indispensable role in directing global capital investment. Corporations can raise funds by selling new shares of stock on a stock market or by borrowing money from creditors (that is, bank loans or corporate bonds). Much investment is funded by credit rather than by selling new shares of stock, but stock markets affect credit-financed investment. Stock markets price capital goods in terms of how these goods are put to use by corporations. Since stock earnings and capital gains represent the profits to corporate owners and shareholders, these earnings reflect the success or failure of corporate strategies. Corporations that invest capital efficiently will earn profits and realize capital gains. Stock prices and dividend payments therefore reflect the value of capital as used by any corporation. Stock markets provide information on the relative value of capital as used by different corporations. Data on the relative value of capital is clearly important to decisions to fund corporate investment through credit.

Competition in stock markets can also promote the efficient management of corporations. Stockholders will likely retain executives who deliver high dividends and capital gains. Shareholders will often remove executives who deliver low dividends and capital losses. Also, decreases in stock prices make it easier for new investors to buy up shares of the stock and replace incumbent executives. Stock markets can therefore redirect the use of capital either by replacing failed executives or by redirecting funds.

If global financial markets operated with perfect efficiency, investment funds would always flow to the most productive and lucrative industrial projects. Competition in stock and other financial markets should equalize the productivity of additional capital investment between nations. What this means is that if an additional increment of capital investment delivers more products in Spain than it does in Portugal, then efficient stock markets will indicate higher returns on investment in Spanish industry, and Portugal will lose capital to Spain.

Inefficiencies in Capital Allocation

Historical experience shows that capital does not always flow to its most productive uses. For example, the productivity of additional capital investment in India is fifty-eight times higher than the productivity of additional capital investment in the United States. What this means is that there is so much capital investment in the United States that the returns on additional capital investment are small. Since people in the United States have already invested heavily to develop areas of potential high productivity, additional investment will not increase the production of goods much more. The relative lack of capital in India, as well as in other less developed nations, means that they have yet to develop many high-productivity areas of their economies. Perfectly efficient global financial markets would redirect some capital from nations with more advanced economies, such as the United States, to less-developed nations, such as India. But capital remains concentrated in relatively few advanced industrial nations.

One possible explanation for the lack of investment in many nations is that stock markets work imperfectly. One of the more common criticisms of stock markets is that they are subject to speculative booms and crashes. While it is obvious that stock markets have had bullish and bearish periods, this does not necessarily explain chronic problems with global investment. Booms and busts exist in both advanced and less developed nations. It is not at all clear that such cycles in stock exchanges should prevent the flow of capital investment to less developed nations. After all, less developed nations lack capital investment during both booms and busts. It is also not clear that booms and busts are inherent to stock exchanges. Of course, there are many examples of stock market booms and crashes. Stock market booms typically take place during credit expansions by central banks. Cen-

tral banks, like the U.S. Federal Reserve, do not seem to have a direct influence on stock market activity. However, they do exert indirect influence through their influence over interest rates and bond prices. Private investors compare bond rates and returns on stocks. For example, the Federal Reserve expanded the money supply 5.9 percent per year during the economically expansive 1920s and kept interest rates low. Low interest rates on bonds made corporate stocks more attractive to investors, fueling the run-up of stock prices. The Federal Reserve also expanded the money supply and kept interest rates low during the more recent dot.com boom of the late 1990s and the housing boom of the early and mid 2000s, again making stocks more attractive and contributing to inflated prices.

Some economists point to imperfect information and "irrational exuberance" among investors as sources of stock market instability. There is some truth to these claims. However, economists do not expect stock markets to attain perfect results. There are also more plausible explanations for the skewed distribution of global capital. Countries with high taxes, heavy-handed regulation, and corruption tend to have low levels of foreign investment. What this suggests is that global stock markets are working effectively to help investors avoid high taxes and other unnecessary burdens. Efficient stock markets should help investors avoid high-risk investment, and the existence of restrictive regulations and corruption pose real risks to investors. Consequently, the skewed distribution of global capital investment might be due in large part to the efficiency of global stock markets. In other words, the actual source of inefficiency in many less developed nations might be excessive taxes and regulation, and corruption in these nations.

History

To fully understand how stock markets work and the role they play in economic development, it is important to look at their history. Stock markets in cities such as London, Tokyo, Amsterdam, New York, and Frankfurt began as informal local institutions in the seventeenth and eighteenth centuries. Trading of financial securities often began in coffee houses and private clubs. With the passage of time, these early stock markets developed into complex institutions with detailed rules and regulations. Stock exchanges in major cities came to direct capital investment. For example, there is much historical evidence indicating that German stock markets, especially the Frankfurt exchange, contributed greatly to German industrialization. For its part, Belgian industry developed rapidly during the nineteenth century, and Belgium's independence in 1830 was key to its financial and industrial development. Liberalization of the Belgian stock market in 1867 accelerated financial and economic development, including that of the Brussels Stock Exchange, and statistics indicate that this in turn drove the country's industrial development.

The German and Belgian examples are not unique. Many statistical studies show that stock market development facilitates industrial development and long-run economic growth. The spread of stock markets globally has increased capital investment and raised productivity throughout the world. In recent decades many developing nations have formed more advanced financial markets, including stock markets. One study of nine African nations indicates that the development of African stock markets has improved economic development. A study of twenty-one developing nations shows that stock market development increases private investment and contributes to economic growth. Such industrial development has brought about gradual increases in living standards for many poor workers around the world.

Government Investment Alternative

The overall record of privately financed and directed investment indicates that stock and other financial markets play an important role in economic development. Of course, there is an alternative to private financing of capital investment. Governments can fund capital investment though taxes and public borrowing. The overall record of government-funded investment is mixed. Many government projects and programs entail waste and corruption. Government investment often benefits politically connected special-interest groups rather than the general population. Many Western nations have provided direct foreign aid to the developing world. Direct foreign aid projects have tended to deliver poor results. Direct aid by foreign governments often benefits political elites within the recipient nation rather than the general population.

Many government investment projects have funded "prestige projects." One example of a government-funded prestige project is the Apollo project to land a man on the moon. Another example was the development of the Concord, the world's fastest jet airliner. Such projects are a source of national pride and attract much attention, but do little to improve the lives of ordinary people. The past success of private investment in the developed countries, combined with the recent but limited success of private investment in developing nations, indicates that stock exchanges are the most effective means of promoting economic development. Thus, stock exchanges appear to be very important to improving economic conditions in developing nations.

Financial Crisis of Late 2000s

Global stock exchanges were deeply affected by the financial crisis of 2008–2009. There was a sharp decline in stock indices with the onset of the recession in late 2007. Such declines in stock prices are not unusual during recessions. The decline in stock indices worsened as the severity of this financial crisis became apparent. Of course, the biggest losses of equity value were sustained by corporations such as Bear Sterns, Lehman Brothers, Citigroup, AIG, and General Motors, which either experienced losses that threatened their solvency or went bankrupt. One could say that share prices did not reflect the true value of these corporations prior to the crisis. Such inaccuracy in stock price is a sign of stock market inefficiency. However, stock prices were generally inflated during the housing boom, and the stocks of some companies, especially AIG, were weak even before the crisis.

The recent crash is in some sense a correction—a return to more accurate values on stock markets around the world. It does not appear that stock trading itself drove the 2008–2009 crisis. It is rather the case that various government policies and private sector miscalculations in derivative markets caused the global crisis. Of course, there has been a great loss of wealth globally, and it is likely that many stocks have fallen "too far." Given time, stock markets will recover and should continue to regulate global investment and production. (Recovery of stock markets in many countries is well under way in late 2009, at the time of this writing.)

Global stock markets emerged with globalization of industry. The emergence of global organization of production was in fact facilitated by the development of stock markets within nations. In modern times stock markets have themselves become increasingly global. While some people see stock markets as centers for greed and financial manipulation, these markets have contributed greatly to economic development and rising living standards around the world. Stock markets were vitally important to early industrialization in developed countries and have more recently contributed to Eastern European and developing-world industrial development. Economists say that the trend toward globalization of stock and other financial markets is likely to continue, with many concluding that this is a good thing. They argue that the public should welcome the trend toward global stock markets and global finance in general, as financial institutions play an indispensable role in promoting economic efficiency and prosperity.

D.W. MacKenzie

See also: Nasdaq; New York Stock Exchange; Souk al-Manakh (Kuwait) Stock Market Crash (1982).

Further Reading
Atje, R., and B. Jovanovic. 1993. "Stock Markets and Development." *European Economic Review* 37: 632–640.

Barro, R.J. "Economic Growth in a Cross Section of Countries." *Quarterly Journal of Economics* 106:2 (1991): 407–443.

Caporale, G.M., P. Howells, and A. Soliman. "Stock Market Development and Economic Growth: The Causal Linkage." *Journal of Economic Development* 29:1 (June 2004): 33–50.

Demirguch-Kunt, A., and R. Levine. "Stock Market Development and Financial Intermediaries: Stylized Facts." *World Bank Economic Review* 10:2 (1996): 291–321.

El-Erian, M.A., and M. Kumar. "Emerging Equity Markets in the Middle Eastern Countries." IMF Staff Papers 42:2 (1995): 313–343.

Greenwood, J., and B. Smith. "Financial Markets in Development and the Development of Financial Markets." *Journal of Economic Dynamics and Control* 21:1 (January 1997): 145–181.

Levine, R. "Stock Markets, Growth, and Tax Policy." *Journal of Finance* 46:4 (1991): 1445–1465.

Levine, R., and S. Zervos. "Stock Markets, Banks, and Economic Growth" *American Economic Review* 88:3 (1998): 537–558.

Stringham, Edward. "The Emergence of the London Stock Exchange as a Self-Policing Club." *Journal of Private Enterprise* 17:2 (Spring 2002): 1–20.

———. "The Extralegal Development of Securities Trading in Seventeenth-Century Amsterdam." *Quarterly Review of Economics and Finance* 43:2 (2003): 321–344.

Stockholm School

The Stockholm school (Stockholmsskolan, or Swedish school of economics) refers to a group of Swedish economists who, during the 1920s and 1930s, made important contributions to the development of dynamic macroeconomic analysis. The chief contributors to this particular "school" were Erik Lindahl (1891–1960), Gunnar Myrdal (1898–1987), Bertil Ohlin (1899–1979), Erik Lundberg (1907–1989), and Dag Hammarskjöld (1905–1961).

The "Stockholm school" label was not applied to this group of men until 1937. The group was a rather loosely organized group of young economists, leading some other economists to argue about whether or not it constituted a school of thought based around a set of ideas and specific research objectives. If a common theme may be discerned through the Stockholm school economists' work, it was their attention to the interaction between economic variables over different time periods (a process referred to as the theory of dynamic processes). It is possible to identify some similarities between the macroeconomic theories of the Stockholm school and those developed by their contemporary, the British economist John Maynard Keynes. However, the extent to which the economists of the Stockholm school anticipated the central tenets of Keynesian analysis remains a contentious subject.

A key contribution of the Stockholm school was the view that decisions by economic agents (households, businesses, governments, organizations) regarding aggregate savings (S) and investment (I) are inherently forward-looking. The recognition of this fact led them to concentrate on the economic importance of future plans or expectations, and ultimately on the distinction between ex ante calculations and ex post results.

Ex ante calculations (basically, calculations that are made before some specified or relevant time period) refer to the situation whereby economic agents will formulate investment and saving decisions on the basis of expected future incomes. Ex post results (those that are known after the specified or relevant time period) are also important, as they form the basis on which subsequent ex ante calculations will be made.

On first examination, the ex ante–ex post distinction appears to be of little consequence. The crucial importance of these terms emerges, however, once it is understood that, in the real world, households and businesses do *not* possess perfect foresight and so, in all probability, will be mistaken in their expectations. For example, even though households and businesses may expect ex ante savings to equal ex ante investment, there is absolutely no certainty that this will be the case. The fundamental difference between subjective forecasts (expectations) and real-world

outcomes (realizations) therefore has important economic implications. Indeed, the Stockholm school regarded anticipations and expectations as the fundamental forces that drove the dynamic process forward. This idea can be explained in the following example.

First, let us assume that there is an ex ante imbalance between savings and investment (in other words, that the ex ante amount of aggregate savings is not equal to the amount of planned investment). This inequality would set in motion important dynamic processes as actual investment, actual savings, and actual income would clearly differ from expected investment, expected savings, and expected income.

Let us now take the scenario in which there is an excess of ex ante investment over savings (*ex ante I > S*). Assuming that there are sufficient unemployed factors of production, this would generate an expansion of the economy, associated with the upswing of the cycle. This upswing, however, would be expected to bring about additional savings through increases in profits and incomes. The result would be that ex post savings would equal investment. Let us now take the opposite scenario, where there is an excess of ex ante savings over investment (*ex ante S > I*). Here the economy would experience a contraction, as businesses and households would find themselves with lower-than-expected profits and incomes. This would clearly be associated with the downswing of the cycle. Once again, however, we must recognize the other forces at play here. As businesses would be unable to sell what they had already produced, they would be forced to reduce their investments. The consequence would be that ex post savings would again equal investment. It can therefore be seen that, in either scenario, a disparity between ex ante savings and investment would set into motion processes that would develop into an ex post equality between the two.

Beyond these general points, it becomes difficult to identify any clear central message within the work of the Stockholm school. Its members never provided a well-defined theory of the movement of the business cycle. One of the key reasons for this was that while the members of Stockholm school sought to highlight the importance of dynamic macroeconomic processes, the economic theories that they constructed proved extremely difficult to analyze. This meant that instead of presenting a detailed examination of the complete movement of the cycle, they were forced to concentrate on a number of separate examples that provided only possible interpretations of the expansion and contraction phases. Having said this, the members of the Stockholm school expressed an interest in policy matters and advocated the use of both fiscal and monetary policies as a means of stabilizing the fluctuation of the cycle. Several members were involved with the Committee on Unemployment, a Swedish government–appointed committee that lasted from 1927 to 1935. Yet due to their inability to fully analyze their own economic system, the Stockholm school possessed no rigid policy prescription regarding the use of stabilizing policies. This led them to argue that the use of different policy measures depended very much on the economic conditions prevailing at a given moment in time.

It is a curious situation that the obvious strengths associated with its ideas of dynamic processes ultimately served to undermine the overall success of the Stockholm school. Put simply, the members of the school did not possess the necessary analytical methods that would enable them to fully examine the interconnections between the various parts of the economic system that they had constructed. Perhaps as a consequence their ideas never formed the basis, in Sweden or elsewhere, for further research into either business cycle theory or stabilization policy.

The Stockholm school did not survive very much beyond the late 1930s, as the young members of the group moved on to other intellectual pursuits. For example, Ohlin served as leader of the Swedish Liberal Party from 1944 to 1967; Myrdal held various economic and political appointments before winning the Nobel Prize in economics in 1974, while Hammarskjöld was elected secretary

general of the United Nations in 1952 (and was posthumously awarded the Nobel Peace Prize in 1961). Lindahl was the only member of the school to pursue an academic career.

Christopher Godden

See also: Keynes, John Maynard; Lundberg, Erik Filip; Myrdal, Gunnar; Sweden.

Further Reading

Hansson, Berg. *The Stockholm School and the Development of Dynamic Method.* London: Croom Helm, 1982.

Laidler, David. *Fabricating the Keynesian Revolution: Studies of the Inter-war Literature on Money, the Cycle, and Unemployment.* Cambridge, UK: Cambridge University Press, 1999.

Patinkin, Don. "On the Relation between Keynesian Economics and the Stockholm School." *Scandinavian Journal of Economics* (1978): 135–143.

Siven, Claes-Henric. "The End of the Stockholm School." *Scandinavian Journal of Economics* 87:4 (1985): 577–593.

Subsidies

Subsidies are government payments to firms or households for the purposes of the lowering the cost of production or encouraging the consumption of goods. Subsides come in two basic types: direct and indirect. Direct subsides include transfers of money to producers and consumers. Farm, research, and export subsidies go to the former and food stamps, rent support, and scholarships to the latter. Direct subsidies may come in the form of cash payments or loans at below-market interest rates. Indirect subsidies, which typically are much more valuable overall than direct subsidies but do not involve transfers of money from governments to households and firms, include things such as copyright and patent protections, tariffs and other trade barriers, and most important, tax deductions, deferments, and rebates.

Governments offer different kinds of subsidies for different reasons. Subsidies to households are usually, but not always, offered to persons near or below the poverty line. They are usually made for reasons of social equity; the argument is that wealthy industrial societies have the resources to make sure that all of citizens have food, shelter, and the other basic necessities of life. In the United States, there are both direct (rent support, welfare, food stamps) and indirect subsidies to poorer households. One of the most significant indirect subsidies is the earned income tax credit, a refund on payroll taxes for workers who are supporting children and other dependent minors. However, it is more likely to be middle- and upper-income households who take advantage of perhaps the largest indirect subsidy in the U.S. economy, the deduction on mortgage payments on primary residences. Even in poorer countries, governments often offer subsidies to bring down the cost of basic necessities. This is done for reasons of social equity but also social peace. In a place where a majority of the people live at the poverty level, cutting off such subsidies can lead to great political instability.

Governments give direct and indirect subsidies to firms for various reasons but usually to encourage desirable economic activity. Copyright and patent protection, for instance, provide incentives for innovation, as do research subsidies. Depreciation allowances, which allow companies to write off the cost of equipment, are designed in part to encourage new investment, as is the lower tax rate on capital gains versus earned income. Farm supports are meant to assure a secure supply of domestically grown food and to keep rural economies afloat.

Economic Impact

Subsidies have a direct impact—sometimes intended and sometimes not—on the functioning of the marketplace. Subsidies to producers increase supply and, all other things being equal, lower the cost of a given good. Subsidies to households increase demand and, again, if all things are equal, can lead to higher prices. In both cases, subsidies create a new price equilibrium of supply and demand that is different from where it would have been if market forces had been left to operate on their own. Free-market-oriented economists usually consider subsidies to be a bad thing, as they distort the smooth functioning of the marketplace through the creation of nonmarket incentives and penalties. Moreover, export subsidies and tariffs also disrupt normal trading patterns, whereby goods are made where production is most efficient.

Subsidies can also have an effect on a country's macroeconomy. By offering generous subsidies, particularly in times of economic crisis, governments are usually forced to borrow money. This can lead to higher interest rates, which make it more difficult for private industry to obtain the funds needed to operate and expand. Deficits can also endanger a government's ability to borrow abroad, which is critical for development in poorer countries. Consequently, multilateral lenders, such as the World Bank and the International Monetary Fund, usually insist on subsidy reduction or elimination for basic necessities before extending new loans to heavily indebted countries.

More Keynesian-oriented economists argue that market forces alone do not always produce healthy equilibriums of supply and demand. Indeed, for a variety of reasons involving the fact that wages and prices do not always adjust smoothly to changes in supply and demand, an equilibrium may be reached at a low supply/low demand level, accompanied by high unemployment and less than maximum utilization of production facilities. To lift that equilibrium to a level at which unemployment falls and productive capacity gets utilized, governments use fiscal policy—direct and indirect subsidies in the form of tax cuts and spending—to bolster supply and demand.

These differing views on subsidies are reflected in the contentious political debate that surrounds them. Various countries take different views on subsidies; in general, European countries tend to be more generous in the direct subsidies they offer to households, while the United States usually emphasizes indirect subsidies in the form of lower taxes. Even within countries, there is much debate over subsidies, with liberals generally favoring more generous household subsidies and conservatives opposing them. In most industrialized countries, producer subsidies generally enjoy more bipartisan support, first because of the argument that they create jobs and second because they often have powerful interest groups fighting for them. That is, once a subsidy is created, an interest group develops around it. That interest group will fight for the subsidy vigorously, while opposition to the subsidy remains more diffuse.

History of Subsidies

Subsidies are as old as government itself. The government of ancient Rome is said to have maintained peace and order in an inequitable society through "bread and circuses," that is, subsidies on food and the provision of free or low-cost diversions. Since medieval times in the West, governments have offered direct subsidies to individuals—albeit parsimonious ones—through the poorhouse. Countries also offered producer subsidies. Among the best known was the land grants the U.S. federal government offered to railroads in the nineteenth century to get them to build lines in the sparsely populated territories and states of the West.

By the late nineteenth and early twentieth centuries, however, there was a growing consensus that government subsidies to the poor were the right thing to do not only to ensure social peace but also to ensure social equity. From its beginning in 1916, the U.S. income tax was meant to tax the well-off more than the poor, partly in order to provide services to the latter. The Great Depression and the manifest suffering it created provided the great impetus for more direct subsidies to individuals and households; among them were jobs programs and welfare payments, though the welfare program did not really become significant until after World War II.

The Great Depression also saw the introduction of federal farm subsidies on a large scale.

However, it was World War II that truly provided the impetus for producer subsidies, largely in the defense sector. In addition, by the early post–World War II era, most governments, including that of the United States, had accepted the Keynesian logic of using subsidies to prevent economies from sinking into recession, where the supply and demand equilibrium resulted in low production and high unemployment. In short, subsidies had become a major tool in the government's effort to smooth out the business cycle.

By the 1980s, however, a new, conservative paradigm arose, particularly in the United States and the United Kingdom, that argued that direct subsidies to households, particularly low-income ones, had a negative effect on society, discouraging people from participating in the marketplace by offering them alternatives to work, and thereby encouraging a "culture of dependence." At the same time, conservatives argued, indirect subsidies (largely in the form of lower taxes) to firms and to the wealthy individuals who provided much of the investment capital in the United States would create accelerated economic growth that would benefit all of society—the so-called supply side"economics argument.

More recent events have prompted a great debate over subsidies. The U.S. war in Iraq, which many believe was fought in part to secure access to critical Middle Eastern energy supplies, demonstrated to many that oil enjoyed a massive subsidy in the form of defense outlays and that these outlays distorted the market, making oil appear cheaper than alternative energy sources. An increased awareness of climate change has also led many to believe that industries responsible for the release of large amounts of carbon dioxide, the chief component of the greenhouse gases that are raising global temperatures, are not paying their fair share for the damage that atmospheric carbon dioxide causes. In other words, they are receiving an indirect subsidy, leading many policy makers to advocate various schemes to address that problem, including fines and taxes, or the more market-oriented cap-and-trade policy.

The recession and financial crisis of 2007–2009 have highlighted the costs of subsidies to the housing and financial sector. Most obvious were the bailouts of financial institutions orchestrated by the United States and other industrialized countries in the wake of the financial market meltdown of September 2008. While most economists agree that the infusion of massive amounts of money—nearly a trillion dollars in the United States alone—was necessary to provide the liquidity banks needed to stay afloat, start lending again, and keep economies from collapsing, they worry about the effects of bailout in terms of moral hazard. That is, they are concerned that aiding banks in this crisis will lead them to act recklessly in the future since they will come to believe that, no matter how risky their behavior, they will be bailed out again.

There are also less obvious and more indirect subsidies that contributed to the crisis, particularly in the housing sector, where the financial meltdown began. One was the above-mentioned mortgage interest tax deduction, which provided a nonmarket incentive for people to buy homes as opposed to renting since they would get a large rebate on their taxes for buying. This helped drive up both demand and prices. In addition, Washington, in effect, backstopped the two government-sponsored enterprises—the Federal National Mortgage Association (Fannie Mae) and the Federal Home Loan Mortgage Corporation (Freddie Mac)—allowing them to insure subprime mortgages to less creditworthy individuals. This helped lead to increasingly reckless lending by financial institutions that left them vulnerable to a drop in housing prices or a rise in unemployment. When both of those occurred, foreclosures mounted, and banks found themselves with lots of nonproducing assets that jeopardized their solvency.

To remedy the crisis, the Barack Obama administration introduced a number of new subsides of its own. In March 2010, for instance, it put out a plan to refinance mortgages when foreclosure was likely, particularly for those borrowers whose homes were worth less than the amount initially borrowed to pay for them.

James Ciment

See also: Fiscal Policy; Political Theories and Models; Tax Policy.

Further Reading

Anderson, Kym. *Distortions to Agricultural Incentives: A Global Perspective, 1955–2007.* New York: Palgrave Macmillan, 2009.

Barth, James R. *The Rise and Fall of the U.S. Mortgage and Credit Markets: A Comprehensive Analysis of the Market Meltdown.* Hoboken, NJ: John Wiley & Sons, 2009.

Laffont, Jean-Jacques. *Incentives and Political Economy.* New York: Oxford University Press, 2000.

Sawyer, James E. *Why Reaganomics and Keynesian Economics Failed.* New York: St. Martin's, 1987.

Van Beers, Ceesm and André de Moor. *Public Subsidies and Policy Failures: How Subsidies Distort the Natural Environment, Equity and Trade, and How to Reform Them.* Northampton, MA: Edward Elgar, 2001.

Zahariadis, Nikolaos. *State Subsidies in the Global Economy.* New York: Palgrave Macmillan, 2008.

Summers, Lawrence (1954–)

One of the most influential U.S. economic policy makers of the late-twentieth and early-twenty-first centuries, Lawrence Summers served as both deputy secretary and secretary of the Treasury in the Bill Clinton administration and director of the National Economic Council, a White House advisory group, in the Barack Obama administration. A controversial figure, Summers has been a strong advocate of financial deregulation and free markets, which has led to charges that he bears a significant share of the blame for the financial crisis that enveloped the global economy beginning in 2007.

Born in Connecticut in 1954, Summers comes from one of the most illustrious lineages in modern American academics; his father, Robert, was a celebrated economic theorist at the University of Pennsylvania, and his mother, Anita, chaired the Department of Public Policy and Management

Economics. In addition, two of his uncles—Paul Samuelson and Kenneth Arrow—are Nobel Prize–winning economists.

Summers himself was a mathematical prodigy, being accepted at the Massachusetts Institute of Technology at age sixteen; he earned a PhD in economics at Harvard in 1982 and then, a year later, became one of the youngest tenured professors in Harvard University's history. Much of Summers's research has been on the role of taxes in economic growth, where he has argued that corporate and capital gains taxes are both inefficient sources of revenue and poor economic policy and thus should be scaled back.

After a brief stint in the early 1980s as a member of President Ronald Reagan's Council of Economic Advisers and as an economic adviser to the unsuccessful Democratic presidential candidate Michael Dukakis in 1988, Summers left Harvard to serve as chief economist for the World Bank. There, in one of a number of controversial statements that has marked his public career, Summers suggested in an internal memo that it made economic sense to ship toxic wastes to underdeveloped countries, though he later claimed the remark was meant to be sardonic.

In 1993, incoming President Bill Clinton appointed Summers deputy secretary of the Treasury under the latter's longtime mentor, Robert Rubin. Given a portfolio that emphasized international economic issues, Summers was an advocate of privatization and liberalization of economies that had long been heavily state directed, such as those of Russia and Mexico.

With his appointment to succeed Rubin as Treasury secretary in 1999, Summers pushed for deregulation in a number of industries and hailed the passage of the Financial Services Modernization Act of 1999, which overturned New Deal–era legislation—specifically, the Glass-Steagall Act of 1933, which prevented commercial banks from dealing in insurance and investment banking.

With the inauguration of George W. Bush in January 2001, Summers left government service to take up the post of president of Harvard Univer-

Lawrence Summers, a former chief economist at the World Bank, Treasury secretary under President Bill Clinton, and president of Harvard University, returned to Washington as part of Barack Obama's economic team but was criticized for his ties to Wall Street. (Mark Wilson/Getty Images)

sity. His five years there were marked by a series of controversies, including his public criticism of noted African-American scholar Cornel West—Summers suggested that the professor's rap album put the university in a bad light—and his implication that women may be underrepresented in the sciences because of "issues of intrinsic aptitude." Widely criticized by faculty, Summers was all but forced to resign in 2006.

His appointment as Obama's director of the National Economic Council also prompted some controversy, particularly on the political left. Many felt that Summers's strong advocacy of financial deregulation in the Clinton administration, including his support for the overturning of much of Glass-Steagall, made him one of the principal agents of the financial meltdown of 2007–2008. By his critics' reasoning, the deregulation that Summers advocated exposed major commercial banks to the kinds of risks normally associated with the less regulated investment banking and insurance industries.

Specifically, it allowed commercial banks to invest in risky financial derivatives, including mortgage-backed securities. Thus, when those derivatives rapidly lost value beginning in 2007, it left major commercial banks with vast quantities of "toxic" assets on their books, requiring the $700 billion financial bailout orchestrated and implemented by the Bush and Obama administrations.

Critics of the appointment, who included Nobel Prize–winning economists Joseph Stiglitz and Paul Krugman, argued that Obama was now going to be advised on how to get the United States out of the economic mess of financial deregulation by the very man who had vigorously advocated policies that created the mess in the first place. Indeed, Summers's advocacy of tax cuts as the best way to stimulate the economy has run counter to liberal economists' arguments that public spending on infrastructure would be a more effective means to that end.

James Ciment

See also: Liberalization, Financial; National Economic Council; Regulation, Financial; Treasury, Department of the.

Further Reading

"Lawrence H. Summers." *New York Times,* June 9, 2009. Available at http://topics.nytimes.com/topics/reference/timestopics/people/s/lawrence_h_summers/index.html. Accessed September 9, 2009.

Lizza, Ryan. "Inside the Crisis: Larry Summers and the White House Economic Team." *The New Yorker,* October 12, 2009. Available at www.newyorker.com/reporting/2009/10/12/091012fa_fact_lizza. Accessed January 2010.

Scheiber, Noam. "Obama's Choice: The Next Larry Summers . . . or Larry Summers." *The New Republic*, November 5, 2008. Available at www.tnr.com/article/politics/obamas-choice?id=c85b418b-5237-4f54-891f-8385243162bd. Accessed January 2010.

"Summers, Lawrence." Available at U.S. Department of the Treasury Web site, www.ustreas.gov/education/history/secretaries/lhsummers.shtml. Accessed September 9, 2009.

Sunspot Theories

In economics, the term "sunspots" refers to extrinsic random variables—that is, noneconomic factors originating outside the economic system under discussion—that affect the economy. Although it is most often used in this general, figurative sense, the term is a specific reference to nineteenth-century work by British economist William Stanley Jevons (1835–1882), who attempted to construct a model linking the eleven-year cycle of sunspot activity observed by astronomers with the business cycle as measured by economists. No crackpot or fringe thinker, Jevons was one of the fathers of modern macroeconomic theory. Literal sunspots do exist, of course, and the term refers to fluctuating regions of lower surface temperature and high magnetic activity. What astronomers call "space weather"—the environmental conditions in space, such as radiation, ambient plasma, and the activity of magnetic fields—is caused by sunspot activity that follows an eleven-year period called the solar cycle or sunspot cycle.

There are legitimate correlations between the sunspot cycle and certain phenomena on Earth. For example, sunspot peaks tend to precede outbreaks of the flu, as they did before the 1918–1919 Spanish flu pandemic. There appear to be at least two reasons for this connection. First, the increase in solar radiation increases the frequency of mutation, allowing the influenza virus to become a more dangerous type of disease that can break through whatever immunity the human population possesses; and second, the increase in solar radiation adversely affects the human immune system, thereby making humans more susceptible to the flu virus. (In this light, it is worth nothing that the swine flu pandemic of 2009 succeeded the minimum, or trough, of the sunspot cycle by less than one year.)

So the idea that sunspots can have a tangible effect on human economic cycles is not as far-fetched as it might seem, particularly if the relationship is indirect—with sunspot activity affecting agricultural yields, for instance. Jevons introduced his sunspot theory in 1875 and presented it in papers to professional associations of scientists and economists three years later. In the afterglow of his major work, *Principles of Science* (1874), Jevons announced that he had found a correlation between the periodicity (timing and duration) of the business cycle and the periodicity of the solar cycle. His major explanation for this related to agricultural effects of solar activity. Thus, he found first a cycle of European harvest yields and price crises, and later one of Indian harvest yields and import price crises. Based on these observations, his sunspot theory posited that solar-cycle minimums—such as that experienced amid the global financial meltdown in late 2008—correspond to stability and steady economic growth.

In the end, the data simply did not support Jevons's conclusions, at least not in any way he could demonstrate, but his attempts were notable because they marked the first time the business cycle had even been examined in any systematic way. Although economists had been well aware of fluctuations in economic activity and even the way extrinsic events can have economic repercussions through very indirect means, the idea of an actual cycle—a periodicity of economic booms and busts—was both compelling and important.

The figurative use of sunspots was popularized by a 1983 paper titled "Do Sunspots Matter?" by economists David Cass and Karl Shell. The paper referred specifically to random events or conditions—such as actual sunspots—that can have economic effects if and when people *think* they matter. Such beliefs affect consumer and business confidence whether or not the event would otherwise affect the economy. Anticipating the twenty-first-century Keynesian revival, Cass and Shell referred to John Maynard Keynes's "animal spirits" and his rejection of the idea that all economic activity can be explained by rational behavior. Quite to the contrary, in Keynes's view and in that suggested in the Cass and Shell paper, a complete model of the business cycle must account for the irrational, for self-fulfilling prophecies, for manic booms and self-destructive panics, and for the importance of human anticipation, perception, and expectation.

Bill Kte'pi

See also: Jevons, William Stanley; Seasonal Cycles.

Further Reading

Benhabib, Jess, Stephanie Schmitt-Grohe, and Martin Uribe. "The Perils of Taylor Rules." *Journal of Economic Theory* 96:1–2 (2001): 40–69.

Cass, David, and Karl Shell. "Do Sunspots Matter?" *Journal of Political Economy* 91: 21 (1983): 193–227.

Duffy, John, and Eric O. Fisher. "Sunspots in the Laboratory." *American Economic Review* 95:3 (2005): 510–529.

Sweden

The third-largest country in the European Union by territory, with a population of just over 9 million people, Sweden is located in the center of Scandinavia in northern Europe. It has a free-market economy, though one in which the state offers a generous package of social welfare programs, paid for by one of the highest tax rates in the world.

Home to the marauding, trade-oriented Vikings in medieval times, the modern state of Sweden emerged as a unified kingdom in the sixteenth century. Within a century, it had become one of the great powers of Europe, extending its control over most of Scandinavia and the Baltic region. But with its relatively small population, it was unable to maintain its hold over these far-flung lands. By the time of the Napoleonic Wars in the early nineteenth century, it had shrunk back to its present size plus Norway, which won its freedom in 1905.

As the leading power in the Baltic region, Sweden became wealthy through the export of fur, timber, and grain (as Russia had done in the early modern era), and began to industrialize and urbanize in the late nineteenth century. By the early twentieth century, Sweden had built one of the most modern financial systems in the world and had emerged as one of the wealthiest countries in Europe.

The Great Depression, which sent Sweden's economy reeling and produced major social unrest among the hard-hit working classes, led to the 1932 victory of the Social Democratic Party, which began to build the modern social welfare system for which the country is now famous.

Neutral in both world wars, Sweden avoided the widespread destruction visited upon much of the rest of the continent and even prospered by selling resources to both sides. (The Swedes leaned politically toward the Allies and offered political refuge to many people fleeing Nazi oppression.)

As a major industrialized country and one with a rich resource base in timber and iron, Sweden took advantage of the postwar economic boom in Western Europe to establish itself as a leading economic force, with much government direction of the economy, including ownership of certain major industries. At the same time, it continued to build on one of the most generous social safety networks in the world, offering full health care, free education through university, and substantial unemployment benefits for its citizens. These programs all came at the cost of one of the highest tax rates in Europe, with the government's share of the gross domestic product (GDP) approaching 50 percent.

The oil shocks and economic stagnation that gripped much of the industrialized world in the 1970s hit Sweden especially hard, as manufacturing declined and tight regulation of the economy, including strict price controls, hampered efforts toward economic reform. Widespread deregulation and privatization under a center-right coalition of parties in the late 1970s and early 1980s helped revive the economy but, according to many economists, in ways that proved damaging in the long run.

Liberalization of lending laws led to bubbles in the housing and financial sectors that burst during the global recession of the early 1990s. With GDP in serious decline, there was a run on the krona, Sweden's national currency, which forced the Swedish Central Bank to dramatically hike interest rates. Unemployment rose significantly, and GDP fell by some 5 percent in 1992 and 1993. By 1994, the government's budget deficit had reach 15 percent of GDP, a level unmatched since the Great Depression.

In response, Stockholm took a number of measures. It scaled back some of the social welfare benefits its citizens enjoyed and privatized a host of industrial concerns. To integrate its economy with that of the rest of the continent, Sweden joined the European Union in 1995, though it did not adopt the euro as its national currency when other countries did in 2002.

The Swedish government also assumed ownership of about 25 percent of the assets of the country's banks during the crisis, attempting to isolate and then liquidate the bad assets that had caused the nation's credit system to freeze up. In retrospect, according to many economists, the so-called Stockholm solution was the key to Sweden's rapid economic recovery in the late 1990s and early 2000s. Indeed, economic policy makers in the United States and elsewhere cited Sweden's policies in the early 1990s as justification for similar measures to confront the more widespread financial panic of 2008–2009.

Meanwhile, many conservatives in Europe pointed to the reduction of Sweden's social welfare system as evidence that, in a modern global economy, such government generosity was unsustainable. Indeed, they said, it had been made possible only by the fact that Sweden had emerged out of World War II with little industrial competition from a devastated Europe. Conversely, defenders of Sweden's social welfare policies argue that the diminution in services was minor and, compared with those in most other industrialized states, Swedish services remained generous. In fact, they maintained, Sweden provides a model for how to sustain social welfare benefits in a global economy, as its unemployment rate remained low and GDP growth strong for an industrialized country.

Because of the banking reforms enacted in the wake of the national financial crisis of the early 1990s, including tighter regulation of lending, liquidity, and leveraging assets, Sweden's financial sector weathered the global financial crisis of 2008–2009 better than many other countries. Indeed, the four largest Swedish banks, which together accounted for 80 percent of banking activity, had not invested in U.S. subprime securities and remained profitable into 2009 (though subsidiaries had actively invested in domestic and commercial activities in the neighboring Baltic states of Estonia, Latvia, and Lithuania, which underwent significant economic downturns). Being outside the euro zone gave the Swedish Central Bank more flexibility in responding both to the crisis and to the recession that followed it. In late 2008 and early 2009, it lowered interest rates four times.

Despite these advantages, Sweden was not able to escape the global recession entirely. During the first quarter of 2009, the country's GDP took its biggest hit in history, dropping 6.5 on an annualized basis, while the manufacturing sector suffered a 24 percent decline in production and exports fell by more than 16 percent. Among the casualties was the automobile manufacturer Saab, which was forced into bankruptcy as a result of the economic woes of its parent company, U.S. auto giant General Motors.

Still, because Sweden avoided the worst of the financial crisis and because the Swedish government had put its fiscal house in order following the national crisis of the early 1990s, most economists were predicting that Sweden would weather the global recession better than many other European economies and might emerge from it more quickly.

James Ciment and Marisa Scigliano

See also: Denmark; Finland; Norway; Stockholm School.

Further Reading

"Bank Bail-outs: Stockholm Syndrome." *Economist*, November 27, 2008.

Economist Intelligence Unit (EIU). *Country Report—Sweden* London: EIU, 2009.

Kent, Neil. *A Concise History of Sweden.* New York: Cambridge University Press, 2008.

Nordstrom, Byron J. *The History of Sweden.* Westport, CT: Greenwood, 2002.

Organisation for Economic Co-operation and Development (OECD). *OECD Economic Outlook*, no. 84. Paris: OECD, 2008.

Switzerland

Apart from its chocolates, cheeses, and watches, Switzerland is well known for its banks. The small, mountainous country is one of the most important financial centers in the world, and its citizens count among the world's wealthiest. As a major financial center, Switzerland is often deeply affected by global booms and busts.

There are several reasons for Switzerland's success in establishing a thriving financial sector. First of all, it lies in the center of Europe, surrounded by Germany, France, Italy, Liechtenstein, and Austria. As commerce revived in the middle of the last millennium, Switzerland became a conduit for much of Western Europe's internal trade. The Swiss earned money through imposing tariffs and guiding foreign businesspeople across the rough and hostile Alps. The trade flows encouraged the development of currency-exchange offices—the precursor of banks. Furthermore, for centuries Switzerland made a significant amount of money through the hiring out of its soldiers; these Swiss mercenaries fought for different kingdoms all around Europe from the Middle Ages up to the seventeenth century. Not only did it profit from the money that was paid in exchange for the soldiers' service, but it also took advantage of the connections that were created thanks to the various trade streams. Despite the fact that many Swiss men fought as mercenaries in different wars around Europe, Switzerland itself has not been involved in any war since 1515. Because of its neutrality and its relatively liberal government, Switzerland remained a neutral country and safe harbor surrounded by countries with often dictatorial laws. Among the famous refugees who came to Switzerland over the course of the centuries are the Huguenots, who brought the watch industry with them, and Henri Nestlé, the founder of the famous food company. Switzerland has typically profited from its immigrants.

Along with England, Switzerland was one of the earliest industrialized countries in Europe. The biggest sector was the textile industry. Thanks to its early industrialization in the eighteenth century, Switzerland was among the wealthiest countries in Europe. In 1770, as a more efficient way of producing cloth in England brought down textile prices, the Swiss textile sector was severely affected. This led to an overall crisis in the Swiss economy that forced the Swiss to also increase the mechanization of the textile sector. Weaving machines replaced traditional looms. These allowed for less labor-intensive production and increased the Swiss per capita income. The industry profited from the abundance of water, taking advantage of hydraulic power. Furthermore, the pharmaceutical and consumption industry emerged and flourished. Likewise, the machine and watch industry grew more important and increased the need for a financial sector to make loans available.

In 1848, Switzerland went from being a loose confederation of cantons (similar to states in the United States) to a federal state. As a consequence, the economic area widened and became unified. At the same time, immigrants exceeded emigrants, leading to a growing population. This was a boom time for Switzerland: The bank and insurance sector flourished; the construction of a nationwide railway system led to employment and later to increased mobility. The federal technical university was introduced and attracted scholars from around Europe.

Switzerland escaped the destruction of the two world wars thanks to its neutrality. The Swiss franc was a highly demanded currency for the neighboring countries involved in the war. World War I and the instability in the financial markets of the war-torn countries turned Switzerland into a significant international financial center; its strong currency, relatively low taxes, and political stability attracted, and still attract, money from all around the world. The introduction of the bank secrecy laws in 1934 increased the attraction of the financial center even more. These laws gave anonymity and thus strict confidentiality to all holders of bank accounts.

Switzerland was also hit by the world economic crisis, which took its greatest toll in the United States through the Great Depression. The Depression and World War II temporarily slowed down the Swiss economy. Just as it had profited from World War I, Switzerland also profited from World War II, again because of its neutrality. During the war, the Swiss franc was the only freely exchangeable currency. This is why Switzerland was able to carry out significant financial transactions—one of the more shameful ones being the purchase of gold that the Nazi regime had stolen from Jewish citizens and the central banks of the occupied countries.

Despite the opposition from the Allied powers, Switzerland managed to maintain its bank secrecy laws in the post–World War II period. This strengthened the reputation of Switzerland as a refuge for capital from around the world, which led to a steady increase in the Swiss gross domestic product (GDP). As a matter of fact, the inflow of capital to Switzerland was so high that the Swiss authorities tried to regulate it.

Along with countries that were dependent on oil, Switzerland suffered a blow during the oil crisis in the 1970s. In addition, the Swiss franc became very strong, which made Swiss exports more expensive for foreigners, thus drastically decreasing exports. At the same time, the watch industry in Switzerland suffered due to the invention of the quartz watch in Japan. Although the watch industry has recovered since—the Swiss brand Swatch was hugely successful—the crisis in the 1970s permanently slowed down the previously fast-growing Swiss economy. Ever since, Switzerland's GDP growth rate has fallen behind that of its neighboring countries. However, because it started out at a high economic level, the country continued to do well economically relative to its neighbors.

For much of the twentieth century, Switzerland's GDP per capita was always higher than that of its European neighbors. In the postwar setting, it passed the U.S. GDP as well. Yet the energy crisis in the 1970s, which hit Switzerland harder than many other countries due to its lack of energy resources and its high energy consumption, caused Switzerland to fall behind the United States. The 1980s and 1990s were also marked by slow economic growth, and Switzerland was hard hit by the global recessions of the early 1990s and early 2000s. Nevertheless, the slow growth came on top of a very high GDP per capita base. Indeed, on the eve of the late 2000s recession, Switzerland

UBS, Switzerland's largest bank, received $60 billion in government bailout funds in 2008. Meanwhile, the United States was suing UBS for using Swiss banking secrecy laws to help American depositors evade taxes; UBS later agreed to pay a fine of $780 million. *(AFP/Stringer/Getty Images)*

had the second highest GDP per capita of European countries with a population above 1 million, second only behind oil-rich Norway.

The financial meltdown of 2007–2009 hit Switzerland very hard. Many Swiss banks had invested in subprime-backed mortgage securities, which led to huge losses. UBS (Union Bank of Switzerland), one of the largest banks in the world, announced losses of approximately $17 billion in 2008. Because the financial sector accounts for more than 13 percent of the overall Swiss economy, it is feared that the crisis in the financial sector will lead to a major slowing of economic growth in the rest of the Swiss economy. It is expected that Switzerland will be in a recession through 2010. As demand from the newly wealthy in emerging markets decreases, 2009 emerged as the worst year for the Swiss watch industry since the 1970s. The Swiss government is trying to decrease the damage of the financial crisis by helping out the banks, and especially UBS, with 68 billion Swiss francs (more than $80 billion). This might seem like a small sum in comparison with the roughly

$1.5 trillion in financial bailout and stimulus money that the U.S. government is spending in an attempt to save its economy in 2008–2009. However, the Swiss rescue package is huge when put into perspective, for it accounts for almost 23 percent of Switzerland's GDP, whereas the U.S. rescue package is barely 10 percent of the income generated within the U.S. borders. This is not the first crisis Switzerland has faced, but it certainly is the most severe.

Christina Zenker

See also: Banks, Commercial; UBS.

Further Reading

Cassis, Youssef. "Banken" (Banks). In *Historisches Lexikon der Schweiz* (Historical dictionary of Switzerland). North Rhine-Westphalia, Germany: Schwabe AG, 2003.

Guex, Sébastien. "Les origines du secret bancaire suisse et son rôle dans la politique de la Confédération au sortir de la seconde guerre mondiale" (The origins of the secret Swiss bank and its role in the politics of the Confederation at the end of World War II). *Genèse. Sciences sociales et histoire* (Genesis: Social sciences and history) 34:34 (1999): 4–27.

Jacquemart, Charlotte. "Finanzkrise nicht allein schuld" (Not solely to blame for financial crisis). Available at www.nzz.ch. Accessed February 2009.

Mottet, Louis. *Geschichte der Schweizer Banken* (History of the Swiss Banks). Zurich: Buchclub Ex Libris, 1987.

Systemic Financial Crises

A systemic financial crisis is the occurrence of significant loss in asset values or failure of financial institutions on a broad scale, triggered by a sudden, unforeseen shock. The triggering event can be the failure of a major financial institution or of government policy, a stock market crash, a foreign investor assault on a national currency, or an external event such as a natural disaster or an act of war that may shut down the financial payment system. The negative shock spreads through declining stock prices, tightening credit lending, frozen liquidity, changes in interest rates, and cascading or chain-reaction effects.

Systemic financial crises have market-wide,

sometimes global effects that are extremely costly. Recoveries are typically slow and painful. Affected nations or regions usually adopt significant changes in financial practices and regulatory reforms after such a crisis. There have been many systemic financial crises in history. Major examples over the last century include the Great Wall Street Crash of 1929, the currency crisis in Asia in 1997–1998, and the global financial crisis of 2008–2009.

The Stock Market Crash of 1929 and the Great Depression

Technological innovations and increased manufacturing productivity throughout the 1920s created the Roaring Twenties, an era in which the United States prospered tremendously. But the wealth was unequally distributed, creating an unstable economy. Excessive speculation in stock markets also generated an artificial boom in the late 1920s, adding more instability to society. When the stock market began to crash in October 1929, it was the triggering event that sent the U.S. and global economies into the Great Depression of the 1930s.

The Wall Street crash led to bank runs that forced widespread bank closures. During the early 1930s, over 9,000 banks failed. Since bank deposits were not insured at that time, people lost all their savings as a result. Surviving banks were unwilling to lend. A reduction in spending by individuals and businesses led to decreased production and rising unemployment. Rising unemployment further reduced spending, and the cycle continued.

According to some economists, some government policy responses may have helped to deepen the Depression. For example, throughout the 1920s, President Herbert Hoover advocated a high-wage policy to prevent incomes from falling. Later, in 1933, President Franklin D. Roosevelt passed the National Recovery Administration (NRA), which aimed at reducing production and raising wages and prices. Both policies increased the real labor cost and, according to critics, resulted in more business failures and unemployment.

More widely accepted by economists as a con-

tributing factor in the global downturn, the U.S. Smoot-Hawley Tariff Act of 1930 was another example of poorly thought through government policy. The act significantly raised U.S. tariffs on over 20,000 imported goods to record levels, causing retaliations from America's trading partners. Countries tried to protect their own industries by raising tariffs and taxes on imports. International trade declined sharply. This led to a collapse of the U.S. farming industry, which depended upon exports of items such as wheat, corn, and other crops to overseas markets.

Furthermore, government tightened monetary and fiscal policies during the Depression and caused the economy to contract further. During 1931–1932, in order to maintain the gold standard, the U.S. Federal Reserve (Fed) increased interest rates at the height of the Depression. Many more banks and businesses failed afterward. In 1932, in an attempt to fill the budget deficit, Congress approved a large increase in taxes. Reduction in household income reduced purchases and economic expansion. These contractionary policies caused even greater damage to an already fragile U.S. economy.

By 1932, the U.S. economy had declined by half. Twenty-five percent of the workforce was unemployed. Ninety percent of stock market values had been wiped out. The United States went through slow and agonizing economic hardship throughout the entire 1930s, and the economy did not fully recover, say most economists, until the World War II, when massive military spending eliminated unemployment and boosted growth.

The Great Depression was one of the most widespread systemic crises. It affected almost all nations in the world. Many countries experienced bank runs and stock market crashes at first. For some countries, such as Britain, France, Canada, the Netherlands, and the Nordic countries, the Depression was less severe and ended by 1931. But in many other countries it lasted until the late 1930s or early 1940s. Poor economic conditions speeded the militarization in Germany, Italy, and Japan, the Axis that plunged the world into World War II.

The Asian Currency Crisis and the Russian Sovereign Default

Many Southeast Asian countries achieved high growth rates in the early and mid-1990s. Thailand, Malaysia, Indonesia, Singapore, and South Korea, for example, experienced gross domestic product (GDP) growth rates of 8 to 12 percent. Fast growth attracted large capital inflows. Almost half of the total global capital inflows to developing countries went to developing Asia during that time.

However, what some had referred to as an Asian "economic miracle" had been in part the result of increasing capital investments developed into bubbles fueled by "hot money"—short-term capital flows that are expensive and often conditioned for quick profits. Further, Asian economies were overly leveraged; that is, extensive borrowing in both the public and private sectors was not supported by sufficient underlying assets. Many Asian governments had adopted a policy to maintain fixed exchange rates in order to protect their exports. The implicit government guarantees of the fixed exchange rate encouraged foreign borrowing and led to excessive exposure to foreign exchange rate risks. For example, Thailand had acquired a large amount of foreign currency–denominated loans that made the country effectively bankrupt even before the crisis. Corporate sectors of South Korea were highly leveraged with foreign debt. Although varying widely from nation to nation, bank credits extended to unhealthy levels in countries such as Thailand, South Korea, Malaysia, and Indonesia. There were other problems underneath the veil of prosperity that destabilized the Asian economies. In Indonesia, for example, there was the additional complication of "crony capitalism," in which development money went only to those individuals who were close to the centers of power.

In the mid-1990s, rising U.S. interest rates reduced capital flows into the Southeast Asian region. Interest rate hikes drove up the value of the U.S. dollar and caused the appreciation of many Asian currencies that were pegged to the dollar. Currency appreciations made exports costly and less competitive in global markets, and Southeast Asia's export growth slowed dramatically starting in the spring of 1996.

The Asian currency crisis started with a drastic devaluation of Thai baht on July 2, 1997, quickly followed by devaluations of the Philippine peso, the Malaysian ringgit, the Indonesian rupiah, and the Singaporean dollar. After the first round of currency attacks took place between July and October of 1997, the second round started in October of 1998, when the Hong Kong stock market lost 40 percent of value and ended with the South Korean won's dramatic devaluation in less than two months.

After frantic attempts to protect their currencies, many countries gave up and let their currencies go into a free fall. Only Hong Kong managed to maintain the peg, but at a cost of more than US$1 billion to defend its currency. Steep devaluations of local currencies increased debt burdens in Asia, since most existing borrowings were made in foreign currencies. As a result, there were massive numbers of bankruptcies.

The International Monetary Fund (IMF) created a series of rescue packages for the most affected countries. However, the aid was conditioned on reforms that called for crisis nations to cut government spending, close troubled banks, and aggressively raise interest rates. Many of these reforms were contractionary and pushed crisis countries further into the recession. The IMF's responses were widely criticized during and after the crisis. As an example, Malaysia refused the IMF's bailout. Instead, it imposed temporary capital controls to deal with the crisis.

Indonesia, Malaysia, South Korea, Thailand, and the Philippines were the countries most affected by the crisis. They suffered permanent currency devaluations, real-estate busts, high unemployment, and social unrest. Nominal U.S. dollar GDP per capita fell 42.3 percent in Indonesia in 1997, 21.2 percent in Thailand, 19 percent in Malaysia, 18.5 percent in South Korea, and 12.5 percent in the Philippines. The crisis had ripple effects throughout the globe, with major impact felt as far and wide as Argentina, Mexico, Chile, Brazil, Russia, and even the United States.

Many viewed the Asian crisis as the trigger of the Russian sovereign default in 1998, as investors fled most developing markets. Recession in Asia had driven down the price of oil. This was devastating to Russia as an oil exporter. The weakening of the Russian economy put pressure on the ruble, resulting in its disastrous decline. By mid-1998 Russia was in need of the IMF's help to maintain its exchange rate. Near the end of that year, Russia's interest payments on its sovereign debt—national debt denominated in foreign currencies—well exceeded its tax revenue. Even though the government hiked interest rates to 150 percent, investors still fled Russia. In late 1998, Russia defaulted on its sovereign debt, sending another shock wave around the globe.

The Subprime Mortgage Meltdown and the Global Financial Crisis of 2008–2009

Beginning in early 2001, the Fed began to lower interest rates and kept them low through 2004. Large capital inflows from Asia and other emerging markets also pushed down U.S. interest rates. Excessively low borrowing costs attracted real-estate investments and created a housing bubble. Many mortgages were originated without the proper risk assessments. Approximately 80 percent of mortgages issued during this boom period were at subprime and/or adjustable rates. These mortgages were then repackaged and sold widely as complex derivative securities with high credit ratings. Many mega-sized financial conglomerates took excessive risks by using borrowed money to invest in mortgage-backed securities.

In mid-2006, U.S. house prices peaked and then started a steep decline. Meanwhile, the Fed had raised benchmark interest rates. Refinancing of home loans became difficult, and mortgage delinquencies soared. With large holdings of assets backed by subprime mortgages, many financial institutions found that their assets lost value significantly. Without adequate capital to cushion against losses, these companies were on the brink of default. Since financial conglomerates were highly interlinked and interdependent, when the Lehman Brothers financial services firm filed for bankruptcy on September 15, 2008, it quickly set off a chain reaction that adversely impacted the entire financial system in the United States.

Investors then became excessively risk-averse, since they could not properly evaluate complex financial products derived from subprime mortgages. As a result, few were willing to lend or invest. Liquidity dried up. Credit markets were tightened, first in the financial sector and then in the nonfinancial sectors. Many companies were unable to finance their daily operations when money markets froze in September 2008. The mortgage market meltdown led to a sharp decline in business activity and rising unemployment nationwide. A financial crisis quickly became an economic recession in the United States.

Between June 2007 and November 2008, Americans lost more than a quarter of their net worth. Total financial losses, including home equity stocks, retirement investments, and savings and investment assets, add up to an astonishing $8.3 trillion. The financial crisis in the United States quickly spread to the rest of the world, resulting in a number of European bank failures and declines in various stock indices. For example, in 2007 there was a consumer run on the British bank Northern Rock, which led to additional financial cracks on the Bank of England. And, adjusted for size, Iceland's banking collapse was the largest sustained by any nation in economic history. The financial crisis also spread through international trade linkages and severely reduced the imports from many Asian and Latin American countries.

Responses by the U.S. Fed, the European Central Bank, and other central banks around the globe were dramatic. In the United States, to prevent a further spread of the systemic crisis, the Fed facilitated the acquisition of several large investment banks. The Treasury Department placed Fannie Mae and Freddie Mac into conservatorship and assumed control of insurance giant AIG in September 2008. To stimulate economic growth, the Fed eased monetary policy by lowering the federal funds rate to historic lows, ranging from 0 percent to 0.25 percent. Many other central banks around the globe followed suit.

In 2008, the U.S. government passed the Emergency Economic Stabilization Act. It authorized $700 billion to the Troubled Asset Relief Program (TARP) for lending funds to banks. On February 17, 2009, President Barack Obama signed the American Recovery and Reinvestment Act of 2009, a $787 billion package that included spending, homeowner assistance, and tax cuts to help stimulate the U.S. economy. The European Union and many individual nations, such as the United Kingdom, Canada, China, India, Russia, Sweden, Mexico, and Brazil, released similar packages to stimulate economic growth. By the end of 2009, governments worldwide had spent or committed trillions of dollars in loans, asset purchases, guarantees, and direct spending in an attempt to revive their economies from the ongoing crisis.

Common Characteristics

Every crisis is unique. There are, however, some commonalities and trends that can be summarized. Systemic financial crises are usually initiated by unforeseen events, but the real causes are not the triggers but systemwide fundamental weaknesses such as asset bubbles, excessive borrowing, fraudulent financial and corporate practices, and regulatory failures.

Many events may trigger a systemic crisis. The failure of a large financial company is more likely to trigger a systemic crisis than the failure of a nonfinancial company. Due to the nature of their businesses, financial institutions are more interlinked and highly leveraged, which makes it more likely for them to transmit and magnify a negative shock. Financial companies, especially banks, finance their long-term assets with short-term debt, causing asset maturity mismatches. This makes them more vulnerable to interest-rate

hikes and liquidity freezes that are common before and during a financial crisis.

Due to financial and technological innovations and increasing globalization, the impact of a systemic financial crisis has become stronger and faster than ever. Incomplete information can help spread a crisis. Recent financial innovations such as financial products derived from subprime mortgages are often complex, opaque, and difficult to value during a crisis. When there is a lack of transparency, investors are more likely to become excessively risk-averse and to engage in herd mentality or contagious behavior that helps drive down asset values steeply. Technological innovations have increased the speed and efficiency of financial transactions, but they leave little time for market participants to digest proper information and to recover losses. Therefore, a crisis becomes more severe as panic selling becomes common.

Globalization increases the linkage of financial institutions and the interdependency of financial markets, which in turn helps spread a crisis to a wider scope and a larger scale. Financial globalization helps savers to earn higher returns and borrowers to obtain cheaper capital worldwide. Easy access to capital helps economic growth as well as attracting financial speculation, and helps build up asset bubbles. Huge amounts of overseas capital can be quickly withdrawn when a bubble bursts. Such capital flight can leave the domestic economy in shock. Globalization also increases international trade among countries. Troubles in one country's financial system often spread to another country's economic sectors through trade linkages during a crisis.

To reduce their vulnerability to a systemic financial crisis, financial institutions have traditionally tried to participate in clearinghouses or trade through financial exchanges. However, since private companies do not bear all the costs of their own failure, say economists, government has a role to play in preventing and managing a crisis.

The failure of the British banking firm Overend & Gurney in 1866 led to a key change in the role of central banks in managing financial crises. Overend

& Gurney was a major London financial institution whose failure caused widespread bankruptcy of many smaller banks. In order to prevent this spillover effect, the Bank of England provided liquidity to the entire British financial system. Since then, it is common for central banks to act as the "lender of last resort" during a systemic financial crisis.

The Great Depression greatly transformed the role of government in the economy. During the Depression, the size and expenditure of the U.S. federal government increased dramatically, and it gained huge power in managing the economy. After the Depression, the government established extensive regulations to prevent future crises from happening; that is, it established the Securities and Exchange Commission and the Federal Deposit Insurance Corporation and separated commercial and retail banking through the Glass-Steagall Act. Many of these rules and regulations helped shape the financial systems in the United States and many other countries today.

The magnitude of government intervention has become stronger through each crisis. Central governments and international organizations, such as the IMF, have played increasingly important roles in preventing and managing crises. International cooperation has also became critical in protecting and reviving the global economy.

Future Issues

It is difficult to predict when, where, how, and why the next systemic financial crisis will occur. Economists and policy makers have studied each past crisis extensively. Many of the lessons learned from the past could help to prevent a future crisis.

Proper responses in managing and recovering from a crisis are equally important. Two related issues deserve attention. First, how should governments manage these too-big-to-fail or too-connected-to-fail companies? Failures of such firms would likely impose severe losses on other firms or markets. A government's bailing out of large, systemically important firms may prevent further spread of a crisis. However, expectations of bailouts by big companies may cause moral hazard and give these companies incentives to take more risks than they otherwise would. Excessive risk taking could thus become one of the causes of another potential crisis.

Second, to what extent and with what financial resources should government intervene in the market to manage a crisis? In the first decade of the twenty-first century, many economists expressed concerns over the enormous U.S. federal deficit and the growing national debt due to various bailout and stimulus packages. Other economists maintained that increased debt was a necessary response to the unprecedented crisis, without which the economic downturn would have been much worse.

It remains to be seen if regulations will be put in place to prevent future excessive risk, and if there will be sufficient government borrowing capacity should another systemic financial crisis occur.

Priscilla Liang

See also: Recession and Financial Crisis (2007–); Regulation, Financial; "Too Big to Fail"; Troubled Asset Relief Program (2008–).

Further Reading

Allen, Franklin, and Douglas Gale. *Understanding Financial Crises.* New York: Oxford University Press, 2009.

Bernstein, Michael A. *The Great Depression: Delayed Recovery and Economic Change in America, 1929–1939.* Cambridge, UK: Cambridge University Press, 1989.

Foster, John B., and Fred Magdoff. *The Great Financial Crisis: Causes and Consequences.* New York: Monthly Review, 2009.

Goldstein, Morris. *The Asian Financial Crisis: Causes, Cures, and Systemic Implications.* Washington, DC: Institute for International Economics, 1998.

Honohan, Patrick, and Luc Laeven, eds. *Systemic Financial Crises: Containment and Resolution.* New York: Cambridge University Press, 2005.

International Monetary Fund. *Global Financial Stability Report, April 2009: Responding to the Financial Crisis and Measuring Systemic Risks.* Washington, DC: International Monetary Fund, 2009.

Shiller, Robert J. *The Subprime Solution: How Today's Global Financial Crisis Happened, and What to Do About It.* Princeton, NJ: Princeton University Press, 2008.

Tirole, Jean. *Financial Crises, Liquidity, and the International Monetary System.* Princeton, NJ: Princeton University Press, 2002.

Tax Policy

Taxes are monetary levies imposed by governments on individuals, households, businesses, and other institutions. While taxes come in a bewildering variety—with levies on income, property, consumption, importation and exportation, capital gains, inheritance, and so on—they basically fall under two broad organizing headings: benefits received and ability to pay. Taxes under the first heading might include highway tolls—the more one benefits from driving on the highway, the more one pays. If highways, however, were funded by an income tax in which the rich pay a higher share than the poor, then the taxation used to pay for the highways would fall under the ability-to-pay heading.

Principles

Two even larger, philosophical principles are also at work in determining tax policy—horizontal and vertical equity. The former principle—nearly universally accepted—says that people or institutions doing the same thing should be treated the same. For example, all other things being equal, the property tax rate on a store selling toys and a store selling stationery should be the same. More controversial but still widely accepted is the principle of vertical equity: that wealthier people should pay higher rates of taxes, particularly on income, than poorer people. When the tax rate is the same for all persons or institutions, it is said to be proportional; when it more heavily taxes the rich, it is called progressive. When it more heavily taxes the poor, it is said to be regressive. An example of the latter is the sales tax. The less wealthy you are, the less you save and the more you spend, as a percentage of your income, on consumption, and hence the greater the percentage of your income you pay in sales taxes. If you earn $1,000 per month, for example, you are likely to spend all of it on consumption, and if the sales tax rate is 8 percent, you would pay 8 percent of your income in sales taxes. However, if you earn $30,000 per month, you might spend only half of it on consumption and save the other half. Thus, you would pay $1,200 (8 percent x $15,000) in sales taxes. Since $1,200 is 4 percent of $30,000, the person with the higher earnings would be paying only 4 percent of her income in sales taxes. This might be partially offset, as in many jurisdictions, by exempting from taxation the items that poorer people spend a higher percentage of their money on, notably nonprepared food.

At the other end of the equation, taxes serve two general purposes. First and foremost, taxes pay for what the government does—national defense, domestic security, transportation, education, health care, social welfare, and any number of other public functions, services, and goods. Second, taxes are a tool of economic and social policy, as governments attempt to maintain growing economies and smoothly running societies by imposing or not imposing taxes on a particular economic good or activity, or by adjusting the level of taxation on a good or activity.

Tax policy, then, attempts to determine all of these things—what kind of taxation is fair and equitable; what serves societal goals; what best promotes sustained and healthy economic growth; and what level provides the government with the revenues it needs to performs its duties, functions, and responsibilities. Looming over all of this is the macroeconomic function of taxation—the shifting of private economic resources to public ends. That is, when government imposes a tax, it is removing the decision-making power over the economic resources in question from the individual or privately owned institution and transferring it to the government itself, which is supposed to represent the public good and, in a democracy, is ultimately controlled by the public. So, to cite a simple example, if the government had a blanket tax of 10 percent on all property and economic activity, then it would be assuming control of 10 percent of a nation's resources.

When it comes to tax policy, the landscape is always shifting and is always subject to political considerations. Populations grow and move about, technology changes economic and social activity, and public sentiment about what is an acceptable level of taxation and what taxes should be used to pay for mutates. Thus, tax policy is always changing as well. Indeed, one of the overriding decisions in elections—where citizens determine the broad outlines of how they want government to operate in the future—concerns tax policy.

Business Cycle

Tax policy also plays a major role in the business cycle. Excessive taxation or the wrong kinds of taxation can contribute to the intensity of the contraction phase of the cycle. High taxes on individuals can lower aggregate demand while various kinds of taxes on business can dampen investment and hiring. Taxes can also distort economic behavior, causing individuals and businesses to make economic decisions based on avoiding or minimizing tax liability rather than as a response to market conditions. This can, then, impede the smooth running of markets and contribute to slower or negative economic growth.

The more important role of tax policy vis-à-vis the business cycle is as a remedy or a response. Taxes represent one of three basic tools at a government's disposal to respond to economic slowdowns and contractions. The others are monetary policy and spending—the latter, with taxation, falling under the rubric of fiscal policy. During these periods of slowdowns and contractions, governments may reduce taxes on business activities in order to leave more money in the private sector for investment and hiring. To this end, the government can use all kinds of targeted tax breaks, tax cuts, and tax rebates. It can also reduce the taxes on individuals or rebate taxes already paid in order to increase aggregate demand.

While lowering taxes seems like an obvious solution to an economic downturn, this policy presents problems of its own because during economic downturns, tax revenues are already declining. Since so much of taxation is based on economic activity—people's income, business profits, consumption—when that activity declines so do tax revenues, as occurred quite dramatically in the recession of 2007 to 2009. At the same time, economic contractions represent a time of increased government expenditures, particularly on things like unemployment compensation and social welfare programs. The combination of lower tax revenue and higher expenditures can lead to ballooning deficits, as was also evidenced in the 2007–2009 recession at the municipal, state, and federal levels in the United States, as well as in many other countries. When the government has to borrow large sums of money, it can make borrowing more expensive for private industry and individuals, dampening consumption, investment, and hiring.

Economists and policy makers vigorously debate the effectiveness of the various tools at the government's disposal in responding to economic downturns, with those on the right emphasizing tax cuts and appropriate monetary policy and those on the left arguing for more government spending. This breakdown, of course, oversimplifies things. Even liberal Post Keynesian economists agree that properly targeted tax cuts and an expansive monetary policy are necessary to combat recessions, while all but the most conservative neoclassical and monetarist economists agree that the government has to spend more on things like unemployment compensation during such times.

The question, then, is the balance, as the debate over the $787 billion economic stimulus package promoted by the Barack Obama administration in early 2009 revealed. The plan included both spending and tax cuts but was largely opposed by Republicans because it emphasized the former, while Democrats supported it for the same reason. In the wake of the stimulus plan, Republicans argued that the emphasis on spending increases over tax cuts resulted in rising unemployment rates while the Obama administration insisted that, absent that spending, the rate would have been much higher. In any case, as unemployment remained in or near double digits, the administration shifted to targeted tax cuts or rebates for business in early 2010, with an emphasis on those, such as cutting the amount small businesses needed to contribute to Social Security taxes for newly hired employees and offering businesses a tax credit on new hires.

James Ciment

See also: Fiscal Policy; Monetary Policy.

Further Reading

Brownlee, W. Elliot. *Federal Taxation in America: A Short History.* 2nd ed. New York: Cambridge University Press, 2004.

Slemrod, Joel, and Jon Bakija. *Taxing Ourselves.* 4th ed. Cambridge, MA: MIT Press, 2008.

Steuerle, C. Eugene. *Contemporary U.S. Tax Policy.* 2nd ed. Washington, DC: Urban Institute, 2008.

Technological Innovation

Technological innovation is the development of new ways to attain the goals of humankind. It can come in two forms: process and product. The former allows firms to make more of a product than before with the same inputs of labor, natural resources, and capital, to or to make the same amount of a product as before with less labor, resources, or capital input. More apparent to persons outside a particular industry is product innovation—that is, the introduction of new or improved products for individual or institutional consumers.

Technological innovation has been a key factor behind the steadily improving living standards of humanity, particularly since the advent of the industrial revolution 250 years ago. At the same time, technological innovation is also disruptive and destabilizing. That is, technological innovation as adapted by entrepreneurs leads to the development of new processes and products but also the destruction of old ones and the economic collateral damage of bankruptcy and unemployment that results from it. In addition, the adaptation of new technology by entrepreneurs, while first creating an economic expansion, can then lead to economic contraction if too many entrepreneurs invest in it, saturating the market and leading to ever lower profit margins and eventual bankruptcy for less efficient firms.

Impact on the Business Cycle

Several aspects of technological innovation have significant bearing on economic cycles. Foremost is the fact that technological innovation occurs unevenly through time. If not for this empirical reality, it would be much less likely that innovation could generate booms and busts. One key reason for the temporal irregularity is that rare "big" innovations spawn a series of small innovations that improve on or extend the big ones. The former are often referred to as "general purpose technologies" (GPTs). Examples include the steam engine and the computer. In both cases, the original device was much improved through time and found application in a wider and wider range of economic activities. Thus, a GPT innovation creates an environment in which rapid innovation can occur. The personal computer, for example, led to a host of software and hardware innovations that have both changed the way virtually all commerce gets done and led to the introduction of a vast array of new consumer products and services.

A second critical characteristic of technological innovation is that it generally, though not always, requires some investment before it can be applied to commerce and industry. That is, new technology often requires the purchase of new machinery and even the construction of new buildings. For example, the assembly line—a process-type innovation—required entrepreneurs to erect factories suitable for its application, while the microchip required the construction of facilities with sterilized "clean rooms." Even when new machines or buildings are not necessary, some upfront investment in the training of workers is generally required.

Thus, technological innovation—along with factors such as the cost of borrowing and the expectations of future growth—is a critical contributor to a firm's decision to increase investment in capital goods. In short, all other factors being equal, investment increases during periods of technological innovation and adaptation and decreases during periods of technological stagnation. With regard to expectations, it is noteworthy that a firm's expectations for the future will depend a great deal on its technological predictions. If it

foresees being able to introduce new products or improve the cost or quality of existing products, it will be confident of the future. Notably, the business press focuses on how innovation might affect economic prospects in the short and medium term.

A third and related characteristic is that technological innovation might also affect consumption decisions. People are more likely to spend rather than save if some new product has just been introduced into the marketplace. This effect is most likely in the case of consumer durables—goods that consumers buy only every several years. Historically, the most important example may be the automobile, which became a mass-market good with the development of assembly-line production. Many economists have suspected that some of the boom-bust cycle of the 1920s and 1930s in the United States and several other countries reflected the fact that the middle class bought automobiles in the late 1920s and did not see any need to buy additional or replacement vehicles in the early 1930s. Automobile manufacturers struggled in response to convince consumers through annual model changes that new cars were superior to the old but had little success in the absence of technological innovation in automobile quality.

Fourth, different types of technological innovation—that is, process versus product innovation—have different effects on investment, consumption, and ultimately employment. Both types of innovation will usually encourage investment. They have quite different effects on consumption, however. As suggested above, new goods or services (or improved quality in existing goods and services) will encourage increased consumption expenditure. A drop in the price of a good already regularly purchased will usually lead to a drop in consumption expenditure. There may be exceptions here, if the drop in price encourages a more-than-proportional increase in the quantity demanded. The above example of assembly lines and automobiles is such an exception. Yet, in general, expenditures fall as prices fall.

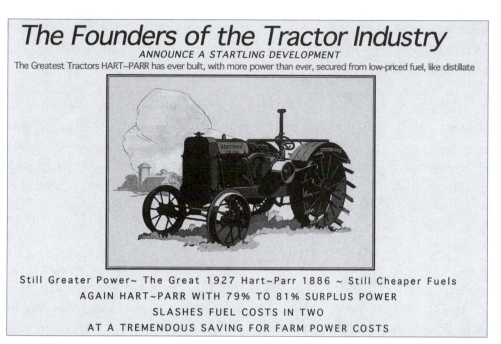

The Founders of the Tractor Industry

ANNOUNCE A STARTLING DEVELOPMENT

The Greatest Tractors HART~PARR has ever built, with more power than ever, secured from low-priced fuel, like distillate

Still Greater Power~ The Great 1927 Hart~Parr 1886 ~ Still Cheaper Fuels
AGAIN HART~PARR WITH 79% TO 81% SURPLUS POWER
SLASHES FUEL COSTS IN TWO
AT A TREMENDOUS SAVING FOR FARM POWER COSTS

Technological innovation has been identified as a primary cause of upswings in the business cycle throughout history. Yet mechanized farming was a mixed blessing for the American farmer in the 1920s, contributing to large crop surpluses and falling prices. *(Buyenlarge/Hulton Archive/ Getty Images)*

Innovation and Employment

The effects on employment of the two types of innovation differ greatly. To produce a new product, firms will generally need to hire workers. If, however, a firm is able to decrease the cost of producing existing goods (and the quantity demanded does not rise by more than the cost falls), the effect will generally be a decrease in employment. In both cases, these within-firm employment decisions may be offset elsewhere in the economy. Consumers spending more, or less, money on the output of the innovating firm may spend less, or more, elsewhere in the economy, and thus, employment may move in the opposite direction in other firms, though adjustments generally do not happen instantaneously.

An economy characterized by a great deal of process innovation and very little product innovation may thus experience increased unemployment. This was exactly the situation in the United States and other developed countries during the interwar period. The only major new product introduced in the decade after 1925 was the electric refrigerator (hundreds of thousands were sold during the depth of the Depression). On the other hand, the interwar period witnessed three of the most important major process innovations of the last century: the assembly line, electrification, and continuous processing (where homogenous outputs like chemicals were produced continuously rather than in batches). As workers were let go by firms introducing these new processes, there were no firms looking to hire workers to make new products. The problem, then, is not process innovation itself. Process innovation is, after all, the main driver of the productivity advance on which economic growth depends. Yet unless accompanied by product innovation, process innovation may yield unemployment, at least in the short and medium term.

While product and process innovation both encourage investment, there is considerable difference across particular innovations with respect to the amount of investment required. The assembly line, electrification, and continuous processing all required a great deal of investment during the 1920s. The most important process innovation of the 1930s was the development of new tungsten carbide cutting tools: these could generally be fitted to existing machines at little cost but allowed cutting operations to be performed several times faster. There was also a great deal of organizational innovation during the 1930s as firms figured out how best to manage the technologies put in place in the 1920s. This also tended to require little investment but produced major advances in worker productivity.

Real Business Cycle Theory

As the above cases make clear, technological innovation plays a role in longer-term boom-bust cycles of capitalist economies. Less obvious—and less studied until the last few decades—has been the role of technological innovation on shorter-term cycles. Real business cycle theory—developed by Norwegian economist Finn Kydland and his American counterpart Edward Prescott in the 1980s (the two would win the 2004 Nobel Prize in Economics for their work)—attempted to address this question. Real business cycle theory posited a link between productivity growth and unemployment that depended on workers choosing not to work for a while if they expected real wages to rise in future. That is, if workers anticipate future process innovation (the theory neglected product innovation), they might decide to put off getting a job until wages rose to reflect the fact that workers could produce more. Not surprisingly, it proved difficult to empirically support the idea that unemployment rates responded to annual changes of a couple of percent in productivity. Moreover, the theory ignored the possibility that firms might hire fewer workers after introducing a process innovation.

Government Policy

Government also plays a significant role in terms of technological innovation, financing both scientific and technological research, encouraging or discouraging innovation through a variety of regulations, and providing patent protection to many sorts of innovation. But given the importance of different types of technological innovation to the business cycle, economists and policy makers debate whether governments should adjust their technology policies to emphasize steadier, long-term growth, which is generally the economic outcome most governments seek to promote.

Governments, say some economists, might indeed be able to encourage both more innovation and a better balance between product and process innovation. The latter could prove difficult in practice because it is difficult to predict the likely result of any research process or how popular any sort of innovation will prove in the marketplace.

The more innovation there is in a society, the more likely that there will be growing firms looking to hire workers displaced by firms that are shedding workers (and vice versa). Expectations of the future are more likely to be positive when lots of innovation is occurring. Governments might thus find that policies that encourage innovation in general not only encourage growth but reduce the severity of booms and busts.

Finally, governments may find, in turn, that policies that reduce the intensity of booms and busts also serve to advance the rate of technological innovation. While certain types of innovation *may be* encouraged during boom or bust periods, a more likely effect is that severe booms and busts discourage innovative activity. Funding for research tends to decline during busts. This reflects both lower firm profitability and lowered expectations of future demand. Firms that are more confident about the future will be more likely to invest in research.

Rick Szostak

See also: Dot.com Bubble (1990s–2000); Information Technology; Real Business Cycle Models; Spillover Effect.

Further Reading

Freeman, Christopher, and Francisco Louçã. *As Time Goes By: From the Industrial Revolutions to the Information Revolution.* New York: Oxford University Press, 2001.

Kleinknecht, Alfred. *Innovation Patterns in Crisis and Prosperity: Schumpeter's Long Cycle Reconsidered.* London: Macmillan, 1987.

Szostak, Rick. *Technological Innovation and the Great Depression.* Boulder, CO: Westview, 1995.

Vivarelli, Marco. *The Economics of Technology and Unemployment.* Cheltenham, UK: Edward Elgar, 1995.

Woirol, Gregory R. *The Technological Unemployment and Structural Unemployment Debates.* Westport, CT: Greenwood, 1996.

Tequila Effect

The "tequila effect" (*efecto tequila*) is a term that refers to the negative effect of the Mexican peso crisis on various Latin American economies in 1995. More broadly, it refers to the diffusion of an economic crash from one Latin American country to other countries in the region. In December 1994, the drastic and sudden devaluation of the Mexican national currency, the peso, affected not only Mexico but several other Latin American countries as well. After the collapse of the peso, many foreign speculators lost confidence in the stability of Latin American economies; this loss of confidence triggered a massive flight of capital from the whole region.

During the administration of President Carlos Salinas de Gortari (1988–1994), the Mexican government tried to attract foreign direct investment (FDI). With his administration opening markets and increasing economic links with industrialized countries, especially the United States, foreign investors brought technological know-how, capital, and jobs to the nation. Prior to President Salinas's administration, almost all investments into Mexico were tied to oil-producing activity. After 1988, investments targeted new industries, and Mexico was able to build a large source of international money reserves.

Beginning in the mid-1980s, Mexico had an apparently reliable economic framework, with relatively low inflation ensured by exchange-rate commitments and a public-sector surplus. Economic reforms had increased the country's productivity and created more jobs and generated more exports, especially to the United States and other members of the Organisation for Economic Cooperation and Development (OECD). Into the 1990s, the peso seemed strong, and Mexico seemed a good place to invest. The signing of the North American Free Trade Agreement (NAFTA) in 1992 helped ensure an apparently bright economic future.

But the Mexican economy proved less stable than many had anticipated, relying on the steady influx of foreign direct investment. As a result of the heavy FDI, Mexico began racking up deficits in the balance of trade. To counterbalance its losses and finance the growing deficit, the Mexican government decided to seek even more outside capital. This led to an even stronger dependency on foreign investments. In the last years of President Salinas's administration, all indications pointed toward a mounting economic crisis, though neither the president nor his successor, Ernesto Zedillo Ponce de León, saw the signs. The main strategy of the Salinas administration was to keep inflation low, even though this inevitably slowed down the economy and increased unemployment. Other economic experts argued that a depreciation of the national currency would enhance economic growth. A devaluation of the peso, they reasoned, could help increase exports, as Mexican products would become cheaper and more competitive on the international market. At the same time, the price of imported goods would increase for Mexicans, resulting in a shift of domestic demand toward local products.

After being elected in August 1994, Zedillo was reluctant to devaluate the peso, but a conflict in the southern state of Chiapas forced him to act. Because of the still-strong peso, many people in Chiapas lost their jobs and were no longer willing to accept promises and excuses by the government. It seemed to many that the country as a whole was getting wealthier but that the poor were not getting their share. When foreign investors heard the news about insurgencies in Chiapas, they began to withdraw their capital. Mexico lost some $16 billion in just ten months, from February to December 1994.

At this point, President Zedillo decided to break his campaign promise of keeping the peso stable and instituted a devaluation in December 1994. The unforeseen change in policy made international investors question whether they could trust the new government and the stability of the Mexican economy. The government, for its part, believed that a decrease in FDI was a normal sign of adjustment and did not anticipate the extent of the coming crisis.

Two days after the investor reaction, the Zedillo administration decided to let the peso float freely against the U.S. dollar. Foreign investors owned about $29 billion in Mexican *tesobonos*, short-term bonds that must be paid back in U.S. dollars. Afraid of losing all their money, they cashed them immediately. Within just a few days, large sums of FDI left the country, and the peso became virtually worthless.

The United States reacted rapidly to the crisis, buying up large amounts of Mexican pesos to stem further depreciation, but the move was only marginally successful. U.S. president Bill Clinton then granted a $20 billion loan to Mexico via the Exchange Stabilization Fund; the United States and Canada offered short-term currency swaps; the Bank for International Settlements offered a line of credit; and the International Monetary Fund (IMF) approved a standby credit agreement that would remain in effect for eighteen months. In total, Mexico received about $50 billion in loans, with other Latin American countries, such as Argentina and Brazil, contributing several million more. As a result of these efforts, the peso remained stable for the next few years, until it was destabilized again by the Asian crisis of 1997–1998.

Because Mexico was required to meet its commitments toward NAFTA and the IMF, it had to introduce tight fiscal policies, keep its market open to free trade, and maintain a floating exchange rate. Thanks to its membership in NAFTA and a weak peso, exports from Mexico increased and kept the country from falling into a long-term recession. By 1996, the country's gross domestic product was showing positive growth, but millions of private households, which took out loans and mortgages at tremendously high interest rates during the economic crisis, had to struggle for several years until they were able to repay their debts.

The following year, 1997, brought international contagion in a number of Latin American countries. In previous years, capital inflows had helped Latin American countries to improve their economies and overcome a recession. But many investors interpreted the Mexican crisis as indicating increased risk in investing in the entire region. Argentina and Brazil were among the countries worst hit by the tequila effect because their economic stability and rapid growth also relied on FDI. As nervous speculators withdrew their funds in the wake of the Mexican crisis, the Argentine stock market plunged and remained bearish for several months; domestic spending declined and an increase in interest rates in March 1995 led to a credit crunch. Although the effects were not as severe as in Mexico, it took Argentina a long time to return to its former interest rate. Even after interest rates reached the precrisis level, output and investment there continued to decline.

Carmen De Michele

See also: Debt; Latin America; Mexico.

Further Reading

Humphrey, Brett M. "The Post-Nafta Mexican Peso Crisis: Bailout or Aid? Isolationism or Globalization?" *Hinckley Journal of Politics* 2:1 (2000): 33–40.

Lustig, Nora. *Mexico: Remaking of an Economy.* 2nd ed. Washington, DC: Brookings Institution, 1998.

Pastor, Manuel, Jr. "Pesos, Policies, and Predictions." In *The Post-NAFTA Political Economy*, ed. Carol Wise. University Park: Penn State University Press, 1998.

Roett, Riordan. *The Mexican Peso Crisis.* Boulder, CO: Lynne Rienner, 1996.

Thorp, Willard Long (1899–1992)

The American Economist Willard Thorp spent much of his career in academia, government, and business researching business cycles in the United

States and around the world. As director of economic research at Dun & Bradstreet, he became a vocal critic of American business's failure to plan effectively to avoid a repetition of the Great Depression, especially as the economy began to improve.

Thorp was born on May 24, 1899, in Oswego, New York, and raised in Chelsea, Massachusetts, and Duluth, Minnesota. He served in the U.S. Army during World War I, after which he earned a bachelor's degree from Amherst College in 1920, a master's degree in economics from the University of Michigan in 1921, and a doctorate from Columbia University in 1924.

In 1923, he joined the new National Bureau of Economic Research, where he compiled centralized economic data on seventeen countries dating to 1890, resulting in the 1926 publication of *Business Annals*, with an introduction by economist Wesley C. Mitchell. A historian and an outspoken advocate for the use of statistics in predicting and evaluating economic events, Thorp, who had become head of economic research at Dun & Bradstreet in 1935, wrote an article titled "Wanted—Industrial Statistics," in which he stated that the use of statistics and analysis had declined since the 1920s, a trend he saw as deplorable. Also in 1935, Thorp became editor of *Dun's Review.*

Researching business cycles in the 1930s, Thorp noted that recovery is the most difficult phase of a business cycle to identify. He stated that recessions are easily defined and are often signaled by "spectacular events." Recoveries, on the other hand, are not marked by spectacular events; additionally, industry and government economies recover at different times and rates. Thorp also criticized the era's lack of sophistication in data gathering and market and industry analysis.

In the 1920s, Thorp had written about the economic growth that occurs during wartime as a result of increasing demand for goods by the government, the maximum use of the workforce, and the elimination of competition as some companies adjust their businesses to support the war effort. Thorp used historical evidence to show that such prosperity is typically marked by inflation and rising prices and followed by severe recession. These views led to various U.S. government appointments from the 1930s to the 1960s.

In 1938, Thorp became an adviser to the U.S. secretary of commerce and an analyst for the National Economic Committee on Monopolies. Beginning in 1945, he served under four U.S. secretaries of state and represented the United States at the General Agreement Tariffs and Trade (GATT) talks in Geneva, Switzerland, and at the Paris Peace Conference. Serving as assistant secretary of state in the administration of President Harry S. Truman, Thorp supported what became known as the Marshall Plan, believing it was the responsibility of the United States to help rebuild Western Europe and to provide aid to noncommunist countries to stop the spread of Soviet communism.

In the 1950s, Thorp returned to academia, teaching primarily at Amherst, from which he retired in 1965. In 1960, he headed a United Nations mission to Cyprus, and in 1961, at the request of President John F. Kennedy, he headed an economic mission to Bolivia.

Thorp spent his later years lecturing, writing, and consulting. Writing in the *New York Times* shortly before his death, he suggested that the U.S. government should adopt a massive infrastructure improvement program to assist the U.S. economy, much as it had during Roosevelt's New Deal. He died in Pelham, Massachusetts, on May 10, 1992.

Robert N. Stacy

See also: Mills, Frederick Cecil; Mitchell, Wesley Clair; National Bureau of Economic Research.

Further Reading

Thorp, Willard Long. *Business Annals.* New York: NBER, 1926.

———. *Economic Institutions.* New York: Macmillan, 1928.

———. *The New Inflation.* New York: McGraw-Hill, 1959.

———. "Wanted—Industrial Statistics." *Journal of the American Statistical Association* 1 (March 1936): 193.

Three-Curve Barometer

After World War I, the study of business cycles emerged as a new field in economic statistics. In 1919, the Harvard University Committee for Economic Research began publishing a periodic business indicator in its general *Review of Economic Statistics* (later *Review of Economics and Statistics*). The three-curve barometer, as the new indicator was called, was developed by Harvard economist Warren Milton Persons (1878–1937) as a means of tracking turns in the business cycle. The three curves measured speculation, business, and money and credit. Because Persons was a member of the Harvard Committee for Economic Research, chaired by Charles Jesse Bullock, his tracking system was also known as the Harvard barometer.

After the turn of the twentieth century, statistical information on economic activity became increasingly available to American businessmen as large corporations, banks, and the government all began to realize that it was to their advantage to have smaller players aware of market conditions. The goal was to minimize disruptions and shocks. Research departments began issuing circulars to maximize investment stability, and before long, specialized private organizations were gathering, processing, and publishing information for the general public. The first business indicators appeared in the years leading up to World War I, generated by such forecasting agencies as the Brookmire Economic Service and Babson Statistical Organization. Because these early services used relatively simple methods to generate their barometers, their analyses were limited.

Roger Babson, a pioneer in the use of statistical charts to forecast business cycles and the founder of the Babson Statistical Organization in Wellesley, Massachusetts, devised a composite called the Babson chart, which graphed weighted indices as an X-Y line equalizing booms and busts. Because Babson's organization buttressed the data with frequent sampling of the opinions of leading businessmen, the Babson chart provided a useful measure of business confidence. Another early business indicator, the Brookmire barometer, devised by James H. Brookmire of St. Louis, forecast changes in the business cycle based on the assumption that banking led the way in significant rises and falls, with stocks following several months later and general business some months after that.

The Harvard three-curve barometer built on the general concept of the Brookmire system. Persons, however, was confident that he could build a better barometer by interpreting and analyzing data rather than just gathering and publishing it. In January 1919, Persons and the Harvard committee began adjusting monthly data since 1903 for seasonal variation and long-term trends. Each corrected series was charted, and the charts of various series were compared. Based on patterns developed from this analysis, the charts were grouped by similar variations in cycle.

At this point, the committee developed a composite for each group and brought the composites together on a single chart. The result was three curves, each related to a specific type of economic activity: speculation (A), business (B), and money and credit (C). Persons and his team immediately recognized that the three curves seemed to maintain similar relations to each other through each type of activity. Nevertheless, to counter the perception that the C curve was less important than the A curve, the Harvard barometer, beginning in 1920, used both A and C to forecast B, with a decline in A and a simultaneous rise in C indicating a serious problem in B.

The three-curve barometer predicted the economic crisis of 1920–1921, putting forecasts by the Harvard group and others in high demand. Businesses relied on Persons's barometer in ordering goods and making other key investment decisions. Even the failure of the barometers to forecast trends of 1923 was excused, as the Federal Reserve sought to modify economic trends by injecting or removing money from the economy.

The Harvard barometer became internationally known, and other institutions adopted its methods. AT&T used it as the basis for its own barometer, and General Motors developed a barometer it was willing to put against Harvard's. Together, Persons's three-curve barometer and the statistical indicators that evolved from it transformed the business report from a tool of individual economic evaluation to a "scientific" document suitable for regulating the entire market. By the end of the 1920s, central banks and governments relied on such measures for their interventions in national economic policy. This was consistent with the growth at the same time of large organizations or divisions devoted to data collection and analysis in order to forecast economic trends and foretell, if not forestall, coming economic crises. Great Britain, France, Russia, Germany, and other European nations based their key economic indicators on the three-curve barometer. Sweden and Italy proceeded with more caution; the League of Nations implemented a committee on business cycle analysis in 1926.

Critics challenged the reliability of cyclic barometers. The Italian statistician and demographer Corrado Gini (originator of the Gini coefficient) noted that they carried the potential for self-fulfilling-prophecy, with businesspeople who relied on the various indicators exaggerating and destabilizing the economic cycle. The Austrian economist Oskar Morgenstern pointed out that the Harvard barometer was not based on true probability—impossible given the nature of the data—and that therefore it should not be used in economic decision making.

The debate culminated in an inconclusive discussion by the International Statistical Institute in 1929. That October, the Harvard Committee first failed to predict the stock market crash and then failed to explain it. The barometer remained flat, indicating no downturn, let alone a depression. Those who depended on the barometers reacted to the initial stock downturn in a manner consistent with their belief that it was only a minor blip before the market stabilized. Nevertheless,

the three-curve barometer retained its hold on the American business community during the early 1930s, leading to a number of erroneous decisions. The ongoing calamity of the Great Depression finally rendered the Harvard indicator and others moot, particularly as they continued to forecast rapid recovery. Publication of the three-curve barometer ceased in 1935.

John Barnhill

See also: Asset-Price Bubble; Credit Cycle; Great Depression (1929–1933); Stock Market Crash (1929).

Further Reading

Glasner, David, and Thomas F. Cooley. *Business Cycles and Depressions.* New York: Taylor and Francis, 1997.

Graf, Hans Georg. *Economic Forecasting for Management: Possibilities and Limitations.* Westport, CT: Quorum, 2002.

Schumpeter, *Joseph A. Ten Great Economists.* New York: Routledge, 1997.

Thrift Supervision, Office of

Established amid the savings and loan crisis of the late 1980s and early 1990s, the Office of Thrift Supervision (OTS) is the primary federal agency charged with overseeing and regulating nationally chartered savings associations (thrifts). Criticized for its lack of supervision of the mortgage practices of savings and loans (S&Ls) during the housing boom of the early and middle 2000s, the OTS has been slated for termination under President Barack Obama's proposed reform package for the regulatory system overseeing the nation's financial system.

The origins of the OTS go back to the Great Depression, when a collapse in the housing market sent many thrifts into bankruptcy. Among the reforms enacted under President Franklin Roosevelt's New Deal was the Federal Home Loan Bank Board, which issued federal charters for thrifts and created a home ownership–promoting regulatory system for the savings and loan industry. Also created at the time was the Federal Savings and Loan Insurance Corporation, a separate agency that provided government guarantees to protect deposits at S&Ls.

The system worked well in the first decades following the end of World War II. While S&Ls were tightly regulated, with high deposit-to-loan ratio requirements, mortgages became increasingly affordable and homeownership expanded dramatically. But when interest rates soared in the 1970s, the restrictions on the interest rates that savings and loans could offer on deposits led to capital flight to banks and into investment options. As a wave of insolvencies threatened the S&L industry, regulations were eased, allowing S&Ls to make more loans on higher-risk investments. By the 1980s, this deregulation led to a crisis, as borrowers proved unable to repay their loans and a wave of bankruptcies hit the S&L industry, ultimately causing Congress to pass a bailout bill that, as of 1999, was estimated by the Federal Deposit Insurance Corporation (FDIC) to have cost taxpayers about $124 billion.

In 1989, Congress passed the Financial Institutions Reform, Recovery and Enforcement Act, a new set of regulatory reforms that moved the S&L deposit insurance to the FDIC (which traditionally provided such insurance to banks) and created the OTS to charter, oversee, and regulate the thrift industry. Unique among the federal financial institution regulatory agencies, the OTS oversees both S&Ls and financial holding companies—that is, companies, including nonfinancial businesses such as General Electric, that own significant stock in financial institutions.

This created a problem. With the financial industry overseen by several agencies—each with its own history and reputation for tight or lax regulation—financial institutions and holding companies were often able to shop around for the regulatory agency that they deemed most likely to allow them to conduct business as they saw fit. For many companies, the OTS fit the bill.

During the housing boom of the early and middle 2000s, the OTS, according to many financial industry experts, took a more lax approach to regulation, allowing financial institutions to maintain ever-lower liquid asset-to-loan ratios. At the same time, the OTS encouraged the development of a variety of higher-risk mortgage options, including adjustable rate mortgages (ARMs) that offered low upfront interest-only payments to borrowers, followed by an adjustment to higher principal-and-interest payments. Potentially, these higher payments could send borrowers into foreclosure. But ever-rising home prices—and ever-rising home equity—allowed borrowers to refinance before the adjustment to a higher monthly payment kicked in.

Still, other federal regulators, including the Office of the Comptroller of the Currency (OCC), issued warnings as early as the mid-2000s that ARMs presented great risk to borrowers, and exposure to such ARMs presented a great risk to the financial institutions that offered excessive amounts of them. However, say experts, the OTS refused to issue new regulations or even warnings to the financial institutions it oversaw.

As the housing bubble burst in 2007 and 2008, many of these financial institutions were hit by a wave of foreclosures and became saddled with bad loans. In 2008, several major thrifts and holding companies overseen by the OTS became insolvent, including the California-based thrift IndyMac Bank and the Washington state–based holding company Washington Mutual. The latter represented the largest failure of a financial institution in American history.

These failures led to renewed scrutiny of the OTS's operations by Congress. But the legislators' concerns went beyond the OTS's history of lax regulation to a questioning of the whole federal financial institution regulatory structure. Many critics argued that overlapping agencies made the system too unwieldy and too prone to manipulation and evasion by financial institutions seeking ways to avoid oversight and regulation.

The incoming Obama administration made reforming and streamlining the federal financial regulatory system a top priority. But while many advocates of reform have applauded the administration's call to fold the OTS into the Office of the Comptroller of the Currency (OCC), they say the plans do not go far enough since that is the only one of the several federal regulatory agencies involved in financial industry regulation and oversight slated for termination.

James Ciment

See also: Regulation, Financial; Savings and Loan Crises (1980s–1990s).

Further Reading

Immergluck, Daniel. *Foreclosed: High-Risk Lending, Deregulation, and the Undermining of America's Mortgage Market.* Ithaca, NY: Cornell University Press, 2009.

Office of Thrift Supervision Web site: www.ots.treas.gov.

White, Lawrence J. *The S&L Debacle: Public Policy Lessons for Bank and Thrift Regulation.* New York: Oxford University Press, 1991.

Tinbergen, Jan (1903–1994)

Dutch economist Jan Tinbergen was a recipient (with Ragnar Frisch of Norway) of the first Nobel Prize in Economic Sciences in 1969 for "having developed and applied dynamic models for the analysis of economic processes." Tinbergen was a founder of the field of econometrics, which he applied to the study of the dynamics of business cycles. (His brother, Nikolaas Tinbergen, a pioneer in the field of ethology, was a co-recipient of the 1973 Nobel Prize for Physiology or Medicine.)

Jan Tinbergen was born on April 12, 1903, in The Hague, Netherlands, to Dirk Cornelis Tinbergen and Jeannette Van Eek. He studied mathematics and physics at the University of Leiden, but redirected his studies and earned a doctorate in economics in 1929. Like many of his generation of economists, Tinbergen worked in both the academic and public-service sectors. While teaching at the Netherlands School of Economics from 1933 to 1973, he also served as a consultant to the League of Nations (1936–1938) and as direc-tor of the Netherlands Central Planning Bureau (1945–1955).

Tinbergen's particular area of interest was the movement and mechanics of business cycles. He began constructing economic models early in his career. Working concurrently with Frisch, he developed the first econometric model of a national economy in the decade before World War II—these efforts mark the beginning of econometrics as a practical and organized field of study. Together with Frisch, Irving Fisher, and thirteen others, Tinbergen founded the Econometric Society in Cleveland, Ohio, in 1930. It was to the development of the science of econometrics, particularly in the study and analysis of business cycles, that Tinbergen made what may be considered his greatest contributions to economics.

Also in 1930, Tinbergen used econometrics to develop a model known as the "cobweb theory," which showed how past and present business-cycle behavior is closely interlinked and can be used to predict future cycles. He built on it the following year with a study of the shipbuilding industry and its cycles. By 1937, Tinbergen was developing a model of the Dutch economy and published *An Econometric Approach to Business Cycle Problems.*

As the decade progressed, Tinbergen developed models of increasing size and complexity. As result of his work for the League of Nations, he created an econometric model of the U.S. economy, published in two volumes (both in 1939), *A Method and Its Application to Investment Activity* and *Business Cycles in the United States of America, 1919–1932.* In *A Method,* he used econometric studies to provide a realistic basis for testing the various theories that attempted to explain the causes and characteristics of the stages of the business cycle. In *Business Cycles,* he showed the results of his large-scale model, which used forty-eight different equations. The work was a landmark both in methodology and in result.

Following World War II, Tinbergen held numerous academic and private-sector positions. In 1965, he was appointed chair of the United Nations Committee for Development Planning.

His knowledge about and effective use of economics to shape public policy, especially in the 1960s and 1970s, drew comparisons to John Maynard Keynes. Increasingly, Tinbergen turned his attention to global economic concerns, including the future availability of natural resources, world security, and Third World development. He died on June 9, 1994, in Amsterdam.

Robert N. Stacy

See also: Fisher, Irving; Frisch, Ragnar.

Further Reading

Hansen, Bent. "Jan Tinbergen: An Appraisal of His Contributions to Economics." *Swedish Journal of Economics* 71:4 (December 1969): 325–326.

Magnus, Jan R., and Mary S. Morgan. "The ET Interview: Professor J. Tinbergen." *Econometric Theory* 3:1 (February 1987): 117–142.

Tinbergen, Jan. *Econometrics.* New York: Routledge, 2005.

———. *Entering the Third Millennium: Some Suggestions.* Rotterdam: Fijan, 1991.

———. *World Security and Equity.* Brookfield, VT: Gower, 1990.

Tobin, James (1918–2002)

An admired Yale University economist and Nobel laureate, James Tobin combined a distinguished academic career with public service. His work on the theoretical formulation of investment behavior provided important insights into financial markets and helped earn him the Nobel Prize in Economics in 1981. He was specifically cited by the nominating committee for "his analysis of financial markets and their relations to expenditure decisions, employment, production, and prices."

Tobin was born on March 5, 1918, in Champaign, Illinois. His father, Michael, was a journalist and his mother, Margaret, a social worker. Coming of age during the Great Depression, and later his introduction to the theories of John Maynard Keynes, had a profound influence on and informed much of Tobin's thinking throughout his career. He attended Harvard University, receiving a bachelor's degree in 1939, and worked as an economist with the Office of Price Administration in 1941–1942. After serving in the U.S. Navy during World War II, he returned to Harvard and earned a doctorate in economics in 1947. Joining the faculty of Yale University in 1950, he was named Sterling Professor of Economics in 1957 and served multiple terms as director of the Cowles Foundation for Research at Yale (1955–1961, 1964–1965). During the John F. Kennedy administration, he served on the Council of Economic Advisers (1961–1962), in addition to several terms on the Board of Governors of the Federal Reserve System.

Tobin's major work involved analysis of financial markets, determining optimal investment strategies and predicting consumer-purchasing patterns. In developing his ideas, Tobin created three major components of financial management theory: portfolio management theory, probit analysis, and the Tobin q value.

Tobin's portfolio management theory was critical to the foundations of modern portfolio theory. In 1958, Tobin wrote a seminal article, "Liquidity Preference as Behaviour Towards Risk," in which he proved that in a world with one safe asset and a large number of risky assets, portfolio choice by any risk-averse individual consists of a choice between a risk-free safe asset and the same portfolio of risky assets. The degree of risk aversion is the only determinant of the shares in the total portfolio accounted for by the safe asset and by the common portfolio of risky assets. When asked to explain his research, Tobin commented in his Nobel Prize acceptance speech that his work could be summarized by the phrase, "Don't put all your eggs in one basket."

Tobin's analysis of household consumption patterns, titled "Liquidity Preference as Behaviour Towards Risk," was published in the *Review of Economic Studies* in 1958. His work used data on individual household income and expenditures that had been collected since the late 1940s but never been put to any meaningful use. Using sophisticated statistical models, Tobin adopted so-called

Nobelist James Tobin argued that economic growth is not ensured purely by market forces and that the economy cannot be managed solely by adjusting the money supply. The government should take steps to control inflation, unemployment, and other factors. *(Hulton Archive/Getty Images)*

Keynesian model, including the necessity of government intervention in economic growth. In the mid-1960s, in a lecture titled "Economic Growth as an Objective of Government Policy," Tobin stated that government policies to promote economic growth represent a collective decision that concerns future generations. Thus, government should take measures to ensure growth because it cannot be done exclusively by private markets.

Tobin studied and wrote about a wide range of topics, including household finances and behavior, macroeconomics (which he maintained had a strong orientation toward public policy), and financial markets. He was the model for Tobit, a minor character in Herman Wouk's novel *The Caine Mutiny*. Tobin died on March 11, 2002, in New Haven, Connecticut.

Robert N. Stacy

See also: Consumption; Keynesian Business Model.

Further Reading

Baumol, William J. *Growth, Industrial Organization and Economic Generalities.* Cheltenham, UK: Edward Elgar, 2003.

Shiller, Robert J. "The ET Interview: Professor James Tobin." *Econometric Theory* 15:6 (December 1999): 867–900.

Tobin, James. *Essays in Economics: Macroeconomics.* Cambridge, MA: MIT Press, 1987.

———. *Full Employment and Growth: Further Keynesian Essays on Policy.* Cheltenham, UK: Edward Elgar, 1996.

———. "Liquidity Preference as Behaviour Towards Risk." *Review of Economic Studies* 25:2 (February 1958): 65–86.

———. *Measuring Prices in a Dynamic Economy: Re-Examining the CPI.* New York: Study Group on the Consumer Price Index, Conference Board, 1999.

———. *Money, Credit, and Capital.* Boston: Irwin/McGraw-Hill, 1998.

———. *Policies for Prosperity: Essays in a Keynesian Mode.* Brighton, Sussex, UK: Wheatsheaf, 1987.

probit analysis to determine the probability of an event occurring. This enabled analysts to estimate not only the likelihood of purchases but also the likely amount of related expenditures.

One of Tobin's innovations, called Tobin's q, can be used to decide whether a firm should invest in an additional unit of capital. Tobin's q is the ratio of the market value of the capital relative to the replacement cost. If q is high, then the firm should invest in more capital because the capital's market value would be greater than its replacement costs. If q is less than 1, the market value of the additional capital is less than its replacement cost, and hence, the firm should not invest. The beauty of Tobin's q is that it provides a simple solution to a complex problem: increase investment only if q is greater than 1.

In addition to his Nobel Prize–winning work, Tobin spent much of his life refining the original

"Too Big to Fail"

"Too big to fail" is a term that was employed by financial pundits and the press during the financial crisis and the subsequent federal bailout of major financial institutions in 2008–2009. It refers to private financial institutions that are so large, so diverse, and so interconnected with other businesses that their failure could create panic in the global financial markets.

History

While the phrase "too big to fail" gained notoriety in recent years, the concept behind it is nothing new. Many of the periodic financial panics of the late nineteenth and early twentieth centuries were triggered by the failure of major banks and financial institutions, often as a result of financial speculation, which caused a cascade of bankruptcies in the financial markets as credit flows froze. In 1907, financier J.P. Morgan orchestrated a $100 million bailout by a consortium of major banks of financial institutions that had been caught up in speculation in the copper market. Though successful, the effort convinced many in the financial community and government that only Washington would have the resources to act as a lender of last resort in the event of an even greater crisis in the future. The result of this thinking was the creation of the Federal Reserve System (Fed) in 1913.

But the Fed proved unable to prevent the avalanche of bank failures in the early 1930s that threatened the U.S. financial system. In response to that unprecedented crisis, the Franklin D. Roosevelt administration created the Federal Deposit Insurance Corporation (FDIC) to insure depositors against losses up to a certain amount, thereby assuring them that their savings were secure and thus preventing depositor runs that could lead to bank failures. Other reforms implemented in the 1930s included new regulations on financial institutions to prevent such failures in the first place, including a law that banned commercial banks from engaging in more speculative investment banking activities.

In the event of a bank failure, the FDIC had three options: close and liquidate the institution's assets, purchase the institution and then sell off its assets to another institution, or provide loans to shore up the institution (this last option was enabled by the Federal Deposit Insurance Act of 1950). The system appeared to work until the early 1980s, when it finally was tested by the potential failure of the Continental Illinois National Bank in 1984. Exposed to liabilities created by collapsing oil prices, America's seventh-largest bank threatened to create a major financial panic if it proved unable to meet its obligations. Normally, federal regulators would have orchestrated its purchase by other institutions, but with the nation in its deepest recession since the 1930s, this proved impossible, forcing the Fed to declare that it would meet any and all of Continental Illinois's liquidity needs.

Despite the Continental Illinois crisis, the 1980s and 1990s saw massive deregulation in the financial industry, a process backed by both Republican and Democratic administrations. Financial industry experts argued that excessive regulations limited the profit-making potential of financial institutions and prevented them from creating new and innovative products that could provide more readily available credit and make financial markets more efficient. Moreover, it was argued that bigger institutions could operate more effectively in increasingly global financial markets.

The result of this deregulatory trend was a wave of consolidation in the financial industry, the rise of multistate banking (banks operating across state lines), and the end of the Depression-era firewall between commercial and investment banking activity. The last move was pushed in 1999 by Citigroup, America's largest financial institution, which sought to operate brokerage, insurance, investment banking, and commercial banking businesses under one roof.

The formation of Citigroup and the creation and expansion of other financial giants led to a perception in the financial community that some banks had become "too big to fail." In other words, if any of these large national banks faced a liquidity crisis or potential insolvency, this would create both unsustainable liquidity demands on other financial institutions as well as a general perception that no institution was safe. Moreover, a failure of such a large institution would cause credit markets to freeze up, making it difficult for financial institutions and businesses to secure the short-term credit they needed to run their daily operations, thereby triggering a financial crisis and recession. With financial markets increasingly integrated across national borders, such a crisis could become global in scope.

During the financial boom years of the late 1990s and early 2000s, few people seemed concerned about such a scenario. Indeed, larger financial institutions benefited from the "too big to fail" notion, as large commercial depositors—unprotected by the FDIC because of the sheer size of their accounts—moved their assets to those institutions, believing that if a crisis came, the federal government would step in to protect the largest banks. At the same time, the managers of the largest banks understood that these perceptions permitted the same managers to offer lower interest rates, thereby increasing the profitability of the biggest banks and allowing them to grow bigger still. In addition, there was the matter of "moral hazard." Simply put, managers of the largest banks, knowing that their institutions would not be allowed to fail, had an incentive to engage in risky—and potentially more profitable—investment activities. Moral hazard, then, created distortions in the financial marketplace competition.

Financial Crisis of 2008–2009

The financial crisis triggered by the collapse of the subprime mortgage market in 2008 set in motion the "too big to fail" scenario. Late in that year, the George W. Bush administration and the Fed convinced Congress to authorize a $700 billion federal bailout plan, known officially as the Troubled Asset Relief Program (TARP). On October 3, 2008, Congress passed and the president signed the Emergency Economic Stabilization Act. The act authorized the U.S. Department of the Treasury to purchase up to $700 billion of

"toxic" mortgage-backed and other securities in order to provide funds to intermediaries so that they could resume lending and prevent further deterioration of the economy. On October 14, 2008, the TARP plan was revised by the Treasury Department, so that the initial $250 billion would be used to purchase preferred stock in American banks under the Capital Purchase Program. The Treasury decided that it would be better to inject capital directly into banks rather than purchase the toxic assets. By the end of October, nine of the largest American banks had applied for and received $125 billion in bailout funds.

The thinking among policy makers was that by shoring up the capital of banks, those institutions would begin lending again, and the financial system would recover. In November 2008, the Treasury authorized the use of $40 billion in TARP funds to purchase preferred stock in the insolvent insurance giant AIG (American Interna-

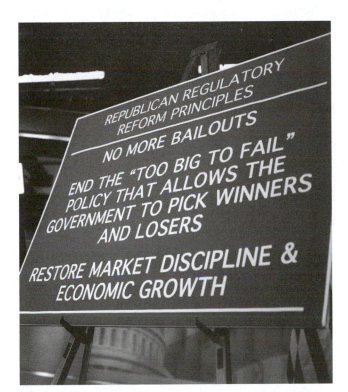

In a 2009 news conference on "lessons learned" a year after federal intervention in the U.S. financial markets, House Republicans call for an end to the "Too Big to Fail" policy under which giant institutions are rescued to avoid panic or other dire consequences. *(Scott J. Ferrell/Congressional Quarterly/Getty Images)*

tional Group), which had been taken over by the federal government two months earlier.

In the same month, three large insurance companies announced plans to purchase depository institutions in order to give them access to TARP funds. Finally, Treasury Secretary Henry Paulson officially announced that the TARP funds would not be used at that time to purchase "toxic" assets, but rather would be used to support the financial system in other ways. In December, the Treasury authorized the use of TARP funds to bail out General Motors and Chrysler.

In December 2008, TARP money was used to buy preferred stock in large and small banks. By early the following January, about $305 billion of the bailout funds had been spent, with approximately $200 billion used to buy preferred stock in banks, $40 billion used to bail out AIG, an additional $45 billion invested in Citigroup and Bank of America (both of which had participated in the Capital Purchase Program), and $20 billion invested with the automakers and their financing subsidiaries. Some analysts charged that the bailout funds were not used for their original purposes and merely supported large institutions that had created the problems in the first place. The argument made at the time was that the failure of any of these institutions would create such a stress on the financial markets that they simply would shut down, triggering an economic downturn rivaling that of the 1930s.

In addition, the government orchestrated the liquidation and/or repurchase of such major financial failures as IndyMac Bank of California and Washington Mutual of Washington State. The bailout came after the federal government refused to rescue Lehman Brothers, a large investment bank, in September 2008, a decision that many financial experts say contributed to the financial crisis.

Ironically, according to some financial experts, the crisis and the bailout contributed to the "too big to fail" phenomenon by reinforcing the gains that large institutions achieved through moral hazard. In other words, large commercial depositors and managers of large financial institutions no longer had to act on faith that the government would step in, knowing that they would be protected and thereby giving these institutions a leg up on their smaller rivals. Moreover, the government, through the bailout and other actions, encouraged larger institutions to buy out smaller and weaker competitors, increasing the size of the former.

While some economists, particularly on the left side of the political spectrum, have argued that these developments necessitate the breakup of the biggest financial institutions, the Barack Obama administration began pushing another option—granting new regulatory powers to the Fed to oversee these "too big to fail" institutions and potentially to intervene should they engage in the kinds of risky behavior that might lead to their failure. In other words, President Obama and his advisers argued that the federal government needs to have a kind of "systemic risk agency" that would prevent a repeat of the financial crisis that unfolded in 2008–2009 and nearly plunged the nation and the world into another Great Depression.

James Ciment

See also: AIG; Moral Hazard; Systemic Financial Crises; Troubled Asset Relief Program (2008–).

Further Reading

Sorkin, Andrew Ross. *Too Big to Fail: The Inside Story of How Wall Street and Washington Fought to Save the Financial System from Crisis—and Themselves.* New York: Viking, 2009.

Stern, Gary F., and Ron J. Feldman. *Too Big to Fail: The Hazards of Bank Bailouts.* Washington, DC: Brookings Institution, 2009.

Transition Economies

A transition economy is an emerging market economy that is in the process of changing from a centrally planned to a free-market economy. Economists usually use the term to describe economies that were once part of the communist bloc, such as those in Eastern Europe and the former

Soviet Union. More loosely, the term is applied to any emerging market economy that was once dominated by state planning and direction, such as India and Iraq.

The transition process in such countries is about more than mere economic change; it is about the society as a whole. According to economists Oleh Havrylyshyn, Thomas Wolf, and Jan Svejnar, the transition encompasses the following changes: limiting the central bank to monetary policy and allowing new private banks to assume commercial banking operations; liberalization of economic activities, including removing barriers to the creation of new firms; ending most government price setting, though government price controls may continue for certain crucial goods and services, such as housing, energy, and medicine; cutting supports for state-owned enterprises so that resources can be allocated by the market; achieving macroeconomic stabilization through market-oriented means, as opposed to direct policy decisions; increasing efficiency and competitiveness through the privatization of state-owned firms; implementing tight budgetary constraints to avoid large public debts; securing property rights; and applying transparent, market-entry regulations for both domestic and foreign-owned firms.

Differences Among Transition Economies

Various authorities and institutions define transition economies somewhat differently and so list different countries as transition economies. The United Nations Statistics Division, for example, identifies eighteen countries from Europe and Asia as transition economies: Albania, Armenia, Azerbaijan, Belarus, Bosnia and Herzegovina, Croatia, Georgia, Kazakhstan, Kyrgyzstan, the Former Yugoslav Republic (FYR) of Macedonia, Moldova, Montenegro, Russia, Serbia, Tajikistan, Turkmenistan, Ukraine, and Uzbekistan. According to the European Bank for Reconstruction and Development (EBRD), a total of thirty countries are classified as transitional: Albania,

Armenia, Azerbaijan, Belarus, Bosnia and Herzegovina, Bulgaria, Croatia, Czech Republic, Estonia, Georgia, Hungary, Kazakhstan, Kyrgyzstan, Latvia, Lithuania, FYR of Macedonia, Moldova, Mongolia, Montenegro, Poland, Romania, Russia, Serbia, Slovak Republic, Slovenia, Tajikistan, Turkey, Turkmenistan, Ukraine, and Uzbekistan. Other countries sometimes classified as transitional include East Germany, Iraq, and China.

Transition economies are historically, politically, geographically, demographically, and economically diverse countries. Their populations range from 678,000 (Montenegro) to 141 million (Russia), and population densities (people per square kilometer) range from 2 (Mongolia) to 134 (Czech Republic). Some transition countries are oil-rich (Azerbaijan and Turkmenistan), while others have no oil reserves at all (Estonia). Some have a relatively warm climate (Turkey and Slovenia), others a cold climate (Lithuania), and still others have highly diverse climates and terrains, including flatlands, steppes, taigas, and deserts (Russia and Kazakhstan). Some countries are located on the ocean or sea (Russia, Croatia, and Latvia), while others are landlocked (Hungary and Mongolia). Such demographic, geographical, and geological differences have had a direct impact on economic development, systems, and structures, among which are the absence of large multinational corporations (which are not easy to establish in a very small country), modes of transport, and the role of agriculture and mining in the economy.

In addition to the above-mentioned differences, the countries also have major historical differences and institutional legacies. A total of fifteen transition economies today belonged to the Soviet Union until 1991: Armenia, Azerbaijan, Belarus, Estonia, Georgia, Kazakhstan, Kyrgyzstan, Latvia, Lithuania, Moldova, Russia, Tajikistan, Turkmenistan, Ukraine, and Uzbekistan. Some of these were generally willing to maintain strong economic and political ties with Moscow, while others (such as Yugoslavia and Hungary) were more autonomous. So, when the Soviet Union dissolved and the Council for Mutual Economic

Assistance—the trading bloc within the Soviet-dominated communist world—was abolished, some countries were affected more strongly than others. Firms in the closer satellite countries, generally state-run, were more apt to lose their markets and shut down. Those that survived and the new ones that were created had little knowledge of Western production systems, lacked contacts with outside distributors, and had few sources of financing for new technology, developing new products, and entering new markets. Thus, most of these economies experienced large declines in total output. Others were less affected because of their weaker connections to—and reliance on—the Soviet Union and their strong ties to capitalist economies of the West.

Economic Progress

The EBRD tracks the economic progress of transition countries according to eight indicators: (1) large-scale and small-scale privatization—the percentage of privately owned firms; (2) governance and enterprise restructuring—the effectiveness of corporate control, tightness of credit and subsidy policy, and enforcement of bankruptcy legislation; (3) price liberalization—the share of price control outside housing, transport, and national monopolies; (4) trade and foreign exchange—the lifting of export and import restrictions and the existence of a fully transparent foreign exchange regime; (5) competition policy—effective enforcement by special institutions; (6) banking reform and interest rate liberalization—the harmonization of banking laws and regulations with international standards, the provision of competitive banking services, the removal of interest rate ceilings; (7) securities markets and nonbank financial institutions—meeting international standards in securities regulation and having well-functioning nonbank financial institutions; and (8) infrastructure reform—the decentralization, commercialization, and effective regulation of electric power, railways, roads, telecommunications, water, and wastewater. According to these indicators, Esto-

nia, Hungary, and Poland have transitioned the quickest while Belarus, Turkmenistan, and Uzbekistan have lagged significantly behind.

Moreover, the EBRD has noted a significant connection between the pace of transition and degree of economic growth, with quicker transitions resulting in faster growth. That is, those countries that have completed basic structural reforms have developed faster than those that have not. At the same time, there is a direct correlation between per capita gross domestic product (GDP) and transition pace, though not a direct cause-and-effect relationship. That is, there is a correlation between higher-income countries and faster paces of transition, but which triggers which is open to debate.

To that end, it is important to note that not all of these countries started on the transition path from the same level of development. Countries that were lagging even before the transition began have generally had more uneven growth than more advanced countries. In addition, which transition measures countries have undertaken has determined their pace of economic growth. Economists have found that countries that encouraged the entry and growth of new firms—as well as encouraging them to innovate and grow faster—did better than countries that did not. Moreover, countries that imposed budgetary constraints on former state-owned enterprises—including denying them access to credit—created economic chaos.

Moreover, say economists at the EBRD and elsewhere, the speed of transition depended on the form of privatization; countries that succeeded in finding successful strategic investors, often from abroad, have developed faster than those that privatized companies to ineffective owners (often, employees or former managers) or continued with state ownership. Also important was the development of new commercial/legal systems and the institutions necessary for the effective functioning of a free-market economy, including the defining and enforcing of private property rights and the means to transfer property. In some transition economies, policy makers were disappointed to find that the free market could not simply take care of itself but needed effective laws and regulatory institutions. In many of these countries, insiders opposed such changes because they were profiting off the privatization and transition processes and wanted a free hand to make their illicit gains. In addition, if existing firms were given special benefits, those who were making money off of them tended to oppose ending such market-distorting subsidies. Finally, those countries that invested more heavily in the social welfare, education, and health systems tended to fare better economically than those that did not.

The Impact of the Financial Crisis and the Recession Since 2007

The financial crisis and recession of 2007–2009 hit many of the transition economies hard. Ironically, those countries, such as Estonia, that had integrated themselves more closely into the global financial markets (a factor that benefited them during the boom years of their early transition period) were the hardest hit, primarily because they had become heavily dependent on foreign investment, which often produced unsustainable growth rates and speculative bubbles in the local real-estate market. When access to that capital disappeared, these economies went into a tailspin. Estonia, for example, saw its annual growth rate plummet from 7.2 percent in 2007 to a depression-level −13.7 percent in 2009. Moreover, as capital fled these countries, private and public debt levels grew, making it more difficult for firms and governments to borrow from abroad to address the social problems exacerbated by the economic downturn.

Most economists agree that for transition economies to emerge from the crisis in better shape than they entered it, they must do the following: improve the governance and structure of their financial sectors and provide them with more liquidity; continue to invest in small and medium-sized firms; fix fiscal imbalances so that future fluctuations in capital flows do not have such a heavy impact on government finances; strengthen competition by removing barriers that obstruct trade and the entry of new firms into the marketplace; support innovation; improve the quality of education; and help firms both diversify and move up the supply chain so that they can produce higher value-added products. At the same time, the private sectors in these economies, say development experts, need to improve their fundamentals as well by cutting costs, developing new and better products, modernizing their marketing strategies, and even restructuring.

Tiia Vissak and James Ciment

See also: China; Eastern Europe; Emerging Markets; India; Latin America; Russia and the Soviet Union; Southeast Asia.

Further Reading

Havrylyshyn, Oleh, and Thomas Wolf. "Determinants of Growth in Transition Countries." Available at www.imf.org/external/pubs/ft/fandd/1999/06/havrylys.htm. Accessed March 2010.

Ichimura, Shinichi, Tsuneaki Sato, and William James. *Transition from Socialist to Market Economies: Comparison of European and Asian Experiences.* New York: Palgrave Macmillan, 2009.

McGee, Robert W., ed. *Corporate Governance in Transition Economies.* New York: Springer, 2008.

Svejnar, Jan. "Transition Economies: Performance and Challenges." *Journal of Economic Perspectives* 16: 1 (2002): 3–28.

Transition Report 2008: Growth in Transition. Norwich, UK: EBRD, 2009. Available at http://transitionreport.co.uk/TRO/b/transition-report/volume2009/issue1. Accessed March 2010.

Transition: The First Ten Years. Analysis and Lessons for Eastern Europe and the Former Soviet Union. Washington, DC: The World Bank, 2002. Available at http://siteresources.worldbank.org/ECAEXT/Resources/complete.pdf. Accessed March 2010.

Treasury Bills

Treasury securities include Treasury bills, Treasury notes, Treasury bonds, and Treasury Inflation-Protected Securities (TIPS); they are issued (sold) by the U.S. Department of the Treasury to investors who are willing to lend money to the federal government. These investors can include other government agencies, the Federal Reserve (Fed), professional investment firms, banks, foreign governments, and individuals. Among these securities, Treasury bills have the shortest term, with a maximum maturity of one year from the time of issue.

The interest that investors usually earn from bonds comes from their coupon payments, which are generally paid semiannually. For example, if a bond promises a 5 percent coupon rate and the face (par) value of the bond is $1,000, then the annual coupon payment is 5 percent x $1,000 = $50 (coupon rate times face value), and the investor receives $25 every six months. Treasury bills, commonly referred to as "T-bills," are zero-coupon bonds, which means they do not make coupon payments and the investor's return is simply the difference between the purchase price and the face (par) value received when the bill matures. Because of this, T-bills are said to be priced and sold at "a discount to par value," or an amount less than their face value, and are quoted on a discount rate basis. Dealers who deal in Treasury securities buy and sell T-bills from investors. An abbreviated T-bill listing from a typical day, February 27, 2009, appears below:

Treasury Bill Prices, February 27, 2009

Maturity	Days to Maturity	Bid	Asked	Chg	Asked Yield
2009 Mar 05	6	0.120	0.095	−0.010	0.096
2009 Mar 12	13	0.130	0.125	Unch.	0.127
2009 Mar 19	20	0.170	0.140	−0.005	0.142
2009 Apr 02	34	0.180	0.160	−0.025	0.162
2009 Apr 09	41	0.190	0.160	−0.020	0.162
2009 May 28	90	0.260	0.250	−0.010	0.254
2009 Jun 04	97	0.285	0.275	Unch.	0.279
2009 Jun 11	104	0.300	0.290	Unch.	0.294
2009 Jun 18	111	0.300	0.290	−0.020	0.294
2009 Jun 25	118	0.320	0.305	−0.010	0.310
2009 Aug 20	174	0.450	0.415	+0.005	0.422
2009 Aug 27	181	0.450	0.440	−0.015	0.447
2009 Sep 03	188	0.485	0.475	Unch.	0.483
2009 Dec 17	293	0.660	0.653	−0.015	0.664
2010 Jan 14	321	0.653	0.643	−0.007	0.654
2010 Feb 11	349	0.690	0.685	−0.013	0.698

Source: Thomson Reuters.

The longest term T-bill outstanding on this day had 349 days to maturity on February 11, 2010. "Bid" and "ask" quotes represent the prices an investor pays to purchase the security (ask) from a securities dealer or the amount an investor receives when selling the security (bid) to a broker. In other words, the bid price is the price at which a dealer will buy T-bills from an investor, and the ask price is the price at which a securities dealer will sell the security to an investor. Bids and asks are usually expressed as prices or percentages of par value, depending on the security being traded; for T-bills, these numbers are discount interest rates. The 0.685 percent "asked" discount rate for the 349-day T-bill corresponds to a price of $993.359. An investor who paid that amount for one of the T-bills receives $1,000 upon maturity on February 11, 2010, which equates to a return over that time period of ($1,000 − $993.359)/$ 993.359 = 0.6685 percent. The asked yield, 0.698 percent, comes from annualizing the 0.6685 percent. Note that for simplicity, in the example a $1,000 T-bill is used. In reality, T-bills are sold in $100 increments with a $100 minimum.

How Treasury Bills Are Sold and Purchased

Investors purchase T-bills by participating in auctions conducted by the Department of the Treasury. Auctions of 4-week, 13-week, and 26-week bills are held every week; 52-week bills are auctioned every 4 weeks. Auction announcements are published in newspapers, issued via press releases or e-mails, and can be found at the Treasury Direct Web site. An auction announcement reveals the important dates and deadlines related to the auction and how much money the government is seeking to borrow. Investors can participate in these auctions either as competitive bidders or noncompetitive bidders. Professional investors tend to be the competitive bidders, and they specify the discount rate they would like to receive along with the dollar amount they are interested in lending. Individuals, who tend to

Treasury Bill Auction Results, February 2009

T-bill	Auction Date	Discount Rate	Amount to Competitive Bidders	Amount to Noncompetitive Bidders
26-week	2/2/2009	0.390%	$27,583,365,500	$1,416,848,500
13-week	2/2/2009	0.270%	$27,188,633,000	$1,811,420,000
4-week	2/3/2009	0.285%	$33,473,458,300	$526,593,300
52-week	2/10/2009	0.610%	$22,851,700,300	$148,610,500
26-week	2/9/2009	0.480%	$28,415,418,600	$1,535,434,400
13-week	2/9/2009	0.340%	$29,326,477,000	$1,673,671,000
4-week	2/10/2009	0.250%	$35,635,089,000	$365,084,600
26-week	2/17/2009	0.470%	$28,532,346,000	$1,467,739,700
13-week	2/17/2009	0.325%	$29,221,190,000	$1,778,860,200
4-week	2/18/2009	0.230%	$35,634,990,000	$365,088,000
26-week	2/23/2009	0.495%	$27,859,875,000	$2,140,250,300
13-week	2/23/2009	0.300%	$28,483,856,500	$2,516,167,400
4-week	2/24/2009	0.205%	$32,609,912,000	$1,390,227,800

Source: John J. Neumann.

be the noncompetitive bidders, submit only the dollar amount they are willing to lend (subject to the maximum of $5 million).

Once the auction's "winning" discount rate is determined, noncompetitive bidders receive the full amount of their bid, while competitive bidders receive all, a portion, or none of their bid dollar amount, depending on how the discount rate they submitted with their bids compares with the winning discount rate. For example, a competitive bidder who submitted a discount rate higher than the winning discount rate may receive nothing because the government wants to minimize borrowing costs and will allocate the T-bills in the auction to investors who bid at lower discount rates first. The results of the auction are made public shortly after the auction closes at 1:00 p.m. Eastern Time. Individuals can participate directly in Treasury auctions at the Treasury Department Web site. The T-bill auction results for a typical month, February 2009, cited above, give a sense of the size and scope of the transactions.

Impact of the 2007–2009 Recession and Financial Crisis

One of the tools available to the Fed in conducting monetary policy is its ability to target the fed funds rate, defined as the overnight lending rate at which depository institutions borrow and lend

reserves from each other to meet their reserve requirements. The fed funds rate is a market determined interest rate. However, the Fed can influence this rate by buying and selling Treasury securities to determine the amount of reserves in the banking system. If the Fed purchases government securities from dealers, it increases the supply of reserves available to the banking system. If the Fed sells government securities to government securities dealers, the supply of reserves decreases. When the supply of reserves increases, the fed funds rate will fall, since with reserves being more plentiful in the system, there is no need to borrow reserves and there is more to lend among depository institutions. Likewise, when the supply of reserves decreases, this puts upward pressure on the fed funds rate because more depository institutions want to borrow reserves and fewer want to lend them. When the Fed lowers the interest target for the fed funds rate, other interest rates also go down because the Fed is pumping more reserves into the banking system which will increase lending. As an overnight rate, the fed funds rate is short-term, so T-bills are the Treasury securities that would be expected to most closely reflect changes in it since they are the shortest term-to-maturity among treasuries.

The figure below plots the fed funds rate against the median/average discount rate from T-

Fed Funds Rate vs. T-Bill Auction Rates: 2000–2008

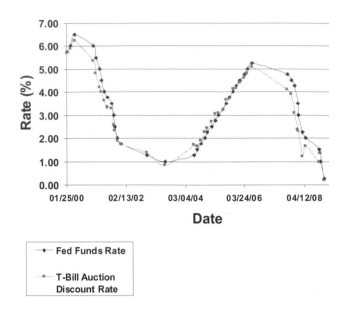

government via T-bill auctions. In June 2008, the fifty-two-week bill was reintroduced for auction after not having been available since 2001.

John J. Neumann

See also: Debt Instruments; Federal Reserve System; Interest Rates; Monetary Policy; Monetary Stability; Treasury, Department of the.

Further Reading

Burghardt, Galen D., Terrence M. Belton, Morton Lane, and John Papa. *The Treasury Bond Basis: An In-Depth Analysis for Hedgers, Speculators, and Arbitrageurs.* 3rd ed. New York: McGraw-Hill, 2005.

Treasury Direct Web site. www.treasurydirect.gov.

United States Government Accountability Office (U.S. GAO). *Report to the Secretary of the Treasury: November 2008 Financial Audit. Bureau of the Public Debt's Fiscal Years 2008 and 2007 Schedules of Federal Debt.* Washington, DC, November 2008.

bill auctions for the period from January 2000 to December 2008. The two lines mirror each other. The two periods that feature steep declines in these rates correspond to the bear market of September 2000 to September 2002 and the financial crisis that began in late 2007. The latter event, and the economic recession it provoked, created great uncertainty in the financial markets. In such climates, investors seek out safe investments like Treasury securities. Investor demand for these securities, like that for any good or service, tends to push prices upward, which corresponds to the decline in T-bill rates depicted in the graph above (since bond prices and rates are inversely related).

The reaction of the U.S. federal government included fiscal policy measures such as TARP (Troubled Asset Relief Program), TALF (Term Asset-Backed Securities Loan Facility), and a $787 billion stimulus package signed by President Barack Obama in February 2009. Without significant tax increases, all of these measures require the government to borrow more money to help pay for them. The additional borrowing was already observable in the increase in T-bill auction dollar amounts from January 2000 to February 2009. The upward trend in borrowing (from the sale of T-bills alone) accelerated at the end of 2008 and into 2009. In February 2009, investors loaned $509 billion to the

Treasury, Department of the

The Federal Reserve and the U.S. Department of the Treasury are without question the two government agencies that have the greatest impact on monitoring, measuring, and affecting the course of U.S. business cycles. The Treasury Department possesses a dizzying array of responsibilities and powers that directly impinge on U.S. economic policy and expansion, both domestic and international. These vital responsibilities and powers have emerged over the past two centuries. Most recently, the department has been charged with overseeing the 2008 Troubled Assets Relief Program (TARP), dispersing some $700 billion in taxpayer funds to financial institutions saddled with nonperforming assets of questionable value, such as mortgage-backed securities.

The History and Main Functions of the U.S. Department of the Treasury

The Treasury Department was established in September 1789 by an act of Congress for managing and improving government revenue (before that, such functions were carried out by other institutions). In the late eighteenth and early nineteenth centuries, the department was rather small, consisting of the secretary of the Treasury, a comptroller, an auditor, a treasurer, a register, and an assistant to the secretary. Currently, the secretary of the Treasury manages more than 100,000 employees. On January 26, 2009, Timothy F. Geithner became the seventy-fifth secretary of the Treasury.

Over the years, the functions of the Treasury have been extended. Currently, it manages federal finances; advises the president and others on economic and financial issues (including domestic and international financial, monetary, economic, trade, and tax, or fiscal policy); collects taxes, duties, and monies paid to and due to the United States; pays all the country's bills; manages government accounts and the public debt (if necessary, borrowing funds for running the federal government); supervises national banks and credit institutions; enforces federal finance and tax laws, investigating and prosecuting tax evaders, counterfeiters, and forgers; and implements economic sanctions against foreign threats to the United States. It is responsible for the production of currency and coinage. Thus, this agency maintains very important systems of the United States and cooperates with other federal agencies, international financial institutions, and foreign governments to advance global economic development and to predict and prevent economic and financial crises. Finally, the Treasury is responsible for ensuring the financial security of the United States, promoting its economic prosperity, and encouraging sustainable economic growth.

The Operating Bureaus and Departmental Offices of the U.S. Department of the Treasury

The Department of the Treasury has twelve operating bureaus carrying out the department's specific operations (about 98 percent of the Treasury's employees work in these bureaus) and nine departmental offices that formulate the Treasury's policy and manage it. The operating bureaus are as follows:

1. Alcohol and Tobacco Tax and Trade Bureau: regulates the production, use, and distribution of alcohol and tobacco products and collects excise taxes for firearms and ammunition;
2. Bureau of Engraving and Printing: designs and manufactures U.S. official certificates and awards, including currency and securities;
3. Bureau of the Public Debt: borrows the funds needed to operate the federal government and also issues and services U.S. Treasury securities;
4. Community Development Financial Institution Fund: provides capital and financial services to distressed communities;
5. Financial Crimes Enforcement Network: cooperates globally to fight against domestic and international financial crimes and also analyzes domestic and worldwide trends and patterns;
6. Financial Management Service: maintains government accounts, receives and disburses all public monies, and makes reports on government finances;
7. Department of the Treasury's Office of Inspector General: provides objective reviews of the department's operations;
8. Treasury Inspector General for Tax Administration: is responsible for the administration of the internal revenue laws and minimizing fraud and abuse;
9. Internal Revenue Service: determines, assesses, and collects U.S. internal revenue;
10. Office of the Comptroller of the Currency: regulates the U.S. banking system;
11. Office of Thrift Supervision: regulates federal- and state-chartered thrift institutions such as savings banks and savings and loan associations;

12. United States Mint: designs and manufactures coins, commemorative medals, and other numismatic items; distributes U.S. coins to the Federal Reserve banks; and protects U.S. gold and silver assets.

The departmental offices include the following:

1. Office of Domestic Finance: is responsible for developing policies and advising banks and other financial institutions on federal debt financing, financial regulations, and capital markets;

2. Office of Economic Policy: reviews and analyzes current and prospective, domestic, and international economic and financial developments and helps to determine appropriate economic policies;

3. Office of General Counsel: coordinates the activities of the Treasury Legal Division and offers advice to the secretary and other departmental staff;

4. Treasury's Office of International Affairs: formulates and executes U.S. international economic and financial policy; for example, financial, trade and development programs;

5. Assistant Secretary for Management and Chief Financial Officer: manages the department; deals with its budget, personnel, information technology, and offers administrative services to departmental offices;

6. Office of Public Affairs: is responsible for the department's communications strategy;

7. Office of Tax Policy: develops and implements tax policies, programs, regulations, and treaties and analyzes the consequences of tax policy decisions; for instance, for the president's budget;

8. Office of Terrorism and Financial Intelligence: combats domestic and international terrorist financing, money laundering, and other financial crimes;

9. Office of the U.S. Treasurer: offers advice on financial education, coinage, and currency of the United States.

The Strategic Plan of the U.S. Department of the Treasury for Fiscal Years 2007–2012

According to its strategic plan for 2007–2012, the U.S. Treasury Department has to concentrate on four strategic priorities. First, it has to manage the government's finances effectively and ensure that sufficient financial resources are available for operating the government. Every year, the Treasury issues more than 960 million payments on behalf of the federal government, collects over $2 trillion, and manages over $8 trillion in debt. An important goal is to reduce the tax gap (the difference between the taxes taxpayers should pay and those they actually pay) by increasing voluntary compliance with tax laws—for instance, through tax simplification—and by reducing evasion opportunities, thus reducing the country's need to borrow. Second, it is responsible for securing the United States' economic and financial future and raising standards of living. The department supports foreign trade liberalization and develops policies for fostering innovation that supports economic growth. It also has to ensure that the U.S. currency is trusted worldwide, that the country is economically competitive, and that financial and economic crises are prevented or mitigated. Moreover, it supports some emerging countries, as this policy increases trade and investment opportunities and ensures regional stability. Third, the Treasury has to strengthen national security. In cooperation with other national and international agencies and governments, but also with private financial institutions, it tries to stop the financers of terrorist groups, drug traffickers, money launderers, and other criminals and rogue regimes that threaten the United States and other free and open economies. Fourth, it has to produce effective management results and guarantee that its programs and activities perform efficiently, transparently, and cost-effectively.

Meanwhile, in 2007–2008, the department, under then secretary Henry Paulson, was faced with the worst financial crisis since the Great

Depression. With financial institutions reeling from the collapse in housing prices and rising fore-closure rates, Paulson sent a request to Congress for hundreds of billions of dollars that could be used to help banks and thrifts that were collapsing under the weight of bad mortgages and mortgage-backed securities.

Initially, Congress balked not just at the size of the rescue plan but at its lack of detail and at the enormous, unchecked latitude it gave the Treasury secretary in deciding what to do with the funds. But as the crisis deepened, Congress was forced to act, passing the Emergency Stabilization Act of 2008 in early October; the act provided $700 billion to the Treasury department to bail out troubled and potentially troubled financial institutions, though with more oversight of the Treasury secretary's actions.

Tiia Vissak

See also: Federal Reserve System; Fiscal Policy; Monetary Policy; National Economic Council; Tax Policy.

Further Reading

"Act of Congress Establishing the Treasury Department." Available at www.ustreas.gov/education/fact-sheets/history/act-congress.shtml. Accessed February 2009.

"Strategic Plan. Fiscal Years 2007–2012. U.S. Department of the Treasury." Available at www.ustreas.gov/offices/management/budget/strategic-plan/2007–2012/home.html. Accessed February 2009.

U.S. Department of the Treasury Web site: www.treasury.gov.

Tribune Company

The Tribune Company is a diversified media corporation with a history stretching back over one-and-a-half centuries. Beginning with the *Chicago Tribune* newspaper, the company's leaders recognized the power and potential of both radio and television when those media first appeared. Aggressive acquisition in large and mid-level markets made the Tribune Company a national force. However, changes in the traditional media mar-kets and questionable business decisions resulted in a serious cash flow problem that caused the Tribune Company to file for bankruptcy protec-tion in December 2008.

The Tribune Company originated on June 10, 1847, with the publication of the first issue of the *Chicago Daily Tribune.* The newspaper struggled through its early years until being acquired in 1855 by Joseph Medill. Medill recognized that Chicago could become a thriving metropolis and that his newspaper might play an important role in that future. He affiliated the paper with the Republican Party and backed Abraham Lincoln's presidential campaign in 1860. During the Civil War, *Chicago Tribune* reporters provided excellent coverage of Union operations across the country. After the war, Medill became a booster of Chi-cago, calling for improvements such as greater fire protection. Although the Tribune building was destroyed by the great fire of October 1871, the newspaper reappeared only two days later, with a prediction that Chicago would rebuild better than ever. Medill was elected mayor soon afterward.

Medill's two grandsons eventually succeeded him at the *Chicago Tribune.* They expanded be-yond Chicago, purchasing a newspaper in New York and founding a national literary magazine. They also recognized that radio could reach new audiences. In 1924, the newspaper purchased a Chicago station whose call letters were changed to WGN. The initials stood for the *Chicago Tribune*'s motto, "World's Greatest Newspaper." Innovative programming on WGN included coverage of the 1925 World Series, the Indianapolis 500, and the Kentucky Derby. Other innovations included live microphones in the courtroom of the so-called Scopes monkey trial in Tennessee and a regular comedy series that came to be nationally broadcast as *Amos 'n' Andy.*

After World War II, the Tribune Company expanded into television. In 1948, both WGN-TV in Chicago and WPIX-TV in New York were launched. WGN started to reach a nationwide audience in 1978, when most cable television systems around the country began carrying it. As a "superstation," WGN could attract advertisers who wanted a national audience. It also carried Chicago Cubs baseball games, giving that team a national following.

Between 1963 and 1985, the Tribune Company continued to expand nationally. Additional newspapers were purchased, including ones in Florida and California. Additional television and radio stations were purchased in other states. The company was reorganized into two divisions, with one concentrating on publishing and the other on broadcasting. Significant resources went into the production of television programs for the cable systems beginning in the 1980s. Shows such as the *Geraldo Rivera Show* and *Gene Roddenberry's Andromeda* were created and sold to broadcasters across the nation. In 1981, the Tribune Company also purchased the Chicago Cubs, building on a relationship that had existed for decades. In 1983, the company went from private to public ownership, with one of the largest stock offerings in history.

In June 2000, the Tribune Company purchased the Times Mirror Company, publisher of the *Los Angeles Times*, for $8.3 billion. The acquisitions included several other major newspapers, including a Spanish-language one in New York. The deal made the Tribune Company the third-largest newspaper publisher in the United States. Expansion into Internet sites and more interactive media also took place.

On April 2, 2007, Chicago-based investor Sam Zell announced his plans to purchase the Tribune Company and make it privately owned. Zell put up $315 million of his own money and financed $8.2 billion from various lenders to purchase the outstanding Tribune Company stock. Experts warned against the deal because it would load the company with a heavy debt when revenues were not increasing. Despite the warning, 97 percent of the stockholders approved the deal on August 21, 2007. Under Zell's leadership, the company purchased its own stock over the next few months. December 20, 2007, was the last day on which Tribune Company stock was traded publicly.

The company soon faced financial difficulties. Although some properties were sold off to raise cash, they were not enough. During the first nine months of 2008, revenue decreased 7.9 percent. Publishing revenue, which provided most of the income, declined 11.6 percent. Part of the reason was competition from the Internet and the public's changing interest in media. Traditional print media, including newspapers, have declined in circulation as more people rely upon the Internet for their news. As circulation declined, advertisers were less interested in using the Tribune Company's newspapers. The recession that began in 2007 only accelerated a trend that began in the 1990s. Broadcasting revenues for the company also failed to increase during this time period. Total revenue for the company was only $3.1 billion, with total liabilities of $13 billion.

On December 8, 2008, the Tribune Company filed for bankruptcy to protect its remaining assets. Under bankruptcy law, the company was allowed to continue operating while a plan to pay back its creditors was worked out. Because some of the original lenders had sold their loans to third parties, many people believed the Tribune Company would be broken up and the parts sold off. In October 2009, for example, the bankruptcy court allowed Thomas Ricketts to buy 95 percent of the Cubs, along with their stadium and broadcasting rights. Zell was criticized for not allowing the sale earlier, when the price might have been better.

In December 2009, the corporate leadership was changed. Zell remained as chairman of the board, while Randy Michaels became chief executive officer.

Tim J. Watts

See also: Information Technology; Technological Innovation.

Further Reading

Madigan, Charles M. *30: The Collapse of the Great American Newspaper.* Chicago: Ivan R. Dee, 2007.

Smith, Richard Norton. *The Colonel: The Life and Legend of Robert R. McCormick, 1880–1955.* Evanston, IL: Northwestern University Press, 2003.

Wendt, Lloyd. *Chicago Tribune: The Rise of a Great American Newspaper.* Chicago: Rand McNally, 1979.

Tropicana Entertainment

A privately owned Las Vegas–based corporation specializing in gambling, hotels, and resorts, Tropicana Entertainment was one of the fastest growing businesses in its sector until the financial crisis and recession that began in 2007 forced the company into bankruptcy. The case of Tropicana, say many industry observers, shows the vulnerability of entertainment-based enterprises during severe economic downturns. This is especially true of companies that have overextended their resources through expansion.

Founded in 1957, during the post–World War II heyday of Las Vegas, the Tropicana began as a hotel and casino complex on the south end of the famed Las Vegas Strip (that hotel became the flagship of a nationwide, eleven-strong resort and casino empire in the mid-2000s). Over the subsequent decades, new additions to the resort were added, including a golf course, new towers, a theater, and other leisure-themed amenities.

In 1979, the national hotel chain Ramada bought the Tropicana Hotel. Two years later, the company opened another Tropicana Casino and Resort in the newly created gambling haven of Atlantic City, New Jersey. In 1989, Ramada spun off a new publicly traded company known as the Aztar Corporation, whose assets included the two hotels. To take advantage of the expansion of legalized gambling across the country, Aztar acquired casinos in several states in the 1990s.

In 2006, Columbia Sussex, a hotel and casino group founded in 1972, created a subsidiary company known as Tropicana Entertainment to run the hotel and casino properties it had acquired when it purchased Aztar for $2.1 billion. Within a year, Tropicana Entertainment had acquired other properties, creating a chain of hotels and casinos in Atlantic City, Las Vegas, other cities in Nevada, and legalized gambling meccas across the South.

Meanwhile, the new company announced plans for a massive expansion of its flagship property in Las Vegas. Initially conceived at the tale end of the Las Vegas boom of the 1990s and early 2000s, which saw dozens of new hotel and casino complexes open on the Strip, the plans were quickly shelved as the recession began to take a major bite out of the city's gambling and tourist trade. A further blow to the company's finances came in 2007, when the New Jersey Casino Control Commission refused to renew the gambling license of the Tropicana property in Atlantic City. After hearing complaints about severe pay cuts and unsanitary conditions at the hotel, the commission decided that neither Columbia Sussex nor Tropicana Entertainment had adequate financial resources to operate the property, also citing the "lack of business ability, good character, honesty, and integrity" of the two companies.

Within months of losing its New Jersey license, Tropicana Entertainment filed for Chapter 11 bankruptcy protection on May 5, 2008, and the president of Columbia Sussex resigned. The Tropicana Atlantic City casino was not included in the filing nor was the Amelia Belle, a riverboat casino operation in Louisiana. Exactly a year after the filing, the Delaware Bankruptcy Court granted Tropicana Entertainment permission, on May 5, 2009, to emerge from bankruptcy as two companies, both of them spun off from Columbia Sussex. One would be the Vegas-based Tropicana Resort and Casino; the other would be a holding company for the remaining casinos. The reorganization plan had to await the approval of the gaming regulatory bodies in the states affected.

Bill Kte'pi and James Ciment

See also: Recession and Financial Crisis (2007–).

Further Reading

"History of the Tropicana." Available at www.tropicanamedia-site.com/history-tropicana.ia. Accessed January 2010.

Krauss, Clifford. "Economic Troubles Affect the Vegas Strip." *New York Times*, May 6, 2008.

Troubled Asset Relief Program (2008–)

The Troubled Asset Relief Program (TARP) was the central component of the federal government's efforts to alleviate the crisis that gripped U.S. and overseas financial markets in late 2008 and to avoid what many economists predicted could be a global slide into a second Great Depression. The enabling legislation—the Emergency Economic Stabilization Act of 2008, signed into law by President George W. Bush on October 3—was a U.S. program initially aimed at buying assets of questionable value and liquidity on the books of major financial institutions. It provided $700 billion to Secretary of the Treasury Henry Paulson and gave him broad, ill-defined powers to act as he saw fit in relieving key financial institutions of various "troubled assets," most notably mortgage-backed securities and collateralized debt obligations (CDOs).

As the financial crisis and resulting recession deepened in the fall of 2008, Paulson shifted his emphasis from purchasing financial institutions' "troubled" or "toxic" assets to taking ownership through equity stakes in collapsing financial institutions themselves, including investment banks, commercial banks, and insurance companies. In addition, the program was expanded by presidential executive order to the troubled U.S. automobile industry.

Much criticized by both the political Left and Right at the time and since, TARP has generally been considered a success by most mainstream economists, who say that the vast amount of bailout money stabilized and restored confidence in the international credit markets, preventing a freezing up in short-term lending that might have brought the global economy grinding to a halt. Still, there has been much criticism as well, focusing on whether the money could have been better spent elsewhere and whether the banks used it to do what the federal government wanted them to—that is, provide more lending.

Causes of the Crisis

TARP's scale was unprecedented. Never before had the U.S. government injected so much capital—or intervened so forcefully—in the financial markets. But, say defenders of the program, not since the Great Depression had the United States faced an equivalently dire financial crisis, the origins of which were many years in the making and rooted in various causes, including: the deregulation of the financial industry; loose monetary policy by the Federal Reserve Board (Fed); the development of new and complicated financial instruments such as mortgage-backed securities and derivatives like collateralized debt obligations; new forms of executive compensation in the financial industry that encouraged risk taking; the rise of hedge funds, which often used derivatives and short selling to offset exposure to ordinary securities investment; and most directly, an unprecedented bubble in housing prices.

Beginning in the late 1970s and accelerating in the 1980s and 1990s, the financial regulatory structure established in the United States during the first half of the twentieth century was dismantled, a trend backed by almost all Republicans and many Democrats in the White House and Congress. Among the most important acts of deregulation was 1999 legislation that overturned a Depression-era law, the Glass-Steagall Act of 1933, forbidding commercial banks from engaging in the investment banking and insurance businesses. Even as regulations were eased, there remained a plethora of competing regulatory agencies, including the Office of Thrift Supervision, created in the wake of the savings and loan crisis of the late 1980s and early 1990s. With regulatory duties spread out among so many different agencies, financial institutions were able to "shop around," in effect, to find the agency that would conduct the least oversight of and allow the greatest flexibility in ever-riskier investment strategies.

Advocates of the deregulatory effort argued that the technological and communications revolutions of the late twentieth century had made information so widely available that markets were capable of regulating themselves far more efficiently than any government agency could. Part of the self-regulation came in the form of new financial instruments that spread risk over ever-greater numbers of investors, thereby smoothing the ups and downs of the financial cycle. Mortgage-backed securities, for example, spread the risk of mortgage default beyond the originator of the mortgage, while derivatives offered a kind of insurance policy against financial losses. Many of these new and "exotic" securities were barely regulated at all. Meanwhile, new forms of compensation—often crafted to avoid tax exposure for the company or the individual being compensated—were too closely tied to the immediate performance of the financial company's stock, encouraging executives to put more of their company's assets in these new, high-performing but high-risk investments.

All of these factors contributed to the unprecedented run-up in U.S. home prices that was at the heart of the financial crisis of 2008–2009. By spreading the risk of mortgage default over a wide investor base—and then insuring the remaining risk through derivatives like CDOs—mortgage-backed securities removed the incentive for mortgage originators to make sure that the people getting the mortgages had the income and credit history to justify lending them tens or hundreds of thousands of dollars. Inevitably, standards declined to the point that many people were receiving mortgages without having to provide evidence of income or assets. Such mortgagees comprised a growing market, known as the subprime market. At the same time, adjustable rate mortgages (ARMs) were being marketed both in the prime and subprime markets. These offered low initial rates against the interest alone, with upward adjustments—sometimes dramatic—to cover principal and higher interest payments after a given period of time.

To some economists during the housing price run-up of the early and mid-2000s, ARMs represented a ticking time bomb, except that the fuse kept being lengthened. With interest rates at historically low levels—a result of Fed policy—more and more people could afford to take on larger and larger mortgages, thus inflating housing prices. With housing prices rising, creating more home equity, homeowners with ARMs could simply refinance before the adjustable rate went up. Eventually, however, the Fed was forced to raise rates to cool the overheated market—home prices in some parts of the country were increasing by 20 percent or more a year—and avoid the inflation that the market might trigger in other sectors of the economy. (Many people were taking out home-equity loans to finance other consumer purchases.)

To the Brink

By late 2006, home prices began to decline, effectively destroying the equity that allowed mortgagors to refinance. As ARMs adjusted upward, many homeowners found themselves unable to meet their monthly mortgage payments, and many were forced into foreclosure. The wave of foreclosures sent home prices down ever farther, finally causing the housing bubble to burst. Mortgage defaults and foreclosure rates shot far above historic norms. This, in turn, undermined confidence in both mortgage-backed securities and the derivatives that insured them. Financial institutions with these securities and derivatives on their books found their assets declining at an accelerating rate, leading to precipitous drops in share prices. Indeed, some of these institutions were unable to obtain credit from other financial institutions, who questioned their solvency. The first to face such a crisis was Bear Stearns, a Wall Street investment bank that found itself on the verge of collapse in March 2008 until the Fed arranged an emergency takeover of the company by the investment bank JPMorgan Chase.

The government and financial community hoped that Bear Stearns was an extreme case—that its exposure to the subprime mortgage market, in the form of mortgage-backed securities and CDOs, was unusually high. By late summer, however, it was becoming increasingly clear that "toxic" or "troubled" assets littered the books of many financial institutions, including major brokerage houses, investment banks, hedge fund companies, and even commercial banks. Events seemed to spin out of control, as worries also arose about the solvency of Fannie Mae and Freddie Mac, two federal government–sponsored private enterprises that insured more than half of the nation's home mortgages. In early September, Secretary Paulson announced a government takeover of the two mortgage insurance giants.

A week later came the collapse of the investment bank Lehman Brothers. Having faced much criticism for its Bear Stearns bailout—and worried that further bailouts would create an expectation in the markets that excessive risk taking would go unpunished and that the government would come to the rescue of over-aggressive players—the Fed opted to let Lehman Brothers fail in what was the largest bankruptcy filing in U.S. history, valued at more than $600 billion. But even as Fed chairman Ben Bernanke was letting Lehman fail, he was moving to shore up the insurance giant AIG with $85 billion, in exchange for a nearly 80 percent government stake in the company. Bernanke and others argued that the unprecedented move to rescue the world's largest insurer of financial instruments was critical, as its failure would create mass panic in the credit markets. Not only was the sum huge, but technically, AIG, as an insurance company, was outside the Fed's purview. In addition, the fact that AIG executives treated themselves to a lengthy retreat at an expensive California resort a mere week after they received government money did not help ease the growing political backlash over the bailout.

Meanwhile, the Fed's decision to let Lehman fail proved disastrous in the short term as panic began to grip the financial markets, freezing up the short-term interbank lending that kept many institutions afloat. In the wake of the Lehman collapse came news that one of the nation's largest bank holding companies, Washington Mutual

(WaMu), was teetering. WaMu was a creation of the 1999 deregulatory law that allowed commercial banks to reform as bank holding companies and to engage in investment banking and other financial services. In the end, the risks assumed by the investment banking division put the rest of the company at risk, and WaMu's commercial banking activities were placed under the receivership of the Federal Deposit Insurance Corporation (FDIC) and many of its assets sold to JPMorgan Chase.

Paulson's Plan

By mid-September 2008, it was becoming clear to both government officials and the financial community that the nation's financial system was experiencing a crisis of major proportions, akin, some said, to that faced in the depths of the Great Depression. On September 20, Secretary Paulson offered the first bailout plan, whereby the Treasury Department would use $700 billion to buy up troubled assets—largely mortgage-backed securities and collateralized debt obligations—on the books of major American financial institutions. Short on details, including how the figure of $700 billion was arrived at, the plan gave Secretary Paulson almost unlimited power to spend the money as he saw fit, with little congressional oversight.

The initial rescue plan raised hackles among both liberals and conservatives in Congress. The former saw it as a giveaway to big banks, the latter as unacceptable government interference in the financial markets. On September 29, the House of Representatives voted down Paulson's plan, sending the stock market reeling as financial stocks collapsed. Fears arose in the markets that the House's rejection of the Paulson plan would freeze up U.S. and global credit markets, making it impossible for companies to obtain the short-term loans they needed to meet payroll. Talk spread in the media of a complete breakdown of the financial markets and a "new Great Depression." Such talk, along with collapsing stock prices and Paulson's efforts to flesh out more details of a bailout plan that would give Congress nominally more oversight, persuaded a still reluctant Congress to pass the Emergency Economic Stabilization Act, the enabling legislation for TARP. The legislation signed into law by President Bush on October 3 called for the release of half the $700 billion immediately and the other half to be authorized by Congress the following January, once the Treasury Department explained more fully how it would be used. Receiving that report, Congress authorized the release of the second $350 billion on January 15, 2009.

Impact and Criticism

TARP's basic goal was simple. No one really knew the value of the troubled assets on the books of the nation's financial institutions nor even exactly what they were. Because mortgages had been bundled and resold so many times, financial institutions themselves did not know what they owned. This made investors reluctant to keep their money in financial institutions and

made the institutions themselves reluctant to lend money to each other. After all, they did not know if the institution to which they were lending would soon become insolvent. Without this modicum of trust and the free flow of credit, the world's financial system could freeze up and bring down the entire global economy. TARP, by taking troubled assets off the books of key financial institutions such as Citigroup (which received $50 billion in TARP money) and Bank of America ($45 billion), would reassure the markets and get credit flowing again. Then, once the markets had stabilized, the government could sell the assets to recoup some of the costs assumed by taxpayers with the bailout.

Secretary Paulson soon came to realize, however, that this approach would not work fast enough to reassure the markets and get credit flowing again. Banks were still reluctant to lend to each other or to nonbanking institutions and individuals. Taking a cue from British Prime Minister Gordon Brown, Paulson quickly shifted gears

During 2009 congressional testimony on TARP by Treasury Secretary Timothy Geithner, members of the Code Pink activist group called on U.S. banks to return taxpayer money. Many banks, eager to escape government restrictions, did just that. *(Bloomberg/Getty Images)*

and took a different approach to financial relief. Rather than use TARP funds to buy up troubled bank assets, he would use the money to buy equity stakes directly in major financial institutions. By November 2008, the immediate crisis seemed to be passing. While most banks remained reluctant to lend for longer-term projects, short-term credit between financial institutions and to nonfinancial institutions was flowing again.

TARP underwent further alteration again in December by President Bush, who used his executive power to expand the program to include major U.S. automobile manufacturers, two of which—General Motors and Chrysler—were on the brink of bankruptcy. Ultimately, GM received some $14 billion in bailout money and Chrysler $4 billion, in exchange for equity stakes. In neither case, however, were the funds enough for the firms to avoid bankruptcy in 2009.

Politically, TARP proved highly controversial, especially after it was revealed that some of the financial institutions being bailed out with taxpayer money were paying large bonuses to top executives and other employees. Economically, the results were mixed. According to most economists, the injection of such a vast amount of capital into the financial marketplace prevented a complete meltdown of the international financial system.

Other criticisms of the plan take three basic forms. Many argued that the TARP money would have been better spent in any number of other ways, including helping distressed homeowners pay their mortgages. These were, it was said, the very people whose financial difficulties were the original source of the crisis. Another group of critics maintained that Secretary Paulson misread the basic problem faced by financial institutions. The problem was not one of liquidity, they maintained, but one of financial irresponsibility. Thus, TARP only encouraged more irresponsibility by rescuing bankers from their own folly. Finally, still other critics of TARP argued that banks inevitably misused the money. Rather than lend the money to businesses and individuals and help lift the economy as a whole, it was said, the banks used

the funds to pay down their own debt and buy up weaker institutions. If one factor of the crisis was the fact that some institutions had grown "too big to fail"—meaning that their collapse posed a systemic risk to financial markets—TARP only made them bigger.

Meanwhile, the government's entire financial rescue plan—of which TARP was the largest part—had contributed to further growth in the already sizable federal debt, which had climbed above $12 trillion by the end of 2009. Such an increase, many feared, was likely to trigger an inflationary spiral in the future and further weaken the economy.

James Ciment

See also: Banks, Commercial; Banks, Investment; Federal Reserve System; Financial Markets; Moral Hazard; Recession and Financial Crisis (2007–); "Too Big to Fail"; Treasury, Department of the.

Further Reading

Acosto, Jarod R., ed. *Assessing Treasury's Strategy: Six Months of TARP.* Hauppauge, NY: Nova Science, 2009.

Board of Governors of the Federal Reserve System. "Troubled Asset Relief Program (TARP) Information." Available at www.federalreserve.gov/bankinforeg/tarpinfo.htm. Accessed October 19, 2009.

Elliott, Douglas J. *Measuring the Cost of TARP.* Washington, DC: Brookings Initiative on Business and Public Policy Fixing Finance Series, January 2009.

Lefebvre, Adelaide D., ed. *Government Bailout: Troubled Asset Relief Program (TARP).* Hauppauge, NY: Nova Science, 2009.

Perkins, Martin Y., ed. *TARP and the Restoration of U.S. Financial Stability.* Hauppauge, NY: Nova Science, 2009.

Tugan-Baranovsky, Mikhail Ivanovich (1865–1919)

The Ukrainian economist Mikhail Ivanovich Tugan-Baranovsky was an early and leading proponent of the idea that economic crises are an unavoidable—and, indeed, intrinsic—aspect of the capitalist system and its surge toward industrialization. His was among the first purely economic theories of business cycles, and his theories of capitalist crises later challenged those of Karl Marx. He was also one of the founders of the National Academy of Science of Ukraine.

Tugan-Baranovsky was born in 1865 in the countryside of Kharkov, Ukraine. After completing his undergraduate studies in Kharkov, he spent some months at the British Museum Library researching the history of the British economy. He received a master's degree in 1894 from the University of Moscow, for which he produced his masterpiece, *Industrial Crises in England*. He earned a doctorate in 1898 and published his thesis, titled *The Russian Factory in the 19th Century*. From 1895 on, he taught economics in various institutions in St. Petersburg, remaining deeply involved in debates on the Russian economy. He made substantial contributions to economic theory and actively participated in the nation's cooperative movement. His renown among Western economists largely rests, however, on his contributions to the theory of industrial crises.

Economic booms and busts were long thought to be accidental, provoked by exogenous factors, including wars, crop failures, and events such as the discovery of gold. Tugan-Baranovsky acknowledged that while this may have been the case before the era of industrialization, it was no longer true in nineteenth-century Great Britain. In *Industrial Crises in England*, he uses historical evidence to support the theory that crises recur with some similarities and striking regularity (every seven to eleven years). He formulated one of the first endogenous theories of economic crises, in which he posited that they are endemic to modern economies. He expanded the notion of a capitalist cycle composed of three phases: expansion, industrial crisis, and stagnation. By emphasizing industrial crises, he discarded widespread theories that disruptions in the monetary or credit systems cause crises. Tugan-Baranovsky did not deny monetary and credit crises, but he viewed them as symptoms that appear during industrial crises.

According to Tugan-Baranovsky, industrial crises emerge from the antagonistic nature of a capitalist economy. Production rules consumption in a capitalist system, whereas in a socialist system, consumption is the aim of production. In capitalist economies, the means of production are mainly intended to create new means of production. Thus, an accumulation of capital takes place, and production strives for infinite and disordered growth. In a capitalist system, the nation's production is disorganized, and the resulting anarchy disrupts growth. The lack of a plan to regulate production between the alternative sectors in the economy (in other words, the disproportionality between production and consumption) is the major cause of modern industrial crises, whereas defective organization in monetary and credit institutions only intensifies them.

Tugan-Baranovsky used the cyclical fluctuations of free available capital to explain the predicted regularity of industrial crises. In a boom period, when prices are high and speculation rises, savings (free capital) is often productively invested. During bust periods, prices are low, and free capital accumulates in banks. Tugan-Baranovsky used the metaphor of the steam engine to illustrate the recurrence of the capitalist cycle. Free capital plays the role of the steam in a steam engine: it accumulates until the evacuation of the pressure becomes unavoidable.

Industrial Crises was translated into several languages, and Tugan-Baranovsky's arguments about the disproportionality in production and the investment-saving fluctuations influenced many economists and authors outside Russia—first German, then French, and eventually British. But he believed his theory was of vital importance to Russia, as well. Vigorous industrialization policies were carried out in Russia in the 1890s that raised questions about the balance between the agricultural and industrial sectors. In *The Russian Factory*, Tugan-Baranovsky shows that economic fluctuations were becoming more and more relevant to the industrial development of prerevolutionary Russia. He died in 1919 near Odessa, Ukraine.

François Allisson

See also: Classical Theories and Models; Over-Savings and Over-Investment Theories of the Business Cycle.

Further Reading

Barnett, Vincent. "Tugan-Baranovsky as a Pioneer of Trade Cycle Analysis." *Journal of the History of Economic Thought* 23:4 (December 2001): 443–466.

Tugan-Baranovsky, M. *The Russian Factory in the 19th Century.* Trans. from the 3rd Russian ed. by Arthur Levin and Claora S. Levin, under the supervision of Gregory Grossman. Homewood, IL: R.D. Irwin, 1970.

Tulipmania (1636–1637)

The seventeenth-century Dutch phenomenon referred to as "tulipmania" is considered the first important financial "bubble" in European history. As the nickname implies, the episode was characterized by rampant speculation in tulip bulbs. More generally, tulipmania has become a metaphor in the economics profession for a highly speculative financial market in which prices for a product or commodity soar irrationally and then, suddenly and often unexpectedly, crash. Despite the numerous boom-and-bust incidents that have occurred since that time, tulipmania remains the event against which all speculative market excesses have been compared. As the noted economic historian Charles P. Kindleberger wrote, tulipmania represented "probably the high watermark in bubbles."

Both the peculiar biology of tulips and the unusual economic circumstances of seventeenth-century Amsterdam contributed to the mania. Tulips can be grown from either seeds or bulbs, the latter representing the faster method. Although growing them from seeds can take up to a dozen years, it is through the budding and seed process that the mosaic virus—which may create spectacular and highly coveted color patterns—propagates itself. Once the particular strain of tulip develops, it naturally clones itself through the bulb. In other words, a highly desired variety is difficult to propagate—and thus is more valuable—but once it is propagated, it is long lasting. In this regard, tulips are akin to gold—rare and beautiful but also durable.

Tulips at the time also had a novelty factor, having been brought to Europe from the Ottoman Empire in the sixteenth century and first propagated in Holland around the turn of the seventeenth. This was just at the time that Holland and its chief city, Amsterdam, were entering their "golden age." A vital center of finance and trade, Amsterdam was arguably Europe's richest city in the first half of the seventeenth century, boasting numerous upper-class merchants and the largest middle class on the continent, both with discretionary income to invest and spend.

By the early 1630s, excess money was washing around the Dutch economy, as the country's trading activities drew in coin and precious metals from around Europe and across the Atlantic. Between January 1636 and January 1637, the height of the tulip boom, deposits in the Bank of Amsterdam rose by more than 40 percent. The rapid run-up in the money supply fostered an atmosphere that was ripe for irrational speculation. Into this feverish climate came the tulip bulb.

Although tulips were popular in the first three decades of the seventeenth century, trade in the bulbs was largely limited to professional growers until the early 1630s. By the middle years of that decade, the bulbs were increasingly being traded among nonprofessionals. A host of new varieties—given grandiose names to enhance their value—were introduced in 1634, which brought prices down for the more common varieties, making them a popular investment for middle-class purchasers. Meanwhile, the upper classes were speculating on the truly rare and spectacular varieties, a popular diversion from the mania for art collection that had gripped wealthy Dutch merchants.

The tulip market was essentially a futures market from September to June each year. Beginning in the summer of 1636, the trading of tulip futures took place in all sorts of public places in Amsterdam, such as taverns and coffee houses.

A Dutch engraving of 1637, titled *The Fool's Cap,* lampoons the speculative frenzy in tulips—and the investors who paid fortunes for them—in The Netherlands that year. The run-up in tulip prices is the first known speculative bubble in history. *(The Granger Collection, New York)*

Groups of traders, called "colleges," created rules that restricted the bidding and fees associated with trading. Only a small fraction of the purchase price of any bulb was required for the down payment, which was known as "wine money."

Upon the arrival of the contract settlement date, buyers typically did not have the required cash to settle the trade, but the sellers did not have the bulbs to deliver either, for they were still in the ground. Thus, the trade was settled with only a payment of the difference between the contract price and the expected settlement price. Such margin buying further exacerbated the speculative fever. By February 1637, when prices hit their peak, tulip bulbs and tulip bulb futures were trading for extraordinary sums. As British journalist Charles Mackay, the first to seriously chronicle the phenomenon, wrote in 1841, a single Viceroy bulb traded for 8,000 pounds of wheat, 16,000 pounds of rye, 4 fat oxen, 8 fat swine, 12 fat sheep, 126 gallons of wine, over a thousand gallons of beer, more than 500 gallons of butter, 1,000 pounds of cheese, a complete bed, a suit of clothes, and a silver drinking cup.

Like all speculative bubbles, tulipmania came to a sudden and spectacular end in the winter of 1637, when new investors could no longer be found. With little intrinsic value, tulip bulb prices plummeted. In January 1637, the common Witte Croonen bulb, which had risen in value by 2,600 percent, fell to one-twentieth of its peak price in a single week. Investors soon tried to dump their bulb futures on the market but found few takers. They then sought help from the government, which allowed investors to get out of their contract by paying 10 percent of the contract's face value. When the sellers sued, the courts offered them little solace, declaring the debts a result of gambling and therefore unenforceable.

The legacy of tulipmania for the Dutch

economy has been debated ever since. Focusing on the small group of relatively well-off investors caught up in the speculation, Mackay insisted that the effects were devastating, citing "[s]ubstantial merchants reduced almost to beggary and many a representative of a noble line saw the fortunes of his house ruined beyond redemption." According to modern historians, however, Mackay was guilty of hyperbole. The mania, as noted above, affected only a small portion of the Dutch population, and its impact on the nation's economy was minimal. Holland remained one of the wealthiest countries in Europe long after the mania dissipated, and its relative decline versus other powers had more to do with geopolitical and other economic factors, such as war, colonial expansion, and the rise of financial and trade centers elsewhere on the continent.

Douglas French and James Ciment

See also: Asset-Price Bubble; Mississippi Bubble (1717–1720); Netherlands, The; South Sea Bubble (1720).

Further Reading

Dash, Mike. *Tulipomania: The Story of the World's Most Coveted Flower and the Extraordinary Passions It Aroused.* New York: Crown, 2001.

Garber, Peter M. *Famous First Bubbles: The Fundamentals of Early Manias.* Cambridge, MA: MIT Press, 2000.

Kindleberger, Charles P. *A Financial History of Western Europe.* London: George Allen and Unwin. 1984.

———. *Manias, Panics, and Crashes: A History of Financial Crises.* New York: John Wiley & Sons, 1978.

Mackay, Charles. *Memoirs of Extraordinary Popular Delusions and the Madness of Crowds.* 1841. Reprint edition. New York: Cosimo Classics, 2008.

Turkey

Located largely on the Anatolian Peninsula in southwestern Asia, with a tiny but demographically and economically important section in southeastern Europe, Turkey—with a majority Islamic population of roughly 74 million—is a major developing country and a political mediator between the West and the Middle East.

Origins of the Turkish Republic

Turkey's economy has experienced a series of highs and lows since the creation of the modern republic in 1923. At that time, the country had an overwhelmingly agricultural economy, and the new government was determined to support more domestic industry. Conservative policies helped Turkey to weather the Great Depression relatively well, but World War II caused a general economic decline. A cycle of rapid expansions and economic downturns followed the war, resulting in several interventions by the army to stabilize the country. Economic reforms in the 1980s improved Turkey's overall economy, but high rates of inflation continued to prevent stability. Modest industrialization, combined with income from services and commodities, helped the Turkish economy to expand during much of the 1990s and early twenty-first century. The worldwide recession beginning in 2007 caused Turkey's economy to contract, with an uncertain outlook for the future.

The multinational Ottoman Empire, of which Turkey was the core, declined militarily and economically during the nineteenth century. Its government borrowed heavily from European lenders, and much of its industry, including railroads, was under foreign control. Beginning in 1912, a decade of warfare devastated the Ottoman economy. By the time the Republic of Turkey was established in 1923, the empire's population had declined by 25 percent. Control over Iraq, Syria, and Palestine was lost, while most Greeks and Armenian inhabitants had been expelled or killed. Agriculture had suffered from the conscription of workers and draught animals. Exports had been curtailed by blockade as well.

During the 1920s, however, an economic recovery took place. Agricultural production returned to prewar levels. In 1924, the medieval practice of using tax farmers to confiscate one-tenth of agricultural production was discontinued, providing significant relief to growers. The government of Turkey's founder, Mustafa Kemal Ataturk, encouraged the development of a Turkish middle class by privatizing various state monopolies and offering incentives and subsidies to industry. State-controlled railroads were constructed to help tie all parts of the country into a unified market.

Beginning in 1929, the Great Depression led to a worldwide economic downturn. Commodity prices declined sharply, harming Turkish growers who depended on the export market. To prop up the Turkish economy, the state assumed more direct control over foreign trade. The amount of goods that could be imported was limited, and tariffs were raised on imports of food products and consumer goods. The government also ceased to make payments on foreign debts and demanded a conference on restructuring the payments. As a result, during most of the 1930s, Turkey had a trade surplus.

Advent of Statist Economics

In 1932, the Turkish government adopted a new economic strategy known as statism. Under statism, the state became a major producer and investor in the urban industrial economic sector, developing an alternative to an export-driven agricultural economy. A five-year plan was set up with assistance from Soviet advisers. Many monopolies that had been privatized during the 1920s, such as transportation and finance, were taken back under state control. Controls over prices and markets were established. Limits on wages and labor activities were also enforced. While state funds were concentrated on heavy industry and transportation, private investment was still encouraged and subsidized. Statism was generally considered a success. Unlike many other economies of the 1930s, the Turkish economy continued to grow slowly. Turkey's statism was adopted after World War II by other countries in the Middle East.

Agriculture also expanded during the Depression. Because commodity prices remained low, Turkish farmers grew more products to achieve the same income. Improvements in transportation gave them a national market. As the world economy improved, agricultural exports also increased, encouraging more growth.

World War II caused stagnation in Turkey's economy. Although the country remained neutral throughout the war, the government ordered a full mobilization to discourage foreign attack. The lack of manpower for farms and industry reduced output. Exports also fell because of blockades and dangers to shipping. State income fell, so expenditures were reduced. The government abandoned statism as an economic policy, and the general standard of living decreased. General dissatisfaction with single-party rule in Turkey led to the adoption of a multiparty system by 1950.

After 1950, Turkey's economy underwent a cycle of boom and bust, with a crisis occurring about every decade. Inflation became a serious problem. During the 1950s, Turkey's economy continued to depend upon exporting agricultural products, particularly wheat. When international prices declined after the Korean War, the Turkish government subsidized wheat farming. Rapid inflation resulted, made worse by the overvaluation of the Turkish lira. Devaluation in 1958 helped bring on a recession. In turn, economic problems led to a military coup in 1960.

During the 1960s, state-owned industries assumed a larger part of the Turkish economy. To promote domestic industrialization, imports of consumer goods were restricted and Turkish industries encouraged. The economy prospered, aided by the many workers who found jobs in other European countries. Inflation again became a problem. During the 1970s, private producers were encouraged to borrow from foreign lenders, with guarantees by the government. The recession caused by increases in oil prices depleted Turkish reserves of foreign currency. Short-term loans were necessary for day-to-day expenses. Inflation reached triple digits by 1979.

Free-Market Reforms

In the 1980s, economic reforms promoted by Turgut Ozal shifted Turkey's economy toward a more export-oriented outlook. Changes included devaluation of the lira, control over money supply and credit, eliminating most subsidies, and allowing prices charged by state industries to reach their market level. The balance of payments improved, and government spending was reduced. A customs arrangement with the European Economic Community, predecessor to the European Union, helped increase exports. Additional income came from charges for pipeline services carrying oil from Iraq to the Mediterranean and from the growth of tourism. Although the reforms caused many hardships at first, the Turkish economy rebounded. As the economy heated up, unemployment and inflation became major problems by the end of the 1980s.

During the 1990s, excessive government borrowing and an overvalued lira led to an economic crisis that peaked in the mid-1990s. Devaluation in 1994 led to renewed growth and foreign investment. By the early 2000s, Turkey's economy grew at an average annual rate of 5 percent. Key industrial sectors included clothing and textiles,

automotive, and electronics. The completion of a pipeline carrying oil from Baku to world markets in May 2006 also provided a major source of income. The Turkish economy was rocked in 2007 and 2008, with the world recession causing a decline in exports. Domestic turmoil also led to uncertainty, as secular and moderate Islamic political parties faced a challenge from Muslim fundamentalists. Aggressive steps by the government to encourage foreign investment and reduce unemployment were expected to help the economy recover by 2011.

Tim J. Watts

See also: Emerging Markets; Middle East and North Africa.

Further Reading

Aydin, Zulkuf. *The Political Economy of Turkey.* London: Pluto, 2005.

Metz, Helen Chapin. *Turkey, a Country Study.* Washington, DC: Federal Research Division, Library of Congress, 1996.

Morris, Chris. *The New Turkey: The Quiet Revolution on the Edge of Europe.* London: Granta, 2005.

UBS

UBS is one of the largest investment banks in the world, with branches and clients in many locations outside its headquarters in Switzerland. Since its formation in 1998, UBS has been rocked by numerous scandals, and it suffered great financial losses in the global recession that began in 2007. Thanks to restructuring and reductions in the number of employees, UBS had returned to a measure of profitability by the second half of 2009.

UBS was created by the merger of two rival Swiss banks. The first was the Swiss Bank Corporation (SBC), which was founded in 1854 by six private bankers in Basel. Known as the Bankverein, the entity was formed to provide funds for increasing demands for credit from Swiss railroad and manufacturing companies. The bank became a joint stock company known as the Basler Bankverein in 1872. The next year, the bank suffered significant financial losses. The Viennese stock exchange collapsed, and borrowers defaulted on a number of large loans. As a result, the Bankverein's leadership refused to issue dividends to investors and adopted a conservative fiscal approach. This caution in business served the bank well, and it prospered over the next quarter-century. Smaller Swiss banks were acquired, and by 1897, the entity became the Schweizerischer Bankverein, known in English as the SBC.

While World War I caused some difficulties, the end of the war offered new opportunities for SBC. Loans were made to countries that were trying to rebuild from the war. Many wealthy foreigners also deposited funds with SBC to protect their wealth from inflation. During the Great Depression, SBC helped support weaker financial institutions. Foreign offices were opened, including one in New York in 1939, giving additional opportunities for international investments. As World War II threatened, many Europeans placed their funds in the bank for safety.

Following the war, SBC concentrated on business with multinational corporations. Additional foreign offices were opened in Europe, North America, and Asia. A less conservative approach to business, including asset management, securities, and investment banking, was adopted during the 1990s, leading to greater profits but also additional risks.

The other partner in the merger that created UBS was the Union Bank of Switzerland. Its roots lay in the Bank of Winterthur, founded in 1872. Unlike SBC, the Union Bank of Switzerland concentrated its efforts on domestic banking operations, including commercial and personal loans, mortgages, and leasing. Its first foreign office was not opened until 1967, and international operations continued at a slow rate after that. During the 1990s, stockholders became unhappy with the bank's conservative leadership and low returns. Battles over the bank's direction resulted in a general weakening of the company.

In 1998, SBC and the Union Bank of Switzerland merged. Although the name originally was to be United Bank of Switzerland, the corporation's official name quickly became UBS. A logo of three keys, standing for confidence, security, and discretion, was taken over from SBC. Although the original Union Bank of Switzerland had greater assets, most leadership positions went to executives from SBC. When the bank was created, it was the second-largest commercial bank in the world, with assets around $600 billion.

Despite its financial strength, the Union Bank of Switzerland suffered both financial and public relations disasters since its creation. One of the most embarrassing and costly episodes had to do with the Holocaust. During the 1930s, after the Nazis came to power in Germany, many wealthy Jewish families deposited their funds in Swiss banks, including the Union Bank of Switzerland, to keep them safe. While some individuals were able to escape and reclaim their wealth, many more perished in the Nazi death camps. Following World War II, the Union Bank of Switzerland, along with other Swiss banks, made no effort to contact the owners of dormant accounts. During the 1990s, Jewish groups accused the Union Bank of Switzerland of cooperating with the Nazis and profiting at the expense of Holocaust victims. The Union Bank of Switzerland refused to make public the account owners' names, justifying this action on the basis of the traditional secrecy surrounding Swiss banks. Eventually, public opinion convinced the Union Bank of Switzerland leadership to release the names of people who had opened accounts before 1945—the assets totaled more than $41 million. Bank president Robert Studer further inflamed public opinion by describing the amount as "peanuts." The ensuing firestorm resulted in Studer's ouster when the Union Bank of Switzerland and SBC merged the following year.

The Union Bank of Switzerland also was embarrassed in 1997, when a security guard found employees shredding files related to the bank's dealings with Nazis. Such activities were forbidden, and criminal proceedings were launched against the bank's archivist. The security guard also was charged with violating bank secrecy. Both prosecutions were dismissed in September 1997, but the public remained suspicious of the Union Bank of Switzerland's activities.

On June 22, 2008, the U.S. Federal Bureau of Investigation announced that it was investigating a tax evasion case involving UBS. Up to 20,000 American citizens were accused of hiding funds with the bank to avoid paying taxes. UBS was accused of marketing tax-evasion schemes to these citizens, with up to $20 billion being deposited. On February 18, 2009, UBS agreed to pay a $780 million fine to the U.S. government and to reveal the names of certain American depositors. The next day, the U.S. government filed suit to force UBS to reveal the names of 52,000 depositors. Under a settlement reached in August 2009, U.S. depositors were granted a grace period in which to report their activities and pay any back taxes and fines without facing criminal prosecution.

UBS, like many banks, was affected by the global recession that began in 2007. Bad loans and mismanagement led to large losses that shook public confidence in the bank. Nearly 10,000 jobs were cut in all divisions worldwide. In 2008, the bank was forced to write off $49 billion in bad investments, with a loss of $15.7 billion for the year. In October 2008, UBS had to accept a bailout from the Swiss government to remain solvent. Losses continued through 2009, as Europe and the world suffered through an economic downturn. In response, UBS put greater emphasis on its traditional wealth management activities and turned away from risky investments—thus returning to mild profitability in late 2009.

Tim J. Watts

See also: Banks, Investment; Switzerland.

Further Reading
Bauer, Hans, and Warren J. Blackman. *Swiss Banking: An Analytical History.* New York: St. Martin's, 1998.
Schutz, Dirk. *The Fall of UBS: The Forces That Brought Down Switzerland's Biggest Bank.* New York: Pyramid Media Group, 2000.
Vincent, Isabel. *Hitler's Silent Partners: Swiss Banks, Nazi Gold, and the Pursuit of Justice.* New York: William Morrow, 1997.

Unemployment, Natural Rate of

The natural rate of unemployment occurs when production of goods and services reflect the full (normal) utilization of an economy's resources. Ultimately there is only one stable rate of unemployment, the natural rate. Deviations from the stable rate come about when there are disturbances in the economy, as during recessions or inflationary booms.

Even under the most balanced supply and demand "normal" conditions, the unemployment rate will not be zero. Labor markets always have unemployment for several reasons. First, labor markets work imperfectly; it takes time for unemployed workers to find new jobs and while they are moving from job to job, they are unemployed. This type of unemployment is not bad but rather reflects the dynamic nature of economy. In addition, certain labor market restrictions create some unemployment. Minimum wage laws raise the wages of some workers, but higher minimum wages also discourage employers from hiring some workers. Minimum wage laws usually result in higher unemployment for teenagers, and high teenage unemployment rates increase the average unemployment rate. Also, some workers become dislocated when their skills become outmoded, such as happened to blacksmiths when the automobile replaced horseback as the preferred way of transportation. Thus, unemployment caused by imperfections and impediments in labor markets—when supply and demand are otherwise well balanced—add up to the natural (stable) rate of unemployment.

The most important studies in the field of the natural rates of unemployment involve the relationship between unemployment and inflation in an economy. This work shows that, all other factors being equal, inflation can cause an economy to deviate from its natural rate of unemployment. In exploring these deviations, economists and governments have attempted to devise policies by which governments can help mitigate the high (unnatural) unemployment rates that occur during economic recessions.

The Phillips Curve

The understanding of how inflation can reduce unemployment below its natural rate began in 1958, when Alban William Phillips published his study of the British economy over the previous century, "The Relationship between Unemployment and the Rate of Change of Money Wages in the United Kingdom, 1861–1957." According to this study, there is a negative relationship between the rate of inflation and unemployment. That is to say, as the prices of goods rise, unemployment falls. This relationship is summarized in what later became known as the Phillips curve. Note that the original study related the unemployment rate and changes in wages. Because there is a strong correlation between changes in wages and changes in prices (inflation), economists quickly substituted inflation for changes in wages.

The Samuelson-Solow Theory

While Phillips's work focused only on Britain in the second half of the nineteenth and first half of the twentieth centuries, American economists Paul Samuelson and Robert Solow—both of whom won the Nobel Prize (in 1970 and 1987, respectively)—maintained that the Phillips study was not a special case but that it revealed a general theoretical principle. In other words, Samuelson and Solow believed that there is always a tradeoff between inflation and unemployment.

If they are correct, then governments can use inflation to control unemployment, that is, to reduce unemployment below its natural rate. Central banks can increase the rate of inflation simply by putting more money in circulation. As the government creates more money, the demand for goods rises and all prices increase. As the price of consumer goods rises, real (i.e., inflation-adjusted) wages fall. This means that the money paid to workers will buy less. Since inflation effectively cuts the wages of workers, employers will want to hire more employees. As employers hire more employees, unemployment rates fall. Hence, higher inflation rates push unemployment below its natural rate.

In the 1970s, economist Arthur Okun of the Brookings Institution refined the theory of the Phillips curve by shifting the focus of decision making from the employer to the worker. Okun pointed out that workers will accept job offers more quickly if wages are increasing. Thus, workers search for jobs with a particular money wage in mind. If inflation is driving up prices and wages, workers will accept job offers more quickly, also lowering unemployment to below its natural rate.

The Phelps-Friedman Theory

Both the Samuelson-Solow and Okun explanations of the Phillips curve rely on the idea that workers do not notice inflation. Milton Friedman and Edmund Phelps (Nobelists in 1976 and 2006, respectively) agreed that inflation causes the unemployment rate to fall below its natural rate, but objected to the idea that workers are so easily fooled. This proved to be a critical distinction with regard to policy options for influencing unemployment rates. According to Phelps and Friedman, workers will not notice inflation imme-

diately. Thus, workers can be fooled by inflation, but only for a short period of time; in the long run, they will take note of inflation. Once they do so, they will push for wage increases to keep up with rising prices or reduce the amount of labor they are willing to supply. Likewise, if employers pay out inflation-adjusted wages, they will hire fewer employees. Thus, inflation-adjusted wages raise the unemployment rate toward its natural level. What Phelps and Friedman argued is that workers adapt to inflation later on, when its negative effects become obvious. Consequently, the only way government can keep unemployment below its natural rate is by increasing inflation over and over again and at an increasing rate. Thus, once workers get used to 5 percent inflation, policy makers would have to take actions to increase inflation by 10 percent to reduce the unemployment rate below its natural rate. This policy would lead to massive inflation in the economy. In fact, in the United States during the 1970s, unemployment rates rose at the same time that inflation rates rose. Many economists see this data as proof that Phelps and Friedman were right about inflation and unemployment.

The Lucas Theory

Phelps and Friedman argued that the Philips study revealed only a temporary tradeoff between inflation and unemployment. Robert Lucas, a student of Milton Friedman, took his ideas about the natural rate of unemployment a step further, arguing that workers learn to anticipate inflation. In the Friedman-Phelps theory of natural unemployment, workers adapt to inflation only after it has been around for a while. Government authorities can therefore use inflation to achieve temporary reductions in unemployment below its natural rate. But Lucas argued that workers will learn to demand wage increases for inflation before it actually happens. If that is the case, then the government cannot use inflation to gain even temporary reductions in unemployment. What Lucas's theory implies is that the natural rate of unemployment prevails not only over the long term, but in the short run as well.

Lucas does not maintain that unemployment is always at its natural rate, but his theory does imply that the government cannot systematically reduce unemployment with inflation. Unemployment will rise above its natural state and fall below its natural state with random events in the economy, but the government cannot be relied upon to use inflation to counteract this problem. Nearly all economists accept either the Lucas theory or the Phelps-Friedman theory.

D.W. MacKenzie

See also: Employment and Unemployment; Samuelson, Paul; Wages.

Further Reading

Fisher, Irving. "I Discovered the Phillips Curve: 'A Statistical Relation between Unemployment and Price Changes.'" *Journal of Political Economy* 81:2 (1973): 496–502. Reprinted from 1926 edition of International Labour Review.

Friedman, Milton. "The Role of Monetary Policy." *American Economic Review* 68:1 (1968): 1–17.

Frisch, Helmut. *Theories of Inflation.* New York: Cambridge University Press, 1983.

Lucas. R.E. "Adjustment Costs and the Theory of Supply." *Journal of Political Economy* 75:4 (1967): 321–334.

Okun, Arthur. *Prices and Quantities: A Macroeconomic Analysis.* Washington, DC: Brookings Institution, 1981.

Phelps, E.S. "Phillips Curves, Expectations of Inflation and Optimal Unemployment Over Time." *Economica* 34 (1967): 254–281.

Phillips, A.W. "The Relationship between Unemployment and the Rate of Change of Money Wages in the United Kingdom, 1861–1957." *Economica* 25:100 (1958): 283–299.

Samuelson, P.A., and R.M. Solow. "Analytical Aspects of Anti-Inflation Policy." *American Economic Review* 50:2 (1960): 177–194.

Tobin, James. "Inflation and Unemployment." *American Economic Review* 62 (1972): 1–18.

United Kingdom

Birthplace of the industrial revolution in the late eighteenth and early nineteenth centuries, the United Kingdom (UK) is a medium-sized island nation of about 60 million people occupying most of the British Isles in northwestern Europe. Once part of the Roman Empire and then conquered by the Normans of France in the eleventh century CE, the modern United Kingdom was created in the early eighteenth century with the political union of England (including Wales) and Scotland, and the addition of Ireland about a century later.

Already a rising power, Great Britain built the most extensive sea-based empire in history by the late eighteenth century, a period in which it also pioneered the industrial revolution. By the nineteenth century, the country had the largest economy in the world. But the rise of rivals, such as Germany and the United States, as well as two world wars, undermined Britain's dominant position and, by the early post–World War II period, it had shed most of its empire and had fallen behind economically, held back by an aging infrastructure.

In the 1980s, the country embarked on major free-market reforms, including privatizing much of the state-owned industrial infrastructure, reducing the power of unions, and deregulating finance. The result was an economic resurgence, albeit marked by increasing inequities in wealth. As one of the world's leading financial centers and with its own housing bubble, Great Britain was hard hit by the financial crisis of 2008–2009 and the accompanying recession.

Economic History Through the Industrial Revolution

Settled as far back as 35,000 BCE, Britain was home to various iron-smelting cultures by the first millennium BCE, at the end of which most of the area was conquered by Rome. With the fall of the Roman Empire in the fifth century CE, the British Isles were subject to invasions by various seafaring peoples, and finally conquered by the Normans of France in 1066. By the sixteenth century, most of what is now England had been united under the Tudor monarchy, which began tentative empire building outside Europe and removed England from the Catholic Church.

Torn by civil war and ruled briefly as a republic in the mid-seventeenth century, England began to assert its political hegemony over Scotland in the north and Ireland across the Irish Sea, officially uniting with the former in 1707 and the latter in 1801. It was also during this time that Britain began to dramatically increase the size of its empire, despite losing its thirteen colonies in North America. By the end of the nineteenth century, Britain ruled lands on every continent, with sovereignty over roughly one in four of the world's people.

World War I and World War II sapped Britain's capacity to rule its far-flung empire. That burden, along with rising nationalist ambitions in colonies, led to the dismemberment of the empire. This process had already begun in the late nineteenth and early twentieth centuries, with independence granted to the settler colonies of Australia, Canada, and South Africa. At the end of World War II, Britain granted independence to its prize colony, India, and, from the late 1950s through the 1970s, saw virtually all of its colonies in the Americas, Africa, and Asia become independent. That process culminated with the return of Hong Kong to China in 1997.

Britain's rise and fall from a land of feuding tribes to unified nation to great empire to former imperial power is evidenced in its economic history. The British Isles were first incorporated into a larger economy with their conquest by Rome, becoming a major exporter of grain and woolen cloth, the latter a product that would remain an important export into the early modern era. With the collapse of the empire in the fifth century, the British Isles reverted to a local barter economy, with the little remaining manufacturing activity centered in monasteries.

With the revival of trade in Europe at the beginning of the second millennium CE, Britain once again became a major exporter of wool and woolen cloth to the continent. By the thirteenth century, a number of English towns from York in the north to Exeter in the south became cloth-producing centers, with London and other port cities thriving on the wool trade.

While causing great immediate suffering and economic dislocation, the Black Death, which reduced the population of the British Isles by as much as one-third in the fourteenth century, had a positive long-term effect on England's economy, according to many historians. By reducing the number of laborers, it gave those who survived higher wages and more freedom, creating greater balances in power and wealth among the different classes. The Black Death thus contributed to the fall of the feudal order, in which semi-enslaved peasants, or serfs, were tied to the land and subjected to the total control of local lords; the end of feudalism allowed more geographic and social mobility.

A second revolution in the English economy occurred in the late seventeenth and early eighteenth centuries with the so-called enclosure movement, in which traditional forms of landholding and farming practices were replaced with more commercial and efficient ones. The process led to more food production even as it displaced many peasants from the land, sending them to towns and cities. Together, these events created the workforce for a new economy based on manufacturing even as they allowed that new workforce to be fed relatively cheaply.

The expansion of empire in the seventeenth and eighteenth centuries also allowed for more overseas trade, which the British government tried to control through mercantilist policies that ensured its colonies would remain captive markets for the mother country's manufactured goods. This trade—as well as less expensive agricultural products—increased the prosperity of the English people, creating greater demand for manufacturing goods such as cloth and shoes. This, in turn, created the impetus for more efficient forms of manufacturing, leading to the factory system of production and the introduction of labor-saving machinery, some of it powered by the newly invented steam engine. By the early nineteenth century, the steam engine had been harnessed for transportation, creating the beginnings of a railroad network that would make for a more integrated national market.

By the mid-nineteenth century, the United Kingdom had become manufacturer to much of the world, producing great capital reserves that were then invested both at home and abroad. By the end of the century, Britain had also emerged as the world's largest foreign investor as well.

War, Loss of Empire, and Economic Decline

Yet even as the British Empire and the British economy were reaching their zenith, new competitors were emerging, most notably Germany and the United States. With larger internal markets (especially true of the United States) and more modern equipment, these two countries gradually came to surpass Britain as manufacturers—the United States by century's end and Germany just before World War I.

The Great War had a profound effect on the British economy, costing Britain many of its most important markets in continental Europe. In addition, it found itself in great debt, much of it owed to the United States, which prevented it from investing in new capital equipment. As its industry became less productive than that of other countries, such as the United States, it lost out in other markets around the world. While there was increasing social equality in Britain after World War I, there was also much unemployment, even as the state began to offer new services, such as housing and medical subsidies, old-age pensions, and unemployment benefits.

Such measures helped Britain escape the worst effects of the Great Depression. While unemployment jumped to 18 percent by 1932, the nation's overall economy recovered faster than that of the United States and France, with production some 20 percent higher in 1937 than it had been on the eve of the Wall Street crash of 1929.

While World War II brought great destruction to Britain's industrial infrastructure and the immediate postwar era saw a weakened mother country give in to nationalist movements around the world and grant independence to the majority of its colonies in Africa, the Americas, and Asia by the 1970s, Britain prospered in the 1950s and early 1960s. Wartime rationing generally ended by the mid-1950s as the economy expanded alongside that of its continental neighbors, as part of the overall boom in Western Europe. Years of shortages had created much pent-up demand even as the government began to spend more on health care, infrastructure, education, and other public services.

For all the gains, there were fundamental flaws in the British economy that began to put a drag on growth by the latter half of the 1960s. The industrial infrastructure was aging, which reduced productivity compared to other industrial powers. The loss of colonies meant a reduced external market for its exports. Many state-run enterprises were inefficient, and unions exerted great sway over the economic decision making of both government agencies and businesses, making it difficult to close down money-losing factories and mines. The oil shocks of the 1970s only added to the economic malaise, leading voters to abandon the Labour Party, which had built the social welfare state of the postwar era, for the more market-oriented Conservative Party, led by Margaret Thatcher, in 1979.

Thatcher and Free-Market Reforms

Over the next decade, Thatcher's government succeeded in changing the face of the UK. Privatization, battles with the trade unions, and economic policy based on monetarism became the new hallmarks of British domestic affairs. Many economists agreed that the UK needed a reality check and that its traditional industries, manufacturing and mining, were no longer competitive. Instead, there was an increased emphasis on the service industries, in particular financial services. The financial services industry was deregulated; loans and mortgages became easier to obtain, and a round of tax cuts led to economic boom times.

The success of the Thatcher government in bringing down inflation and unemployment while generating economic growth came to a grinding halt in the late 1980s. In his efforts to conquer inflation, Chancellor of the Exchequer Nigel Lawson had pinned his faith on linking the UK pound with the German deutschmark. By shadowing the deutschmark, Lawson hoped to impose some monetary discipline on British businesses. If the prospect of currency depreciation were removed, he reasoned, then firms would be forced to become more competitive by controlling costs and increasing productivity.

The logical conclusion to this policy was for the UK to join the Exchange Rate Mechanism (ERM), which it did in October 1990. The pound was allowed to float within a range of £1 = DM2.83 and DM3.13. At the time of entry, UK inflation was running at 10.9 percent; wages were rising at 10 percent; and unemployment, after 44 months of successive falls, started to rise again to over 1.6 million. Interest rates stood at 14 percent, having been cut by 1 percent in October 1990.

In the mid- to late 1980s, a strong housing market had led many people to take the risk of buying near the peak of the market. However, the need to maintain high interest rates finally began to impact borrowing and investment. Britain's gross domestic product (GDP) fell by 0.77 percent between 1989 and 1990, and then by 0.6 percent between 1990 and 1991.

The number of house repossessions rose dramatically: 247,000 from 1990 to 1993. Unemployment rose to 2.6 million by the end of 1991, and inflation stood at 4.6 percent. In the face of the recession, the government had only limited room to maneuver given its membership in the ERM. Any major cut in interest rates to stimulate the economy would have put pressure on the sterling and risked it moving out of its range to the deutschmark. The government cut interest rates to

10.5 percent by September 1991, and the sterling ended the year near its lowest level.

The year 1992 brought a continuation of the recession. Economic growth was still negative, and unemployment reached 2.87 million, with 1,200 businesses closing every week. Inflation fell to 3 percent, helped by the cuts in interest rates. In September, the sterling began to be sold heavily and fell below its ERM floor; the government attempted to prop up the value of the pound by increasing interest rates, which it raised as high as 15 percent. On the evening of September 16, 1992, dubbed Black Wednesday, Chancellor of the Exchequer Norman Lamont announced to the press that the UK was withdrawing from the ERM. Speculators seemed to know that the government simply did not have the funds to support the pound indefinitely, and keeping interest rates at such a high level would have exacerbated the recession.

The withdrawal of the UK from the ERM marked a major change in economic policy. The recession had reduced inflationary pressures, but the cost in terms of high unemployment and business failures was significant. At the end of 1992, the total number of failed businesses had reached 61,767 for the year. Without the constraints of the ERM, Lamont cut interest rates to 7 percent, which heralded the start of a slow recovery. In 1993, GDP rose by 1.75 percent, but unemployment, ever the lagging indicator, peaked at over 3 million. Inflation also fell rapidly, dropping to 1.2 percent by the end of the year.

The government faced additional problems as a result of the recession. Tax revenue fell as unemployment continued to rise, business profits fell, and consumer spending slowed markedly. At the same time, spending on public benefits increased. Government borrowing rose to £50 billion. To address this problem, the government increased the value-added tax (VAT) on fuel and power, and then made changes to mortgage tax relief and personal allowances that had the effect of adding to the income-tax burden. Interest rates, however, were reduced to 5.5 percent by the end of 1993, providing some relief for homeowners and encouraging borrowing by both businesses and individuals.

The recovery continued to gather pace in 1994, with GDP growth at 4 percent; inflation remained manageable at just over 2.0 percent, and unemployment fell to under 2.5 million. The tax increases also started to have their effect on public borrowing, which fell to £40 billion. Throughout 1994 and 1995, while the key economic variables seemed to be moving in the right direction, the problem for the government was that the feel-good factor seemed to be missing in the minds of many of the population. In 1995, GDP growth was 2.5 percent, unemployment was falling, and retail sales were flat, but there were signs that consumer credit was starting to rise.

The same trends continued into 1996. House prices rose at an annual rate of about 5 percent, and unemployment fell to below 7 percent of the workforce. The inflation rate of 2.8 percent exceeded the government's target of 2.5 percent, but it was still a significant improvement from the levels of the late 1980s and early 1990s. Consumer confidence finally seemed to be picking up, but there were concerns that much of the spending was being financed by credit.

Labour Government and Economic Boom

The general election of May 1997 returned the Labour Party to power. One explanation for the cycles of boom and bust in the United Kingdom over the previous thirty years was the fact that the power to change interest rates lay in the hands of the government. There was always a temptation to manipulate interest rates for political gain, as opposed to pure economic reasons. Reducing interest rates at the wrong time, however, could have a direct effect on inflation and economic growth, leading to knee-jerk reactions rather than considered policy. The temptation to reduce rates before an election—whatever the state of the economy—was, it was argued, too great. The inevitable consequence was that government would

A proponent of retaining the British pound writes "No EMU" (European Monetary Union) during the "Give a Pound to Save Our Pound" campaign in 1998. As a member of the European Union, Great Britain could join the euro but opted against doing so. *(Sinead Lynch/AFP/Getty Images)*

have to raise taxes or interest rates—or both—in the aftermath of an election. This, in turn, led to the lurches in economic activity that characterize boom-and-bust economies.

The answer, it was determined, was to put decision-making power regarding interest rates in the hands of the Bank of England. In the first week of the new government, the Bank was given operational authority over monetary policy. The chancellor of the exchequer set a target for inflation, and it was the responsibility of the Bank of England to adjust interest rates to help meet this target. A meeting of the Monetary Policy Committee (MPC), made up of members of the bank itself and external members (nine in all), would be held every month to review the prospects for inflation and make the decision about interest rates. If inflation rose above its target level by more than 1 percent, the governor of the Bank of England was required to write an open letter to the chancellor giving an explanation and an outline of the strategy to bring inflation back under control.

One of the main benefits of this system would be to influence inflationary expectations. The rational expectations model had gained some currency in economic theory. If businesses and individuals knew that the Bank of England would keep a firm hold on inflation—raising interest rates in the face of rising inflationary expectations and lowering them to keep inflation at target level in times of economic slowdown—decision making would be affected. No more would interest rate changes be at the whim of a chancellor seeking electoral popularity.

The initial test for the bank came when inflation rose above the target level of 2.5 to 3.7 percent. In response, the MPC raised interest rates to a seven-year high of 7.25 percent by the end of 1997—by which time unemployment had fallen to around 1.4 million and growth stood at 3.1 percent. In many respects, then, the improving economic climate inherited by the new exchequer, Gordon Brown, was largely due to the policies of his Conservative predecessors. Brown's challenge was to maintain that momentum. In his first budget, in 1997, he announced that the government would set in place a number of fiscal rules to guide policy. The "Golden Rule" stated that there would be a commitment that over the period of the economic cycle, government borrowing would be made only to finance investment and not to fund current spending. This meant that the burden of current spending would be shouldered by those who would benefit from it—current taxpayers rather than future taxpayers.

The other major fiscal rule Brown introduced was the so-called sustainable investment rule, according to which public sector debt as a proportion of GDP would be held at a prudent level, or below 40 percent. In addition, Brown cut corporation taxes, the tax on business profits, and the VAT on gas and electricity and imposed a windfall tax on privatized utilities that would raise £5.2 billion over two years from twenty-eight companies.

Over the next ten years, Brown presided over a period of unprecedented economic stability. Unemployment fell to below 1 million, and inflation remained within the target range redefined in 2003 at around 2 percent. The Bank of England varied interest rates by only a quarter point on the vast majority of occasions it felt the need to change them. Economic growth remained positive throughout the first ten years of the Labour government.

Increased Speculation and Financial Crisis

Improved public finances meant there was room to cut income taxes and increase public spending, including heavy increases for health and education. Consumer confidence was high and the housing market, in particular, was booming. The effects of financial deregulation back in the 1980s meant that banks and building societies competed to provide ever more attractive mortgage products. Money was being lent under ever more generous terms, and the housing market continued to strengthen. Although some cautioned that the housing market was bound to crash, their worries appeared ill founded as home prices continued to rise.

The use of credit to finance purchases also continued to expand. The initial signs that consumers were using the increased range of credit facilities being offered by banks and financial institutions began in the mid-1990s under the Conservative government. By 2008, UK consumers had built up credit debt of £1.4 trillion. One of the reasons put forward for the buildup was that homeowners were able to use the equity in their properties as security for additional borrowing. The availability of credit and debit cards also made it much easier to spend now and worry later. All in all, public finances had improved, inflation seemed well under control, and years of continued economic growth seemed to breed the expectation that the good times could only continue.

The global financial meltdown of 2007–2008

showed all too clearly that this was not the case. The United Kingdom, whose financial-services sector had helped devise and market many of the more exotic credit swap derivatives and mortgage-backed securities that were at the heart of the crisis, was especially hard hit. At first, the British government, now led by Prime Minister Gordon Brown, seemed to take the lead in confronting the crisis, rescuing a collapsing Northern Rock Bank, one of the country's largest financial institutions, and offering huge amounts of government capital to shore up the financial system.

Soon, however, the crisis proved too much for even these aggressive measures. The underlying problems were simply too great. One of the problems had to do with housing. During the boom years of the 1990s and especially during the early and middle 2000s, the United Kingdom had seen a dramatic increase in housing prices, which severely deflated again with the contraction of the credit markets in the wake of the crisis.

Indeed, the credit crunch went beyond the housing sector. Household debt had grown dramatically in the 1990s and 2000s, as Britons tried to maintain their standard of living despite falling exports and a growing trade imbalance with the rest of the world. Moreover, the British economy had been boosted by significant inflows of capital as London came to rival New York as the world's financial capital. But this, too, shrank in the wake of the financial crisis and the freezing up of the credit markets beginning in late 2007 and accelerating in 2008.

Large amounts of household debt, rising foreclosure rates, increasing unemployment, and the decline in the critical financial sector of the economy all sent the United Kingdom into its first recession in more than a decade. In the second quarter of 2008, the nation's economy began to contract for the first time since the recession of the early 1990s. By the first quarter of 2009, the contraction had reached 2.5 percent, though it eased to just 0.5 percent in the second quarter. The worst appeared to have passed, as the economy emerged from recession in the fourth quarter of 2009, albeit with an anemic growth rate of just 0.3 percent.

Andrew Ashwin and James Ciment

See also: France; Germany; Italy; Northern Rock.

Further Reading
Alford, B.W.E. *Britain in the World Economy Since 1880.* New York: Longman, 1996.

"Banking Crisis Timeline: How the Credit Crunch Has Led to Dramatic, Unprecedented Events in the City, on Wall Street and Around the World." *The Guardian*, October 30, 2008.

Chapman, Stanley. *Merchant Enterprise in Britain: From the Industrial Revolution to World War I.* New York: Cambridge University Press, 1992.

Dellheim, Charles. *The Disenchanted Isle: Mrs. Thatcher's Capitalist Revolution.* New York: W.W. Norton, 1995.

Gilmore, Grainne, and Gary Duncan. "Credit Crisis: The Cracks Are Opening in UK's Debt Mountain." Available at http://business.timesonline.co.uk/tol/business/industry_sectors/banking_and_finance/article3579142.ece. Accessed February 2009.

Lawson, Nigel. *The View from No. 11: Britain's Longest-Serving Cabinet Member Recalls the Triumphs and Disappointments of the Thatcher Era.* New York: Doubleday, 1993.

Romano, Flavio. *Clinton and Blair: The Political Economy of the Third Way.* New York: Routledge, 2006.

Roy, Subroto, and John Clarke, eds. *Margaret Thatcher's Revolution: How It Happened and What It Meant.* New York: Continuum, 2005.

Trentmann, Frank. *Free Trade Nation: Commerce, Consumption, and Civil Society in Modern Britain.* New York: Oxford University Press, 2008.

United States

With the world's largest gross domestic product (GDP) and most diversified economy, the United States—population just over 300 million—boasts a major manufacturing infrastructure, the world's most productive agricultural system, a well-developed service sector, and a globally influential financial sector. In the years following World War II, the United States emerged as the world's largest importer and exporter and the dollar became the world's key currency.

The origins of the modern United States date back to the establishment of European colonial settlements in eastern North America in the early seventeenth century. After achieving independence from Great Britain in the late eighteenth century, the United States embarked on a vast geographic expansion that ultimately would span the North American continent.

In the nineteenth century, the nation became one of the pioneers of the industrial revolution, creating a major manufacturing and transportation infrastructure that, by century's end, would render the country the world's largest economy. Victory in two world wars in the first half of the twentieth century helped turned the United States into a military and geopolitical superpower with strategic interests around the globe.

With its entrepreneurial dynamism and high social mobility, the United States has enjoyed buoyant economic growth through much of its history but at the price of great economic volatility, with booms and busts marking the period from the early nineteenth through the early twenty-first centuries. Most recently, the United States—particularly its housing and financial sectors—has been at the epicenter of the crisis that brought down the world's financial markets in 2008.

For much of its history, the United States has adhered to a more laissez-faire approach to economic policy than many other industrialized countries, leaving the free market to allocate economic resources and eschewing the elaborate welfare system erected in many European countries in the twentieth century. Still, it has erected a regulatory infrastructure—enhanced since the Depression of the 1930s by a slew of social welfare programs—designed to smooth out and ease the impact of the boom-and-bust capitalist cycle.

Colonial Era, Revolution, and Constitution

What is now the United States of America has been home to indigenous peoples since at least 15,000 BCE, and by the time of first contact with Europeans in the sixteenth century, a number of different kinds of cultures had emerged, with some tribes practicing agriculture and others existing as hunters and gatherers. In many areas, elaborate trading networks had been established. In the Southwest, for example, native peoples, some of whom had built small-scale urban settlements, traded as far away as the Aztec Empire of central Mexico.

Aside from a few Spanish settlements in the Southwest and Florida, the first European colonizers came from Northern Europe in the early seventeenth century—primarily from England, though the Dutch settled what would later become New York. The colonies they founded varied significantly, from the religious settlements of New England, to the commercial agriculture and trading colonies of New Netherland (later New York) and Pennsylvania, to the plantation agriculture–based colonies of Virginia and the Carolinas.

By the eighteenth century, the thirteen British colonies had thriving and diversified economies (the Dutch were ousted from New York by the 1670s). New England was a center of fishing, whaling, and trade, while the mid-Atlantic colonies boasted the major trading ports of New York, Philadelphia, and Baltimore, where grains and other agricultural products of the hinterland were exchanged for manufactured goods from Europe. Most lucrative of all were the southern colonies. Utilizing slave labor imported from Africa and the Caribbean, Virginia became a major exporter of tobacco, while South Carolina and Georgia shipped out ever growing quantities of rice and cotton.

Under British mercantilist policy, the colonies were meant to be suppliers of raw materials for the mother country and to serve as a captive market for English manufactured goods. But the policy was honored more in the breach through the mid-eighteenth century when, to pay the costs of imperial defense, the British began imposing higher taxes and tighter restrictions on colonial trade. The impositions rankled many colonists, particularly influential merchants in the North and planters in the South.

Leading a coalition that would eventually encompass most of the white colonial population, patriotic leaders first petitioned the British government to change its policies and allow colonial representation in Parliament. Then, upon being turned down, they declared independence from Britain while launching an armed insurrection. After six years of often bitter fighting, the thirteen colonies defeated the much more powerful British military, signing a peace treaty in 1783 that gave the new United States of America control not just of the Atlantic seaboard but of most of territory south of the Great Lakes and east of the Mississippi River.

While the new republic had much in its favor economically—vast and rich farmlands in the North, a lucrative plantation system in the South, thriving ports, a well-developed artisan manufacturing system, and an entrepreneurially minded mercantile community—it was plagued with problematic public finances. The war had impoverished the country, ruined its currency, and saddled both the central and individual colonial governments with enormous debts. Adding to the new nation's woes, in the opinion of many of the republic's early leaders, was the weakness of the central government, which, because it had virtually no ability to raise revenues, could not deal with these many economic problems. In 1787, proponents of a more powerful central government fashioned a Constitution that granted far greater authority to the federal government, though still leaving a significant amount of policy-making power to the individual states.

A great debate then ensued about what kind of national economy should be promoted. Southern planters, led by Secretary of State Thomas Jefferson, argued for an economy based on small-scale farming, limited manufacturing, a minimal financial sector, and a small, low-taxing, low-debt government, especially at the federal level. Arrayed against Jefferson and his allies were the merchants of the North, led by Treasury Secretary Alexander Hamilton, a key confidant of President George Washington.

Maritime trade and shipbuilding were the foundations of the New England colonial economy. Agricultural products and other raw materials were exported to Europe in exchange for manufactured products—and for African slaves through the Triangle Trade. *(MPI/Stringer/Hulton Archive/Stringer/Getty Images)*

Interpreting the Constitution loosely—meaning that its mandate to "promote the general welfare" should be understood as allowing government to expand its role in setting economic policy—Hamilton argued for a plan that would allow the central government to assume and pay off state debts, thereby putting it on sound financial footing, and establish a central bank to regulate the nation's currency and financial system. Hamilton ultimately won the day, though his plan for using the federal government to encourage manufacturing was resisted by those who believed America's economic future lay with agriculture and trade.

Booms and Busts of the Early Republic and Antebellum Eras

Despite the setbacks to trade caused by the Napoleonic Wars in Europe—which triggered a brief but devastating trade embargo on the part of the Jefferson administration in 1807—the U.S. economy prospered during the first two decades of the nineteenth century. With improvements in transportation, particularly in the form of canals, more farmers turned to raising commercial crops, selling them on the open market for cash to buy manufactured goods and foodstuffs, such as sugar or coffee, which they were unable to grow themselves. There was also an expansion in domestic manufacturing, particularly in New England, where the first water-powered, machine-driven textile mills began to open as early as the 1790s. Increasingly, the United States was developing a national marketplace for goods, a process aided by a series of Supreme Court decisions in the early nineteenth century upholding contracts and limiting the power of state governments to regulate trade.

With the end of European and transatlantic war in 1815, the economy took off; trade increased and manufacturing capacity expanded significantly. As wages and prices rose, a speculative real-estate frenzy swept many parts of the country, particularly in the West, fueled by easy credit as state banks issued far more bank notes—a form of currency—than their assets suggested they should. When manufacturing and trade began to fall off in 1818 and prices dropped, panic set in as speculators tried to get rid of their real-estate holdings in order to meet debt obligations. The result was the Panic of 1819, the first national financial panic in U.S. history and one that sent unemployment and insolvency proceedings soaring. (Under the Constitution, only Congress could pass bankruptcy legislation; after a brief experiment in 1800, it declined to do so until 1841.)

By the mid-1820s, the national economy had revived, spurred by continued improvements in transportation, increasing factory output, and westward expansion. A key development was the completion of the Erie Canal in 1825, linking the Great Lakes to the Atlantic Ocean and turning New York City, where the Hudson River/Erie Canal waterway met the ocean, into the nation's preeminent port and financial center. This period also saw an increase in the number of corporations, as investors began to pool their money in order to undertake projects whose capital requirements were too great for any single entrepreneur to meet. Further, corporations offered the protection of limited liability, so that, should they fail, the stockholders were liable only for the money they had invested, leaving their personal fortunes intact. Because corporations offered this protection and because they possessed great financial power, they were limited at first, with investors required to petition state legislatures for charters that often had time limits and other restrictions. Meanwhile, laws against imprisonment for debt were overturned, lifting the fear of jail time from the minds of risk-taking entrepreneurs.

As business was expanding, so, too, was democracy. By the 1820s and 1830s, virtually all property restrictions on voting had been removed, granting nearly all white adult males the franchise. This development led to increasingly populist-tinged politics, culminating in the 1828 victory of the war hero Andrew Jackson, who campaigned as a man of the people who would fight the economic elites of the major eastern cities. Among his pledges was to do away with Hamilton's creation, the Bank of the United States. (Actually, it was the Second Bank of the United States, the re-chartered heir to Hamilton's original institution.) In 1832, Jackson vetoed the bill that would re-charter the institution—though the bank would not close until 1836—thus ending federal regulation of the nation's money supply and financial system for the rest of the century.

The bank's closing could not have come at a worse time. During much of the 1830s, yet another speculative real-estate bubble had been inflating as state banks, many of them poorly capitalized, offered easy credit to purchase lands in the ever-expanding western states and territories. Prices skyrocketed for rural land and especially for plots in future cities, many of them nothing more than plans on paper. But with the closing of the Bank of the United States, credit suddenly dried up, prices collapsed, bankruptcies multiplied, and unemployment soared in a new panic—beginning in 1837—that was even more economically devastating and long lasting than the one of 1819. Indeed, its effect would continue to be felt into the early 1840s. In response to the Panic of 1837, many states decided that the solution lay in more competition. Legislatures passed new bank chartering laws that allowed anyone who met certain capital requirements and followed certain rules regarding how much they loaned against assets to open a bank. Previously, persons interested in starting a bank had to petition the legislature for a special charter, a process that often restricted the granting of this lucrative opportunity to political insiders.

Again, the economy expanded dramatically in the late 1840s and 1850s, as manufacturing centers began to emerge outside New England, linked to national and international markets by a rapidly expanding railroad system, itself a source of much economic investment. Indeed, despite the ever gloomier political climate—as sectional rivalries over slavery threatened secession—the economy largely boomed right up to the opening salvoes at Fort Sumter in 1861, the first battle of the Civil

The California gold rush of the late 1840s and early 1850s gave rise to boomtowns such as San Francisco and Sacramento, California; to an influx of wealth seekers from across America and overseas; and to the reality of riches for some. (*The Granger Collection, New York*)

War. There had been a sharp panic and economic downturn in 1857, triggered by an investor loss of confidence in the financial system, the failure of a major Ohio bank, and the loss to shipwreck of a major gold shipment from California. Although short in duration, the Panic of 1857 did point out one fact: the country's reliance on foreign, and especially British, capital to fund its economic expansion. The withdrawal of British capital from U.S. banks is what most historians cite as the panic's single most important cause.

From the Civil War to the 1920s

While the Civil War was primarily about slavery and race, other economic factors were involved. Many Southerners, particularly the planters who led the charge to war, were angry that while they produced the cotton and other commercial crops that earned the foreign capital that helped make the nation's dramatic economic expansion possible, most of the profits—and the economic development made possible by those profits—accrued to merchants, traders, bankers, and other middlemen of Northern cities such as New York, Boston, and Philadelphia. By becoming independent, the South hoped to be able to exert more control over its economic destiny.

The Civil War had a more profound effect on the economy than any other single event in nineteenth-century American history, disrupting internal trade and finance, closing off regional markets, and halting the flow of commodities. Southern producers of agricultural goods such as cotton, sugar, and tobacco were hit particularly hard and would never fully recover. Some Northern businesses, particularly textile mills that relied on cotton from the South, also suffered. Merchants and banks were hurt as well, since they could not recover their debts from Southerners.

Soon, however, much of the economy had recovered from the initial shock, spurred by unprecedented government spending on war supplies. The war revived the fortunes of the financial industry, as the government issued vast quantities of bonds through New York financiers. Free from the resistance of Southern legislators, Congress passed a series of laws favoring Northern businesses and farmers, including acts to build a transcontinental railroad and to offer free western lands to homesteading farmers. Indeed, agriculture also got a short-term fillip from the war, as Northern farmers not drafted into or volunteering for the army prospered as food prices climbed due to shortages and demand. A lack of farm labor also encouraged the use of labor-saving agricultural machinery, increasing output and creating demand among manufacturers of this equipment.

The war also accelerated economic divisions. Because the government needed to ramp up production quickly, it sought out manufacturers capable of meeting the demand, contributing to the growth of the kinds of large-scale businesses that would dominate the economy through the rest of the nineteenth century. At the same time, rising prices led to demand for higher wages and

encouraged the growth of a labor movement that would come to blows with big business time and again during the late nineteenth and early twentieth centuries.

With the Union victorious in 1865, the country was poised for another period of rapid expansion. Between 1865 and 1913, the United States underwent the largest economic expansion in human history to that time, as the gross national product (GNP) climbed more than 700 percent, from less than $7 billion in the former year to about $50 billion in the latter. By 1900, the United States had come to surpass Great Britain as the largest economy in the world.

The economic growth was fueled by several factors. One was heavy manufacturing, as a second wave of industrialization threw up vast steelmaking works in the Midwest and a ready-to-wear clothing industry in the Northeast, a food processing industry in the Midwest, and manufacturing plants of various types throughout the country. Even the economically backward South participated, as textile manufacturers moved to the region to take advantage of its cheaper labor. The country also became increasingly urbanized (the number of people in towns would come to surpass those living in rural areas by the 1920 census), creating a population of people whose consumer demand fueled economic growth. The national population also skyrocketed, both because of high birth rates (though they were actually falling slightly), improved mortality rates, and massive waves of immigrations. A larger population meant a larger domestic market, contributing further to economies of scale.

But the economic boom of the period was not without its problems and setbacks. First, there were the growing inequalities in wealth between those who owned the means of production and those who came to work for them. Such disparities often led to widespread and sometimes violent labor unrest, particularly during economic downturns when companies tried to cut their costs by lowering wages and accelerating production.

Indeed, the late-nineteenth-century economy

of the United States was an especially volatile one. Two major panics—and several smaller ones—triggered long-term economic recessions in every decade between the 1870s and 1890s. These panics were usually triggered by speculative excess. But unlike the panics of the antebellum era, which were fueled by real-estate crises, the panics of the late nineteenth century were caused by unsustainable run-ups in the price of railroad stocks. As the speculative bubbles burst and share prices collapsed, overextended financial institutions suddenly found themselves unable to meet their financial obligations, leading to depositor runs on bank assets, which further contributed to the panic. The result was a dramatic contraction of credit that undermined investment and hiring, leading to wage cuts and higher unemployment. This, in turn, led to deflationary pressure that produced a further loss in confidence and continued reductions in investment.

Many people, particularly in the South and West, came to believe that the heart of the problem lay in the nation's money supply. With the dollar backed by gold exclusively—and gold in limited supply until major discoveries were made in the mid-1890s in the Yukon and South Africa—money became increasingly valuable. That is, there was a limited amount of money in an ever-expanding economy, which reduced prices and wages. The solution, opponents of the gold standard argued, was to monetize silver, which, because it was relatively plentiful, would increase the money supply, raise prices, and make it easier for borrowers—especially farmers—to pay their debts. Opposed by major financiers and the pro-business Republican establishment that dominated national politics in the late nineteenth and early twentieth centuries, the silver solution was largely ignored by policy makers.

With the expansion of the gold supply in the 1890s, however, the issue became less economically pressing, even if the politics surrounding it reached their crescendo in the heated presidential campaign of 1896. Still, while the money question began to fade in importance and the Populists who thrived on it lost their political footing, a new economic issue arose—the power of the huge corporations that had emerged in manufacturing and transportation in the years since the Civil War.

While the social welfare of the poor and working classes—many of them laboring for big business—was at the heart of local and state reform efforts of the early twentieth century (federal involvement in such issues was still decades in the future), the Progressive movement at the national level focused largely on how to control the excessive power of big business to affect political decision making and hinder economic competition. Progressives, such as President Theodore Roosevelt, achieved this either by breaking monopolistic corporations into smaller competing companies, as in the case of Standard Oil in 1909–1911, or by passing regulations to make sure that corporations behaved more responsibly vis-à-vis consumers, workers, and the environment.

In short, Progressives believed that government played an important role in shaping economic behavior and steering economic activity in socially beneficial directions. This included reducing the excessive financial speculation that triggered panics and produced economic downturns. In the wake of the short but sharp recession of 1907, many business and government leaders came to the conclusion that it was time to create a central bank, like those in many European countries. The Federal Reserve System, which came into being in 1913, was created to ease volatility by maintaining control over the money supply, raising interest rates to cut back on speculative excess, and lowering them to spur economic growth during downturns.

But in its first two decades, the Fed, as it came to be called, was less than effective. During the booming 1920s, it maintained an artificially low interest rate that spurred speculative excess, first in the real-estate market and then, when prices there fell back to Earth in the middle years of the decade, in the stock market, which saw unprecedented run-ups in the price of corporate securities. In fact, the 1920s were a time of great economic prosperity for some and economic hardship for others, as wealth and income became ever more inequitably distributed, both between classes and between rural and urban areas.

Crash, Depression, and War

The great Wall Street crash of 1929 was grounded in both aspects of economic life in the 1920s—the run-up in share prices and the growing inequality in wealth. As for the former, much of the skyrocketing price of corporate securities could be traced to too much easy credit, as brokerages borrowed money from banks to lend to investors, who would buy stock on margin (pay a small portion of the stock price and use the full value as collateral against the loan). This worked as long as stock prices were climbing. But when they began to fall in late 1929, the house of cards collapsed, as brokerages called in their margin loans to pay back panicky banks.

The crash might have been confined to Wall Street investors, still a tiny minority of the population in 1929, if it had not been for the underlying weaknesses of the national economy. As credit dried up, so did investment, sending unemployment rising and bankruptcies soaring. Because most consumers lived on the financial edge—having failed to be included in the prosperity of the 1920s—demand for the goods being produced by manufacturers plummeted.

The result was the worst economic downturn in American history—the Great Depression of the 1930s. Making things worse were the actions of government, in particular the Fed. Indeed, some economic historians blame the severity of the economic downturn of the early 1930s—when overall economic output fell by some 40 percent and unemployment topped 25 percent—on the tight money policy of the Fed. Believing that overcapacity was the major problem facing the country, the Fed decided to lower interest rates slowly beginning in early 1930, a pace that many economists have argued contributed to the severity of the Depression. This policy not only con-tributed to the fall in economic output, but sent many banks to the edge financially, creating panic among depositors, who tried to withdraw their money. This, in turn, caused a wave of bankruptcies in the financial sector.

The landslide victory of Democrat Franklin Roosevelt in the 1932 presidential election ushered in an era of enhanced government involvement in the economy. The New Deal, as Roosevelt's domestic agenda was called, consisted of two major parts. The first focused on business and included such programs and institutions as the Federal Deposit Insurance Corporation, to protect bank depositors and prevent runs on banks; the Securities and Exchange Commission, to regulate Wall Street and prevent the kind of excesses that had led to the stock market crash of 1929; and the National Recovery Administration, an ambitious program to prevent "destructive competition" by setting wage and price standards that was ultimately ruled unconstitutional by the Supreme Court. The "second New Deal," as it came to be known, was not inaugurated until late in Roosevelt's first term. It consisted of laws and programs designed to bolster the demand side of the economic equation, including the National Labor Relations Act, which made unionization easier, and the Social Security Act, which set a national, government-run pension system. Meanwhile, the federal government tried to ease unemployment by hiring thousands of citizens to work on infrastructure and other projects through the Works Progress Administration and other programs.

While Roosevelt did not explicitly invoke the name of John Maynard Keynes, the ideas of that pioneering English economist were increasingly at the heart of what his administration was trying to achieve. Keynes, focusing on the demand side of the economic equation, argued that government spending, even if it causes deficits, is critical in lifting an economy out of a slump. Prior to Keynes, most economists held to the idea that deficit spending dried up capital necessary for private investment. And indeed, with the economy recovering by the mid-1930s, Roosevelt took such conventional advice and cut back on government spending. That, most economic historians agree, sent the nation's economy into the steep recession of 1937–1938.

But Keynes's ideas were invoked by Roosevelt, if obliquely, at decade's end, as the country mobilized for war. Economists continue to debate the role of World War II in lifting the economy out of the Depression. Some argue that massive defense spending was not exactly what Keynes recommended—he preferred more socially productive spending, on things such as infrastructure—but it did the trick, boosting industrial output and dramatically slashing unemployment. Others, however, contend that employment was lowered by the fact that more than 16 million Americans were removed from the labor force by entering the military, while output was artificially sustained by defense spending.

Boom and Recession in the Postwar Era

There is no argument about the reality of the prolonged economic boom that followed the war. Aside from occasional recessions and bouts of inflation, the U.S. economy enjoyed unprecedented expansion between the late 1940s and the early 1970s—an acceleration of growth fueled by pent-up demand after years of depression and war; large government outlays for housing, education, and defense; and limited foreign competition, as other major industrial powers focused on rebuilding after the devastation caused by World War II. The postwar boom was also one in which the U.S. government explicitly pursued Keynesian counter-cyclical economic policy, reducing taxes and increasing spending during downturns. Meanwhile, the United States emerged from World War II as the dominant global economic player—or, at least, the dominant player outside the Communist bloc. When the U.S. economy boomed, it tended to lift other economies with it; when it contracted it usually created recessionary conditions in much of the rest of the world.

In the mid-1970s, however, the country entered a period in which recessions became deeper and more frequent. In addition, they were accompanied not by falling prices, as was usually the case during downturns, but by galloping inflation. This pattern of "stagflation" (a combination of "stagnation" and "inflation") was caused by multiple oil price hikes by OPEC and a wage-price spiral (cost-push inflation instead of demand-pull inflation); expansion of the money supply by the Fed served to accelerate inflation rather than ease unemployment and reverse slow or negative growth. Post Keynesian economists then suggested that taxes and other government measures be imposed on large corporations to prevent them from hiking wages and prices. But such an approach was not implemented, other than a 90-day freeze on wages and prices instituted by President Richard Nixon in 1971.

While all economists agree that the oil shocks of the 1970s, which sent crude prices spiking, contributed to the "malaise," other factors are highly debated. In particular, economists point to a still not well-explained decline in productivity. On the left, economists pointed to the end of a period of labor peace in which capitalists had granted higher wages in return for more productivity. However, more influential politically was the claim by conservatives that excessive workplace, environmental, and other forms of regulation were undermining productivity, limiting investment, and restricting the country's competitiveness. With millions of Americans hurting from unemployment, high interest rates, and inflation, the message hit home, propelling conservative Republican Ronald Reagan into the White House in the 1980 election.

The Reagan administration's "supply-side" solution to the country's economic problems was premised on the idea that lowering tax rates on corporations and wealthy individuals would spur investment, which would eventually "trickle down" to benefit all Americans in the form of higher employment and wages. In addition, it was argued—counter to previous conservative economic thinking—the deficits produced by lower revenues would be only temporary, as a booming economy would soon produce even more revenues. And, indeed, Reagan dramatically lowered tax rates across the board, which meant that most of the savings accrued to those who proportionately paid the most in taxes—that is, the business sector and wealthy individuals. The Reagan administration also initiated a policy of laxer enforcement of government regulations, refused to give in to an air traffic controllers' strike—thereby sending a signal to unions to rein in their wage demands—and eased up on antitrust enforcement.

At the same time, Fed chairman Paul Volcker began to dramatically hike interest rates—thereby contracting the growth in the money supply—in an effort to wring inflation out of the system. The immediate result was the worst economic downturn since the Great Depression, with national unemployment topping 10 percent for the first time in more than four decades. The recession proved relatively short-lived, however, and did wring inflation out of the system. Meanwhile, the economy began to boom by the mid-1980s, though at the cost of growing inequalities in wealth.

In addition, the anti-regulatory policies of the 1980s also contributed to one of the greatest financial crises in American history, as much of a once-staid savings and loan (S&L) industry—freed from requirements about what it could invest in and how much money institutions must maintain against their loans—nearly collapsed, requiring a massive government bailout and liquidation of distressed assets. While the S&L debacle of the late 1980s and early 1990s did result in specific reforms to prevent a recurrence, the overall trend toward deregulation of the financial industry accelerated during the 1990s.

After a brief recession in the early part of the decade—triggered in part by dramatically lower defense spending as the cold war wound down—the economy entered the longest period of continuous sustained growth in U.S. history, propelled by the great productivity gains made possible by the spread of computers, more advanced telecommunications technology, and better management techniques, including just-in-time inventory and improved quality control.

With moderate Democrat Bill Clinton in the White House and conservative Republicans in charge of Congress, the country continued on a generally conservative economic path through the end of the century. The national welfare system was significantly restructured, with a new emphasis on pushing recipients into the workforce (1996), the telecommunications industry was deregulated (1996), the federal deficit was turned into a surplus (beginning in 1998), and legislation from the New Deal era barring commercial banks from engaging in brokerage and insurance activity was repealed (1999).

Booms and Busts of the 1990s and 2000s

Meanwhile, the boom of the 1990s was not without its flaws. Most pronounced was a price bubble in the high-tech industry. By the late 1990s, it was becoming increasingly apparent that the Internet was going to revolutionize the way business was conducted. Hundreds of billions of dollars were invested in companies set up to take advantage of the new technology, both privately and through initial public offerings on securities exchanges, most notably, the National Association of Securities Dealers Automated Quotations (NASDAQ). Valuations soared, padding the paper fortunes of investors. But many of the dot.com firms lacked a realistic, profit-making business model. By 2000, these weaknesses became increasingly glaring, leading to a dramatic collapse in valuations that, along with the terrorist attacks of September 11, 2001, contributed to recession in 2001 and 2002.

To counteract the downturn, the Fed began to dramatically lower the interest rates it charged member banks—to historic lows of 3 percent or less—from late 2002 to mid-2005. These low rates, passed on to consumers, encouraged millions of Americans to buy homes or refinance their mortgages, fueling a boom in the construction industry and housing prices that peaked in late 2006 and early 2007. As with the high-tech boom of the 1990s, however, there were underlying problems that few noticed in the midst of what many thought was a sustained expansion of the housing sector. First, many financial institutions—facing less oversight and regulation by the government—began to lower their lending standards, offering mortgages to prospective homebuyers who ordinarily would not be qualified. Many of these so-called subprime mortgages—as well as many ordinary mortgages—had graduated payment clauses in which they started off low and then jumped after a set period of time, or were set up as adjustable rate mortgages with higher payments due if interest rates increased. As long as housing prices rose, mortgagors could simply refinance with a new adjustable rate, using the rising equity in their homes to cover the closing costs.

Abetting this phenomenon was the securitization of mortgages. That is, mortgages were increasingly being bundled into packages and sold to investors, both in the United States and abroad. The idea was that, by bundling mortgages, the losses caused by foreclosures were spread around, thereby limiting the risk for those holding the mortgages. Reducing risk even further—or so investors thought—were credit default swaps, essentially insurance policies taken out against mortgage-backed securities. But there was a basic flaw in the system. For in selling the mortgages to other investors, the initiators of the mortgage—whether brokers or lending institutions—no longer had to worry about the creditworthiness of those taking out the mortgages, contributing to the lowering of lending standards.

For a while, no one in the industry or among government regulators seemed overly concerned, as housing prices continued to soar. As in the case of all financial bubbles, however, confidence in ever-rising prices eventually evaporated and real-estate valuations began to fall. With home equity disappearing, marginal homeowners could not refinance, which led to accelerated foreclosures and the so-called subprime mortgage crisis, which began in 2007.

The contagion inevitably spread to the financial institutions holding the mortgage-backed securities and collateral debt obligations, leading to the collapse of several major investment banks on Wall Street and precipitating the financial crisis of late 2008. The crisis—which prompted a $700 billion bailout of major financial institutions by the George W. Bush and Barack Obama administrations—contributed, along with collapsing home prices, to the longest and deepest recession, as measured by negative GDP growth, since the Great Depression. Nor was the crisis confined to the United States, since so many of the troubled, mortgage-related assets had been purchased by financial institutions around the world.

While the crisis and recession led to great immediate suffering by individuals and businesses alike—including the bankruptcy of two of America's three leading carmakers—it also prompted longer-term changes in government economic policy. Never before in U.S. history had the government taken such large equity stakes in financial institutions and other corporations, such as General Motors, in order to keep them afloat. Nor had the federal government ever spent more on an economic stimulus package than the one Obama pushed through Congress in early 2009, which amounted to $787 billion, prompting economists and the media to talk of a revival of Keynesian economics at the federal level. And with Democrats in control of both the White House and Congress after the 2008 elections, there appeared to be a new consensus in Washington that tighter regulation of the financial industry, including more consumer protections and stricter limits on executive compensation, was needed if the country was to avoid a repeat of the kind of financial crisis that nearly pushed the country and the world into a new Great Depression.

James Ciment

See also: Boom, Economic (1920s); Boom, Economic (1960s); Canada; Dot.com Bubble (1990s–2000); Great Depression (1929–1933); New Deal; Panic of 1901; Panic of 1907; Recession and Financial Crisis (2007–); Recession, Reagan (1981–1982); Recession, Roosevelt (1937–1939); Recession, Stagflation (1970s); Savings and Loan Crises (1980s–1990s).

Further Reading

Andreano, Ralph L., ed. *The Economic Impact of the American Civil War.* Cambridge, MA: Schenkman, 1962.

Badger, Anthony J. *The New Deal: The Depression Years, 1933–1940.* Chicago: Ivan R. Dee, 2002.

Bluestone, Barry, and Bennett Harrison. *The Deindustrialization of America: Plant Closings, Community Abandonment, and the Dismantling of Basic Industry.* New York: Basic Books, 1982.

Cassidy, John. *Dot.con: The Greatest Story Ever Sold.* New York: HarperCollins, 2002.

Chandler, Alfred D. *The Visible Hand: The Managerial Revolution in American Business.* New York: Arno, 1977.

Fishlow, Albert. *American Railroads and the Transformation of the Ante-Bellum Economy.* Cambridge, MA: Harvard University Press, 1965.

Freidman, Benjamin. *Day of Reckoning: The Consequences of American Economic Policy Under Reagan and After.* New York: Random House, 1988.

Galbraith, John Kenneth. *The Affluent Society,* 40th anniversary ed. Boston: Houghton Mifflin, 1998.

———. *The Great Crash: 1929.* Boston: Houghton Mifflin, 1997.

Henretta, James A. *The Origins of American Capitalism.* Boston: Northeastern University Press, 1991.

Keller, Morton. *Regulating a New Economy: Public Policy and Economic Change in America, 1900–1933.* Cambridge, MA: Harvard University Press, 1990.

Nettels, Curtis. *The Emergence of a National Economy, 1775–1815.* Armonk, NY: M.E. Sharpe, 1989.

Perkins, Edwin J. *The Economy of Colonial America.* New York: Columbia University Press, 1988.

Solomon, Robert. *Money on the Move: The Revolution in International Finance Since 1980.* Princeton, NJ: Princeton University Press, 1999.

Tedlow, Richard. *The Rise of the American Business Corporation.* Philadelphia: Harwood, 1991.

Veblen, Thorstein (1857–1929)

Thorstein Veblen, a Norwegian-American social critic and economist, was best known for his 1899 book *The Theory of the Leisure Class.* In that work, he coined the term "conspicuous consumption" to describe the acquisition of consumer goods and services for the purpose of attaining and reflecting social status.

He was born Tosten Bunde Veblen on July 30, 1857, in Cato, Wisconsin, and raised in Minnesota. He received a bachelor's degree in economics from Carleton College in 1880, where he studied under John Bates Clark, a leading American neoclassical economist. Later he studied philosophy and political economy at Johns Hopkins University and at Yale, from which he received a PhD in 1884.

Veblen was greatly influenced by the work of British philosopher of biological and social evolution Herbert Spencer and British naturalist Charles Darwin; Veblen later developed the field of evolutionary economics based on Darwin's principles as well as on the then new thinking in the areas of psychology, anthropology, and sociology. After recovering from a long illness, Veblen studied economics at Cornell University from 1891 to 1892, leaving there to take a position as a professor of political economy at the University of Chicago and as managing editor of the *Journal of Political Economy.* In 1906 he moved to Stanford University; then, from 1911 to 1918, he joined the economics department at the University of Missouri. Finally, in 1918, he moved to New York. There, he became an editor of *The Dial* and, in 1919, co-founded the New School for Social Research with Charles Beard, John Dewey, and James Robinson.

Veblen's academic career was marked by turmoil and rumors of scandal. Although his published work brought great success, he was not highly regarded as a teacher and was viewed as something of an outsider by the academic establishment. This, combined with his so-called sociological or "nonscientific" approach to economics, resulted in Veblen's less than spectacular rise through the ranks of academia.

After helping found the New School for Social Research in 1919, Veblen became part of Howard Scott's Technical Alliance (later Technocracy Incorporated), one of the first think tanks in the United States. He remained at the New School until 1927. He returned to his home in Palo Alto, California, where he died on August 3, 1929.

In *The Theory of the Leisure Class*, Veblen defines and analyzes conspicuous consumption. Contrary

Known for his concept of "conspicuous consumption"—that consumers care more about the status conferred by material goods than about their utility—Thorstein Veblen argued that public institutions must ensure the proper distribution of resources because people waste them. *(The Granger Collection, New York)*

to the newly developed neoclassical economics of the period, which viewed the consumer as a rational being whose behavior was driven by utility and self-interest, Veblen suggested the revolutionary theory that consumers' buying behavior—and, by extension, consumerism and economic expansions and contractions—is driven by social institutions, tradition, and a desire for social status. He argued that in a modern society's leisure class, wealth is determined by the possession of "useless" things—or the ability to spend money on things that do not provide any real utility to the consumer.

Thus, social context is prominent in Veblen's consumption theory. People, he argued, consume to emulate and impress others; so consumption is socially determined, not decided by individuals on a rational basis. This notion became the foundation of his twentieth-century evolutionary economics. According to Veblen, when consumers purchase useless products that they cannot afford instead of

essentials, or necessities of high utility, problems arise in the economy. He questioned how the conspicuous consumer can justify, for example, living in a big house to impress neighbors and friends when the loan repayments are prohibitive and, in times of financial crises, the consumer is faced with possible unemployment, rising interest rates, and the threat of losing the family home.

Veblen's critique went even further. He claimed that the production of such conspicuous goods for nonutility consumption wastes valuable economic resources. The state, he argued, must ensure the availability of public goods; it must tax the nonutility goods to redistribute economic resources. This insight made Veblen a prominent representative of the "institutionalist" school of economics. According to this view, because individual incentives for consumption waste resources, public institutions must—in modern society—make sure that resources are properly distributed for optimal economic use.

Sabine H. Hoffmann

See also: Consumption; Institutional Economics.

Further Reading

Dorfman, Joseph. *Thorstein Veblen and His America.* New York: A.M. Kelley, 1972.

Tilman, Rick, ed. *The Legacy of Thorstein Veblen.* Northampton, MA: Edward Elgar, 2003.

Veblen, Thorstein. *The Theory of Business Enterprise.* New York: A.M. Kelley, 1975. First published 1904.

———. *The Theory of the Leisure Class.* New York: Dover, 1994. First published 1899.

———. "Why Is Economics Not an Evolutionary Science?" *Cambridge Journal of Economics* 22:4 ([1898] 1998): 403–414.

Venture Capital

Venture capital (VC) is a form of financial capital typically provided to high-risk, early-stage, high-growth-potential companies dealing with high technology. This type of capital is usually invested in enterprises that are too risky for standard capital markets or for bank loans. A venture capital firm is a private governmental or semigovernmental organization that provides early-stage or growth-equity capital and/or loan capital, seeking returns significantly higher than accepted market return rates.

Venture capital activity has been increasingly associated with technological growth and economic growth in developed countries. By the same token, economic recessions tend to have a devastating effect on the level of venture capital investments, resulting in a slowdown in the pace of innovation and, in turn, the rate of economic growth.

Origins and Evolution

In the first half of the twentieth century, capital investment (originally known as "development capital") was not a regular source of funding. Private equity was mostly provided by wealthy individuals and families. In 1938, for example, Laurance S. Rockefeller helped finance the creation of both Eastern Air Lines and Douglas Aircraft. Entrepreneurs at the time who had no wealthy friends or family had little opportunity to fund their ventures.

The modern VC industry was established in 1946, when a U.S. general named George Doriot returned from World War II to Harvard University and founded the American Research and Development Corporation (ARD), a venture capital firm created to raise private-sector investments in businesses launched by returning soldiers. Doriot was followed by the industrialist and philanthropist John Hay Whitney, who established the J.H. Whitney & Company venture capital firm later that same year.

The development of the venture capital industry in the United States was encouraged by passage of the Small Business Investment Act in 1958, which established the Small Business Administration (SBA) "to aid, counsel, assist and protect . . . the interests of small business concerns." The legislation allowed the SBA to license small business investment companies (SBICs) to help the financing and management of small entrepreneurial businesses in the United States. During the 1960s and 1970s, venture capital firms focused their investment activity primarily on high-tech ventures, mostly in computer-related, data-processing, electronic, and medical companies.

The public successes of the venture capital industry in the 1970s encouraged the proliferation of venture capital investment firms across the country and in diverse sectors of the economy. During the 1980s, the number of venture capital firms operating in the United States surged to over 650; the capital they managed increased to more than $31 billion. During the late 1980s and early 1990s, however, the industry's growth was hampered by sharply declining profits.

With the emergence and proliferation of the global information technology (IT) industry, the mid-1990s was a boom time for the venture capital industry. Initial public offerings (IPOs)—by which firms become public by selling stock—on the NASDAQ stock exchange for technology and other growth companies were thriving, with venture-backed firms enjoying large windfalls. The good times ended abruptly in 2001, however, with the bursting of the so-called dot.com bubble.

The recovery arrived in 2004, and the industry grew to about $31 billion within three years. In 2008, however, VC investments in the United States dropped to $28 billion due to the world financial crisis that started in the last quarter of the year.

Corporate Venture Capital

Following the emergence and growth of VC firms in the post–World War II period, corporate venture capital (CVC) programs—in which corporations invest directly in other firms—began appearing in the mid-1960s. The successful private VCs were believed to be the drivers of this first CVC wave. The next wave occurred during the first half of the 1980s, driven by new technological opportunities and favorable changes in legislation. The third wave came with the Internet boom in the mid- to late 1990s, when 400 CVC programs were operated by such major players as Intel and Siemens, among others.

VC funding is most attractive for new companies with limited operating history. It is a vital tool of economic development in market economies and plays a key role in facilitating access to finance for small and medium enterprises (SMEs). It also plays a vital role in the creation and growth of public corporations. In addition to providing capital at critical stages of development, VC firms add value to the process of going public through screening, monitoring, and decision-support functions. Since VC firms usually specialize by industry and stage of development, their knowledge, experience, and contacts assist entrepreneurs in strategic, financial, and operational planning. These activities, in addition to the capital invested, are critical to ensuring that a steady stream of well-prepared firms goes public. Research results also indicate that VC involvement improves the survival profile of firms. A VC-backed enterprise will usually survive longer than a non-VC-backed operation.

Venture capital activity also contributes directly to productivity growth. VC firms have an indirect impact on productivity growth by improving the output and outcomes of research and development activities. Increased VC participation makes it easier for a firm to absorb the knowledge generated by universities and firms, thereby improving a country's economic performance.

Structure of VC Firms

The investors in VC firms are called "limited partners" because of their limited legal responsibility. Their financial resources usually come from large institutional players such as pension funds and insurance companies. The limited partners pay the general partners—those who manage the VC firm—an annual management fee of 1 to 2 percent and a percentage of profits, typically up to 20 percent; this is referred to as the "two and 20 arrangement." The remaining 80 percent of prof-

its are paid to the fund's investors. The life span of each fund raised for investment by the VC firm is usually six to eight years. Because a fund may run out of capital before the end of its life, larger venture capital firms try to have several overlapping funds at the same time.

Each fund typically invests in a number of new ventures. The fund managers select two to five out of hundreds of opportunities presented to them through a process of screening and due diligence (checking out the favorability of a possible investment). Selection criteria include a solid business plan, a product or service with clear competitive advantage, capable and highly motivated entrepreneurs and management team, and of course, the likelihood of profits and growth.

Unlike with public companies, information regarding entrepreneurial business plans is typically confidential and proprietary. As part of the due diligence process, most venture capitalists require significant detail with respect to the proposed business plan. Entrepreneurs must remain vigilant about sharing information with venture capitalists who are potential investors or current shareholders in their competitors. Venture capitalists are also expected to nurture the companies in which they invest in order to increase the likelihood of a successful exit.

VC Investment Cycle

Venture capital investments are illiquid—they cannot be readily turned into cash—and generally require three to seven years to harvest, or receive a return on investment. Corresponding to the life cycle of a firm, there are six different stages of financing offered by venture capital:

- Seed money: low-level financing needed to prove a new idea
- Early stage: funding for expenses mainly needed for market research and product development
- First round: early sales and manufacturing funds

- Second round: working capital for early-stage companies that are selling product but not yet turning a profit
- Third round (a stage also called mezzanine financing): expansion money for a newly profitable company
- Fourth round: referred to as "bridge" financing as it leads to the initial public offering (IPO)

Many VC firms will consider funding only after a firm passes the early stage, when the company can prove at least some of its claims about the technology and/or market potential for its product or services. Therefore, many entrepreneurs who are just starting out seek initial funding from "angel investors" or "technology incubators" prior to VC funding.

Angel investors provide an informal source of capital from wealthy businesspeople, doctors, lawyers, and others who are willing to take an equity, or ownership, stake in a fledgling company in return for their funding. In recent years, more and more angel investors have been previous successful high-tech entrepreneurs themselves.

Technology incubators are usually government-driven sources of early-stage financing at the federal, state, or local level. Their main contribution, in addition to funding, is marketing, legal, and administrative support for the new venture. Initially, in order to prove at least some of its claims about the technology and/or market potential for its product or services, many start-ups seek self-finance, a practice called "bootstrapping."

Activities of Venture Capitalists

The activities of venture capitalists in a start-up enterprise include investing and monitoring, aimed at "exiting" on their investment. The exit, or harvest, is the Holy Grail for venture capitalists, achieved by selling their shares in the business and realizing their profits. The shares are usually sold to a large corporation or offered to the public after a successful IPO.

In most cases, venture capitalists make investments of cash in exchange for shares in the invested company. Since venture capitalists assume high risk while investing in smaller and less mature companies, they generally retain a measure of control over company decisions through board membership, in addition to owning a significant portion of the company's shares. Many of the most successful American high-tech companies today, such as Microsoft, Intel, and Apple Inc., were backed at their early stage by venture capital funds, such as Benchmark, Sequoia, and others.

The return rates on VC investment are generally between 36 percent and 45 percent for early-stage investments and 26 and 30 percent for expansion and late-stage investments. The average rate of return varies according to the anticipated time of exit and the maturity level (age) of the venture. In individual cases, of course, the return varies much more significantly, based on the success of the product or service, market conditions, and management of the company.

Banks and large corporations also have capital investment units; notable early players included General Electric, Paine Webber, and Chemical Bank. Companies that make strategic investments seek to identify and exploit the complementary relationship that exists between themselves and a new venture. For example, a corporation looking at a financial investment seeks to do as well as or better than private VC investors because of what it sees as its superior knowledge of markets and technologies, its strong balance sheet, and its ability to be a patient investor. The endorsement of a major corporate brand is regarded as a sign of quality for the start-up, helping bring in other investors and potential customers.

Global VC Industry

American firms have traditionally been the largest participants in venture deals. In 1996 the U.S. venture capital pool was about three times larger than the total venture capital pool in twenty-one other countries where it existed. Moreover, about

70 percent of the venture capital in the rest of the world was concentrated in three countries with strong ties to the U.S. economy: Israel, Canada, and the Netherlands.

It may be argued that in countries with strong banking systems, such as Germany and Japan, there is less need for venture capital. In recent years, however, non-U.S. venture investment has been growing, and the number and size of non-U.S. venture capitalists has been expanding. The European venture capital industry has followed the U.S. model of VC investment, as have the industries in such Asian countries as Singapore, Taiwan, and China. Policy makers in these areas also believe that venture capital should be encouraged, as it is a boost to high-tech growth, general entrepreneurship, and overall economic growth.

The global competitiveness report of 2006–2007 of the World Economic Forum ranked the United States first and Israel second for venture capital availability. In 2008 there were about fifty venture capital funds operating in Israel. Since the mid-1990s, the total capital raised was about $10 billion, with investments made in more than 1,000 Israeli start-up companies. The average size of the leading Israeli venture capital fund jumped from $20 million in 1993 to more than $250 million in 2007. As elsewhere, investments have focused on technological innovation with global application in the areas of communication, computer software and IT, semiconductors, medical equipment and biotechnology, and homeland security.

In 2008, American VC firms invested about $28.3 billion in 3,908 deals, down a bit from $30.9 billion in 3,952 deals during 2007. According to the European Private Equity and Venture Capital association, €3.01 billion of VC cash was invested by European VCs in 2007, an increase of 80 percent from 2006. However, following the worldwide economic recession that started in late 2008, returns deteriorated for most VC firms, and the industry encountered one of the most radical shakeouts in its history.

Eli Gimmon

See also: Dot.com Bubble (1990s–2000); Information Technology; Technological Innovation.

Further Reading
Chesbrough, H.W. "Making Sense of Corporate Venture Capital." *Harvard Business Review* 80 (2002): 90–99.
Dushnitsky, G. "Corporate Venture Capital: Past Evidence and Future Directions." *The Oxford Handbook of Entrepreneurship.* New York: Oxford University Press, 2006.
Metrick, Andrew. *Venture Capital and the Finance of Innovation.* Hoboken, NJ: John Wiley & Sons, 2007.
National Venture Capital Association Web site: www.nvca.org.
Timmons, J., and S. Olin. *New Venture Creation: Entrepreneurship for the 21st Century.* Boston: McGraw-Hill, 2004.

VeraSun Energy

Once the largest producers of the corn-based renewable fuel ethanol in the United States, South Dakota–based VeraSun Energy was founded in the early 2000s to take advantage of the growing interest in and market for alternative fuels that would allow the country to cut its dependence on foreign oil. Despite high fuel prices and passage of federal legislation requiring oil refiners in the United States to use billions of gallons of renewable fuel, VeraSun has struggled financially, filing for bankruptcy protection in late 2008, a victim of the notoriously volatile energy and agricultural industries and the global financial crisis.

Ethanol, also known as grain alcohol, is a flammable hydrocarbon liquid produced from a variety of crops, mainly sugarcane and corn. From the dawn of the automobile age, it has been technically possible to run motor vehicles on a flex fuel basis, that is, either on gasoline alone or on a mix of gasoline and renewable fuels, such as ethanol. Over the years, however, gasoline came to predominate and renewable fuels fell by the wayside. But with the oil shocks of the 1970s came new interest in such fuels to counter growing U.S. dependence on sources of oil in politically volatile parts of the world.

In recent years, many manufacturers have produced cars that run on what is known E85, a mixture of 15 percent gasoline and 85 percent ethanol, though regular cars can run on a mix of 10 percent ethanol and 90 percent gasoline, known as gasohol. (There is also a 70 percent ethanol mix for use in cold temperatures.) By the late 2000s, most new automobiles, vans, SUVs, and pick-up trucks had been made available in flexible-fuel versions, allowing them to use either gasoline or E85.

VeraSun was founded in Sioux Falls, South Dakota, in 2001 to produce ethanol. The goal of the company, beyond making a profit, was to provide the United States with a source of domestic energy that would at the same time boost rural economies, both by buying up corn from farmers and by employing people at local refineries where that corn was turned into ethanol.

In 2003, VeraSun opened its first ethanol production facility in Aurora, South Dakota. The first company to surpass the 100-million-gallon annual production milestone, VeraSun also created the first branded E85 fuel, which it trademarked as V85. Over the next several years, the company opened several new plants, and in 2006 it went public with a listing on the New York Stock Exchange. Soon, VeraSun was acquiring smaller producers, and by 2008 had seventeen production facilities across the corn-growing Upper Midwest and Great Lakes region. Meanwhile, the company benefited from passage of the Energy Policy Act of 2005, which required that oil refiners use 4 billion gallons of ethanol by 2006, 6.1 billion gallons by 2009, and 7.5 billion gallons by 2012.

But such legislation and the record high fuel prices of 2008, when crude hit nearly $150 a barrel, could not prevent VeraSun from experiencing financial troubles; in the end, VeraSun was a victim of its own industry's success.

The demand for ethanol forced up the price of corn from roughly $4 a bushel to $7 a bushel over the spring and summer of 2008, as farmers could not keep up with the demand for ethanol, a result of the 2005 legislation. To protect itself against what it expected to be continuing rises in the price of corn, VeraSun locked itself into contracts to buy large amounts of the commodity at those inflated prices. But when corn prices came down in the fall of 2008, VeraSun found itself in an uncompetitive position, especially when fuel prices began to fall in the late summer and autumn of 2008. The locked-in corn contracts added to the company's debt load of hundreds of millions of dollars. Then came the financial crisis of September 2008. With credit markets freezing up, VeraSun found itself unable to service its debts, and over the course of 2008, the company's share price fell from nearly $18 to under $1. On October 31, VeraSun filed for protection under Chapter 11 of the U.S. bankruptcy code, allowing it to stay in business as it reorganized and found ways to meets its obligation to creditors. In early 2009, Texas-based Valero, the largest oil refiner in North America, purchased VeraSun for just under half a billion dollars.

James Ciment and Bill Kte'pi

See also: Agriculture; Oil Shocks (1973–1974, 1979–1980).

Further Reading

Asplund, Richard W. *Profiting from Clean Energy: A Complete Guide to Trading Green in Solar, Wind, Ethanol, Fuel Cell, Carbon Credit Industries, and More.* New York: John Wiley & Sons, 2008.

Rubino, John. *Clean Money: Picking Winners in the Green Tech Boom.* New York: John Wiley & Sons, 2008.

"VeraSun Seeks Bankruptcy Protection." *Wall Street Journal*, November 2, 2008. Available at http://online.wsj.com/article/SB122552670080390765.html. Accessed August 31, 2009.

Viner, Jacob (1892–1970)

Known in the economics community as "the outstanding all-rounder of his generation," as one colleague put it, Jacob Viner is especially noted for his work on the history of economic thought and international trade theory. Viner's other important contributions to the field include an analysis of the proper role of the government during economic recessions.

Viner was born on May 3, 1892, in Montreal, Canada. He received a bachelor's degree in 1914 from McGill University and a doctorate in 1922 from Harvard University, where he studied under the noted economist Frank Taussig. In 1916 he became an instructor at the University of Chicago and was named a full professor in 1925. Although he was never a member of the Chicago school of economic thought, he did teach at Chicago until 1946, also editing, along with Frank Knight, the *Journal of Political Economy.* After leaving Chicago, he moved to Princeton University—where he contributed greatly to the school's intellectual life and where he was known as a tough but generous teacher—and remained there until his retirement in 1960.

In addition to his academic work, Viner held a number of government positions. During World War I, he served on the U.S. Tariff Commission and the Shipping Board. In the 1930s, he contributed to the original plans for the Social Security program at the Treasury Department, where he served again during World War II. Later he was a consultant to the State Department and to the Board of Governors of the Federal Reserve System. Perhaps because of his government service, Viner believed that while research and theoretical studies are useful, the functional and practical help that economists, trained as scholars, can offer outweigh the benefits of pure research.

An anti-Keynesian (although he acknowledged the significant contributions of Keynes's work), Viner favored government intervention and inflation as a means to successfully fight the Great Depression. He believed that the Depression's corresponding deflation resulted directly from the prices of outputs falling faster than the fall in the costs of outputs. In contrast to Keynesian theory, he opposed monetary expansion, although he favored deficit spending. In 1931, Viner and other economists on the faculty at the University of Chicago issued a memorandum advocating heavy deficit spending to increase jobs as a way to help improve the depressed economy. In the mid-1930s, Viner attacked Keynesian economics as being effective in the short run but ineffective as a long-run solution, stating that a short-term solution would be "a structure built on shifting sands." This emphasis on the difference between short-term versus ultimately better long-term solutions is a consistent theme throughout his writing.

Viner's early publications dealt chiefly with international economics. His first book, *Dumping: A Problem in International Trade* (1924), was followed the next year by *Canada's Balance of International Indebtedness.* Although he pursued other interests, Viner continued his research in the area of international trade. In the late 1930s, he published what many considered his most important work on the subject, *Studies in the Theory of International Trade*, which was acknowledged by some economists as the main source of historical knowledge in the field.

In 1962 Viner received the Francis A. Walker Medal from the American Economic Association for his contributions to economics. He taught for a year at Harvard as the Taussig research professor and continued to write and lecture. He was a member of the Institute for Advanced Study in Princeton and an honorary fellow of the London School of Economics. Viner died on September 12, 1970.

Robert N. Stacy

See also: Fiscal Policy; Great Depression (1929–1933); Keynes, John Maynard.

Further Reading

Bloomfield, Arthur I. "On the Centenary of Jacob Viner's Birth: A Retrospective View of the Man and His Work." *Journal of Economic Literature* 30:4 (December 1992): 2052–2085.

Robbins, Lionel. *Jacob Viner: A Tribute.* Princeton, NJ: Princeton University Press, 1970.

Rotwein, Eugene. "Jacob Viner and the Chicago Tradition." *History of Political Economy* 15:2 (1983): 265–280.

Viner, Jacob. *Balanced Deflation, Inflation, or More Depression.* Minneapolis: University of Minnesota Press, 1933.

———. *The Long View and the Short: Studies in Economic Theory and Policy.* New York: Free Press, 1958.

———. *Problems of Monetary Control.* Princeton, NJ: Department of Economics, Princeton University, 1964.

Winch, Donald. "Jacob Viner." *American Scholar* 50:4 (January 1981): 519–525.

Volcker, Paul (1927–)

American economist Paul Volcker served from 1979 to 1987 as chairman of the Federal Reserve System. He is credited with reducing the runaway inflation of that period with historic increases in interest rates. His influence on U.S. economic policy continued into the early twenty-first century, when he served as head of the Economic Recovery Board under President Barack Obama, charged with helping navigate the U.S. economy through the global financial crisis that began in 2007.

Born on September 5, 1927, in Cape May, New Jersey, Volcker grew up in Teaneck, New Jersey. He graduated in 1949 from Princeton University and, in 1951, earned a master's degree in political economy and government from Harvard University's graduate schools of Arts and Sciences and Public Administration. He attended the London School of Economics from 1951 to 1952.

Volcker started his career in 1952 as an economist with the Federal Reserve Bank of New York. He joined Chase Manhattan Bank in 1957 (returning in 1965 as a director of planning) and in 1962 joined the U.S. Treasury Department as a director of financial analysis, becoming undersecretary for monetary affairs in 1963.

Volcker next served in the Department of the Treasury as undersecretary for international monetary affairs from 1969 to 1974, where he was involved in deliberations surrounding the U.S. decision to devalue the dollar that resulted in the collapse of the Bretton Woods system (which pegged foreign currencies to the dollar, which in turn was pegged to gold). After leaving the Treasury, he became president of the Federal Reserve Bank of New York from 1975 to 1979.

In *The Rediscovery of the Business Cycle* (1978), Volcker stated his view that business cycles last for periods of ten to twenty years, considerably shorter than the Kondratieff cycles of just over fifty years.

Former Federal Reserve Board chairman Paul Volcker, credited with taming inflation in the early 1980s by raising interest rates to above 20 percent, returned to government in 2009 as head of President Barack Obama's Economic Recovery Advisory Board. *(Win McNamee/Getty Images)*

The shorter cycles, according to Volcker, do not occur in any predictable pattern or length. He also noted that since the end of World War II, recessions generally have been milder than those before the war, largely because of government interventions. One of the greatest challenges of the time, he believed, was restoring price stability without adversely affecting economic stability. Volcker's belief that the control of the money supply is crucial because of the cause-and-effect relationship between inflation and money growth became a point of contention in the early 1980s. Volcker believed that there were limits on the extent to which the curtailment of the money supply could be accomplished without having a negative impact on business.

As chairman of the Federal Reserve, Volcker took an activist approach to eliminating inflation. Record-high interest rates in the late 1970s and early 1980s resulted in a dramatic economic downturn and made it increasingly difficult for consumers and businesses to obtain credit. In 1982, the number of business failures in the United States was almost 50 percent greater than in any year since 1945; two years later, the number had doubled. In addition, unemployment rates were higher than at any time since the end of World War II. Volcker was criticized by both Republicans and Democrats, many of whom urged a lowering of interest rates; some sought his removal. Opponents of his activist approach argued that the Federal Reserve should not adjust interest rates to affect business cycles.

By the mid-1980s, however, Volcker's policy, which had continued under two administrations—that of Democrat Jimmy Carter and that of Republican Ronald Reagan—began to show signs of success. The economic recovery that had begun in 1983 continued to 1990. By then, inflation was so low that it was no longer a concern. Volcker returned to the service of the White House in February 2009 as an economic adviser to President Barack Obama. Volcker was named chairman of the President's Economic Recovery Advisory Board, a panel of academics, businessmen, and other private-sector experts charged with reporting to the president on the economic crisis and policies to reverse it.

Robert N. Stacy

See also: Federal Reserve System; Inflation; Recession and Financial Crisis (2007–); Recession, Reagan (1981–1982).

Further Reading

Neikirk, William. *Volcker: Portrait of the Money Man.* New York: Congdon & Weed, 1987.

Samuelson, Robert J. *The Great Inflation and Its Aftermath: The Past and Future of American Affluence* New York: Random House, 2008.

Treaster, Joseph B. *Paul Volcker: The Making of a Financial Legend.* Hoboken, NJ: John Wiley & Sons, 2004.

Volcker, Paul A. *The Rediscovery of the Business Cycle.* New York: Free Press, 1978.

———. *The Triumph of Central Banking?* Washington, DC: Per Jacobsson Foundation, 1990.

Von Neumann, John (1903–1957)

Regarded as one of the most brilliant and influential mathematicians of the twentieth century, John von Neumann made notable contributions in such diverse fields as quantum mechanics, computer science (he was part of the team that constructed the ENIAC computer at the University of Pennsylvania), and statistics. He was also involved in the Manhattan Project and the building of the first nuclear bomb. In economics, he is known for his work in game theory and the modeling of supply-demand equilibrium.

He was born Neumann János Lajos on December 28, 1903, in Budapest, Hungary, and raised in a privileged household. His father, Max Neumann, a successful banker in Budapest, purchased the honorific "von," which János later applied to his name. In 1911, von Neumann entered Budapest's Lutheran gymnasium, where his remarkable skills in mathematics were quickly recognized. After studying at the University of Berlin and earning a degree in chemical engineering from the Technical Institute in Zürich, he went on to obtain a PhD in mathematics from Pázmány Péter University (Budapest University) in 1926 with a thesis on the method of inner models in set theory. Along the way, he published in 1923 what became the lasting definition of ordinal numbers.

After a year of postdoctoral study as a Rockefeller fellow at the University of Göttingen, von Neumann taught mathematics at the University of Berlin (1926–1929) and the University Hamburg (1929–1930). He went to the United States as a visiting professor at Princeton University in 1930 and was appointed to a professorship in mathematical physics the following year. He was invited to join the prestigious Institute for Advanced Study at Princeton in 1933 and taught mathematics there until his death some twenty-two years later. In the meantime, he became a U.S. citizen in 1937.

Von Neumann had already become interested in the application of mathematical analysis to economic problems, especially after extensive conversations with economist Nicholas Kaldor. In the 1930s, von Neumann published two papers that had a great impact on the study of economics. The first was on game theory, or the use of complex simulations to solve difficult quantitative problems. While the paper did not deal with economics directly, it formed the basis of his later collaboration with Oskar Morgenstern, *Theory of Games and Economic Behavior* (1944). In what would become a classic in the field, the book built on von Neumann's work in game theory. Von Neumann's original studies explored the mathematics of two-person, zero-sum card games in which the players know the cards. One area of particular focus was the strategies other players should follow to minimize their maximum possible losses ("minimax"). Game theory emerged as a compelling new means of exploring nonmathematical disciplines such as economics and politics.

Von Neumann's second important paper on economic theory was originally presented in 1932, published five years later, and translated into English in 1945 as "A Model of General Economic Equilibrium" (also known as the "Expanding Economic Model"). In it, von Neumann presented a highly mathematical approach to the study of market equilibrium, in which supply and demand combine to achieve maximum price stability—a sophisticated model that helped explain the dynamics of the business cycle. This idealized model was based on production, profitability, and wages in a hypothetical economic environment without external influences. While it was generally agreed that the model of economic equilibrium was brilliantly conceived, it was also criticized for being too abstract and removed from economic reality. The approach proved valuable, however, in that it provided a new method, based on mathematical models, to examine questions of economic growth and equilibrium between inputs and outputs.

During and after World War II, von Neumann served as a consultant to the Allied armed forces. He helped develop the implosion method for bringing nuclear fuel to explosion and played a key role in the development of both the atomic and hydrogen bombs. In 1940, he became a member of the Scientific Advisory Committee at the Ballistic Research Laboratories in Aberdeen, Maryland. He served on the Navy Bureau of Ordnance from 1941 to 1955 and as a consultant to the Los Alamos Scientific Laboratory from 1943 to 1955. From 1950 to 1955, he was also a member of the Armed Forces Special Weapons Project in Washington, DC. In 1955, President Dwight Eisenhower appointed him to the Atomic Energy Commission. Von Neumann died in Washington, DC, on February 8, 1957.

Robert N. Stacy

See also: Kaldor, Nicholas; Morgenstern, Oskar.

Further Reading

Aspray, William. *John von Neumann and the Origins of Modern Computing.* Cambridge, MA: MIT Press, 1990.

Dore, Mohammed, Sukhamoy Chakravarty, and Richard Goodwin, eds. *John von Neumann and Modern Economics.* Oxford, UK: Oxford University Press, 1989.

Macrae, Norman. *John von Neumann.* New York: Pantheon, 1992.

Pierre, Andrew J., ed. *Unemployment and Growth in the Western Economies.* New York: Council on Foreign Relations, 1984.

Von Neumann, John. *John von Neumann: Selected Letters*, ed. Miklós Rédei. Providence, RI: American Mathematical Society, 2005.

———. *Theory of Games and Economic Behavior.* Princeton, NJ: Princeton University Press, 2004.

Wachovia

The Wachovia Corporation, created from the 2001 merger of two major North Carolina–based banks, was a wide-ranging financial services company with branches in twenty-one states coast to coast. With assets in the hundreds of billions of dollars by the mid-2000s, the Wachovia Corporation was one of the largest and most prominent victims of the financial crisis of 2008–2009. Having expanded aggressively in the early and mid-2000s, Wachovia was forced, in the face of mounting losses and a collapsing share price, to sell itself to Wells Fargo for a mere $15 billion.

Before the buyout, Wachovia offered a variety of financial services beyond commercial banking, including mortgage banking, home equity lending, investment advisory services, insurance, securities brokering, investment banking, and asset-based lending and leasing through its various subsidiaries.

The origins of the bank go back to 1866, when a banker named William Lemly founded the First National Bank in Salem, North Carolina. Thirteen years later, the company moved to nearby Winston and was renamed Wachovia National Bank, after the original German land grant in the region. In 1893, textile and railroad entrepreneur Francis Fries opened a separate company known as Wachovia Loan and Trust Company, North Carolina's first trust, in what would soon become the merged city of Winston-Salem. In 1911, the two Wachovias also merged, becoming the Wachovia Bank and Trust Company. The new company derived a large portion of its deposits from the wealth generated by the state's growing textile and tobacco industries.

For much of the twentieth century, the business was known for its conservative banking style, specializing in low-risk lending. So sterling was the company's reputation that at the beginning of the 1990s, it was one of very few banks in the United States to earn a triple-A credit rating, having avoided some of the more speculative real-estate lending that triggered the savings and loan crisis of the late 1980s and early 1990s.

Even after the U.S. Supreme Court's 1985 *Northeast Bancorp, Inc. v. Governors, Federal Reserve System* decision opened the door to interstate banking, Wachovia proceeded cautiously in its acquisitions, buying up a few banks around the South between the mid-1980s and mid-1990s. By the mid-1990s, that strategy had changed, however, as the company began to buy up not just other banks, but a variety of financial services companies around the country.

One of the five largest bank holding companies in the United States, Wachovia was highly exposed to the home mortgage crisis of 2007–2008 and forced to sell or shut down. Wells Fargo bought the bank for $15 billion and began to absorb the Wachovia brand. *(Bloomberg/Getty Images)*

Its future partner, First Union, had nearly as long a history. Founded as the Union National Bank of Charlotte in 1908, it merged fifty years later with the First National Bank and Trust Company of Asheville to form the First Union National Bank of North Carolina. In 1964, First Union acquired the Raleigh-based national mortgage and insurance firm Cameron-Brown Company. By the 1990s, First Union was also expanding rapidly, and by 2000 had banking operations in East Coast states and the District of Columbia. First Union was also the home of the sixth-largest securities broker-dealer network in the country, operating in forty-seven states. But First Union's expansion also created strains as it earned a reputation for poor service and experienced shaky share prices on Wall Street.

In September 2001, First Union merged with Wachovia, keeping the more highly esteemed name of the latter, as part of a wave of mergers in the financial industry made possible by changes in regulatory law and a belief among players in the industry that to survive in the globalized financial marketplace, companies had to get big. To do that, the newly merged company acquired other banks, including the Golden West Financial Corporation of California in 2006.

It was this last purchase that left Wachovia vulnerable, as Golden West was heavily exposed to the subprime and adjustable rate mortgages that were at the heart of the financial crisis that hit in late 2007. In the second quarter of 2008, Wachovia posted nearly $9 billion in losses, a record for the company and an amount far greater than analysts had predicted. New management was brought in, but the company's share price continued to plummet in September as a result of the failure of rival Washington Mutual.

Rumors began to spread that Wachovia was in serious trouble, leading depositors to reduce their holdings in the bank to the $100,000 limit the Federal Deposit Insurance Corporation (FDIC) will protect. (Later during the crisis, the insurance limit was increased to $250,000.) The depositor run made Wachovia's collapse all but inevitable. Because of its size, however, and the drain its failure would exact on the FDIC's available funds, federal regulators declared Wachovia "systematically important." In other words, the federal government decided for the first time that it would seek a buyer for a collapsing bank rather than a mere liquidation of its assets. On September 29, 2008, the FDIC announced that Citigroup would purchase Wachovia and that the federal government would absorb up to $42 billion in losses Citigroup would suffer from its purchase.

But Wachovia's management and shareholders balked at the deal, complaining that Citigroup was offering too low a price for Wachovia stock. Just four days after the FDIC announced the Citigroup deal, Wachovia itself announced that it was merging with Wells Fargo, a transaction that was completed by the end of 2008.

James Ciment and Frank Winfrey

See also: Banks, Commercial; Banks, Investment; Recession and Financial Crisis (2007–).

Further Reading

Brubaker, Harold. "Wachovia Latest to Seek Merger Rescue." *Philadelphia Inquirer*, September 18, 2008.

Dash, Eric. "Wachovia Reports $23.9 Billion Loss for Third Quarter." *New York Times*, October 23, 2008.

de la Merced, Michael J. "Regulators Approve Wells Fargo Takeover of Wachovia." *New York Times*, October 10, 2008.

"Outclassed." *The Economist*, April 21, 2001.

Singletary, Michelle. "Wachovia: Taking a Great Leap Northward." *Washington Post*, October 20, 1997.

Trigaux, Robert. "Bank Built on Tradition, Patience." *St. Petersburg Times*, May 15, 1999.

———. "First Union Buys New Name and, Maybe, Some Time." *St. Petersburg Times*, April 17, 2001.

Wages

Jobs and wages are vital indicators of business cycles. Both closely shadow and are heavily influenced by the economic forces at play during recessions and periods of expansion. Wages are defined as money paid or received for work or services, usually determined and reported on an hourly, weekly, or monthly basis.

Determining Factors

Wages vary significantly across occupations, which, according to economic theory and considerable research, are determined largely by two factors: the supply of workers who are willing and able to do a particular job and employer demand for workers in that job.

In general, the more people with the education, training, and desire to perform a job, the lower the wage rate; a larger supply depresses the price of labor. This explains why, for example, low-skilled jobs—such as entry-level positions in the fast-food industry—pay less than jobs requiring an advanced level of skill and education—such as that of engineer or doctor. The advanced skill and educational requirements of a job tend to limit the number of people who are able to do the job, which pushes up the wage rate.

In addition to the wage level, the desire of a worker to do a job for a particular employer may be determined by working conditions and other aspects of the job, such as benefits, hours, location, and other factors. In general, dangerous or otherwise undesirable working conditions or a geographically undesirable work location tend to limit the supply of workers willing to work for certain employers, putting upward pressure on wages. By the same token, all else being equal, workers are more likely to supply their labor to an employer who offers more generous benefits, such as health insurance and a retirement plan, which tends to depress the wage rate. In general, there is often an inverse relationship between wage levels and the availability of favorable benefits.

Wage levels are also affected by the local demand for workers, or lack thereof. In general, the greater the demand by employers for a particular job skill, the higher the wage. If a job within the organization is deemed essential, the business is willing to pay a higher salary to the employee in that job than to an employee in a less essential role. For example, a professional baseball team is willing to offer a player a high salary if that player attracts fans to the stadium, which raises total revenue for the franchise. The player is deemed much more essential to the organization than a clerical worker in the front office or a peanut vendor, for example, and will be compensated more generously—much more.

The productivity of labor is also positively related to employer demand. Labor productivity is defined as the number of units of output per unit of labor input, usually measured in hours of labor. Employers value and compensate productive labor, which is directly related to education, training, and experience; the use of equipment—such as computers—that allows workers to produce more per hour; improvements in production technologies and management organizational techniques; and public policies and societal attitudes that allow workers to make the best use of their skills and talents. Labor productivity and, thus, wages, are generally pro-cyclical, meaning that they decrease during recessions and increase during economic upturns. This is because companies are reluctant to lay off workers during recessions and hesitant to hire when the economy begins to recover.

The demand for workers is a derived demand, meaning that it is driven by market demand for the product or service being provided. For example, the demand for autoworkers—and hence their wages—is driven by consumer demand for new cars and trucks. The relatively high wages paid in the health care professions today are derived from the increasing demand for health care services caused in part by the aging of the population. Similarly, the relatively high wages in computer-science occupations are derived by the increasing demand for computers both in businesses and at home.

Unions strive to raise the wages of their members through collective bargaining with employers. However, union membership in the United States has been declining since the mid-1950s, when 33 percent of nonagricultural workers were members; by 2008, the figure had fallen to 12.4 percent.

Researchers also observe that wages vary based on worker characteristics unrelated to job productivity, including age, gender, and ethnicity. For example, in 2008, the median weekly earnings of females working full time were only 80.5 percent of the median weekly earnings of males working full time; the black-white wage differential was 79.3 percent, and the Hispanic-white wage differential was 71.3 percent. Such gaps are a

function of a variety of factors, and not entirely of employer discrimination. The wage differentials may be explained in part by differences among the groups in type and level of schooling, training, and experience, and other social factors.

Wages also play a key role in the economic cycle. According to classical economics, wages should decline during economic downturns when unemployment increases. Theoretically, a greater number of workers looking for jobs should lower wages, both for new hires and existing employees. Ultimately, according to this model, wages should fall to a level that entices employers to hire, eliminating involuntary unemployment and lifting wages. However, as the early-twentieth-century British economist John Maynard Keynes and others have pointed out, wages are sticky, responding very slowly to economic downturns. Falling wages, then, do not clear the labor market of excess idle workers, and this stickiness leads to persistent unemployment during economic downturns and often slow hiring during recoveries. Moreover, some believe that falling wages, rather than clearing the labor market, would make the situation worse. This is because debts such as mortgages are denominated in dollars, and when wages fall, the real value of household debt increases—forcing many households into bankruptcy. Also, falling wages and the crisis in confidence that they may engender can cause households to further reduce spending, leading to a reduction in demand and further layoffs.

Among the chief reasons why wages respond slowly to economic fluctuations is that wages are not determined by what economists call an "auction market," but by an "administered market." In the former, buyers and sellers of goods or services bargain with each other freely, with little constraint. In the case of employers and employees, however, most companies have fixed pay scales that do not adapt immediately to changing economic circumstances. Employers fear that constantly lowering wages might sap employee morale. In unionized industries, wages are also affected by "outside" parties representing workers. Finally, labor laws of various kinds, including minimum wage rules and, in some localities, "living wage" laws, also reduce wage flexibility. In short, employee wages constitute an administered, rather than an auction, market.

Labor Laws

Laws enacted to ensure fair labor and wage practices in response to discriminatory and other unfair practices on the part of employers include the Fair Labor Standards Act (FLSA), passed in 1938 and administered by the U.S. Department of Labor. The legislation established minimum wage, overtime pay, and child labor standards for most private and government employees. Workers employed as executive, administrative, professional, and outside sales employees who are paid on a salary basis are exempt from minimum wage and overtime laws. In the many states that have their own minimum wage requirements, employers are required to pay the higher of the two (state or federal). As of July 24, 2009, the U.S. federal minimum wage was $7.25 per hour. Employers can pay workers less than the minimum wage if the employee receives tips, but the total compensation must equal or exceed the hourly minimum. Employers may legally pay less than the federal minimum wage to workers younger than twenty years of age for the first ninety days of employment and only if their work does not replace other workers. Other programs that allow for payment of less than the full federal minimum wage apply to workers with a disability, full-time students, and vocational education students.

Federal legislation prohibiting wage discrimination based on worker characteristics unrelated to productivity, enforced by the Equal Employment Opportunity Commission (EEOC), include the Equal Pay Act of 1963, Title VII of the Civil Rights Act of 1964, the Age Discrimination in Employment Act of 1967, Title I of the Americans with Disabilities Act of 1990, and the Lilly Ledbetter Fair Pay Act of 2009.

Donna Anderson

See also: Employment and Unemployment; Income Distribution; Productivity.

Further Reading

McConnell, Campbell R., Stanley L. Brue, and David A. Macpherson. *Contemporary Labor Economics*. 8th ed. New York: McGraw-Hill/Irwin, 2009.

U.S. Bureau of Labor Statistics. *Usual Weekly Earnings of Wage and Salary Workers: Fourth Quarter 2008*. Washington, DC: U.S. Department of Labor, 2009.

U.S. Department of Labor. "Wages." www.dol.gov/dol/topic/wages.

Washington Mutual

Washington Mutual, often abbreviated as WaMu, was a primary player in the financial meltdown of 2008 and a telling example of how the failure of one major bank can have unexpected consequences for a major economy and help to spur on economic recession.

WaMu was the sixth-largest bank in the United States, and the largest savings and loan, until its 2008 failure—the largest bank failure in American history. "WaMu" refers either to Washington Mutual Bank, which went into receivership and had its assets sold to JPMorgan Chase, or Washington Mutual Inc., the holding company that formerly owned the bank and has since filed for Chapter 11 bankruptcy.

Prefailure History

Originally the Washington National Building Loan and Investment Association, incorporated in Seattle in 1889, WaMu changed its name to the Washington Mutual Savings Bank in 1917. Long a successful regional bank, its major growth came after it demutualized in 1983. Demutualization is a process by which a mutual company (such as a bank jointly owned by its depositors) converts to a publicly traded company owned by shareholders. Demutualization was especially common in the 1980s in the wake of bank deregulation, as financial institutions were eager to take advantage of the greater opportunities offered by the new legal landscape.

WaMu first acquired Murphey Favre, a Washington brokerage firm, in 1983, and by so doing, doubled its assets between 1983 and 1989. More acquisitions rapidly followed—fifteen in all between 1990 and 2006, including savings and loans and banks—partly in response to the Interstate Banking and Branching Efficiency Act of 1994, which allowed bank holding companies to acquire branches outside of the state holding their charter.

These acquisitions changed not only the scale of WaMu's operations but also their character, as the company became the ninth-largest credit card issuer and third-largest mortgage lender in the country. Chief Executive Office (CEO) Kerry Killinger in 2003 explicitly compared the company's mission with Starbucks, Wal-Mart, and Costco, companies that had gone from regional presences to well-known national corporate icons. "Five years from now," he said, "you're not going to call us a bank." The company's heavy interest in high-risk mortgages to poor borrowers and subsequent securitization and sale of those loans amid the escalating subprime mortgage market resulted in Killinger's prediction being correct, albeit in ways he clearly did not intend.

The Failure of WaMu

At the end of 2007, in the midst of a subprime mortgage crisis the scale of which was not yet evident, WaMu made drastic cuts to its home loan division, eliminating a quarter of its staff and half of its offices. Layoffs in the holding company followed, with further closures of offices and loan processing centers. Killinger rejected a secret deal offered by JPMorgan Chase to buy out the company, considering the offer too low. Killinger himself stepped down as chairman in June 2008 and was dismissed as CEO in early September. Stock prices were falling, and shareholders were perturbed at the capital influx by outside investors funded by TPG Capital, which diluted the ownership stake of existing shares.

The JPMorgan Chase offer had been for $8 a share. In 2007, WaMu stock had traded for $45 a share, but by the middle of September 2008 it had plummeted to close to $2 and WaMu was quietly courting potential buyers, with no success. The obvious struggles of the company led to a massive ten-day run on the bank as customers panicked, with nearly $17 billion taken out in deposits, primarily through electronic means. The Treasury Department insisted WaMu find a buyer, and the Federal Deposit Insurance Corporation (FDIC) took over the search. On the night of September 25, 2008, the 119th anniversary of WaMu's founding, the Treasury Department's Office of Thrift Supervision (OTS) put Washington Mutual Bank (but not the holding company) into receivership and sold its assets to JPMorgan Chase for $1.9 billion.

The new owners acquired WaMu's assets, but not its equity obligations, which meant existing WaMu stock was nearly worthless, dropping to $0.16 a share and prompting the bankruptcy filing of the holding company and an as-yet unresolved protest by existing shareholders (first quarter of 2010), who have been exploring the possibility of a lawsuit over what they declare an illegal takeover by the Treasury. The takeover required the OTS to declare that WaMu was unstable and unable to meet its obligations; the contention of the potential lawsuit is that while the bank was troubled, it had not lost enough liquidity to require receivership.

Account holders formerly with WaMu have been unaffected by the change; deposits have been transferred to JPMorgan Chase, and WaMu customers can bank with Chase branches and use Chase ATMs without the usual fees for noncustomers. The conversion of WaMu branches to Chase branches was completed by the first quarter of 2010.

Washington Mutual Inc. was delisted from the New York Stock Exchange; its remaining subsidiary, WMI Investment Corporation, is a partner in various capital funds, which it has been selling off as part of WaMu's Chapter 11 proceedings.

Bill Kte'pi

See also: Banks, Commercial; JPMorgan Chase; Recession and Financial Crisis (2007–).

Further Reading

Krugman, Paul. *The Return of Depression Economics and the Crisis of 2008.* New York: W.W. Norton, 2009.

Shiller, Robert J. *The Subprime Solution: How Today's Global Financial Crisis Happened, and What to Do About It.* Princeton, NJ: Princeton University Press, 2008.

Soros, George. *The New Paradigm for Financial Markets: The Credit Crisis of 2008 and What It Means.* New York: PublicAffairs, 2008.

Wealth

Wealth is defined in economic terms as the amount of tangible and financial assets, minus liabilities, owned by a person, household, enterprise, community, or nation. Thus, in economic terms, everyone and every country has wealth, even if they are not "wealthy" in the popular sense of the word, meaning affluent. Moreover, wealth is time-sensitive: it is the stock of what a person or collective possesses at a given point in time. Wealth is different from income, which measures the flow of money or assets earned over a given period of time.

Types of Wealth

Wealth can take either of two basic forms: tangible assets and financial assets. Tangible assets include real property, or land, structures, precious metals, capital equipment, paid-for inventory, and personal property, such as jewelry, vehicles, furniture, and so on. Financial assets include cash, bank deposits, stocks, bonds, and other financial instruments. Certain types of property—particularly tangible property, such as houses, cars, and jewelry—are more likely to be owned by private individuals and families, while other types of assets, such as capital equipment, are more likely to be owned by businesses. For the economy as a whole, the net amount of financial assets is equal to the amount of domestic and foreign financial assets owned less the amount of domestic and foreign financial assets owed. In a closed economy with no foreign trade or capital flows, net financial assets would be equal to zero, since every financial asset is a financial liability for someone else. Thus it is only the excess of financial assets owned by economics actors in a country over the amount of financial liabilities owed by the same actors that add to national wealth.

In capitalist countries, most of the wealth is privately owned, whether by individuals and households, business owners, or shareholders of publicly held corporations. In the United States, for example, some 80 percent of all wealth is held by the private sector, with about 80 percent of this owned by private organizations and corporations (both profit and nonprofit) and 20 percent by private persons. The other 20 percent of all wealth is held by various governments—local, state, and federal.

Aside from tangible and financial assets, wealth can be divided into three basic types. Some wealth generates income directly. Among financial assets, there are instruments that pay annuities, or regular payments to share owners. Among tangible assets, there are assets such as apartment buildings that bring the owner rent income that exceeds the total cost of the building's mortgage, maintenance, and depreciation. Other forms of wealth do not produce income but tend to increase in value over time, such as corporate securities, land, artwork, and so on. Finally, there are forms of wealth that lose value. A computer is a form of wealth, but one that sheds its value, or depreciates, relatively rapidly. In short, wealth accrues in two basic ways, through savings and through asset appreciation.

On the other hand, the ordinary depreciation of a tangible asset is not the only way that wealth disappears. Assets can also lose market value, of course. In the housing crash of the late 2000s, for example, most Americans saw the value of their homes decline appreciably. In stock market crashes, securities lose value rapidly as well. In all of these cases, wealth simply disappears. But other forces can work to redistribute wealth as well. For example, governments that tax wealth through inheritance and property taxes, as well as other levies, often redistribute a portion of that wealth as income to the poor.

Inflation also works to redistribute wealth. A critical type of asset—and one that is owned by many corporations and financial institutions—are loans and bonds of various types. For example, a bank that has loaned $10,000 to an individual to buy a car can list that $10,000 loan as an asset on its books. But if inflation eats away half the value of the money over the life of the loan, then, all other things being equal, $5,000 in wealth has shifted from the bank to the borrower. Inflation can also erode the value of tangible items. If, for example, someone were to purchase a home worth $100,000 and, for whatever reasons particular to the local market, the home went up in value only $20,000, or 20 percent, over ten years, it would lose value if the cumulative inflation over the same time period were 40 percent.

Wealth Distribution

Finally, wealth is never evenly distributed. Even in the most egalitarian societies, some individuals and households enjoy greater wealth than others. Economists use a mathematical formula known as the Gini coefficient to measure wealth (as well as income) distribution on a zero-to-one scale, with zero representing perfectly equal distribution of wealth (everyone owns exactly the same amount) and one representing perfect inequality (one individual owns all of the wealth).

Wealth distribution varies greatly across regions and through history. Economically developed regions of the world, of course, claim a far greater portion of global wealth than developing regions. Europe, for example, is home to just under 10 percent of the world's population but owns more than 25 percent of the world's wealth. Africa, by contrast, is home to just over 10 percent of the world's people but owns just 1.5 percent of the world's wealth.

Generally speaking, then, the more advanced the nation is economically, the more evenly distributed its wealth. Thus, industrialized economies tend to have lower Gini coefficients than do developing world countries. There are a number of reasons for this. Developed nations usually have much larger middle classes than developing nations. Workers in developed nations are more highly skilled, meaning they can command more of the income their labor produces; and by commanding more income, they can save more or invest in assets that appreciate in value, thereby increasing their wealth. Finally, developed nations tend to have more advanced social welfare networks and tax systems to even out income and wealth distribution. Yet even among developed nations, there are differences in wealth distribution. Countries with more generous social welfare systems—and redistributive tax schemes to pay for them—tend to have greater wealth equality. Scandinavian countries, for example, have relatively low Gini coefficient numbers.

Social factors within countries can have a major impact on wealth distribution as well. For example, in the United States, white households have about ten times the wealth of African-American households, even though African-American incomes were roughly 60 percent those of whites. There are two basic reasons for this. Lower income means less opportunity for savings and investment, and a history of discrimination has meant that African-Americans have lacked the opportunity to build up inherited wealth that they can pass on to their children.

Wealth distribution also changes over time. There have been periods in U.S. history, for example, where wealth has been more equally distributed and periods when it has been less equally distributed. Industrialization and the rise of large corporations in the late nineteenth and early twentieth centuries led to growing wealth inequality, while the Great Depression, which destroyed the value of many assets, and the post–World War II boom, which saw a rapid expansion of the middle class, saw greater wealth equality, at least through the 1970s. Since then, however, there has been a trend toward greater wealth inequality. Economists point to a variety of factors: a weakened labor movement, which depresses wages; tax cuts for the wealthy; and globalization, which increases corporate profits, much of which accrue to the wealthiest portions of society.

Another great shift has been in the composition of household wealth. Whereas in the 1920s, less than one in ten American households owned corporate securities, by the early 2000s, the figure had climbed to 50 percent, with a good portion of that increase accruing since the 1980s. Whereas stocks represented just 6 percent of household wealth in the late 1980s, by the early 2000s it had climbed to 15 percent. Note, however, that the bulk of household stock market wealth is not held by stock ownership directly, but rather through ownership of a mutual fund, a retirement account, or a pension plan that invests in the stock market.

Finally, the importance of wealth distribution to overall economic performance is an issue hotly debated among economists. Some, particularly those on the right of the political spectrum, tend to see wealth inequality as a less important factor in economic performance than those on the left. Indeed, they sometimes argue, more wealth accumulating at the top creates more wealth available for investment, which spurs economic growth to the benefit of all. Economists on the left side of the political spectrum argue that a more equal distribution of wealth assures more sustained growth since it provides security to households, allowing them to spend money on consumer goods—a crucial factor given that consumer spending generates some 70 percent of all economic activity in the United States. In addition, it is argued, greater distribution of wealth allows households to spend more on education, which assures a productive workforce in the future.

James Ciment

See also: Consumption; Income Distribution; Poverty.

Further Reading

Clark, John Bates. *The Distribution of Wealth: A Theory of Wages, Interest, and Profits.* New York: Cosimo Classics, 2005.

Collins, Robert M. *More: The Politics of Economic Growth in Postwar America.* New York: Oxford University Press, 2000.

Dowd, Douglas. *U.S. Capitalist Development Since 1776: Of, By, and For Which People?* Armonk, NY: M.E. Sharpe, 1993.

Ferguson, Niall. *The Ascent of Money: A Financial History of the World.* New York: Penguin, 2008.

Oliver, Melvin L., and Thomas M. Shapiro. *Black Wealth, White Wealth: A New Perspective on Racial Inequality.* New York: Routledge, 2006.

Ornstein, Allan. *Class Counts: Education, Inequality, and the Shrinking Middle Class.* Lanham, MD: Rowman & Littlefield, 2007.

Reynolds, Alan. *Income and Wealth.* Westport, CT: Greenwood, 2006.

World Bank

The World Bank provides fiscal and technical support to developing countries and development programs (such as for building schools, roads, and bridges), with the objective of reducing poverty. The role of the World Bank is to provide aid in various forms to countries stuck in economic stagnation, with the purpose of helping them gain stability and build long-term economic growth in the context of globalization. As part of its mission, the World Bank conducts ongoing research on the causes and profiles of booms and busts during the business cycles of both developed and developing countries.

The World Bank was one of two institutions (with the International Monetary Fund, or IMF) created in July 1944 at the United Nations Monetary and Financial Conference under the Bretton Woods Agreement, with the primary goal of rebuilding Europe after World War II. In the years and decades that followed, the goals and efforts of both organizations expanded to rebuilding the infrastructure of Europe's former colonies.

The World Bank today is headquartered in Washington, D.C., with 186 member nations as of year-end 2009 and more than 100 offices worldwide. Its declared mission is "to fight poverty with passion and professionalism for lasting results and to help people help themselves and their environment by providing resources, sharing knowledge, building capacity and forging partnerships in the public and private sectors." The institution—sometimes referred to as the World Bank Group—is composed of the International Bank for Reconstruction and Development (IBRD) and the International Development Association (IDA), as well as three lesser-known agencies: the International Finance Corporation (IFC), the Multilateral Investment Guarantee Agency (MIGA), and the International Centre for Settlement of Investment Disputes (ICSID). The specific duties of the World Bank are overseen by twenty-four executive directors, including one each from the five largest shareholders—France, Germany, Japan, Great Britain, and the United States—and the nineteen others selected from the remaining member nations.

The World Bank is active in a number of economic development areas, and includes the following departmental programs: Agriculture and Rural Development; Conflict Prevention and Reconstruction; Education; Energy; Environment; Gender Issues; Governance; Health, Nutrition, and Population; Industry; Information, Computing, and Telecommunications; International Economics and Trade; Labor and Social Protections; Law and Justice; Macroeconomic and Economic Growth; Mining; Poverty Reduction; Private Sector, Public Sector Governance; Rural Development; Social Development; Social Protection; Trade; Transport; Urban Development; Water Resources; and Water Supply and Sanitation.

World Bank president Robert Zoellick attends the opening of a new office in Berlin, Germany, in 2007. A specialized agency of the UN, the World Bank provides financial and technical assistance to middle-income and poor nations. (*Andreas Rentz/ Getty Images*)

IBRD and IDA

The International Bank for Reconstruction and Development (IBRD) primarily works with middle-income and creditworthy poorer countries to promote equitable and sustainable job growth, while simultaneously alleviating poverty and addressing issues of regional and global importance. The agency is structured like a cooperative, delivering flexible, timely, and tailored financial products, knowledge and technical services, and strategic advice. Clients of the IBRD also have access to financial capital in larger volumes and more favorable terms with longer maturities through the World Bank Treasury.

Specifically, the IBRD preserves borrowers' financial strength by providing support during bust periods, when poorer individuals are likely to be most adversely affected; helping meet long-term human and social development needs that the world's private financial markets do not support; using the leverage of financing to promote key policy and institutional reforms (such as social safety net programs and anticorruption efforts); and providing financial support (in the form of grants) in areas that are critical to the well-being of poor people.

While IBRD serves middle-income countries, the International Development Association (IDA) is the single largest donor for social services in the world's seventy-nine poorest countries, about half of which are located in Africa. The agency was established in 1960 with the aim of reducing poverty and financial inequality, boosting economic growth, and improving people's living conditions. The money is lent on concessional terms with no interest charges and repayments stretched over 35 to 40 years, including a 10-year grace period. Since its inception, the IDA grants and credits have well exceeded $200 billion, reaching an average of some $12 billion annually in the early twenty-first century. About half of the funding goes to countries in Africa.

Research on Booms and Busts

Research by the World Bank on economic expansions and contractions worldwide shows that the first global real-estate boom was reached around 1990 in most countries associated with the Organisation for Economic and Co-operation and Development (OECD). Asset inflation—the condition in which the prices of assets such as real estate have increased to far higher values than can be justified by underlying economic conditions—was extraordinarily high at the time. In some European markets, real-estate values rose by almost 400 percent in just one decade, followed by a sharp decline of almost 50 percent from peak values in the following five years. Such volatility has been shown to be costly and destructive, with negative effects on the banking system, households, and the economy in general. Given the irreversible globalization of the financial markets, World Bank research also indicated that, to help avoid future financial and economic crises, governments should limit incentives that lead to overvalued assets and should more tightly regulate the banking and finance industry to limit the flow of cash into overly risky projects.

Mortgage Recommendations

The World Bank also has issued recommendations for lending in emerging markets based on the subprime mortgage boom and bust that occurred in the United States in 2008–2009. That crisis raised the question of extending mortgage loans to low- and moderate-income households. In most emerging markets, mortgage financing is still considered a luxury, restricted to upper-income individuals and households. As policy makers in these markets seek to regulate lending practices, the World Bank has recommended that they should adopt more flexible policies that incorporate a wider variety of financing methods in order to steer many accounts out of the subprime mortgage trap. Beyond that, the World Bank has recommended rules and regulations that force lenders to more closely link rental or purchase agreements to the real and long-term financial capacity of the household.

Criticisms

According to some critics, the World Bank has failed in its mission to promote development in the Third World by failing to take into account the particular economic circumstances of a given country; instead, the bank imposes a one-size-fits-all approach based on Western models. Moreover, the bank has sometimes been seen as promoting export-oriented development over the needs of the local economy. Because of this emphasis on developing exports—often low-priced ones intended for rich-country markets—some critics of the institution, particularly on the political left, have accused it of primarily serving the economic and even political needs of the developed world.

Critics charge that through all of its practices, the bank has unfairly placed a burden on the world's poorer, ill-equipped nations to compete against the more developed countries. As a result, the critics claim, the World Bank has actually increased poverty in the poorer countries and has been detrimental to the environment, public health, and cultural diversity.

Even the organizational structure of the World Bank has come under criticism, since the president of the institution is always a U.S. citizen nominated by the president of the United States (subject to the approval of the other member countries). It is also alleged that the decision-making structure of the World Bank is undemocratic, since the United States has veto power on some constitutional decisions despite having only 16 percent of shares in the bank. Reflecting that concern, seven Latin American nations have formed the Bank of the South to minimize U.S. influence in the region. The issue of U.S. dominance aside, at least in part, critics charge that the internal governance of the World Bank lacks transparency regarding the politics of how it conducts business.

Abhijit Roy

See also: International Development Banks; International Monetary Fund.

Further Reading

Bret, Benjamin. *Invested Interests: Capital, Culture, and the World Bank.* Minneapolis: University of Minnesota Press, 2007.

Gilbert, Christopher, and David Vines. *The World Bank: Structure and Policies.* New York: Cambridge University Press, 2000.

Goldman, Michael. *Imperial Nature: The World Bank and Struggles for Social Justice in the Age of Globalization.* New Haven, CT: Yale University Press, 2005.

Kaufmann, Daniel, and Aart Kraay. "Governance Indicators: Where Are We, Where Should We Be Going?" *World Bank Research Observer* 23:1 (2008): 1–30.

Kulshreshtha, Praveen. "Public Sector Governance Reform: The World Bank's Framework." *International Journal of Public Sector Management* 21:5 (2008): 556–567.

Mallaby, Sebastian. *The World's Banker: A Story of Failed States, Financial Crises, and the Wealth and Poverty of Nations.* New York: Penguin, 2004.

World Bank Web site: www.worldbank.org.

WorldCom

WorldCom, Inc., provided a sobering example to the global business community of a very large company brought down by overextension, gross mismanagement, and unethical corporate behavior in the unregulated markets of the late twentieth and early twenty-first centuries—the years leading up to the financial meltdown of 2007–2009.

WorldCom was the second-largest long-distance telecommunications provider in the United States, second only to AT&T, in the late 1980s—when the importance of long-distance telephone service had not yet been greatly diminished by the expansion of cellular telephone service. The company's merger with MCI Communications in 1997 was the largest in American history to that time—as was its Chapter 11 bankruptcy filing in 2002. After emerging from bankruptcy, WorldCom was acquired by Verizon Communications in February 2005, a month before former chief executive officer (CEO) Bernard Ebbers was found guilty of fifteen counts of fraud and conspiracy in yet another notorious landmark for the storied company—the largest accounting scandal in history.

WorldCom was founded as Long Distance Discount Services (LDDS) in 1983, amid the divestiture of AT&T into seven regional operating companies (the "Baby Bells"). Ebbers, a motel chain operator, was soon hired as CEO, and LDDS prospered. It aggressively acquired other small telecommunications companies, picking up sixty before changing the firm's name to WorldCom in 1995. The acquisitions included not only long-distance companies, but also Internet companies such as MFS Communications, which owned UUNET Technologies, one of the largest Internet service providers in the world.

In 1997, seemingly out of the blue, Ebbers and WorldCom announced an intention to acquire MCI Communications. Founded as Microwave Communications, Inc., in 1963, MCI was originally devoted to building microwave relay stations to transmit the signals from two-way radios used by the transportation industry. The company went public in 1972 to raise money for infrastructure, using what it learned along the way to move into other forms of telecommunications. It established a vast fiber-optic network during the 1980s and became the second-largest telecommunications company by the end of the decade. MCI's influence was instrumental in spurring the antitrust case against AT&T that opened up the industry to other competitors.

WorldCom's move to acquire MCI came on the heels of buyout offers from GTE and British Telecom, both of which Ebbers successfully outbid. After a stock-swap deal of $34.7 billion, the restructured MCI WorldCom began business on September 15, 1998. A further merger, with the Sprint Corporation, was immediately considered, and a $129 billion deal worked out by the following fall—sufficient to catapult the resulting company past AT&T. Although no official action was taken against the company, the merger was terminated at the urging of the European Union and the U.S. Justice Department on antitrust grounds. WorldCom's stock began declining, losing the gains it had attained in anticipation of the Sprint merger, as well as suffering from the general slump of the telecommunications industry.

Much of Ebbers's personal wealth came from his MCI WorldCom stock, whose declining prices eroded his fortune. To continue financing his other businesses, Ebbers secured hundreds of millions of dollars of loans from the WorldCom board of directors. The board worried that without such loans, Ebbers would begin selling his stock, further reducing the price. But the loans proved insufficient for Ebbers, who before long was forced to resign as CEO. His debts to the company at the time totaled $408.2 million.

Meanwhile, internal auditors working after hours had discovered widespread fraud and financial misreporting on the part of corporate management and notified the board of directors. Ebbers, Chief Financial Officer Scott Sullivan, Controller David Myers, and Director of General Accounting Buddy Yates had artificially inflated the price of WorldCom stock by overreporting revenues and underreporting costs, among other cases of fraudulent accountancy. Sullivan was immediately fired, and the Securities and Exchange Commission (SEC) began an investigation. After eighteen months, the SEC established that the fraud had exaggerated WorldCom's assets by $11 billion. Ebbers was eventually convicted of multiple felonies and sentenced to twenty-five years in prison; WorldCom investors brought a class-action lawsuit against him and the other defrauders, which was settled out of court for just over $6 billion. Sullivan, Myers, Yates, and Accounting Managers Betty Vinson and Troy Normand all were convicted of related felonies.

A month after the SEC investigation began, on July 21, 2002, WorldCom filed for Chapter 11 bankruptcy. The proceedings were held during the same months as those for Enron's bankruptcy; the filings by the companies constituted the two largest corporate bankruptcies in U.S. history. In the bankruptcy, MCI WorldCom shed the WorldCom from its name and began doing business as MCI, Inc.—although most of its business consisted of paying off its debts. Just months after MCI emerged from bankruptcy in 2004, Verizon Communications acquired the company for $7.6 billion.

Bill Kte'pi

See also: Corporate Corruption; Technological Innovation.

Further Reading

Cooper, Cynthia. *Extraordinary Circumstances: The Journey of a Corporate Whistleblower.* Hoboken, NJ: John Wiley & Sons, 2008.

Jeter, Lynne W. *Disconnected: Deceit and Betrayal at WorldCom.* Hoboken, NJ: John Wiley & Sons, 2003.

Zarnowitz, Victor (1919–2009)

Victor Zarnowitz was a leading scholar in the fields of economic forecasting, business cycles, and economic indicators whose influence extended well beyond academia. He was a senior fellow and economic counselor for the Conference Board, an economist at the National Bureau of Economic Research (NBER), and a professor of economics and finance at the University of Chicago's graduate school of business.

Zarnowitz was born on November 3, 1919, in Lancut, Poland. He studied at the University of Krakow from 1937 to 1939, when he and his brother were forced to flee Poland during the Nazi invasion. The brothers were captured by Soviet Russians and imprisoned in a Siberian labor camp, where Zarnowitz's brother died. Zarnowitz escaped and was reunited with his family; he later wrote about the experience in *Fleeing the Nazis, Surviving the Gulag and Arriving in the Free World* (2008).

Zarnowitz earned a doctorate in economics in 1951 from the University of Heidelberg in West Germany, for which he produced a thesis titled "Theory of Income Distribution." While a student at Heidelberg, Zarnowitz also tutored in econom-

ics at the university and at the Graduate School of Business in Mannheim, Germany.

Zarnowitz moved with his family to the United States in 1952 and took a position as a research economist at the NBER in New York City. From 1956 to 1959, he was a lecturer and visiting professor at Columbia University. He was appointed associate professor of economics and finance at the University of Chicago's Graduate School of Business, becoming a full professor in 1965 and professor emeritus following his retirement in 1989.

In his research, Zarnowitz concluded that economic forecasters were rarely accurate in predicting the turning points of business cycles, since their data tended to be faulty or incomplete. He attempted to measure the length of business cycles himself in order to help predict the durations of economic booms and busts. He advocated the use of forecast averages instead of individual forecasts, and his approach later became standard practice in the preparation of government budgets and predicting revenue streams from taxation. Zarnowitz's method has also been used by businesses to anticipate recruitment needs and expansion plans.

Zarnowitz was active in helping guide U.S. economic policy, serving as director of the Study of Cyclical Indicators at the U.S. Department of

Commerce's Bureau of Economic Analysis from 1972 to 1975. He was a fellow of the National Association of Business Economists, the American Statistical Association, an honorary fellow of the International Institute of Forecasters, and an honorary member of the Centre for International Research on Economic Tendency Surveys.

A prolific author, Zarnowitz wrote a number of books that integrated theoretical and practical understandings of business cycles and their behavior, including *Orders, Production, and Investment: A Cyclical and Structural Analysis* (1973); *Business Cycles: Theory, History, Indicators, and Forecasting* (1992), and *What Is a Business Cycle?* (1992). He also co-authored and edited *The Business Cycle Today* (1972) and contributed numerous academic papers, including "Recent Work on Business Cycles in Historical Perspective" in 1985; "Has the Business Cycle Been Abolished?" in 1998; "Theory and History Behind Business Cycles" in 1999, and "The Old and the New in U.S. Economic Expansion" in 2000.

As a member of the NBER's Business Cycle Dating Committee, Zarnowitz was one of the seven economists who officially identified the recession that began in late 2007. With a career that spanned six decades, he witnessed firsthand every U.S. recession since the Great Depression. Zarnowitz died on February 21, 2009, in New York City.

Justin Corfield

See also: Confidence, Consumer and Business.

Further Reading

Zarnowitz, Victor. *Business Cycles: Theory, History, Indicators, and Forecasting.* Chicago: University of Chicago Press, 1992.

———. *Fleeing the Nazis, Surviving the Gulag and Arriving in the Free World.* Wesport, CT: Praeger, 2008.

———. *Orders, Production, and Investment: A Cyclical and Structural Analysis.* New York: Columbia University Press, 1973.

———. "Recent Work on Business Cycles in Historical Perspective: A Review of Theories and Evidence." *Journal of Economic Literature* 23:2 (1985), 523–580.

Zarnowitz, Victor, and G.H. Moore. "Major Changes in Cyclical Behavior." In *The American Business Cycle Today: Continuity and Change*, ed. R.J. Gordon. Chicago: University of Chicago Press, 1986.

Chronology

1630s Speculators send the price of exotic tulip bulbs soaring in newly wealthy Amsterdam, the Netherlands, before market forces cause them to collapse; the episode, known as "tulipmania," is widely viewed by historians as the first great speculative bubble in the history of capitalism.

1668 The Sveriges Riksbank (Bank of the Swedish Realm) opens as the world's first central bank.

1694 The Bank of England, which serves as the model for most other central banks, is founded in London.

1716– After it wins a royal charter giving it a mo-
1720 nopoly on trade with French North America, the Paris-based Compagnie d'Occident (Company of the West) draws thousands of investors; its soaring stock price turns many investors into "millionaires," a newly coined term, before the bubble bursts, wiping out many fortunes.

1720 In an episode known as the South Sea Bubble, British investors bid up the share price of the South Sea Company, a joint-stock company that had been given a royal monopoly on trade with Latin America, by nearly 1,000 percent before lack of credit causes it to tumble; the collapse wiped out the fortunes of thousands of middle- and upper-class investors.

1776 Scottish economist Adam Smith publishes *The Wealth of Nations*, which laid the foundation for the classical economic tradition.

1791 Congress establishes the First Bank of the United States, the country's first central bank; its charter is allowed to lapse twenty years later.

1792 A group of merchants and financiers found the New York Stock Exchange.

1798 British economist and demographer Thomas Malthus publishes his influential *Essay on the Principle of Population*, on demographic cycles, in which he theorizes that population growth inevitably outstrips agricultural production, leading to famines.

1812 City Bank of New York, the predecessor institution of Citigroup, is founded.

1815– The end of the Napoleonic Wars in Europe
1819 triggers an economic boom in the United States.

1816 Congress establishes the Second Bank of the United States; its proposed rechartering is vetoed by President Andrew Jackson twenty years later; Jackson saw the bank as an institution that served the interests of wealthy eastern merchants and financiers rather than those of small businessmen and farmers in the West and South.

1819 The United States experiences its first major nationwide bank panic and recession.

1833– Expanding credit creates an economic boom
1837 and an unsustainable bubble in real-estate prices.

1837– A currency crisis and bank panic triggers
1843 the worst economic depression in U.S. history to date.

1844   The Bank of England, Britain's central bank, is granted a monopoly on the issuance of banknotes, or paper money.

1857   The collapse of an Ohio bank triggers a nationwide panic that plunges the country into a brief but sharp recession.

French economist Clément Juglar publishes an article laying out one of the first theories on the cyclical nature of capitalist economies.

1858   German immigrant Mayer Lehman moves to Montgomery, Alabama, and joins his brother Henry Lehman in founding the partnership that would eventually become the investment bank Lehman Brothers.

1860   Henry Varnum Poor publishes his *History of Railroads and Canals in the United States*, which includes the first major credit rating of corporate securities.

1862   British economist William Stanley Jevons publishes a paper entitled "On the Study of Periodic Commercial Fluctuations," one of the first major analyses of business cycles.

1867   German economist Karl Marx publishes *Das Kapital (Capital)*, a critique of capitalist economics that helps lay the foundation for the various communist revolutions of the twentieth century.

1869   German immigrant businessman Marcus Goldman founds the investment bank that became Goldman Sachs in 1882, when his son-in-law Samuel Sachs became a partner.

1871   Carl Menger, founder of the Austrian school of economics, publishes *The Principles of Economics*, the first major text to explore the concept of marginal utility, a key component of modern economic thinking.

Financiers Andrew Drexel and J.P. Morgan found Drexel, Morgan & Company, predecessor of the investment bank portion of the financial services company JP Morgan Chase.

1873   A major bank panic sets off a recession that grips the U.S. economy through 1877; it creates high unemployment and lower wages, and sets off major labor unrest.

1874   British economist William Stanley Jevons publishes *Principles of Science*, in which he lays out his theory connecting fluctuations in the business cycle to sunspot activity.

1886   Charles Dow, founder of the *Wall Street Journal*, publishes an index of eleven leading companies, the forerunner of the Dow Jones Industrial Average.

1890   British economist Alfred Marshall publishes *Principles of Economics,* a seminal text of neoclassical economics.

1893–   One of the worst economic downturns in
1897   history grips the U.S. economy and much of the industrialized world.

1899   American sociologist Thorstein Veblen publishes *The Theory of the Leisure Class*, in which his contention that consumer behavior is often driven by irrational impulses challenges neoclassical assumptions that consumers are rational agents.

1901   A struggle over control of the Northern Pacific Railroad triggers a major panic on Wall Street.

1904   What is now the Bank of America is founded in San Francisco, as the Bank of Italy, by Italian immigrant Amadeo Giannini.

1907   A failed effort to corner the market in copper leads to a major financial panic, prompting financier J.P. Morgan to arrange a $100 million infusion of capital to free up credit markets; the panic prompts economists and investors to call for a U.S. central bank to provide stability in the credit market, which leads six years later to creation of the Federal Reserve System.

1908   Horse-carriage manufacturer William Durant founds General Motors; the company was the world's largest automobile producer through most of the twentieth century.

1913   The Federal Reserve Bank (Fed), America's modern central bank, is founded; in a nod to

America's federalist heritage and regional interests, the bank consists of twelve regional banks, though the New York branch becomes the pacesetter of Fed policy.

1914 Financier Charles E. Merrill founds his eponymous company, predecessor of the brokerage firm and investment bank Merrill Lynch.

1919 American Insurance Group (AIG) is founded in China by American businessman Cornelius Vander Starr.

The Harvard University Committee for Economic Research begins publishing what comes to be known as the three-curve barometer, one of the first econometric tools for measuring the financial system.

1919– Italian immigrant Charles Ponzi sets up an
1920 investor scheme involving international postage, in which he pays existing clients with funds from new investors; the illegal pyramid scheme quickly collapses, costing investors millions and putting Ponzi behind bars and attaching his name to all similar pyramid schemes in the future.

1921– A major recession hits the United States,
1922 partly as a result of too-rapid demobilization efforts following World War I.

1922– The Florida land boom sends real-estate
1925 prices in South Florida dramatically upward; the boom ends as financial analysts begin to question whether land and home prices are too high for their underlying value.

1923 Germany undergoes a bout of hyperinflation in which the mark, the national currency, is rendered virtually worthless, creating economic havoc and contributing to the political instability that would give rise to the Nazi Party.

1926 Soviet economist Nikolai Kondratieff publishes an article stating that the major capitalist economies of the West experience long-term economic cycles, based on the interplay of entrepreneurial activity and technological innovation; the article proved influential, and the cycles of roughly sixty years in length were eventually named in his honor.

1927– A stock market boom sends prices soaring on
1929 Wall Street; the Dow Jones Industrial Average rises from roughly 150 at the beginning of 1927 to more than 380 at its peak in September 1929.

1929 Over several weeks in October and November, securities listed on the New York Stock Exchange plummet in value, resulting in billions of dollars of lost investor assets and triggering an economic panic that led to the Great Depression.

1929– Following a crash in U.S. corporate securities
1933 prices, the United States and much of the rest of the world is plunged into the Great Depression, the worst economic downturn in history.

1930 Following the great Wall Street stock market crash of 1929, corporate securities prices revive significantly (later economists described the revival as an "echo bubble") before plunging to even greater losses from 1931 to 1933.

1931 In one of the first major works on monetary theory, *Prices and Production,* Austrian school economist Friedrich von Hayek argues that monetary stability is key to avoiding the excesses of the boom-bust cycle in capitalist economics.

1933 In the wake of widespread bank failures, the Franklin Roosevelt administration creates the Federal Deposit Insurance Corporation (FDIC) to insure deposits at commercial banks and prevent bank panics; the FDIC is one of a variety of agencies, programs, and policies initiated by the Roosevelt administration to counter the Great Depression through regulatory reform and countercyclical spending.

American economist Irving Fisher publishes his article "The Debt Deflation Theory of Great Depression"; it describes how high debt during boom periods can lead to a vicious cycle of debt and deflation during economic downturns.

In the wake of revelations about the speculative excesses of banks and the role they played in the Great Stock Market Crash of 1929, Congress passes the Banking Act, better known as the Glass-Steagall Act, which, among other things, prevents banks from engaging in such investment bank activities as underwriting corporate securities.

Investment bank Morgan Stanley is created as a result of the Glass-Steagall Act requiring J.P. Morgan and Company to divest itself of its commercial banking activities.

1934   Hungarian-born economic Nicholas Kaldor first formulates his "cobweb theory," which challenged the conventional economic thinking that disruptions to agricultural and other markets did not always correct themselves automatically.

Congress and the Roosevelt administration create the Federal Housing Administration to insure mortgages offered by commercial institutions, thereby making those mortgages more affordable.

In the wake of the 1929 stock market crash and revelations of securities fraud on Wall Street, Congress passes the Securities Exchange Act, establishing the Securities and Exchange Commission to oversee and regulate the securities trading industry.

1936   British economist John Maynard Keynes publishes *The General Theory of Employment, Interest and Money*; it critiques the equilibrium paradigm of classical and neoclassical economic thinking and emphasizes the importance of aggregate demand to economic growth and the role of government fiscal and monetary policies in addressing downturns in the economic cycle.

1937–
1939   Responding to fears that the federal deficit will dry up funds needed for private investment, President Franklin Roosevelt cuts back on stimulus spending even as the Federal Reserve, fearing renewed inflation, hikes interest rates; the result is a two-year economic downturn known as the Roosevelt recession.

1938   The federal government creates the Federal National Mortgage Association (Fannie Mae), an agency that buys and securitizes mort-

gages in order to make them more affordable; it would be turned into a private shareholder-owned company in 1968.

1939   The National Association of Security Dealers, predecessor of the National Association of Securities Dealers Automated Quotation, now officially known as Nasdaq, is founded.

1942   In his book *Capitalism, Socialism and Democracy*, Austrian school economist Joseph Schumpeter popularizes the term "creative destruction" to describe how innovation drives capitalist growth.

1944   Amid the waning days of World War II, Allied powers meet at Bretton Woods, New Hampshire, where they hammer out plans for the international economic order, including rules on currency exchange and trade; they also lay the foundations for the International Monetary Fund (IMF) and the World Bank to provide capital for investment in war-damaged and underdeveloped parts of the globe.

1947   Twenty-three major economies agree to establish a global free-trading regime known as the General Agreement on Tariffs and Trade (GATT), the predecessor of the World Trade Organization (WTO).

1948   Australian-born American economist Alfred Jones establishes the first hedge fund; a flattering 1966 article on the fund in the business magazine *Fortune* helps launch the hedge fund industry.

1952   American economist George Katona begins publishing the quarterly *Survey of Consumer Attitudes*, the first major measurement of consumer confidence.

1957   Standard & Poor's, a credit rating agency, creates the widely watched S&P 500 Index of representative large companies.

1960   American financier Bernard Madoff founds a broker-dealer firm that soon becomes a Ponzi scheme, paying dividends to existing clients with the investment funds of new clients; losses to investors had come to $65 billion when the scheme was exposed in 2008.

1963 American economists Milton Friedman and Anna Schwartz publish *A Monetary History of the United States, 1867–1960*, a book that helped establish monetarism as a major school of economic thinking.

1964 President Lyndon Johnson signs into law the biggest tax cut as a percentage of gross domestic product (GDP) in U.S. history; the cut, along with heavy defense spending on the Vietnam War, contributes to the economic boom of the late 1960s.

1966 An article in the business magazine *Fortune* highlighting the success of a hedge fund spreads the popularity of this investment strategy.

1967 Entrepreneur Alan Turtletaub founds The Money Store, a monoline lender that helps pioneer the subprime mortgage.

1969 Countrywide Financial, which will become one of the largest originators of subprime mortgages, is founded in California.

1969– Following discoveries of nickel deposits by
1970 Poseidon NL, an Australian mining firm, investors run up prices on Australian mining shares; the so-called Poseidon bubble collapses when returns on investment prove lower than expected.

1970 Congress creates the Federal Home Loan Mortgage Corporation (Freddie Mac) to buy home mortgages and to provide competition for the newly privatized Fannie Mae.

In the largest bankruptcy in American history to the time, railroad giant Penn Central collapses, a victim of changes in transportation patterns and the decline in the American railroad industry.

1971 As an inflation-fighting measure, President Richard Nixon imposes a ninety-day freeze on wages and prices; Nixon cancels the direct convertibility of U.S. dollars into gold, allowing the dollar to float against other currencies and ending the international financial order set in place at the Bretton Woods Conference in 1944.

The National Association of Security Dealers, the predecessor of Nasdaq, sets up the first electronic securities exchange.

1973– A sudden hike in oil prices helps to set off a
1974 global recession and begins a period marked by "stagflation," in which slow or negative growth is accompanied by inflation.

1973– Oil-price hikes create vast fortunes for a
1981 number of oil-exporting countries, particularly in the Middle East, which they plow into investments in the United States and other Western countries.

1977 Congress passes the Community Reinvestment Act, encouraging commercial banks and savings and loans to make credit and mortgages more available to low-income borrowers.

1978 To enhance competition in the industry, the U.S. Congress passes the Airline Deregulation Act, which lowers prices and expands services but also contributes to the eventual bankruptcy of several major carriers.

Chinese Communist Party chairman Deng Xiaoping pushes for the introduction of market forces, launching China on its path to economic modernization and liberalization.

1979 Deeply in debt and on the verge of bankruptcy, Chrysler, a major American automobile manufacturer, receives billions of dollars in federal bailout money, helping to return the company to profitability.

The Iranian Revolution pushes up oil prices; this second "oil shock" contributes to slow and negative economic growth in much of the industrialized world in the late 1970s and early 1980s.

1981– A dramatic hike in interest rates designed
1982 to wring inflation out of the economy contributes to the worst economic downturn in American history since the Great Depression; the recession is often referred to as the Reagan recession, after the sitting U.S. president Ronald Reagan.

1982 Congress passes the Garn–St. Germain Depository Institutions Act, freeing savings and loans to move beyond their traditional role of financing home mortgages to invest in riskier commercial real-estate and business financing, which would contribute to the savings and loan crisis of the late 1980s and early 1990s.

Congress passes the Alternative Mortgage Transaction Parity Act, which allows for the adjustable interest rates and balloon payments at the heart of subprime mortgages.

Having borrowed heavily in foreign markets on the back of rising prices for its oil exports, Mexico is pushed to the verge of sovereign default as oil prices plunge, forcing the government to devalue the peso; with the plunge of the Mexican economy into recession, foreign investment in Mexico and other Latin American markets is frozen.

The alternative and unregulated Souk al-Manakh stock exchange in Kuwait crashes, wiping out billions of dollars in assets; the crash comes after several years in which newly oil-rich Middle East investors plowed funds into securities listed on the exchange.

1983 The first collateralized debt obligation, a financial instrument that pools debt securities, is offered to investors.

1985 Natural gas pipeline company Internorth and Houston Natural Gas merge to form a company that is soon called Enron.

1986 American economist Hyman Minsky publishes the first of his studies on what would become known as Minsky's financial instability hypothesis, in which he argues that, contrary to mainstream economic thinking, financial markets are prone to instability as opposed to equilibrium.

1987 In the worst single-day percentage loss in its history, the Dow Jones Industrial Average falls 508 points, or 22.6 percent, on October 19, known as Black Monday, triggering a cascade of stock market crashes around the world.

1989 Having aggressively moved into speculative

commercial real-estate lending—newly permitted under 1982 deregulation legislation—some 327 savings and loans, with assets of $135 billion, go bankrupt in what would come to be called the savings and loan crisis. Congress then passes the Financial Institutions Reform Recovery and Enforcement Act, providing tens of billions of dollars in bailout money to savings and loans and setting up the Office of Thrift Supervision to oversee the industry.

1989– Revolutions in Eastern Europe and the
1991 collapse of the Soviet Union cause the collapse of command-style communist economies in countries throughout the region and their replacement by market-oriented ones.

1990 After a dizzying rise in real-estate and securities prices, the Japanese economy enters a period of deflation and nearly flat economic growth that lasts through the rest of the century, a period that would come to be known as the "lost decade."

1992 The U.S. Congress establishes the Office of Federal Housing Enterprise Oversight to oversee the quasi-governmental mortgage insurers Fannie Mae and Freddie Mac.

In the wake of a speculative real-estate boom gone bust, Sweden's banking system experiences near collapse; the government responds by forcing the bank shareholders to take major losses and then takes major equity stakes in leading commercial banks.

1994 A series of political shocks shake foreign investor confidence in Mexico, causing capital outflows; with the government on the verge of defaulting on its foreign loans, the U.S. government, the International Monetary Fund, and other countries and institutions put together a $50 billion bailout package.

1995 An initial public offering of stock in Netscape, an early Internet browser, rakes in billions, and helps set off a boom in high-tech and Internet stocks, the so-called dot.com boom of the late 1990s.

Mexico's dramatic devaluation of the peso causes foreign investors to pull out of bonds and securities not only in that country but throughout Latin America; the phenomenon of Mexico's financial troubles infecting other Latin American markets comes to be called the "Tequila effect."

1996   Federal Reserve chairman Alan Greenspan utters his now-famous "irrational exuberance" remark about how overly optimistic investors were driving securities prices to unsustainable levels.

1997   Investment bank J.P. Morgan & Co. issues the credit default swap, a contract that transfers the risk of default from the purchaser of a financial security to a guarantor.

1997–
1998   Fearing a collapse in the baht, Thailand's national currency, foreign investors begin to pull capital out of securities markets in Thailand and other Asian countries, setting off the Asian financial crisis and plunging much of Southeast Asia, South Korea, and other Asian economies into a steep recession.

1998   The European Union establishes a common central bank, the European Central Bank, followed by the introduction of an electronically traded common currency, the euro; printed euros appeared in 2002 and replaced most European national currencies.

To prevent what it fears could become a global financial crisis, the Federal Reserve coordinates a multi-billion-dollar bailout by major U.S. banks of the hedge fund giant Long-Term Capital Management.

Falling oil and natural resource prices damage Russian finances, leading to a $22 billion loan from the International Monetary Fund, but it is not enough to prevent Moscow from defaulting on its foreign debt obligations and imposing a ninety-day moratorium on loan payments to nonresident lenders.

1999   The U.S. Congress passes the Financial Services Modernization Act, or Gramm-Leach-Bliley, overturning Depression-era restrictions on commercial banks engaging in investment banking activities, as laid out in the Glass-Steagall Act of 1933.

2000   As investors grow increasingly leery of poorly run, overhyped high-tech and Internet stocks, securities prices plunge, putting many start-up companies out of business and signaling the end of the so-called dot.com boom of the late 1990s.

In response to the recession triggered in part by the collapse of the dot.com boom, the Fed reduces the prime interest rate, lowering the price of credit and helping to fuel the housing boom of 2003–2006.

2001   American manufacturer Bethlehem Steel declares bankruptcy, marking a major milestone in the deindustrialization of the United States.

As accounting and other scandals expose its faulty finances, Enron, a Houston-based energy provider, declares bankruptcy.

2002   In response to several high-profile corporate corruption incidents, Congress passes the Sarbanes-Oxley Act, requiring more transparency in corporate accounting.

In the wake of the collapse in high-tech stocks and revelations of corporate scandals, the telecommunications giant WorldCom declares bankruptcy, becoming the largest firm in U.S. history to do so up to that date.

2003–
2006   Low interest, easy credit, and loose lending standards fuel a dramatic run-up in housing prices, particularly in the urban Northeast, the Southwest, and Florida, with the national median price peaking in July 2006.

2007   **March:** After months of declining U.S. home prices and waves of subprime mortgage defaults, Fed chairman Ben Bernanke attempts to reassure international credit markets that he believes the growing crisis will not spread beyond the subprime mortgage market.

August–September: A series of high-profile subprime lenders—including Ameriquest Financial and Luminent Mortgage Capital—declare bankruptcy.

September: To stimulate the economy, the Federal Reserve begins cutting interest rates for the first time in four years; the cuts, which continued through 2009, brought the effective rate to near zero.

October: The Dow Jones Industrial Average reaches its all-time peak of 14,164.53 on October 9.

October–December: A contracting economy ushers in the beginning of a U.S. recession—the worst of the post–World War II era—that will continue through the second quarter of 2009.

2008   January: Bank of America buys out the struggling Countrywide Financial, the nation's largest mortgage lender; home sales fall to their lowest level in twenty-five years.

February 13: As a recession-fighting measure, President George W. Bush signs a $170 billion stimulus package, largely consisting of tax cuts, credits, and rebates.

February 28: The British bank Northern Rock, a major but now struggling player in its country's mortgage market, is taken over by the government, an indication that the bursting housing bubble is not confined to the United States.

March: Having grown dramatically in the credit boom of the early 2000s, Icelandic banks begin to fail, causing a collapse in the nation's currency and a rescue from the International Monetary Fund, a rarity for a developed-world country.

May: In an effort to prevent panic in international credit markets, Treasury Secretary Henry Paulson coordinates the sale of investment bank Bear Stearns to fellow investment bank JPMorgan and provides a $29 billion federal loan to facilitate the deal.

July: Following a run by bank depositors, the Federal Deposit Insurance Corporation (FDIC) seizes California's IndyMac Bank.

September 7: The federal government announces it is assuming control of Fannie Mae and Freddie Mac, two government-sponsored but privately held entities that insured or owned roughly half the mortgages in the country.

September 14: Under federal government prodding, Bank of America agrees to buy Merrill Lynch, a major investment bank on the verge of collapse.

September 15: Lehman Brothers, the oldest investment bank in the United States, fails after the federal government declines to bail it out.

September 18: The federal government provides $85 billion in capital to American International Group (AIG), the world's largest insurance company and one heavily invested in credit default swaps; the Federal Reserve and other major central banks pump $180 billion into the global financial system as a means of preventing a freezing up of international credit markets.

September 19: To prevent a collapse in the prices of financial stocks, the Securities and Exchange Commission bans short selling of such stocks.

September 21: The Federal Reserve approves the decision of Goldman Sachs and Morgan Stanley, the last two standing investment banks, to convert themselves into bank holding companies; this move gives them better access to Fed lending but also subjects them to more regulatory scrutiny.

September 24: Runs on international money market funds raise fears that interbank lending, a key component of the international financial system, will freeze up.

September 25: A depositor run forces the FDIC to put Washington Mutual, the nation's largest savings and loan, into receivership.

September 26: The Federal Reserve and other central banks conclude two days of injecting billions more into financial markets around the world.

September 29: Citing a lack of specifics and oversight, the House of Representatives rejects Treasury Secretary Henry Paulson's $700 billion bailout package for the financial system; the vote sends the Dow Jones Industrial Average plummeting 777 points—the largest point drop in its history—on fears of a collapse of global financial markets.

October 3: Chastened by collapse in securities prices and reassured that it will be given more oversight, Congress passes the Emergency Economic Stabilization Act, which provides $700 billion in bailout money to financial institutions as part of the Troubled Assets Relief Program (TARP); global financial markets begin to stabilize.

December: Failing automakers Chrysler and General Motors receive roughly $25 billion of TARP money, but with the condition that they reorganize their operations.

2009 **February 4:** Responding to public outrage over large compensation packages, President Barack Obama caps executive pay at firms receiving federal bailout money at $500,000 a year.

February 17: In a recession-fighting move, President Obama signs the American Recovery and Reinvestment Act; it provides roughly $787 billion in stimulus money, approximately one-third consisting of tax cuts and two-thirds in government spending, about half of the latter in grants to financially strapped states and local governments.

February 18: President Obama announces the Homeowner Affordability and Stability Plan, which provides $75 billion to lenders to modify mortgage terms to aid homeowners threatened with default.

March 9: The Dow Jones Industrial Average bottoms out at 6547.05, down more than 53 percent from its peak in October 2007.

April 2: Leaders of the G-20 group of the world's largest economies meet in London and pledge a collective $1.1 trillion to help emerging markets fight the global recession.

May 7: The Federal Reserve releases the results of its Supervisory Capital Assessment Program, popularly known as the "stress test," which tested 19 major banks' ability to withstand a severe economic downturn; of

the 19, 9 are deemed to have adequate capital while the rest are told they would need to add $185 billion in capital to bring them up to the standards set by the program.

June–September: The U.S. economy experiences an annualized 3.5 percent growth rate, marking the end of the 2007–2009 recession.

October: The seasonally adjusted unemployment rate in the United States peaks at 10.1 percent, the highest level since the early 1980s.

October 14: The Dow Jones Industrial Average climbs above 10,000 for the first time in more than a year.

December 1: AIG begins to pay back the bailout money it received from the federal government in 2008.

December 2: Bank of America announces that it will begin paying back the $45 billion it received from TARP.

2010 **February:** On the verge of sovereign default, Greece is offered a major bailout by the European Central Bank, which fears that the eurozone member's default would create panic in financial markets and undermine investor faith in the twelve-year-old currency.

March 26: The Obama administration announces a new $75 billion initiative to help the unemployed and also to help those who owe more than their homes are worth to stay in their homes; the money is to come from unused and repaid TARP funds.

April 2: The Department of Labor announces that the U.S. economy created 162,000 jobs in March, the biggest gain in three years, but with thousands of unemployed once again seeking work, the unemployment rate remains at the same level as in February, 9.7 percent.

April 20: The Securities and Exchange Commission votes to charge the investment bank Goldman Sachs with fraud for its involvement in the sale of mortgage-backed securities.

Glossary

A

AAA. The highest rating offered on a corporate bond by most credit-rating agencies.

ABS. *See* asset-backed security.

acquisition. The purchase of one company by another.

adjustable rate mortgage. A mortgage in which a low initial interest rate is followed, after a set period of time, by an interest rate pegged to an index.

aggregate demand. Total spending in an economy at a given time: consumption, investment, government, and net exports (amount exports exceed imports).

aggregate supply. Total amount of goods and services businesses would like to produce over a given period of time.

algorithm. A step-by-step procedure for solving a mathematical problem. In finance, a mathematical formula or computer program for estimating the future performance of securities or markets.

Alt-A. A mortgage offered to someone with good credit but an inability to document his or her income.

alternative trading system. A government-approved, nonexchange venue for the trading of securities.

amortization. The steady reduction in the principal of a loan over the term of the loan so that the balance is fully repaid by maturity.

animal spirits. John Maynard Keynes's term for optimistic expectations by investors and business managers.

annuity. An insurance contract that pays a given stream of income for a given period time or for the life of the beneficiary.

arbitrage. The purchase of a good or asset in one market and its immediate sale in another, with the purchaser earning a profit based on a discrepancy in prices between the two markets.

ARM. *See* adjustable rate mortgage.

asset. A tangible or intangible item of value; buildings, financial assets, and brand names are all assets.

asset-backed security. A security that is collateralized by assets such as credit card borrowings, auto loans, school loans, or home mortgages.

audit. An examination and verification of a company's or individual's financial records.

automated trading system. A system in which computers and computer programs determine the buying and selling of securities.

B

bailout. Money provided to a firm or individual when that firm or individual is threatened with default; the term is usually used when the money comes from the government.

balance of payments. A statement measuring the monetary transactions or flows between residents of one country and those of another.

bank cycle. *See* credit cycle.

bank holding company. A bank that controls one or more commercial banks or other holding companies by owning 25 percent or more of the equity in each.

bankruptcy. The legal action of resolving unpaid liabilities and dispersing assets to creditors.

barrier to trade. A policy designed to limit imports.

bear market. A securities market where sellers outnumber buyers, driving prices down.

black swan. An event that is highly improbable but whose consequences, if it does occur, dwarf the consequences of more probable outcomes.

bond. A financial security for which a borrower (issuer of the bond) agrees to pay the lender (purchaser of the bond) interest payments based on the principal of the bond and coupon rate (usually in semiannual payments), as well as the face value of the bond at maturity.

boom. A period of rapid economic growth and rising expectations often initiated by new economic developments. In the first phase, investor expectation usually corresponds with economic realities. In the second phrase, investor euphoria results in speculative investment leading to a turning point, where precipitous selling causes asset values and economic activities to decline rapidly.

brokerage house. A firm that buys and sells securities for clients.

bubble. The rapid and unsustainable inflation of asset values.

building cycle. A business cycle related to construction.

bull market. A securities market where buyers outnumber sellers, driving prices up.

bullion. Precious metal in noncoin form.

business cycle. Fluctuations in the output of national economies, usually marked by the period from high output to low output and back to high output.

bust. A precipitous fall in economic activity brought on by the sudden realization by investors that the preceding boom is unsustainable. A financial bust is quickly followed by business contraction, bankruptcies, and unemployment.

buying long. The conventional form of purchasing a security (the expectation is that it will increase in value); buying long is the opposite of selling short.

C

call. In economics, a demand for immediate payment on a debt, usually before the debt is due.

capital. In economics, all assets, aside from land and labor, utilized in production; produced goods used to produce other goods.

capital account. The statement measuring the inflow and outflow of financial capital from a given country.

capital flight. The sudden withdrawal of financial capital from a given market (a term usually used in reference to a particular national market).

capital flow. The flow of money across international borders.

capital goods. Produced goods used to produce other goods, including factories, equipment, tools, and so forth.

capital inflow. The flow of funds into a given market; the term is usually used in reference to a national market.

capital market. The market for equity and debt securities with an original maturity greater than one year.

capital outflow. The flow of funds out of a given market; usually used in reference to a national market.

capital-intensive. Referring to economic activity that requires large amounts of capital.

capitalization. The process in which companies get the funds they need to operate and expand.

cartel. A group of firms or countries producing a similar good or commodity that work together to set quantity supplied and/or to determine price.

CDO. *See* collateralized debt obligation.

CDS. *See* credit default swap.

central bank. A government-operated bank that sets a nation's monetary policy.

CMO. *See* collateralized mortgage obligation.

collateral. The assets offered to secure a loan.

collateralization. The bundling and selling of collateral or debt obligations, usually mortgages, as security.

collateralized debt obligation. A security created from the bundling together of a pool of financial assets where the payments made on the underlying financial assets are passed on to the investors in the security.

collateralized mortgage obligation. A security created from the bundling together of a pool of mortgages where the mortgage payments are passed on to the investors in the security.

command economy. An economy where resources are allocated primarily by government dictate.

commercial bank. A bank that takes deposits and makes loans. It provides checking, savings, and money market accounts (as distinct from an investment bank).

commercial paper. Short-term debt instruments issued by financial and nonfinancial institutions.

commodity. A good for which there is a demand.

common stock. Equity claims representing ownership of the net income and assets of a corporation; common stock holders are last in line to receive any payments from the corporation after all other lenders and creditors have been paid.

confidence. In economics, the belief by individuals or businesses that economic conditions will improve.

consumption. In economics, the total amount of spending on consumer goods.

cooperative. A jointly owned enterprise that produces or sells goods or services for the benefit of its owners.

cornering. The act of trying to control the supply of a given commodity in order to set prices and derive large profits.

corporation. A legal entity separate and distinct from its owners, usually established to conduct business and earn profit.

cost-push inflation. General inflation triggered by the upsurge in the price of a critical good or commodity, such as oil, or else caused by a wage-price spiral in which wages rise at a faster rate than productivity in a critical sector of the economy, such as auto manufacturing; the result in either case is a rise in prices.

countercyclical. Something that runs counter to the direction of the economy at a given point in time.

creative destruction. In capitalism, the process by which innovation creates new products, firms, and markets while destroying old ones; the term was coined by Joseph Schumpeter.

credit. The use of someone else's capital, with the promise of repayment, usually plus interest, at a future date.

credit cycle. Period of expanding and contracting credit.

credit default swap. A contract that, for a fee, transfers the default risk on a given security from the purchaser of that security to the guarantor.

credit rating. A mutually agreed-upon measure of the creditworthiness of an issuer of debt or of a debt instrument, usually set by a credit-rating agency.

credit union. Cooperatively owned depository institution whose members usually have a common affiliation, such as a common employer.

crowd behavior. In booms and busts, the tendency of investors to buy when others are buying and sell when others are selling.

current account. The statement measuring the value of exports and the value of imports of goods and services, as well as transfer payments, of a given country.

cyclical unemployment. Unemployment that results from contractions in the business cycle.

D

debt deflation. A phenomenon in which excessive debt leads to deflation of prices, causing the real value of the debt to rise.

debt instrument. A financial instrument representing debt rather than equity of the issuer.

debt-to-equity ratio. The ratio of debt obligations to financial and real assets held.

decoupling. In international economics, the process by which developing-world economies become less affected by fluctuations in developed-world economies.

default. The failure of a borrower to make an agreed-upon payment of interest and/or principal when due.

deficit. In finance, the gap by which expenditure exceeds income.

deficit finance. Deficit spending by a government in an economic downturn in order to offset a decline in private sector demand. The concept was originated by John Maynard Keynes.

deficit spending. Spending by government that exceeds government revenues.

defined benefit plan. A retirement or pension plan in which an individual receives a set amount per a given time period once he/she has retired from work.

defined contribution plan. A retirement or pension plan in which an individual (or the corporation in the name of the individual) puts aside a portion of her/his income at each pay period.

deflation. A broad decrease in prices over time.

deindustrialization. The reduction or removal of manufacturing capacity and the economic change wrought by that process.

delinquency. In economics, the falling behind in payments on the interest and/or principal of a loan.

demand-pull inflation. A classic form of inflation that is caused when aggregate demand outpaces an economy's productive capacity.

demographic cycle. Fluctuations in human populations over time and the impact of those fluctuations on economies.

deposit insurance. Government guarantee to make good on deposits at banks and other depository institutions up to a certain level should those institutions become insolvent.

depository institution. A financial institution that issues checkable deposits and uses them to make loans. The institution earns a profit on the spread, the difference between what the institution earns on its assets and pays for its liabilities.

depreciation. The falling value of a good, asset, or currency.

deregulation. The removal of government regulations on economic activities.

derivative. A financial instrument that derives its value from other assets or securities.

devaluation. A reduction by monetary authorities of a currency's value relative to other currencies.

development bank. A multilateral financial institution that receives money from developed-world countries and distributes it in the form of loans or grants to developing-world countries.

discount rate. The interest rate a central bank charges on loans to commercial banks.

diversification. For the purposes of risk management, the putting together of a portfolio of investments whose returns are relatively uncorrelated.

dividend. A payment made to stockholders from a company's after-tax profits.

E

earnings-to-price ratio. The ratio of dividends paid on a share of stock plus retained earnings to the share price.

echo bubble. A smaller asset price bubble that follows a larger asset price bubble after a short period of time.

econometrics. The application of mathematics and statistics to the study of economic behavior.

economic contraction. A decrease in the output of goods and services in an economic system.

economic cycle. *See* business cycle.

economic growth. An increase in the output of goods and services in an economic system.

economic indicators. Measures of aspects of the economy that help determine future performance of the economy as a whole.

economic policy. The fiscal and monetary policy of a government, designed for the purposes of assuring sustainable economic growth, full employment, and stable prices.

effective demand. In microeconomics, the ability of an individual or firm to pay combined with the desire to buy; in macroeconomics, a synonym for aggregate demand.

elasticity. In economics, the degree to which prices and wages react to market forces; the less they react, the more inelastic they are.

emerging market. The financial market in a developing country.

endogenous. Generated from within an economic system, model, or theory, as opposed to being determined outside the system, model, or theory.

entrepreneurialism. The act of starting a business and assuming the financial risks associated with that business in the hopes of gleaning profit.

equilibrium. The state in which various economic forces balance one another so that there is no tendency to change; for a business, the point at which the firm is maximizing profit and therefore has no incentive to change; for consumers, the point at which utility is maximized; in macroeconomics, the point at which aggregate quantity demanded and aggregate quantity supplied are in balance.

equities. Shareholder stakes (shares of stock) in a company.

equity. The difference between the market value of an asset and what is owed on that asset; in finance, a shareholder stake in a company.

ergodic axiom. The argument that past economic history is a reliable basis for predicting future economic activity.

exchange rate. The value of a national currency in relation to the value of other national currencies.

exogenous. Generated from outside an economic system, model, or theory as opposed to being determined within the system, model, or theory.

exposure. The total amount of credit committed to a borrower; also, the potential for gains or losses due to market fluctuations.

extensive growth. Growth in aggregate gross domestic product.

externalities. *See* spillover effect.

externality. An activity that affects others for good or ill, without those others paying for or being compensated for the activity.

F

face value. *See* nominal value.

factors of production. The resources—land, labor, capital (buildings, equipment, tools, and so forth)—utilized to produce goods and services.

FICO score. A person's credit-risk rating as established by the Fair Isaac Corporation and used as a basis to determine if credit will be extended and, if so, at what interest rate.

financial crisis. A period when credit becomes tight, or less available, usually because of widespread fears of default by borrowers.

financial deepening. *See* financial development.

financial development. The growth in the quantity of financial assets relative to the growth of gross domestic product; also, the increase in the variety of assets available to savers and investors.

financial fragility. The degree to which a financial system is vulnerable to collapse.

financial friction. Occurs when a nonmarket force or thing hampers business, trade, or exchange.

financial innovation. The development of new financial operations, instruments, and institutions in response to regulatory and market challenges and opportunities, and to changes in technology.

financial integration. The integration of one country's financial markets with that of another country or countries.

financial intermediation. Borrowing for the purpose of re-lending, where the profit is the difference between what the intermediary earns on its assets and what it pays for its liabilities.

financial market. A figurative place where various forms of securities are bought and sold.

financial modeling. The use of financial data to determine future expansions or contractions in the economy.

financial regulation. Government oversight of the financial markets and government enforcement of the rules governing financial markets.

financial services institution. A company that provides a host of financial services, which may include commercial and investment banking, insurance, brokerage, underwriting, and others services.

fiscal balance. The state at which a government's revenues and expenditures are equal, producing neither a deficit nor a surplus.

fiscal policy. The taxing and spending policy of a government.

fixed business investment. The amount of money businesses invest in capital assets, primarily buildings and equipment with a lifespan of one year or more.

flexible. In economics, the ability or willingness to respond to market forces.

flipping. Slang for the rapid buying and reselling of real property, ideally at a profit.

foreclosure. The legal process by which a lender seizes the collateral of a borrower, usually a home, after the latter defaults on the loan.

foreign direct investment. Investment by foreigners in the productive assets of a given country.

foreign exchange. The currency of a foreign country.

free market economy. An economy in which resources are allocated primarily by market forces.

fungible. In economics, referring to the interchangeability of an asset or a commodity with a similar item of value; for example, stocks and bonds are fungible in that one can be exchanged for the other.

furlough. The temporary laying off of a worker or the shortening of the hours an employee works for the purposes of saving on labor costs.

futures agreement. In economics, an agreement to buy or sell a standardized quantity of a commodity or financial asset, at a price determined today, on a standardized date in the future.

G

galloping inflation. A rapid increase in prices, usually in an annual range of 20 to 1,000 percent.

game theory. A theory about competition based on gains and losses of opposing players and their strategic behavior.

GDP. *See* gross domestic product.

Gini coefficient. A measure of inequality, usually of income or wealth, that ranges between zero and one. A score approaching zero indicates greater equality; a score approaching one indicates greater inequality.

globalization. The integration of markets around the world, implying a freer flow of goods and services, physical capital, people, and financial capital.

government-sponsored enterprise (GSO). A privately owned company established under government aegis and with the explicit or implicit guarantee that the government will assume the enterprise's liabilities should that enterprise become insolvent. Fannie Mae and Freddie Mac, which make mortgage loans, are examples.

gross domestic product (GDP). The total market value of the goods and services produced in a nation in the course of a year.

gross substitution axiom. The idea that every item in the market is a good substitute for every other item.

GSE. *See* government-sponsored enterprise.

H

hedge. In finance, an investment made to limit the risk of other investments.

hedge fund. An investment fund in which high-net-worth investors pool their funds to purchase a basket of high-risk investments designed, collectively, to cushion market fluctuations.

hoarding. The acquisition and holding of resources in expectation of future demand or future lack of supply.

holding company. A legal entity created to hold a controlling interest in other companies.

home equity loan. A loan secured by the equity in a home, usually secondary to a mortgage.

hyperinflation. An extremely high rate of inflation, usually measured in thousands or millions of percent per annum and the result of excessive printing of money by the government.

I

import substitution. A government policy for creating industries to supply goods and services that were previously imported.

income. The flow of wages, dividends, interest payments, and other monies during a given period of time.

index. A composite of values that measures the changes in a given market or economy.

inflation. A broad increase in overall prices over time.

information asymmetry. An economic exchange in which one individual or firm (usually the seller or borrower) has more information than the other about the exchange (usually the buyer or lender).

initial public offering (IPO). The first offering of a company's shares to the investing public.

innovation. The introduction of a new or improved product, production technique, or market.

insider trading. The illegal trading of securities by persons who have knowledge unavailable to the investing public.

insolvency. The inability to meet financial obligations.

intensive growth. Aggregate economic growth driven by increased productivity (higher output per unit than input), often a result of technological advances.

interest. The price paid to borrow money at a given point in time, usually set as a percentage of the total borrowed. Also the return on money lent.

international development bank. A multilateral institution that collects money from developed countries in order to make loans to developing economies.

inventory. Goods kept on hand by retailers and wholesalers to meet future demand.

inventory cycle. A business cycle related to the building up and drawing down of business inventories.

investment. The money firms spend on newly produced tangible and intangible goods and services for the purposes of earning more revenues; also the money spent by households on newly constructed housing or on purchases of real estate with the intent of reselling at a higher price; also government spending on durable projects such as roads and schools.

investment bank. A bank that specializes in financial market activities rather than lending money to or holding money for customers.

investment-grade bond. A corporate bond receiving a rating of BBB/Baa or above from a credit-rating agency, signifying that the bond is safe and has a very low probability of default.

invisible hand. An expression coined by Adam Smith referring to the presumed self-regulating character of the market.

irrational exuberance. A term used by Alan Greenspan to describe extreme investor optimism divorced from market realities.

irreversibility effect. The reluctance to make large purchases or to loan money for others to make large purchases for fear that the commitment of money cannot be reversed should earnings fall in the future.

J

junk bond. A very risky bond that pays a high interest rate to compensate for the risk.

L

labor discipline. A body of policies designed to ensure that people will seek work rather than more leisure time.

labor-Intensive. Referring to economic activity that requires large inputs of labor.

lag. The delaying of the settlement of a debt in international trade.

lagging indicator. An economic indicator that lags behind the performance of the economy as a whole.

laissez-faire. The notion that economic performance is best achieved when the government interferes as little as possible in the workings of markets.

lead. The expediting of the settlement of a debt in international trade.

leading indicator. An economic indicator that anticipates the performance of the economy as a whole.

leveraging. In economics, borrowing money to make an investment.

liability. A debt or other financial obligation owed to another firm or individual.

liberalization. In economics, the process of freeing an economy from government regulation and control.

liquidation. The selling of assets by a bankrupt firm to pay off creditors.

liquidity. Holding cash or near-cash, such as government securities; the ability of having ready access to invested money; the ability to sell an asset for cash.

liquidity preference. In a slump, the preference of households, businesses, and banks to hold money or near-money, such as government securities, as the safest way to preserve assets otherwise available for spending or investment.

liquidity trap. A situation in which the expansion of the money supply fails to stimulate the economy because the demand for money has become perfectly inelastic; that is, the demand for money remains flat no matter how far interest rates are lowered.

loan-to-value ratio. The ratio of a loan amount to the value of the asset being purchased with money from the loan.

long wave theory. The theory that economies undergo long-term fluctuations in the rate of growth.

M

macroeconomics. The study of the behavior of the economy as a whole.

marginal utility. The amount of satisfaction received from consuming an additional unit of a good or service.

mark to market. Pricing an asset at its current market value.

market correction. A drop in the value of a traded asset or security or of an index when investors decide it has been overvalued.

market reform. The introduction of market forces into an economy.

maturity. In economics, the length of time between a security's issuance and the date on which it can be redeemed at face value.

MBS. *See* mortgage-backed security.

mercantilism. An archaic economic theory based on the idea that national prosperity results from a positive balance of payments.

merger. The fusion of two or more companies.

microeconomics. The study of the behavior of individual units such as firms and households within an economy.

mixed economy. An economy dominated by private enterprise but where the government exerts significant influence on and control of economic activity.

monetary policy. The activities of a central bank in determining the money supply, interest rates, and credit conditions in order to affect the overall level of economic activity and prices.

monetary stability. A goal of monetary policy, in which the value of a currency remains relatively stable over time.

money illusion. The process by which individuals mistake the nominal value of money for the real value of money.

money market. Financial market for short-term financial instruments; that is, those with an original maturity of one year or less.

money supply. Narrowly defined as M1 (the amount of currency in circulation plus the amount of checkable deposits) or M2 (broadly defined as M1 plus liquid assets and quasi monies, such as savings deposits, money market funds, and so on).

monoline institution. An institution specializing in one form of financing.

monopoly. A market in which there is only one seller.

monopsony. A market in which there is only one buyer.

moral hazard. A situation that leads individual investors or firms to take excessive risks because they believe that possible losses will be absorbed in part or in full by others, particularly by government or insurance companies.

mortgage. A loan taken out for the purchase of property, which is secured by the property.

mortgage-backed security. A security that is collateralized by a pool of mortgages.

multiplier mechanism. The process by which changes in investment or government spending trigger successive rounds of spending that lead to subsequent and expanding changes in income and output.

mutual company. A company owned by its customers.

mutual fund. An open-ended investment trust that pools investors' capital to buy a portfolio of securities.

N

nationalization. The process by which privately owned companies are acquired by the government of the country where they are located, with or without compensation.

natural rate of unemployment. The unemployment level associated with an economy utilizing all of its productive resources.

neutrality of money. An economic concept that states that changes in the money supply only affect prices in an economy and not the output of goods and services.

NINA. Abbreviation for "no income, no assets"; a mortgage obtained by a borrower who does not have to document income or assets.

NINJA. Abbreviation for "no income, no job or assets"; a mortgage obtained by a borrower who does not have to document income, assets, or employment.

nominal value. Non-inflation-adjusted value, also known as face value.

nonperforming loan. A loan in which neither the interest is being paid nor the principal is being paid down.

O

oligopoly. A market in which there are only a few sellers or where a few sellers dominate.

opportunity cost. The value that a person or firm places on a commodity or investment compared with the value that a person or firm places on alternative commodities or investments that are declined because the one chosen is expected to result in greater satisfaction or higher returns.

option. An agreement giving an investor the right—as opposed to the obligation—to buy a financial asset or commodity at a given point in the future at a price determined today.

overinvestment. A situation in which businesses increase the level of investment beyond the equilibrium level of aggregate investment in an economy.

overproduction. Excessive production that causes a lowering of profits and a slowing or contraction of the economy.

oversavings. A situation in which households are saving so much of their income that it lowers aggregate demand.

over-the-counter. Referring to the trade of a security directly between buyer and seller, outside an established stock or other exchange.

overvaluation. A situation in which an asset's price exceeds its intrinsic value.

P

Phillips curve. That element of an economics graph that shows the trade-off between employment and inflation, indicating that when unemployment goes down, wage inflation goes up.

political cycle. In economics, a business cycle that is determined by political events.

Ponzi scheme. An illegal financial arrangement in which current investors are paid profits or interest out of the capital invested by new investors.

portfolio investment. The purchase by foreigners of stocks, bonds, and other financial instruments of a given country, which does not result in foreign management, ownership, or control.

poverty level. An official level of income below which individuals or households cannot afford the basic necessities of life as defined by a given society.

preferred stock. Stock whose holders have priority in the payment of a fixed dividend if the corporation earns a profit.

price equilibrium. The point where quantity demanded and quantity supplied meet, determining the price and quantity of a given good or service.

price stability. A situation in which prices remain relatively unchanged over a given period of time.

principal. The amount of money borrowed.

private placement. A stock or bond issue offered directly to investors.

privatization. The process by which government-owned assets and firms are sold off to private investors.

production. The process whereby economic inputs are turned into economic outputs.

production cycle. The period of time required by a firm to provide a good or service and receive compensation for that good or service.

productivity. The ratio of output to input, usually used in reference to labor.

profit. Total revenue minus total costs.

public debt. The amount owed by a government to bondholders.

public goods. Goods that provide benefits to large sectors of society or society as a whole that cannot be profitably created in optimum amounts by private industry.

public works. The creation of public goods by the government.

publicly traded company. A company that has received legal permission to sell its shares to the public.

purchasing power parity. A comparison showing how much a given amount of money buys in various national economies.

pyramid scheme. *See* Ponzi scheme.

Q

quant. Slang term for a person who uses training in the hard sciences or mathematics to calculate risk, uncertainty, and other financial investment variables.

quantitative analysis. The use of mathematics to determine investment strategy in securities.

R

random walk. The process by which the price of an

asset varies in unpredictable ways as a result of new information about the value of that asset.

real business cycle. Fluctuations in economic activity triggered by changes in technology.

real economy. The nonfinancial sector of the economy, where real goods and services are produced and sold.

real-estate investment trust (REIT). An open-ended investment trust that pools investors' capital to buy a portfolio of real-estate properties.

real value. Inflation-adjusted value.

recession. A period of economic contraction, usually lasting two successive quarters or longer.

redlining. The process, usually illegal, in which banks refuse to offer loans or offer them at higher interest rates to minority or low-income neighborhoods.

refinancing. Borrowing money to pay back a loan, usually on different terms.

REIT. *See* real-estate investment trust.

resource allocation. The means by which a society distributes its factors of production.

retirement instrument. A tax-deferred private financial instrument or plan that provides income for an individual once he or she retires from work or is rendered disabled.

revenue. Income derived from the normal operations of a business; also, the funds obtained by a government through taxes, fees, and other means.

reverse mortgage. A type of mortgage designed for senior citizens who want to convert the equity in their homes to monthly cash payments from a lender.

risk. In economics, the possibility that an investment will experience a loss or a less-than-expected return in the future.

risk-based pricing. Determining loan terms using the credit history of the borrower.

S

S&L. *See* savings and loan bank.

savings. Income not spent on consumption.

savings and loan bank (S&L). A bank that accepts savings deposits and primarily makes mortgage loans.

seasonal cycle. A business cycle determined by weather or other seasonal variables.

secured loan. A loan secured by assets.

securitization. The process by which various types of loans are bundled and sold to investors as securities.

security. An investment instrument issued by a government, corporation, or other organization.

share. A share of ownership in a company that entitles the owner to receive a share of profits.

shock. In economics, an exogenous event that has a dramatic effect on the performance of an economy or disturbs an economic equilibrium.

short sale. The sale of the collateral used to obtain a loan, usually a home, for less than the value of the loan; a short sale allows a mortgagor to avoid foreclosure.

short-selling (also known as "shorting"). Borrowing financial securities and selling them in anticipation of a drop in the price of the securities. In such a case a profit can be made by repaying the loan of the securities with the securities purchased at a price lower than the price at which the short seller originally borrowed the securities.

sinusoidal. In economic terms, wavelike deviations from long-term trends.

social responsibility. A belief that economic agents, including businesses, should look beyond profits and act in ways that enhance social goals.

sovereign default. The failure of a government to make timely payments on the principal or interest of a loan or bond.

sovereign risk. The degree to which investors feel that a nation will be unable to meet the financial obligations of its sovereign debt.

special-purpose vehicle. A limited liability company or other legal entity created for a specific economic activity.

speculation. Based on the prediction of future performance, the act of making an investment in the hope of receiving large rewards.

speculative-grade bond. *See* junk bond.

spillover effect. Also known as externalities. Positive or negative external effects created by the activities of firms or individuals.

stabilization policies. Efforts by a government to achieve economic stability in the wake of endogenous or exogenous shocks.

stagflation. An economic phenomenon in which inflation coincides with slow or negative growth in the economy.

sticky. In economics, the inability or unwillingness of workers, employers, and consumers to respond to market forces when setting or accepting wages and prices.

stimulus. Government spending or tax reductions designed to revive or spur demand.

stochastic model. A business-cycle model that takes into account random, unexpected shocks.

stock. An ownership share in a company.

stock exchange. A real (physical location) or virtual (electronic) auction market for the buying and selling of stocks.

stock market. A market for buying and selling stocks, whether in a physical stock exchange, through a network of dealers, or more recently, electronically over the Internet.

stock market crash. The sudden collapse in the valuation of a broad array of stocks on a given exchange.

structured investment vehicle (SIV). An arrangement in which an investment firm borrows money by selling short-term securities at low interest rates and then buys long-term securities that pay higher interest rates, making a profit for the investment firm.

stylized fact. In economics, the simplified presentation of empirical data.

subprime mortgage. A mortgage loan requiring little or no down payment made to a borrower with a poor credit history, usually at a teaser (low) interest rate that is adjusted sharply upward after a few years.

subsidiary. A company in which controlling interest is held by another company.

subsidy. A government payment to firms or households for the purposes of lowering the cost of production or encouraging the consumption of goods.

sunspot theory. The theory that extrinsic random variables (variables outside the system, such as sunspots) affect economic activity.

surplus. In finance, the gap by which income exceeds expenditure.

surplus value. The value created by the production of goods by workers that is not returned to workers as compensation.

synthetic CDO. A complex financial derivative in which the underlying assets of the collateralized debt obligation (CDO) are not owned by the creator (such as an investment firm); a synthetic CDO "references" a group of assets.

systemic financial crisis. A crisis that affects a broad sector of a national financial system or of the international financial system as a whole.

T

tariff. A tax on imported goods.

tax. A levy charged by government on products, activities, assets, or income for the purposes of raising revenues for the government and influencing economic and social behavior.

T-bill. *See* treasury bill.

thrift. *See* savings and loan bank.

tiger. Slang for a fast-growing economy in the developing world.

too big to fail. An expression for a firm whose financial collapse would so destabilize financial markets that the government becomes obligated to ensure its solvency.

toxic asset. Slang for an asset of questionable value whose presence on a firm's balance sheet leads others to question the solvency of that firm.

trade cycle. *See* business cycle.

tranche. A portion or allocation of the returns on an investment, often based on risk.

transition economy. A national economy undergoing transition from a command-style economy to a free-market economy.

transparency. In business, the act of opening up the operations of a firm to the public to ensure that the firm is operating in a fair and legal manner.

treasury bill. A government debt security with a maturity date of one year or less.

treasury bond. A government debt security with a maturity date of at least ten years in the future.

troubled asset. *See* toxic asset.

trust. In economic history, a combination of companies under one board of directors created for the purpose of controlling an industry and dictating prices to consumers.

U

uncertainty. In economics, the possibility of profit or loss on an investment in the future.

underconsumption. A lack of consumer demand that causes a slowing or contraction of the economy.

undervaluation. A situation in which an asset's intrinsic value exceeds its price.

underwater mortgage. Slang for a mortgage with a face value that is greater than the value of the house it has financed.

underwriting. A form of insurance in which an individual or institution agrees to take a fee for guaranteeing the purchase of a specific quantity of a new security issue should public demand be insufficient.

unemployment. The state of being available—and looking—for work but unable to find it.

unsecured loan. A loan whose repayment is not secured by real or financial assets.

upside-down mortgage. *See* underwater mortgage.

V

velocity. In economics, the speed at which money circulates in an economy.

venture capital. Private equity financial capital directly invested in the early stages of a new firm with high growth or profit potential.

volume-weighted average price. The ratio of the combined value of all stocks traded (price of each stock times the number of shares traded) over the course of a trading session divided by the total number of shares traded.

W

wages. Money received by labor for work performed or service rendered.

wealth. The amount of tangible and financial assets, minus financial liabilities, owned by an individual, household, firm, or nation.

windfall profit. Large, sudden, and/or unexpected profit.

Selected Bibliography

The following is a selective list of books and Web sites covering a range of topics pertaining to booms, busts, and economic cycles. Please see the Further Reading list accompanying each article for additional sources on specific subjects and people.

Books

Abelshauser, Werner. *The Dynamics of German Industry: Germany's Path Towards the New Economy and the American* Challenge. Oxford, UK: Berghahn, 2005.

Acharya, Viral, and Matthew Richardson, eds. *Restoring Financial Stability: How to Repair a Failed System.* Hoboken, NJ: John Wiley & Sons, 2009.

Acosto, Jarod R., ed. *Assessing Treasury's Strategy: Six Months of TARP.* Hauppauge, NY: Nova Science, 2009.

Agarwal, Monty. *The Future of Hedge Fund Investing: A Regulatory and Structural Solution for a Fallen Industry.* Hoboken, NJ: John Wiley & Sons, 2009.

Aghion, Philippe, and Peter Howitt. *Endogenous Growth Theory.* Cambridge, MA: MIT Press, 1998.

Ahamed, Liaquat. *Lords of Finance: The Bankers Who Broke the World.* New York: Penguin, 2009.

Akerlof, George A., and Robert J. Shiller. *Animal Spirits: How Human Psychology Drives the Economy, and Why It Matters for Global Capitalism.* Princeton, NJ: Princeton University Press, 2009.

Akerman, Johan. *Economic Progress and Economic Crises.* Philadelphia: Porcupine, 1979.

———. *Theory of Industrialism: Causal Analysis and Economic Plans.* Philadelphia: Porcupine, 1980.

Albrecht, William P. *Economics.* Englewood Cliffs, NJ: Prentice-Hall, 1983.

Aldcroft, Derek H. The European Economy, *1914–2000.* London: Routledge, 2001.

Alexander, Kern, Rahul Dhumale, and John Eatwell. *Global Governance of Financial Systems: The International Regulation of Systemic Risk.* New York: Oxford University Press, 2006.

Alexander, Nicholas. *International Retailing.* New York: Oxford University Press, 2009.

Alford, B.W.E. *Britain in the World Economy Since 1880.* New York: Longman, 1996.

Aligica, Paul Dragos, and Anthony J. Evans. *The Neoliberal Revolution in Eastern Europe: Economic Ideas in the Transition from Communism.* New York: Edward Elgar, 2009.

Allen, Franklin, and Douglas Gale. *Financial Innovation and Risk Sharing.* Cambridge, MA: MIT Press, 1994.

———. *Understanding Financial Crises.* New York: Oxford University Press, 2009.

Allen, Robert Loring. Opening Doors: The Life and Work of Joseph Schumpeter. 2 vols. New Brunswick, NJ: Transaction, 1991.

Altman, Morris. *Handbook of Contemporary Behavioral Economics: Foundations and Developments.* Armonk, NY: M.E. Sharpe, 2006.

Altucher, James. *SuperCash: The New Hedge Fund Capitalism.* Hoboken, NJ: John Wiley & Sons, 2006.

Al-Yahya, Mohammed A. *Kuwait: Fall and Rebirth.* New York: Kegan Paul International, 1993.

Ammer, Christine, and Dean Ammer. *Dictionary of Business and Economics.* New York: Free Press, 1977.

Anderson, Kym. *Distortions to Agricultural Incentives: A Global Perspective, 1955–2007.* New York: Palgrave Macmillan, 2009.

Antczak, Stephen, Douglas Lucas, and Frank Fabozzi. *Leveraged Finance: Concepts, Methods, and Trading of High-Yield Bonds, Loans, and Derivatives.* Hoboken, NJ: John Wiley & Sons, 2009.

Ardagh, John. *France in the New Century: Portrait of a Changing Society.* London: Penguin, 2000.

Ariff, Mohamed, and Ahmed M. Khalid. *Liberalization, Growth and the Asian Financial Crisis: Lessons for Developing and Transitional Economies in Asia.* Northampton, MA: Edward Elgar, 2000.

Arndt, H.W., and Hal Hill, eds. *Southeast Asia's Economic Crisis: Origins, Lessons and the Way Forward.* St. Leonards, Australia: Allen and Unwin, 1999.

Arnold, Lutz G. *Business Cycle Theory.* New York: Oxford University Press, 2002.

Aron, Janine, Brian Kahn, and Geeta Kingdon, eds. *South African Economic Policy Under Democracy.* New York: Oxford University Press, 2009.

Aronowitz, Stanley. *Just Around the Corner: The Paradox of the Jobless Recovery.* Philadelphia: Temple University Press, 2005.

Arvedlund, Erin. *Too Good to Be True: The Rise and Fall of Bernie Madoff.* New York: Portfolio, 2009.

Asimakopulos, A. *Investment, Employment and Income Distribution.* Boulder, CO: Westview, 1988.

Aspray, William. *John von Neumann and the Origins of Modern Computing.* Cambridge, MA: MIT Press, 1990.

Auletta, Ken. *Greed and Glory on Wall Street: The Fall of the House of Lehman.* New York: Random House, 1986.

Aydin, Zulkuf. *The Political Economy of Turkey.* Ann Arbor, MI: Pluto, 2005.

Badger, Anthony J. *The New Deal: The Depression Years, 1933–1940.* Chicago: Ivan R. Dee, 2002.

Baer, Werner. *The Brazilian Economy: Growth and Development.* 4th ed. Westport, CT: Praeger, 1995.

Balen, Malcolm. *The King, the Crook, and the Gambler: The True Story of the South Sea Bubble and the Greatest Financial Scandal in History.* New York: Fourth Estate, 2004.

Bamber, Bill, and Andrew Spencer. *Bear-Trap: The Fall of Bear Stearns and the Panic of 2008.* New York: Brick Tower, 2008.

Banks, Erik. *Risk and Financial Catastrophe.* New York: Palgrave Macmillan, 2009.

Barber, William J. *Designs Within Disorder: Franklin Roosevelt, the Economists, and the Shaping of American Economic Policy, 1933–1945.* New York: Cambridge University Press, 1996.

Barlett, Bruce R. *The New American Economy: The Failure of Reaganomics and a New Way Forward.* New York: Palgrave Macmillan, 2009.

Barnett, Vincent L. *Kondratiev and the Dynamics of Economic Development: Long Cycles and Industrial Growth in Historical Context.* New York: St. Martin's, 1998.

Barth, James. *The Rise and Fall of the U.S. Mortgage and Credit Markets: A Comprehensive Analysis of the Market Meltdown.* Hoboken, NJ: John Wiley & Sons, 2009.

Baskin, Jonathan Barron. *A History of Corporate Finance.* New York: Cambridge University Press, 1997.

Bauer, Hans, and Warren J. Blackman. *Swiss Banking: An Analytical History.* New York: St. Martin's, 1998.

Beatty, Jack, ed. *Colossus: How the Corporation Changed America.* New York: Broadway, 2001.

Bellofiore, Riccardo, and Piero Ferri. *The Economic Legacy of Hyman Minsky. Vol. 1, Financial Keynesianism and Market Instability.* Northampton, MA: Edward Elgar, 2001.

———. *The Economic Legacy of Hyman Minsky. Vol. 2, Financial Fragility and Investment in the Capitalist Economy.* Northampton, MA: Edward Elgar, 2001.

Belobaba, Peter, Amedeo Odoni, and Cynthia Barnhart. *The Global Airline Industry.* Chichester, UK: John Wiley & Sons, 2009.

Ben-Bassat, Avi, ed. *The Israeli Economy, 1985–1998: From Government Intervention to Market Economics.* Cambridge, MA: MIT Press, 2002.

Benston, George J. *The Separation of Commercial and Investment Banking: The Glass Steagall Act Revisited and Reconsidered.* New York: Oxford University Press, 1999.

Bergsman, Steve. *Maverick Real Estate Financing.* Hoboken, NJ: John Wiley & Sons, 2006.

Berlin, Isaiah. *Karl Marx: His Life and Environment.* Oxford, UK: Oxford University Press, 1978.

Bernanke, Ben. *Essays on the Great Depression.* Princeton, NJ: Princeton University Press, 2000.

Bernstein, Irving. *The Lean Years: A History of the American Worker, 1920–1933.* Boston: Houghton Mifflin, 1960.

Bernstein, Michael A. *The Great Depression: Delayed Recovery and Economic Change in America, 1929–1939.* Cambridge, UK: Cambridge University Press, 1989.

Bernstein, Peter L. *A Primer on Money, Banking, and Gold.* Hoboken, NJ: John Wiley & Sons, 2008.

Blanchard, Olivier. *Macroeconomics.* 5th ed. Upper Saddle River NJ: Prentice Hall, 2009.

Blaug, Mark. *Economic Theory in Retrospect.* London: Cambridge University Press, 1978.

———. *Great Economists Before Keynes. An Introduction to the Lives and Works of One Hundred Great Economists of the Past.* Atlantic Highlands, NJ: Humanities, 1986.

Bodie, Z., A. Kane, and A. Marcus. *Essentials of Investments.* Boston: McGraw-Hill/Irwin, 2008.

Bonner, William, and Addison Wiggin. *Empire of Debt: The Rise and Fall of an Epic Financial Crisis.* Hoboken, NJ: John Wiley & Sons, 2006.

Bookstaber, Richard. *A Demon of Our Own Design: Markets, Hedge Funds, and the Perils of Financial Innovation.* Hoboken, NJ: John Wiley & Sons, 2007.

Borcherding, Thomas E., ed. *Budgets and Bureaucrats: The Sources of Government Growth.* Durham, NC: Duke University Press, 1977.

Borjas, George. *Heaven's Door: Immigration Policy and the*

American Economy. Princeton, NJ: Princeton University Press, 1999.

Borthwick, Mark. *Pacific Century: The Emergence of Modern Pacific Asia.* 3rd ed. Boulder, CO: Westview, 2007.

Boughton, James M., and Domenico Lombardi, eds. *Finance, Development, and the IMF.* New York: Oxford University Press, 2009.

Boyes, Roger. *Meltdown Iceland: How the Global Financial Crisis Bankupted an Entire Country.* New York: Bloomsbury, 2009.

Braun, Hans-Joachim. *The German Economy in the Twentieth Century: The German Reich and the Federal Republic.* New York: Routledge, 1990.

Bresnan, John, ed. *Crisis in the Philippines: The Marcos Era and Beyond.* Princeton, NJ: Princeton University Press, 1986.

Bret, Benjamin. *Invested Interests: Capital, Culture, and the World Bank.* Minneapolis: University of Minnesota Press, 2007.

Brian, Harvey W., and Deborah L. Parry. *The Law of Consumer Protection and Fair Trading.* London: Butterworths, 2000.

Brigham, Eugene F., and Michael C. Ehrhardt. *Financial Management: Theory and Practice.* Mason, OH: South-Western, 2008.

Bronner, Stephen Eric. *Rosa Luxemburg: A Revolutionary for Our Times.* University Park: Pennsylvania State University Press, 1997.

Brown, Lester R., Gary Gardner, and Brian Halweil. *Beyond Malthus: Sixteen Dimensions of the Population Problem.* Washington, DC: Worldwatch Institute, 1998.

Brownlee, W. Elliot. *Federal Taxation in America: A Short History.* 2nd ed. New York: Cambridge University Press, 2004.

Bruner, Robert F., and Sean D. Carr. *The Panic of 1907: Lessons Learned from the Market's Perfect Storm.* New York: John Wiley & Sons, 2009.

Brunner, Karl. *Money and the Economy: Issues in Monetary Analysis.* New York: Cambridge University Press, 1993.

Bullock, Charles Jesse. *Economic Essays.* Freeport, NY: Books for Libraries Press, 1968 (reprint ed.).

———. *Essays on the Monetary History of the United States.* New York: Greenwood, 1969 (reprint ed.).

Burchardt, F.A., et al. *The Economics of Full Employment: Six Studies in Applied Economics.* Oxford, UK: Basil Blackwell, 1944.

Burdekin, Richard C.K., and Pierre L. Siklos, eds. *Deflation: Current and Historical Perspectives.* New York: Cambridge University Press, 2004.

Burns, Arthur F. *Wesley Clair Mitchell: The Economic Scientist.* New York: National Bureau of Economic Research, 1952.

Burns, Arthur F., and Wesley C. Mitchell. *Measuring Business Cycles.* New York: National Bureau of Economic Research, 1946.

Burton, Dawn. *Credit and Consumer Society.* New York: Routledge, 2007.

Burton, Katherine. *Hedge Hunters: How Hedge Fund Masters Survived.* New York: Bloomberg, 2010.

Burton, Maureen, and Bruce Brown. *The Financial System and the Economy.* 5th ed. Armonk, NY: M.E. Sharpe, 2009.

Burton, Maureen, Reynold Nesiba, and Bruce Brown. *An Introduction to Financial Markets and Institutions.* 2nd ed. Armonk, NY: M.E. Sharpe, 2010.

Butler, Eamonn. *Milton Friedman: A Guide to His Economic Thought.* New York: Universe, 1985.

Buzo, Adrian. *The Making of Modern Korea.* New York: Routledge, 2007.

Bye, Raymond T. *An Appraisal of Frederick C. Mills' The Behavior of Prices.* New York: Social Science Research Council, 1940.

Calder, Lendol. *Financing the American Dream: A Cultural History of Consumer Debt.* Princeton, NJ: Princeton University Press, 1999.

Caldwell, Bruce. *Hayek's Challenge: An Intellectual Biography of F.A. Hayek.* Chicago: University of Chicago Press, 2004.

Calit, Harry S., ed. *The Philippines: Current Issues and Historical Background.* New York: Nova, 2003.

Callaghan, Paul T. *Wool to Weta: Transforming New Zealand's Culture and Economy.* Auckland, NZ: Auckland University Press, 2009.

Carlson, Mark. *A Brief History of the 1987 Stock Market Crash with a Discussion of the Federal Reserve Response.* Washington, DC: Board of Governors of the Federal Reserve, 2006.

Cassidy, John. *Dot.con: The Greatest Story Ever Sold.* New York: HarperCollins, 2002.

Cate, Thomas, ed. *An Encyclopedia of Keynesian Economics.* Cheltenham, UK: Edward Elgar, 1997.

Cecchetti, Stephen G. *Money, Banking and Financial Markets.* Boston: McGraw-Hill/Irwin, 2006.

Center for Economic and Policy Research. *Slow-Motion Recession.* Washington, DC: CEPR, 2008.

Cento, Alessandro. *The Airline Industry: Challenges in the 21st Century.* New York: Springer Heidelberg, 2008.

Chancellor, Edward. *Devil Take the Hindmost: A History of Financial Speculation.* New York: Farrar, Straus and Giroux, 1999.

Chapman, Stanley. *Merchant Enterprise in Britain: From the Industrial Revolution to World War I.* New York: Cambridge University Press, 1992.

Chernow, Ron. *The Death of the Banker: The Decline and Fall of the Great Financial Dynasties and the Triumph of the Small Investor.* New York: Vintage, 1997.

———. *The House of Morgan: An American Banking Dynasty and the Rise of Modern Finance.* New York: Simon & Schuster, 2010.

Chipman, John S. *The Theory of International Trade.* Cheltenham, UK: Edward Elgar, 2008.

Chorafas, Dimitris N. *Financial Boom and Gloom: The Credit and Banking Crisis of 2007–2009 and Beyond.* New York: Palgrave Macmillan, 2009.

Clapham, Sir John. *The Bank of England: A History.* London: Cambridge University Press, 1970.

Clark, John Bates. *The Distribution of Wealth: A Theory of Wages, Interest, and Profits.* New York: Cosimo Classics, 2005.

Clarke, Peter. *The Keynesian Revolution and Its Economic Consequences.* Cheltenham, UK: Edward Elgar, 1998.

———. *The Keynesian Revolution in the Making, 1924–1936.* New York: Oxford University Press, 1988.

Clauretie, Terrence M., and G. Stacy Sirmans. *Real Estate Finance: Theory and Practice.* Mason, OH: Cengage Learning, 2010.

Coatsworth, John H., and Alan M. Taylor. *Latin America and the World Economy Since 1800.* Cambridge, MA: Harvard University, 1998.

Cohan, William D. *House of Cards: A Tale of Hubris and Wretched Excess on Wall Street.* New York: Doubleday, 2009.

Colander, David C., and Harry Landreth. *History of Economic Thought.* 4th ed. Boston: Houghton Mifflin, 2002.

Collins, Robert M. *More: The Politics of Economic Growth in Postwar America.* New York: Oxford University Press, 2000.

Commons, John R. *Institutional Economics: Its Place in Political Economy.* New York: Macmillan, 1934.

Cooper, George. *The Origin of Financial Crises: Central Banks, Credit Bubbles and the Efficient Market Fallacy.* New York: Vintage, 2008.

Corkill, David. *The Portuguese Economy Since 1974.* Edinburgh, UK: Edinburgh University Press, 1993.

Cottrell, Allin F., Michael S. Lawlor, and John H. Wood, eds. *The Causes and Costs of Depository Institution Failures.* New York: Springer, 1995.

Cukierman, Alex. *Central Bank Strategy, Credibility, and Independence: Theory and Evidence.* Cambridge, MA: MIT Press, 1992.

Cumings, Bruce. *Korea's Place in the Sun: A Modern History.* New York: W.W. Norton, 2005.

Dale, Richard. *The First Crash: Lessons from the South Sea Bubble.* Princeton, NJ: Princeton University Press, 2004.

Dash, Mike. *Tulipomania: The Story of the World's Most Coveted Flower and the Extraordinary Passions It Aroused.* New York: Crown, 1999.

Davidson, Paul. *The Keynes Solution: The Path to Global Economic Prosperity.* New York: Palgrave Macmillan, 2009.

Dawiche, Fida. *The Gulf Stock Exchange Crash: The Rise and Fall of the Souq Al-Manakh.* Dover, NH: Croom Helm, 1986.

De Goede, Marieke. *Virtue, Fortune and Faith: A Genealogy of Finance.* Minneapolis: University of Minnesota Press, 2005.

Deacon, John. *Global Securitisation and CDOs.* Chichester, UK: John Wiley & Sons, 2004.

Dellheim, Charles. *The Disenchanted Isle: Mrs. Thatcher's Capitalist Revolution.* New York: W.W. Norton, 1995.

Demeny, Paul, and Geoffrey McNicoll. *The Political Economy of Global Population Change, 1950–2050.* New York: Population Council, 2006.

Desruelle, Dominique, and Alfred Schipke, eds. *Economic Growth and Integration in Central America.* Washington, DC: International Monetary Fund, 2007.

Dimand, Robert W., and John Geanakopolos, eds. *Celebrating Irving Fisher: The Legacy of a Great Economist.* Oxford, UK: Blackwell, 2005.

Dimitrakopoulos, Dionyssis G., and Argyris G. Passas. *Greece in the European Union.* New York: Routledge, 2004.

Doganis, Rigas. *The Airline Business.* New York: Routledge, 2005.

Dore, Mohammed, Sukhamoy Chakravarty, and Richard Goodwin, eds. *John von Neumann and Modern Economics.* Oxford, UK: Oxford University Press, 1989.

Dorfman, Joseph. *Thorstein Veblen and His America.* New York: A.M. Kelley, 1972.

Dormois, Jean-Pierre. *The French Economy in the Twentieth Century.* New York: Cambridge University Press, 2004.

Dowd, Douglas. *U.S. Capitalist Development Since 1776: Of, By, and For Which People?* Armonk, NY: M.E. Sharpe, 1993.

Downs, Anthony. *Real Estate and the Financial Crisis: How Turmoil in the Capital Markets Is Restructuring Real Estate Finance.* Washington, DC: Urban Land Institute, 2009.

Drucker, Peter. *What Business Can Learn from Nonprofits.* Boston: Harvard Business Review, 1989.

Duesenberry, James S. *Income, Saving, and the Theory of Consumer Behavior.* Cambridge, MA: Harvard University Press, 1962.

Dunn, Donald. *Ponzi: The Incredible True Story of the King of Financial Cons.* New York: Broadway, 2004.

Durlauf, Steven N., and Lawrence E. Blume. *Behavioural and Experimental Economics.* Hampshire, UK: Palgrave Macmillan, 2010.

Dutzler, Barbara. *The European System of Central Banks:*

An Autonomous Actor? The Quest for an Institutional Balance in EMU. New York: Springer, 2003.

Dymski, Gary, and Robert Pollin, eds. *Monetary Macroeconomics: Explorations in the Tradition of Hyman P. Minsky.* Ann Arbor: University of Michigan Press, 1994.

Eastman, Lloyd. *Family, Fields, and Ancestors: Constancy and Change in China's Social and Economic History.* New York: Oxford University Press, 1988.

Ebenstein, Lanny. *Milton Friedman: A Biography.* New York: Palgrave Macmillan, 2007.

Eckstein, Otto. *The Great Recession.* Amsterdam, NY: North-Holland, 1978.

Economic Commission for Latin America and the Caribbean. *Economic Survey of Latin America and the Caribbean: 2008–2009.* Santiago: ECLAC, 2009.

Economist Intelligence Unit (EIU). *Country Report—Denmark.* London: EIU, 2009.

———. *Country Report—Finland.* London: EIU, 2009.

———. *Country Report—Norway.* London: EIU, 2009.

———. *Country Report—Sweden* London: EIU, 2009.

Edwards, George. *The Evolution of Finance Capitalism.* New York: Augustus M. Kelley, 1938. Reprint, 1967.

Edwards, John. *Australia's Economic Revolution.* Sydney: University of New South Wales Press, 2000.

Eichengreen, Barry. *The European Economy Since 1945.* Princeton, NJ: Princeton University Press, 2007.

———. *Golden Fetters: The Gold Standard and the Great Depression, 1919–1939.* New York: Oxford University Press, 1992.

Elias, Victor J. *Sources of Growth: A Study of Seven Latin American Economies.* San Francisco: ICS Press, 1989.

Elliott, Douglas J. *Measuring the Cost of TARP.* Washington, DC: Brookings Initiative on Business and Public Policy Fixing Finance Series, January 2009.

Elliott, Larry. *The Gods That Failed: How Blind Faith in Markets Has Cost Us Our Future.* New York: Nation, 2009.

Ellis, Charles D. *The Partnership: The Making of Goldman Sachs.* New York: Penguin, 2008.

Enderwick, Peter. *Understanding Emerging Markets: China and India.* New York: Routledge, 2007.

Endlich, Lisa. *Goldman Sachs: The Culture of Success.* New York: A.A. Knopf, 1999.

Fabozzi, Frank J., ed. *Accessing Capital Markets Through Securitization.* Hoboken, NJ: John Wiley & Sons, 2001.

———. *The Handbook of Mortgage-Backed Securities.* New York: McGraw-Hill, 2006.

Fabozzi, Frank J., and Vinod Kothari. *Introduction to Securitization.* Hoboken, NJ: John Wiley & Sons, 2008.

Fabozzi, Frank J., and Franco Modigliani. *Capital Markets: Institutions and Instruments.* 4th ed. Upper Saddle River, NJ: Prentice Hall, 2008.

Fabozzi, Frank J., Franco Modigliani, and Frank J. Jones. *Foundations of Financial Markets and Institutions.* 4th ed. Upper Saddle River, NJ: Prentice Hall, 2009.

Farber, David. *Sloan Rules: Alfred P. Sloan and the Triumph of General Motors.* Chicago: University of Chicago Press, 2002.

Feinstein, Charles H. *An Economic History of South Africa: Conquest, Discrimination, and Development.* New York: Cambridge University Press, 2005.

Feinstein, Charles H., Peter Temin, and Gianni Toniolo. *The European Economy Between the Wars.* Oxford, UK: Oxford University Press, 1997.

Feiwel, George R., ed. *Joan Robinson and Modern Economic Theory.* Hampshire, UK: Macmillan, 1989.

Feldman, David Lewis, ed. *The Energy Crisis: Unresolved Issues and Enduring Legacies.* Baltimore, MD: Johns Hopkins University Press, 1996.

Felix, David. *Biography of an Idea: John Maynard Keynes and the General Theory of Employment, Interest and Money.* New Brunswick, NJ: Transaction, 1995.

———. *Keynes: A Critical Life.* Westport, CT: Greenwood, 1999.

Fellner, William J. *Competition Among the Few: Oligopoly and Similar Market Structures.* New York: Alfred A. Knopf, 1949.

———. *Towards a Reconstruction of Macroeconomics: Problems of Theory and Policy.* Washington, DC: American Enterprise Institute for Public Policy Research, 1976.

Fenton-O'Creevy, Mark, Nigel Nicholson, Emma Soane, and Paul Willman. *Traders: Risks, Decisions, and Management in Financial Markets.* Oxford, UK: Oxford University Press, 2005.

Ferguson, Niall. *The Ascent of Money: A Financial History of the World.* New York: Penguin, 2008.

Feser, Edward. *The Cambridge Companion to Hayek.* New York: Cambridge University Press, 2006.

Fisher, Irving. *Booms and Depressions: Some First Principles.* New York: Adelphi, 1932.

Fiske, Frank S., ed. *The Mississippi Bubble: A Memoir of John Law; to Which Are Added Authentic Accounts of the Darien Expedition, and the South Sea Scheme.* New York: Greenwood, 1969.

Flaschel, Peter, and Michael Landesmann, eds. *Mathematical Economics and the Dynamics of Capitalism: Research in Honor of Richard M. Goodwin.* New York: Routledge, 2008.

Fleckenstein, William A., and Frederick Sheehan. *Greenspan's Bubbles: The Age of Ignorance at the Federal Reserve.* New York: McGraw-Hill, 2008.

Fletcher, Gordon. *Dennis Robertson.* Basingstoke, UK: Palgrave Macmillan, 2008.

Ford, J.L. *G.L.S. Shackle: The Dissenting Economist's Economist.* Northampton, MA: Edward Elgar, 1994.

Foster, John B., and Fred Magdoff. *The Great Financial Crisis: Causes and Consequences.* New York: Monthly Review, 2009.

Foster, Richard, and Sarah Kaplan. *Creative Destruction: Turning Built-to-Last into Built-to-Perform.* New York: Currency, 2001.

Fox, Justin. *The Myth of the Rational Market: A History of Risk, Reward, and Delusion on Wall Street.* New York: HarperBusiness, 2009.

Fox, Loren. *Enron: The Rise and Fall.* Hoboken, NJ: John Wiley & Sons, 2003.

Frank, Robert H. *Falling Behind: How Rising Inequality Harms the Middle Class.* Berkeley: University of California Press, 2007.

Freeman, Christopher, and Francisco Louçã. *As Time Goes By: From the Industrial Revolutions to the Information Revolution.* New York: Oxford University Press, 2001.

Freeman, Richard B. *America Works: Critical Thoughts on the Exceptional U.S. Labor Market.* New York: Russell Sage Foundation, 2007.

Freidman, Benjamin. *Day of Reckoning: The Consequences of American Economic Policy Under Reagan and After.* New York: Random House, 1988.

Friedman, Milton. *A Theory of the Consumption Function.* Princeton, NJ: Princeton University Press, 1957.

Friedman, Milton, and Anna Jacobson Schwartz. *The Great Contraction, 1929–1933.* Princeton, NJ: Princeton University Press, 2009.

———. *A Monetary History of the United States, 1867–1960.* Princeton, NJ: Princeton University Press, 1963.

Friedman, Walter A. *The Seer of Wellesley Hills: Roger Babson and the Babson Statistical Organization.* Boston: Harvard Business School, 2008.

Frisch, Helmut: *Theories of Inflation.* Cambridge, UK, and New York: Cambridge University Press, 1983.

Furtado, Celso. *The Economic Growth of Brazil: A Survey from Colonial Times to Modern Times.* Berkeley: University of California Press, 1963.

Galbraith, John Kenneth. *The Affluent Society.* 40th anniversary ed. Boston: Houghton Mifflin, 1998.

———. *The Great Crash: 1929.* Boston: Houghton Mifflin, 1997.

———. *The New Industrial State.* Boston: Houghton Mifflin, 1967.

———. *A Short History of Financial Euphoria.* New York: Whittle Books, in association with Viking, 1993.

Gali, Jordi. *Monetary Policy, Inflation, and the Business Cycle: An Introduction to the New Keynesian Framework.* Princeton, NJ: Princeton University Press, 2008.

Garber, Peter M. *Famous First Bubbles: The Fundamentals of Early Manias.* Cambridge MA: MIT Press, 2000.

Garrison, Roger. *Time and Money: The Macroeconomics of Capital Structure.* New York: Routledge, 1999.

Geanuracos, John, and Bill Millar. *The Power of Financial Innovation.* New York: HarperCollins Business, 1991.

Geisst, Charles R. *Wall Street, a History: From Its Beginnings to the Fall of Enron.* New York: Oxford University Press, 2004.

Gilbert, Christopher, and Vines, David. *The World Bank: Structure and Policies.* New York: Cambridge University Press, 2000.

Gilpin, Robert. *Global Political Economy: Understanding the International Economic Order.* Princeton, NJ: Princeton University Press, 2001.

Glade, William P. *The Latin American Economies: A Study of Their Institutional Evolution.* New York: American Book, 1969.

Glasner, David, ed. *Business Cycles and Depressions: An Encyclopedia.* New York: Garland, 1997.

Gold, Gerry, and Paul Feldman. *A House of Cards: From Fantasy Finance to Global Crash.* London: Lupus, 2007.

Goldman, Michael. *Imperial Nature: The World Bank and Struggles for Social Justice in the Age of Globalization.* New Haven, CT: Yale University Press, 2005.

Goldstein, Morris. *The Asian Financial Crisis: Causes, Cures, and Systemic Implications.* Washington, DC: Institute for International Economic, 1998.

Goodhart, C.A.E., and Boris Hofmann. *House Prices and the Macroeconomy: Implications for Banking and Price Stability.* New York: Oxford University Press, 2007.

Goodman, Laurie S., Shumin Li, Douglas J. Lucas, Thomas A. Zimmerman, and Frank J. Fabozzi. *Subprime Mortgage Credit Derivatives.* Hoboken, NJ: John Wiley & Sons, 2008.

Goodwin, Richard M. *Chaotic Economic Dynamics.* New York: Oxford University Press, 1990.

Gordon, John Steele. *The Great Game: The Emergence of Wall Street as a World Power, 1653–2000.* New York: Simon & Schuster, 1999.

Gould, Bryan. *Rescuing the New Zealand Economy: Where We Went Wrong and How We Can Fix It.* Nelson, NZ: Craig Potton, 2008.

Grabowski, Richard, Sharmistha Self, and Michael P. Shields. *Economic Development: A Regional, Institutional, and Historical Approach.* Armonk, NY: M.E Sharpe, 2006.

Graf, Hans Georg. *Economic Forecasting for Management: Possibilities and Limitations.* Westport, CT: Quorum, 2002.

Gramlich, Edward M. *Subprime Mortgages: America's Latest Boom and Bust.* Washington, DC: Urban Institute, 2007.

Gray, Joanna, and Jenny Hamilton. *Implementing Financial Regulation: Theory and Practice.* Hoboken, NJ: John Wiley& Sons, 2006.

Greenspan, Alan. *The Age of Turbulence: Adventures in a New World.* New York: Penguin, 2007.

Greider, William. *Secrets of the Temple: How the Federal Reserve Runs the Country.* New York: Simon & Schuster, 1989.

Groenewagen, Peter. *A Soaring Eagle: Alfred Marshall, 1842–1924.* Cheltenham, UK: Edward Elgar, 1995.

Gros, Daniel, and Alfred Steinherr. *Economic Transition in Central and Eastern Europe: Planting the Seeds.* 2nd ed. New York: Cambridge University Press, 2004.

Gross, Daniel. *Pop! Why Bubbles Are Great for the Economy.* New York: Collins Business, 2007.

Gup, Benton E., ed. *Too Big to Fail: Policies and Practices in Government Bailouts.* Westport, CT: Praeger, 2004.

Haas, Jeffrey J. *Corporate Finance in a Nutshell.* St. Paul, MN: Thomson/West, 2004.

Haas, Peter M. *Knowledge, Power, and International Policy Coordination.* Columbia: University of South Carolina Press, 1997.

Haberler, Gottfried. *Prosperity and Depression: A Theoretical Analysis of Cyclical Movements.* 5th ed. New York: Atheneum, 1963.

———. *The Theory of International Trade: With Its Applications to Commercial Policy.* Trans. Alfred Stonier and Frederick Benham. New York: Augustus M. Kelley, 1968.

Hall, Peter A., and David Soskice, eds. *Varieties of Capitalism: The Institutional Foundations of Comparative Advantage.* New York: Oxford University Press, 2001.

Hamilton, Carolyn, Bernard Mbenga, and Robert Ross, eds. *The Cambridge History of South Africa.* New York: Cambridge University Press, 2009.

Hamouda, O.F. *John R. Hicks: The Economist's Economist.* Oxford, UK: Blackwell, 1993.

Hanke, John E., and Dean Wichern. *Business Forecasting.* 9th ed. Upper Saddle River, NJ: Pearson Prentice-Hall, 2005.

Hansen, Alvin Harvey. *Guide to Keynes.* New York: McGraw-Hill, 1953.

Hansson, Berg. *The Stockholm School and the Development of Dynamic Method.* London: Croom Helm, 1982.

Harris, Ethan S. *Ben Bernanke's Fed: The Federal Reserve After Greenspan.* Boston: Harvard Business, 2008.

Harrison, Joseph, and David Corkill. *Spain: A Modern European Economy.* Burlington, VT: Ashgate, 2004.

Hartley, James E., Kevin D. Hoover, and Kevin D. Salyer, eds. *Real Business Cycles: A Reader.* London: Routledge, 1998.

Hayek, Friedrich A. *Monetary Theory and the Trade Cycle.* New York: Harcourt, Brace, 1933.

———. *The Pure Theory of Capital.* London: Macmillan, 1941.

Head, Simon. *The New Ruthless Economy: Work and Power in the Digital Age.* New York: Oxford University Press, 2005.

Hearder, Harry, and Jonathan Morris. *Italy: A Short History.* 2nd ed. New York: Cambridge University Press, 2001.

Heertje, Arnold. *Schumpeter on the Economics of Innovation and the Development of Capitalism.* Cheltenham, UK: Edward Elgar, 2006.

Heffernan, Shelagh. *Modern Banking in Theory and Practice.* Hoboken, NY: John Wiley & Sons, 1996.

Heilbroner, Robert, and Peter Bernstein. *The Debt and the Deficit: False Alarms/Real Possibilities.* New York: W.W. Norton, 1989.

Henn, R., and O. Moeschlin, eds. *Mathematical Economics and Game Theory: Essays in Honor of Oskar Morgenstern.* New York: Springer, 1977.

Henretta, James A. *The Origins of American Capitalism.* Boston: Northeastern University Press, 1991.

Henriques, Diana B. *The White Sharks of Wall Street: Thomas Mellon and the Original Corporate Raiders.* New York: Scribner, 2000.

Henwood, Doug. *After the New Economy.* New York: New Press, 2003.

Hetzel, Robert L. *The Monetary Policy of the Federal Reserve.* New York: Cambridge University Press, 2008.

Hicks, John Richard. *Collected Essays on Economic Theory.* 3 vols. Cambridge: Harvard University Press, 1981–1983.

Hill, Charles. *International Business: Competing in the Global Marketplace.* 7th ed. New York: McGraw-Hill/Irwin, 2009.

Hirschmeier, Johannes, and Tsunehiko Yui. *The Development of Japanese Business, 1600–1980.* Boston: G. Allen & Unwin, 1981.

Hixson, William F. *Triumphs of the Bankers: Money and Banking in the Eighteenth and Nineteenth Centuries.* Westport, CT: Praeger, 1993.

Hollander, Samuel. *The Economics of John Stuart Mill.* Toronto: University of Toronto Press, 1985.

———. *The Economics of Karl Marx: Analysis and Application.* New York: Cambridge University Press, 2008.

———. *The Economics of Thomas Robert Malthus.* Toronto: University of Toronto Press, 1997.

Hollis, Martin, and Edward J. Nell. *Rational Economic Man: A Philosophical Critique of Neo-Classical Economics.* New York: Cambridge University Press, 1975.

Homer, Sidney, and Richard Sylla. *A History of Interest Rates.* Hoboken, NJ: John Wiley & Sons, 2005.

Honohan, Patrick, and Luc Laeven, eds. *Systemic Financial Crises: Containment and Resolution.* New York: Cambridge University Press, 2005.

Hooshmand, A. Reza. *Business Forecasting: A Practical Approach.* 2nd ed. New York: Routledge, 2009.

Horowitz, Daniel. *The Anxieties of Affluence: Critiques of American Consumer Culture, 1939–1979.* Amherst: University of Massachusetts Press, 2004.

Horwich, George, and Paul Samuelson, eds. *Trade, Stability, and Macroeconomics: Essays in Honor of Lloyd A. Metzler.* New York: Academic, 1974.

Hough, J.R. *The French Economy.* New York: Holmes & Meier, 1982.

Houseman, Gerald L. *America and the Pacific Rim: Coming to Terms with New Realities.* Lanham, MD: Rowman & Littlefield, 1995.

Hudis, Peter, and Kevin B. Anderson, eds. *The Rosa Luxemburg Reader.* New York: Monthly Review, 2004.

Hughes, Jonathan, and Louis P. Cain. *American Economic History.* 8th ed. Boston: Addison-Wesley, 2010.

Humphreys, Norman K. *Historical Dictionary of the International Monetary Fund.* Lanham, MD: Scarecrow, 1999.

Hunt, E.K. *History of Economic Thought.* 2nd ed. Armonk, NY: M.E. Sharpe, 2002.

Hurewitz, J.C., ed. *Oil, the Arab-Israeli Dispute, and the Industrial World: Horizons of Crisis.* Boulder, CO: Westview, 1976.

Hutchinson, T.W. *The Politics and Philosophy of Economics: Marxians, Keynesians, and Austrians.* New York: New York University Press, 1981.

Ichimura, Shinichi, Tsuneaki Sato, and William James. *Transition from Socialist to Market Economies: Comparison of European and Asian Experiences.* New York: Palgrave Macmillan, 2009.

Immergluck, Daniel. *Foreclosed: High-Risk Lending, Deregulation, and the Undermining of America's Mortgage Market.* Ithaca, NY: Cornell University Press, 2009.

Ingebretsen, Mark. *NASDAQ: A History of the Market That Changed the World.* Roseville, CA: Forum, 2002.

International Monetary Fund (IMF). *Balance of Payments and International Investment Position Manual.* 6th ed. Washington, DC: International Monetary Fund, 2008.

———. *Balance of Payments Statistics Yearbook.* Washington, DC: International Monetary Fund, 2008.

———. *Global Financial Stability Report.* Washington, DC: International Monetary Fund, 2009.

———. *World Economic Outlook: Housing and the Business Cycle.* Washington, DC: International Monetary Fund, 2008.

Issing, Otmar, Vitor Gaspar, and Oreste Tristani. *Monetary Policy in the Euro Area: Strategy and Decision Making at the European Central Bank.* New York: Cambridge University Press, 2001.

Jackson, Walter. *Gunnar Myrdal and America's Conscience: Social Engineering and Racial Liberalism, 1938–1987.* Chapel Hill: University of North Carolina Press, 1990.

Jevons, William Stanley. *Investigations in Currency and Finance.* London: Macmillan, 1909.

Johnson, Chalmers, ed. *The Industrial Policy Debate.* San Francisco: ICS Press, 1984.

Johnson, Harry G. *The Canadian Quandary: Economic Problems and Policies.* Montreal: McGill-Queen's University Press, 2005.

Johnson, Moira. *Roller Coaster: The Bank of America and the Future of American Banking.* New York: Ticknor & Fields, 1990.

Jones, Charles I. *Macroeconomics.* New York: W.W. Norton, 2008.

Jones, Stuart, ed. *The Decline of the South African Economy.* Northampton, MA: Edward Elgar, 2002.

Juglar, Clement. *A Brief History of Panics: And Their Periodical Occurrence in the United States.* 3rd ed. New York: Forgotten Books, 2008.

Kalaitzidis, Akis. *Europe's Greece: A Giant in the Making.* New York: Palgrave Macmillan, 2010.

Kaldor, Nicholas. *Essays on Economic Stability and Growth.* 2nd ed. New York: Holmes & Meier, 1980.

Kansas, Dave. *The Wall Street Journal Guide to the End of Wall Street As We Know It: What You Need to Know About the Greatest Financial Crisis of Our Time—and How to Survive It.* New York: HarperBusiness, 2009.

Karier, Thomas. *Great Experiments in American Economic Policy: From Kennedy to Reagan.* Westport, CT: Praeger, 1997.

Kates, Steven. *Say's Law and the Keynesian Revolution.* Cheltenham, UK: Edward Elgar, 2009.

Kaufman, Henry. *The Road to Financial Reformation: Warnings, Consequences, Reforms.* Hoboken, NJ: John Wiley & Sons, 2009.

Kaufman, Perry J. *New Trading Systems and Methods.* Hoboken, NJ: John Wiley & Sons, 2005.

Kautsky, John H. *Karl Kautsky: Marxism, Revolution & Democracy.* New Brunswick, NJ: Transaction, 1994.

Keaney, Michael, ed. *Economist with a Public Purpose: Essays in Honor of John Kenneth Galbraith.* New York: Routledge, 2001.

Kehoe, Timothy J., and Edward C. Prescott, eds. *Great Depressions of the Twentieth Century.* Minneapolis, MN: Federal Reserve Bank of Minneapolis, 2007.

Keller, Morton. *Regulating a New Economy: Public Policy and Economic Change in America, 1900–1933.* Cambridge, MA: Harvard University Press, 1990.

Kemp, Murray C. *International Trade Theory*. London: Routledge, 2008.

Kendall, Leon T., and Michael J. Fishman, eds. *A Primer on Securitization*. Cambridge, MA: MIT Press, 2000.

Kent, Neil. *A Concise History of Sweden*. New York: Cambridge University Press, 2008.

Kenton, Lawrence V., ed. *Manufacturing Output, Productivity, and Employment Indications*. New York: Novinka/Nova Science, 2005.

Keynes, John Maynard. *The General Theory of Employment, Interest and Money*. New York: Harcourt, Brace, 1936.

———. *A Treatise on Money*. New York: Harcourt, Brace, 1930.

———. *A Treatise on Probability*. Vol. 8, *The Collected Writings of John Maynard Keynes*, ed. D. Moggeridge and E. Johnson. London: Macmillan, 1973, 1921.

Killingsworth, Mark R. *Labor Supply*. New York: Cambridge University Press, 1983.

Kindleberger, Charles P. *A Financial History of Western Europe*. London: George Allen and Unwin, 1984.

———. *The World in Depression, 1929–1939*. Berkeley: University of California Press, 1973.

Kindleberger, Charles, and Robert Z. Aliber. *Manias, Panics, and Crashes: A History of Financial Crises*. 6th ed. Basingstoke, UK: Palgrave Macmillan, 2010.

King, John Edward. *Nicholas Kaldor*. Basingstoke, UK: Palgrave Macmillan, 2008.

Kirtzman, Andrew. *Betrayal: The Life and Lies of Bernie Madoff*. New York: HarperCollins, 2009.

Kirzner, Israel M. *Ludwig von Mises: The Man and His Economics*. Wilmington, DE: ISI Books, 2001.

———. *The Meaning of Market Process: Essays in the Development of Modern Austrian Economics*. New York: Routledge, 1992.

Klein, Maury. *Rainbow's End: The Crash of 1929*. New York: Oxford University Press, 2001.

Kleinknecht, Alfred. *Innovation Patterns in Crisis and Prosperity: Schumpeter's Long Cycle Reconsidered*. London: Macmillan, 1987.

Klingaman, William K. *1929: The Year of the Great Crash*. New York: Harper & Row, 1989.

Knoop, Todd. *Recessions and Depressions: Understanding Business Cycles*. Westport, CT: Praeger, 2004.

Koo, Richard C. *The Holy Grail of Macroeconmics: Lessons from Japan's Great Recession*. Hoboken, NJ: John Wiley & Sons, 2008.

Koopmans, Tjalling. *Three Essays on the State of Economic Theory*. New York: McGraw-Hill, 1957.

Kose, M., C. Otrok, and E. Prasad. *Global Business Cycles: Convergence or Decoupling?* Washington, DC: International Monetary Fund, 2008.

Kriesler, Peter. *Kalecki's Microanalysis: The Development of Kalecki's Analysis of Pricing and Distribution*. New York: Cambridge University Press, 1987.

Krugman, Paul. *Geography and Trade*. Cambridge, MA: MIT Press, 1991.

———. *The Return of Depression Economics and the Crisis of 2008*. New York: W.W. Norton, 2009.

Krugman, Paul R., and Maurice Obstfeld. *International Economics: Theory and Policy*. Boston: Pearson Addison-Wesley, 2009.

Kuenne, Robert E. *Eugen von Böhm-Bawerk*. New York: Columbia University Press, 1971.

Kuznets, Simon S. *Capital in the American Economy: Its Formation and Financing*. Princeton, NJ: Princeton University Press, 1961.

———. *Economic Change: Selected Essays in Business Cycles, National Income, and Economic Growth*. New York: W.W. Norton, 1953.

Lachmann, Ludwig Maurits. *Capital and Its Structure*. London: Bell and Sons, 1956.

Laffont, Jean-Jacques. *Incentives and Political Economy*. New York: Oxford University Press, 2000.

Laider, David. *Fabricating the Keynesian Revolution: Studies of the Inter-war Literature on Money, the Cycle, and Unemployment*. Cambridge, UK: Cambridge University Press, 1999.

Langdana, Farrokh K. *Macroeconomic Policy: Demystifying Monetary and Fiscal Policy*. New York: Springer, 2009.

Langley, Lester D. *The Americas in the Modern Age*. New Haven, CT: Yale University Press, 2003.

Lawson, Tony, J. Gabriel Palma, and John Sender, eds. *Kaldor's Political Economy*. London: Academic, 1989.

Lefebvre, Adelaide D., ed. *Government Bailout: Troubled Asset Relief Program (TARP)*. Hauppauge, NY: Nova Science, 2009.

Lerner, Abba. *Selected Writings of Abba Lerner*, ed. David Colander. New York: New York University Press, 1983.

Leuchtenburg, William. *Franklin Roosevelt and the New Deal*. New York: Harper & Row, 1963.

———. *The Perils of Prosperity, 1914–1932*. Chicago: University of Chicago Press, 1958.

Lewis, Michael. *The Big Short: Inside the Doomsday Machine*. New York: W.W. Norton, 2010.

Lewis, William W. *The Power of Productivity: Wealth, Poverty, and the Threat to Global Stability*. Chicago: University of Chicago Press, 2004.

Lindbeck, Assar, ed. *Nobel Lectures: Economics, 1969–1980*. Singapore: World Scientific, 1992.

Lowe, Adolph. *Essays in Political Economics: Public Control in a Democratic Society*. New York: New York University Press, 1987.

———. *On Economic Knowledge: Toward a Science of Political Economics*. Armonk, NY: M.E. Sharpe, 1977.

Lowenstein, Roger. *When Genius Failed: The Rise and Fall of Long-Term Capital Management.* New York: Random House, 2000.

Lowy, Michael. *High Rollers: Inside the Savings and Loan Debacle.* New York: Praeger, 1991.

Lucas, Douglas J., Laurie S. Goodman, and Frank J. Fabozzi. *Collateralized Debt Obligations: Structures and Analysis.* 2nd ed. Hoboken, NJ: John Wiley & Sons, 2006.

Lucas, Douglas J., Laurie S. Goodman, Frank J. Fabozzi, and Rebecca Manning. *Developments in Collateralized Debt Obligations: New Products and Insights.* Hoboken, NJ: John Wiley & Sons, 2007.

Lundberg, Erik Filip. *The Development of Swedish and Keynesian Macroeconomic Theory and Its Impact on Economic Policy.* Cambridge, UK: Cambridge University Press, 1996.

———. *Instability and Economic Growth.* New Haven, CT: Yale University Press, 1968.

Lustig, Nora. *Mexico: The Remaking of an Economy.* Washington, DC: Brookings Institution, 1998.

Lys, Thomas, ed. *Economic Analysis and Political Ideology: Selected Essays of Karl Brunner.* Cheltenham, UK: Edward Elgar, 1996.

Mackay, Charles. *Memoirs of Extraordinary Popular Delusions and the Madness of Crowds.* New York: Cosimo Classics, 2008. First published 1841.

Macrae, Norman. *John von Neumann.* New York: Pantheon, 1992.

Maddison, Angus. *Monitoring the World Economy 1820–1992.* Paris: OECD, 1995.

———. *The World Economy: A Millennial Perspective.* Paris: OECD, 2001.

Madura, Jeff. *Financial Markets and Institutions.* Mason, OH: South-Western, 2008.

Magdoff, Fred, and Michael Yates. *The ABCs of the Financial Crisis.* New York: Monthly Review, 2009.

Maksakovsky, Pavel V. *The Capitalist Cycle,* trans. Richard B. Day. Chicago: Haymarket, 2009.

Mallaby, Sebastian. *The World's Banker: A Story of Failed States, Financial Crises, and the Wealth and Poverty of Nations.* New York: Penguin, 2004.

Malthus, Thomas Robert. *An Essay on the Principle of Population,* ed. Philip Appleman. New York: W.W. Norton, 2004.

———. *Principles of Political Economy,* ed. John Pullen. Cambridge, UK, and New York: Cambridge University Press, 1989.

Mandel, Ernest. *Long Waves of Capitalist Development: A Marxist Interpretation.* New York: Verso, 1995.

Mankiw, N. Gregory. *Principles of Macroeconomics.* 5th ed. Mason, OH: South-Western, 2009.

Manzetti, Luigi. *Neoliberalism, Accountability, and Reform Failures in Emerging Markets: Eastern Europe, Rus-*

sia, Argentina, and Chile in Comparative Perspective. University Park: Pennsylvania State University Press, 2009.

Marcuzzo, Maria Cristina, Luigi L. Pasinetti, and Alessandro Roncaglia, eds. *The Economics of Joan Robinson.* London: Routledge, 1996.

Markham, Jerry W. *A Financial History of Modern U.S. Corporate Scandals: From Enron to Reform.* Armonk, NY: M.E. Sharpe, 2005.

———. *A Financial History of the United States.* 3 vols. Armonk, NY: M.E. Sharpe, 2002.

———. *A Financial History of the United States: From Enron-Era Scandals to the Subprime Crisis (2004–2006); From the Subprime Crisis to the Great Recesion (2006–2009).* Armonk, NY: M.E. Sharpe, 2010.

Marshall, Alfred. *Industry and Trade.* London: Macmillan, 1919.

———. *Money, Credit and Commerce.* London: Macmillan, 1923.

———. *Principles of Economics.* Amherst, NY: Prometheus, 1997. First published 1890.

Marx, Karl. *Capital: A Critique of Political Economy,* trans. Ben Fowkes. New York: Vintage, 1976–1981.

———. *Das Kapital.* 3 vols. London: Penguin, 2004.

Matusow, Allen J. *Nixon's Economy: Booms, Busts, Dollars, and Votes.* Lawrence: University Press of Kansas, 1998.

Mavrotas, George, and Anthony Shorrocks, eds. *Advancing Development: Core Themes in Global Economics.* New York: Palgrave Macmillan, 2007.

Mayer, Martin. *The Greatest-Ever Bank Robbery: The Collapse of the Savings and Loan Industry.* New York: Scribner, 1990.

Mayer, Thomas. *Monetary Policy and the Great Inflation in the United States: The Federal Reserve and the Failure of Macroeconomic Policy, 1965–1979.* Northampton, MA: Edward Elgar, 1999.

Mayer, Thomas, James S. Duesenberry, and Robert Z. Aliber. *Money, Banking, and the Economy.* New York: W.W. Norton, 1996.

McCarthy, Dennis. *International Economic Integration in Historical Perspective.* New York: Routledge, 2006.

McConnell, Campbell R., and Stanley L. Brue. *Economics: Principles, Problems, and Policies.* 17th ed. New York: McGraw-Hill/Irwin, 2006.

McConnell, Campbell R., Stanley L. Brue, and David A. Macpherson. *Contemporary Labor Economics.* 8th ed. New York: McGraw-Hill/Irwin, 2009.

McCraw, Thomas K. *Prophet of Innovation: Joseph Schumpeter and Creative Destruction.* Cambridge, MA: Harvard University Press, 2007.

McDonald, Lawrence G., with Patrick Robinson. *A Colossal Failure of Common Sense: The Inside Story of the Collapse of Lehman Brothers.* New York: Crown Business, 2009.

McDougall, Derek. *Asia Pacific in World Politics*. New Delhi: Viva, 2008.

McGrane, Reginald. *The Panic of 1837: Some Financial Problems of the Jacksonian Era*. New York: Russell & Russell, 1965.

McGregor, Andrew. *Southeast Asian Development*. New York: Routledge, 2008.

McLellen, David. *Karl Marx: His Life and Thought*. London: Macmillan, 1973.

McLeod, Ross, and Ross Garnaut, eds. *East Asia in Crisis: From Being a Miracle to Needing One?* London: Routledge, 1998.

Means, Gardner, ed. *The Roots of Inflation: The International Crisis*. New York: B. Franklin, 1975.

Meijer, Gerrit. *New Perspectives on Austrian Economics*. New York: Routledge, 1995.

Mengkui, Wang, ed. *China in the Wake of Asia's Financial Crisis*. New York: Routledge, 2009.

Metrick, Andrew. *Venture Capital and the Finance of Innovation*. Hoboken, NJ: John Wiley & Sons, 2007.

Metz, Tim. *Black Monday: The Catastrophe of October 19, 1987, and Beyond*. New York: William Morrow, 1988.

Metzler, Lloyd A. *Collected Papers*. Cambridge, MA: Harvard University Press, 1973.

———. *Income, Employment and Public Policy: Essays in Honor or Alvin H. Hansen*. New York: W.W. Norton, 1948.

Michaelson, Adam. *The Foreclosure of America: The Inside Story of the Rise and Fall of Countrywide Home Loans, the Mortgage Crisis, and the Default of the American Dream*. New York: Berkley, 2009.

Milgate, Murray and Shannon C. Stimson. *After Adam Smith: A Century of Transformation in Politics and Political Economy*. Princeton, NJ: Princeton University Press, 2009.

Mill, John Stuart. *The Collected Works of John Stuart Mill*, ed. J.M. Robinson. Toronto: University of Toronto Press, 1963–1991.

———. *Principles of Political Economy*. New York: Oxford University Press, 1998.

Miller, Sally M., A.J.H. Latham, and Dennis O. Flynn, eds. *Studies in the Economic History of the Pacific Rim*. Routledge Studies in the Growth Economies of Asia. London and New York: Routledge, 1998.

Mills, Frederick C. *The Behavior of Prices*. New York: Arno, 1975.

———. *Statistical Methods Applied to Economics and Business*. 3rd ed. New York: Holt, 1955.

Milonakis, Dimitris, and Ben Fine. *From Political Economy to Economics: Method, the Social and the Historical in the Evolution of Economic Theory*. New York: Routledge, 2008.

Minsky, Hyman P. *Can "It" Happen Again? Essays on Instability and Finance*. Armonk, NY: M.E. Sharpe, 1982.

———. *John Maynard Keynes*. New York: Columbia University Press, 1975.

———. *Stabilizing an Unstable Economy*. New Haven, CT: Yale University Press, 1986.

Minton, Robert. *John Law, The Father of Paper Money*. New York: Association, 1975.

Mises, Ludwig von. *The Theory of Money and Credit*. London: J. Cape, 1934.

Mitchell, Wesley Clair. *A History of the Greenbacks: With Special Reference to the Economic Consequences of Their Issue, 1862–65*. Chicago: University of Chicago Press, 1960.

———. *What Happens During Business Cycles, a Progress Report*. New York: National Bureau of Economic Research, 1951.

Moffett, Michael, Arthur I. Stonehill, and David Eiteman. *Fundamentals of Multinational Finance*. Boston: Pearson Prentice Hall, 2009.

Mommen, Andre. *The Belgian Economy in the Twentieth Century*. London: Routledge, 1994.

Moreno-Brid, Juan Carlos, and Jaime Ros. *Development and Growth in the Mexican Economy: A Historical Perspective*. New York: Oxford University Press, 2009.

Morris, Charles R. *The Trillion Dollar Meltdown: Easy Money, High Rollers, and the Great Credit Crash*. New York: PublicAffairs, 2008.

———. *The Tycoons: How Andrew Carnegie, John D. Rockefeller, Jay Gould, and J.P. Morgan Invented the American Supereconomy*. New York: Holt, 2006.

Morris, Chris. *The New Turkey: The Quiet Revolution on the Edge of Europe*. London: Granta, 2005.

Mosk, Carl. *Japanese Industrial History: Technology, Urbanization, and Economic Growth*. Armonk, NY: M.E. Sharpe, 2001.

Motamen-Samadian, Sima, ed. *Capital Flows and Foreign Direct Investments in Emerging Markets*. New York: Palgrave Macmillan, 2005.

Mullineux, A.W. *The Business Cycle After Keynes: A Contemporary Analysis*. Brighton, UK: Wheatsheaf, 1984.

Muolo, Paul, and Mathew Padilla. *Chain of Blame: How Wall Street Caused the Mortgage and Credit Crisis*. Hoboken, NJ: John Wiley & Sons, 2008.

Murphy, Antoin E. *John Law: Economic Theorist and Policy-Maker*. New York: Oxford University Press, 1997.

Nadeau, Kathleen. *The History of the Philippines*. Westport, CT: Greenwood, 2008.

Nardini, Franco. *Technical Progress and Economic Growth: Business Cycles and Stabilization*. New York: Springer, 2001.

Naughton, Barry. *The Chinese Economy: Transitions and Growth*. Cambridge, MA: MIT Press, 2007.

Naylor, R.T. *Canada in the European Age, 1453–1919.* 2nd ed. Montreal: McGill-Queen's University Press, 2006.

Neikirk, William. *Volcker: Portrait of the Money Man.* New York: Congdon & Weed, 1987.

Nell, Edward J., and Willi Semmler, eds. *Nicholas Kaldor and Mainstream Economics: Confrontation or Convergence?* New York: St. Martin's, 1991.

Nettels, Curtis. *The Emergence of a National Economy, 1775–1815.* Armonk, NY: M.E. Sharpe, 1989.

Nettl, J.P. *Rosa Luxemburg.* London: Oxford University Press, 1966.

Niskanen, William A. *Reaganomics: An Insider's Account of the Policies and the People.* New York: Oxford University Press, 1988.

Nitzan, Jonathan, and Shimshon Bichler. *The Global Political Economy of Israel.* Sterling, VA: Pluto, 2002.

Norton, Hugh S. *The Quest for Economic Stability: Roosevelt to Bush.* 2nd ed. Columbia: University of South Carolina, 1991.

Obay, Lamia. *Financial Innovation in the Banking Industry: The Case of Asset Securitization.* London: Taylor & Francis, 2001.

OECD. *Economic Survey of Iceland 2006: Policy Challenges in Sustaining Improved Economic Performance.* Paris: Organisation for Economic Co-operation and Development, 2006.

Okun, Arthur M. *Equality and Efficiency: The Big Tradeoff.* Washington, DC: Brookings Institution, 1975.

Olson, Mancur Lloyd, Jr. *The Rise and Decline of Nations: Economic Growth, Stagflation, and Social Rigidities.* New Haven, CT: Yale University Press, 1982.

Overton, Rachel H. *China's Trade with the United States and the World.* Hauppage, NY: Nova Science, 2009.

Owen, Norman G., ed. *The Emergence of Modern Southeast Asia: A New History.* Honolulu: University of Hawai'i Press, 2005.

Page, Alan C., and R.B. Ferguson. *Investor Protection.* London: Orion, 1992.

Panayiotopoulos, Podromos. *Immigrant Enterprise in Europe and the USA.* New York: Routledge, 2006.

Parker, Richard. *John Kenneth Galbraith: His Life, His Politics, His Economics.* New York: Farrar, Straus and Giroux, 2005.

Parthasarathi, P. *The Transition to a Colonial Economy: Weavers, Merchants, and Kings in South India 1720–1800.* New York: Cambridge University Press, 2001.

Paulson, Henry. *On the Brink: Inside the Race to Stop the Collapse of the Global Financial System.* New York: Business Plus, 2009.

Pauly, Louis W. *Who Elected the Bankers? Surveillance and Control in the World Economy.* Ithaca, NY: Cornell University Press, 1997.

Peart, Sandra. *The Economics of W.S. Jevons.* London and New York: Routledge, 1996.

Peláez, Carlos M., and Carlos A. Peláez. *Regulation of Banks and Finance: Theory and Policy After the Credit Crisis.* New York: Palgrave Macmillan, 2009.

Perkins, Edwin J. *The Economy of Colonial America.* New York: Columbia University Press, 1988.

Perkins, Martin Y., ed. *TARP and the Restoration of U.S. Financial Stability.* Hauppauge, NY: Nova Science, 2009.

Philion, Stephen E. *Workers' Democracy in China's Transition from State Socialism.* New York: Routledge, 2009.

Pierre, Andrew J., ed. *Unemployment and Growth in the Western Economies.* New York: Council on Foreign Relations, 1984.

Pizzo, Steven, Mary Fricker, and Paul Muolo. *Inside Job: The Looting of America's Savings and Loans.* New York: McGraw-Hill, 1989.

Posner, Richard A. *A Failure of Capitalism: The Crisis of '08 and the Descent into Depression'.* Cambridge, MA: Harvard University Press, 2009.

Power, Michael. *Organized Uncertainty: Designing a World of Risk Management.* New York: Oxford University Press, 2007.

Prebisch, Raúl. *The Economic Development of Latin America and Its Principal Problems.* Lake Success, NY: United Nations Department of Social Affairs, 1950.

Pressman, Steven. *Fifty Major Economists.* 2nd ed. London and New York: Routledge, 2006.

Rao, Bhanoji, *East Asian Economies: The Miracle, a Crisis and the Future.* Singapore: McGraw-Hill, 2001.

Ravenhill, John, ed. *APEC and the Construction of Pacific Rim Regionalism.* Cambridge, UK: Cambridge University Press, 2002.

Rebonato, Riccardo. *Plight of the Fortune Tellers: Why We Need to Manage Financial Risk Differently.* Princeton, NJ: Princeton University Press, 2007.

Reekie, W. Duncan. *Markets, Entrepreneurs, and Liberty: An Austrian View of Capitalism.* New York: St. Martin's, 1984.

Reich, Robert B. *The Next American Frontier.* New York: New York Times Books, 1983.

Reinhart, Carmen M., and Kenneth S. Rogoff. *This Time Is Different: Eight Centuries of Financial Folly.* Princeton, NJ: Princton University Press, 2009.

Reinis, August, ed. *Standards of Investment Protection.* New York: Oxford University Press, 2008.

Reisman, David. *The Economics of Alfred Marshall.* London: Macmillan, 1986.

Ricklefs, M.C. *A History of Modern Indonesia Since c. 1200.* Palo Alto, CA: Stanford University Press, 2008.

Rigg, Jonathan. *Southeast Asia: The Human Landscape of Modernization and Development*. 2nd ed. New York: Routledge, 2003.

Rima, Ingrid H., ed. *The Joan Robinson Legacy*. Armonk, NY: M.E. Sharpe, 1991.

Robbins, Lionel. *The Great Depression*. London: Macmillan, 1934.

————. *Jacob Viner: A Tribute*. Princeton, NJ: Princeton University Press, 1970.

Robertson, Dennis H. *A Study of Industrial Fluctuations: An Enquiry into the Character and Causes of the So-Called Cyclical Movements of Trade*. London: P.S. King, 1915.

Robinson, Joan. *Collected Economic Papers*. Oxford, UK: Blackwell, 1980.

————. *Further Contributions to Modern Economics*. Oxford, UK: Blackwell, 1980.

Robinson, Michael A. *Overdrawn: The Bailout of American Savings*. New York: Dutton, 1990.

Robinson, William. *Transnational Conflicts: Central America, Social Change, and Globalization*. New York: Verso, 2003.

Roett, Riordan. *The Mexican Peso Crisis*. Boulder, CO: Lynne Rienner, 1996.

Romano, Flavio. *Clinton and Blair: The Political Economy of the Third Way*. New York: Routledge, 2006.

Romer, Christina D. *Changes in Business Cycles: Evidence and Explanations*. Cambridge, MA: National Bureau of Economic Research, 1999.

————. *Monetary Policy and the Well-Being of the Poor*. Cambridge, MA: National Bureau of Economic Research, 1998.

Roncaglia, Alessandro. *The Wealth of Ideas*. New York: Cambridge University Press, 2005.

Röpke, Wilhelm. *The Crisis of European Economic Integration*. Zurich: Swiss Credit Bank, 1963.

————. *A Humane Economy: The Social Framework of the Free Market*. Chicago: H. Regnery, 1960.

Rose, Peter S., and Sylvia C. Hudgins. *Bank Management and Financial Services*. New York: McGraw-Hill, 2008.

Rosen, Elliot A. *Roosevelt, the Great Depression, and the Economics of Recovery*. Charlottesville: University of Virginia Press, 2005.

Rosenof, Theodore. *Economics in the Long Run: New Deal Theorists and Their Legacies, 1933–1993*. Chapel Hill: University of North Carolina Press, 1997.

Ross, Ian Simpson. *The Life of Adam Smith*. New York: Oxford University Press, 1995.

Ross, Stephen A., Randolph W. Westerfield, and Bradford Jordan. *Fundamentals of Corporate Finance*. 9th ed. New York: McGraw-Hill, 2009.

Røste, Ole Bjørn. *Monetary Policy and Macroeconomic Stabilization: The Roles of Optimum Currency Areas, Sacrifice Ratios, and Labor Market Adjustment*. New Brunswick, NJ: Transaction, 2008.

Rostow, W.W. *Concept and Controversy: Sixty Years of Taking Ideas to Market*. Austin: University of Texas Press, 2003.

————. *The Process of Economic Growth*. New York: W.W. Norton, 1952.

Rowley, C., and Y. Paik, eds. *The Changing Face of Korean Management*. London: Routledge, 2009.

Roy, Subroto, and John Clarke, eds. *Margaret Thatcher's Revolution: How It Happened and What It Meant*. New York: Continuum, 2005.

Rubin, Robert E., and Jacob Weisberg. *In an Uncertain World: Tough Choices from Wall Street to Washington*. New York: Random House, 2004.

Ryscavage, Paul. *Rethinking the Income Gap*. New Brunswick, NJ: Transaction, 2009.

Sachs, Jeffrey D. *The End of Poverty: Economic Possibilities for Our Time*. New York: Penguin, 2005.

Sadowski, Zdzisław, and Adam Szeworski, eds. *Kalecki's Economics Today*. New York: Routledge, 2004.

Safford, Frank, and Marco Palacios. *Colombia: Fragmented Land, Divided Society*. New York: Oxford University Press, 2002.

Salvadori, Massimo L. *Karl Kautsky and the Socialist Revolution, 1880–1938*. London: NLB, 1979.

Samii, Massood, and Gerald Karush, eds. *International Business and Information Technology: Interaction and Transformation in the Global Economy*. New York: Routledge, 2004.

Samuelson, Paul. *Foundations of Economic Analysis*. Enlarged ed. Cambridge, MA: Harvard University Press, 1983.

Samuelson, Paul A., and William D. Nordhaus. *Economics*. Boston: McGraw-Hill/Irwin, 2009.

Samuelson, Robert J. *The Great Inflation and Its Aftermath: The Past and Future of American Affluence* New York: Random House, 2008.

SarDesai, D.R. *Southeast Asia: Past and Present*. 6th ed. Boulder, CO: Westview, 2010.

Saunders, Anthony, and Marcia Millon Cornett. *Financial Markets and Institutions: An Introduction to the Risk Management Approach*. New York: McGraw-Hill, 2007.

Sawyer, James E. *Why Reaganomics and Keynesian Economics Failed*. New York: St. Martin's, 1987.

Sawyer, Malcolm C., ed. *The Legacy of Michał Kalecki*. Cheltenham, UK: Edward Elgar, 1999.

Schama, Simon. *The Embarrassment of Riches: An Interpretation of Dutch Culture in the Golden Age*. New York: Alfred A. Knopf, 1987.

Schedvin, C.B. *Australia and the Great Depression*. Sydney: Sydney University Press, 1970.

Schiere, Richard. *China's Development Challenges: Public Sector Reform and Vulnerability to Poverty.* New York: Routledge, 2010.

Schiller, Bradley R. *The Economics of Poverty and Discrimination.* 10th ed. Upper Saddle River, NJ: Pearson/Prentice Hall, 2008.

Schioppa, Fiorella P. *Italy: Structural Problems in the Italian Economy.* New York: Oxford University Press, 1993.

Schlefer, Jonathan. *Palace Politics: How the Ruling Party Brought Crisis to Mexico.* Austin: University of Texas Press, 2008.

Schlesinger, Arthur M. *The Coming of the New Deal.* London: Heinemann, 1960.

Schneider, Ben Ross. *Business Politics and the State in Twentieth-Century Latin America.* New York: Cambridge University Press, 2004.

Schofield, Neil C. *Commodity Derivatives: Markets and Applications.* Hoboken, NJ: John Wiley & Sons, 2007.

Schumpeter, Joseph. *Business Cycles: A Theoretical, Historical and Statistical Analysis of the Capitalist Process.* 2 vols. New York: McGraw-Hill, 1939.

———. *The Theory of Economic Development.* New Brunswick, NJ: Transaction, 1983.

Seidman, L. William. *Full Faith and Credit: The Great S&L Debacle and Other Washington Sagas.* New York: Times Books, 1993.

Sena, Vania. *Credit and Collateral.* New York: Routledge, 2007.

Senor, Dan, and Saul Singer. *Start-Up Nation: The Story of Israel's Economic Miracle.* New York: Twelve, 2009.

Shackle, George L.S. *Epistemics and Economics: A Critique of Economic Doctrines.* Cambridge, UK: Cambridge University Press, 1972.

———. *Keynesian Kaleidics: The Evolution of a General Political Economy.* Edinburgh, UK: Edinburgh University Press, 1974.

Sharpe, Myron E. *John Kenneth Galbraith and the Lower Economics.* 2nd ed. White Plains, NY: International Arts and Sciences, 1974.

Shefrin, Hersh. *Beyond Greed and Fear: Understanding Behavioral Finance and the Psychology of Investing.* New York: Oxford University Press, 2007.

Shiller, Robert J. *Irrational Exuberance.* 2nd ed. New York: Currency/Doubleday, 2005.

———. *The Subprime Solution: How Today's Global Financial Crisis Happened and What To Do About It.* Princeton, NJ: Princeton University Press, 2008.

Shlaes, Amity. *The Forgotten Man: A New History of the Great Depression.* New York: Harper Perennial, 2008.

Sicilia, David, and Jeffrey Cruikshank. *The Greenspan Effect.* New York: McGraw-Hill, 2000.

Siebert, Horst. *The German Economy: Beyond the Social Market.* Princeton, NJ: Princeton University Press, 2005.

Siklos, Pierre L., ed. *The Economics of Deflation.* Northampton, MA: Edward Elgar, 2006.

Simon, Julian L., ed. *The Economics of Population: Classic Writings.* New Brunswick, NJ: Transaction, 1998.

Singh, Dalvinder. *Banking Regulation of UK and US Financial Markets.* Farnham, UK: Ashgate, 2007.

Skidelsky, Robert. *John Maynard Keynes: A Biography.* London: Macmillan, 1983.

———. *Keynes: The Return of the Master.* New York: Public Affairs, 2009.

Skott, Peter. *Kaldor's Growth and Distribution Theory.* New York: Peter Lang, 1989.

Smith, Adam. *An Inquiry into the Nature and Causes of the Wealth of Nations.* Chicago: University of Chicago Press, 1977.

———. *The Theory of Moral Sentiments,* ed. Knud Haakonssen. Cambridge, UK: Cambridge University Press, 2002.

Smith, John, ed. *The Rescue and Repair of Fannie Mae and Freddie Mac.* Hauppauge, NY: Nova Science, 2009.

Snider, David, and Chris Howard. *Money Makers: Inside the New World of Finance and Business.* New York: Palgrave Macmillan, 2010.

Soloki, E. Cary, and Robert M. Brown. *Paul Samuelson and Modern Economic Theory.* New York: McGraw-Hill, 1983.

Solomon, Robert. *Money on the Move: The Revolution in International Finance Since 1980.* Princeton, NJ: Princeton University Press, 1999.

Solomou, Solomos. *Phases of Economic Growth, 1850–1973: Kondratieff Waves and Kuznets Swings.* New York: Cambridge University Press, 1988.

Sorkin, Andrew Ross. *Too Big to Fail: The Inside Story of How Wall Street and Washington Fought to Save the Financial System from Crisis—and Themselves.* New York: Viking, 2009.

Soros, George. *The New Paradigm for Financial Markets: The Credit Crisis of 2008 and What It Means.* Jackson, TN: PublicAffairs, 2008.

Sowell, Thomas. *On Classical Economics.* New Haven, CT: Yale University Press, 2006.

Spence, Jonathan. *The Search for Modern China.* New York: W.W. Norton, 1999.

Spencer, Peter D. *The Structure and Regulation of Financial Markets.* New York: Oxford University Press, 2000.

Spencer, Roger W., and John H. Huston. *The Federal Reserve and the Bull Markets: From Benjamin Strong to Alan Greenspan.* Lewiston, NY: Edwin Mellen, 2006.

Spotgeste, Milton R., ed. *Securitization of Subprime Mortgages.* Hauppauge, NY: Nova Science, 2009.

Spotton Visano, Brenda. *Financial Crises: Socio-economic Causes and Institutional Context.* New York: Routledge, 2006.

Sprague, O.M.W. *History of Crises Under the National Banking System.* Washington, DC: Government Printing Office, 1910.

———. *Theory and History of Banking.* New York: Putnam, 1929.

Spulber, Nicolas. *Managing the American Economy, from Roosevelt to Reagan.* Bloomington: Indiana University Press, 1989.

Steindl, Josef. *Economic Papers, 1941–88.* London: Macmillan, 1990.

———. *Maturity and Stagnation in American Capitalism.* Oxford, UK: Basil Blackwell, 1952.

Stern, Gary F., and Ron J. Feldman. *Too Big to Fail: The Hazards of Bank Bailouts.* Washington, DC: Brookings Institution, 2009.

Stiglitz, Joseph E. *Free Fall: America, Free Markets and the Sinking of the World Economy.* New York: W.W. Norton, 2010.

———. *Globalization and Its Discontents.* London: Penguin, 2002.

Stiglitz, Joseph E., and Shahid Yusef, eds. *Rethinking the East Asian Miracle.* New York: Oxford University Press, 2001.

Strasser, Susan, Charles McGovern, and Matthias Judt. *Getting and Spending: European and American Consumer Societies in the Twentieth Century.* New York: Cambridge University Press, 1998.

Stridsman, Thomas. *Trading Systems That Work: Building and Evaluating Effective Trading Systems.* New York: McGraw-Hill, 2000.

Strober, Deborah H. *Catastrophe: The Story of Bernard L. Madoff, the Man Who Swindled the World.* Beverly Hills, CA: Phoenix, 2009.

Strouse, Jean. *Morgan: American Financier.* New York: Harper, 2000.

Swedberg, Richard. *Schumpeter: A Biography.* Princeton, NJ: Princeton University Press, 1991.

Syrett, Stephen. *Contemporary Portugal: Dimensions of Economic and Political Change.* Aldershot, UK: Ashgate, 2002.

Szenberg, Michael, Lall Ramrattan, and Aron A. Gottesman, eds. *Samuelsonian Economics and the Twenty-First Century.* New York: Oxford University Press, 2006.

Szostak, Rick. *The Causes of Economic Growth: Interdisciplinary Perspectives.* Berlin: Springer, 2009.

Tavakoli, Janet M. *Structured Finance and Collateralized Debt Obligations: New Developments in Cash and Synthetic Securitization.* Hoboken, NJ: John Wiley & Sons, 2008.

Taylor, John B., ed. *Monetary Policy Rules.* Chicago: University of Chicago Press, 2001.

Tedlow, Richard. *The Rise of the American Business Corporation.* Philadelphia: Harwood Academic, 1991.

Teichman, Judith A. *Policymaking in Mexico: From Boom to Crisis.* New York: Routledge, 1988.

Temin, Peter. *Lessons from the Great Depression.* Cambridge, MA: MIT Press, 1989.

Thomas, Gordon, and Max Morgan-Witts. *The Day the Bubble Burst: A Social History of the Wall Street Crash of 1929.* New York: Penguin, 1980.

Thorp, Rosemary. *Progress, Poverty, and Exclusion: An Economic History of Latin America in the 20th Century.* Washington, DC: Inter-American Development Bank, 1998.

Thorp, Willard Long. *Economic Institutions.* New York: Macmillan, 1928.

———. *The New Inflation.* New York: McGraw-Hill, 1959.

Tibman, Joseph. *The Murder of Lehman Brothers: An Insider's Look at the Global Meltdown.* New York: Brick Tower, 2009.

Tilman, Rick, ed. *The Legacy of Thorstein Veblen.* Northampton, MA: Edward Elgar, 2003.

Tily, Geoff. *Keynes's General Theory, the Rate of Interest and 'Keynesian' Economics.* New York: Palgrave Macmillan, 2007.

Timmons, J., and S. Olin. *New Venture Creation: Entrepreneurship for the 21st Century.* Boston: McGraw-Hill, 2004.

Tinbergen, Jan. *Econometrics.* New York: Routledge, 2005.

Tirole, Jean. *Financial Crises, Liquidity, and the International Monetary System.* Princeton, NJ: Princeton University Press, 2002.

Tobin, James. *Essays in Economics: Macroeconomics.* Cambridge, MA: MIT Press, 1987.

———. *Full Employment and Growth: Further Keynesian Essays on Policy.* Cheltenham, UK: Edward Elgar, 1996.

Topik, Steven, Carlos Marichal, and Zephyr Frank, eds. *From Silver to Cocaine: Latin America Commodity Chains and the Building of the World Economy, 1500–2000.* Durham, NC: Duke University Press, 2006.

Treaster, Joseph B. *Paul Volcker: The Making of a Financial Legend.* Hoboken, NJ: John Wiley & Sons, 2004.

Trentmann, Frank. *Free Trade Nation: Commerce, Consumption, and Civil Society in Modern Britain.* New York: Oxford University Press, 2008.

Tuch, Hans N. *Arthur Burns and the Successor Generation: Selected Writings of and About Arthur Burns.* Lanham, MD: University Press of America, 1999.

Turner, Graham. *The Credit Crunch: Housing Bubbles, Globalisation and the Worldwide Economic Crisis.* London: Pluto, 2008.

Turner, Marjorie S. *Nicholas Kaldor and the Real World.* Armonk, NY: M.E. Sharpe, 1993.

Turner, Michael, ed. *Malthus and His Time.* Houndmills, UK: Macmillan, 1986.

Tvede, Lars. *Business Cycles: History, Theory, and Investment Reality.* New York: John Wiley & Sons, 2006.

Van Overtveldt, Johan. *The Chicago School: How the University of Chicago Assembled the Thinkers Who Revolutionized Economics and Business.* Chicago: Agate, 2007.

Veblen, Thorstein. *The Theory of Business Enterprise.* New York: A.M. Kelley, 1975. First published in 1904.

———. *The Theory of the Leisure Class.* New York: Dover, 1994. First published in 1899.

Viner, Jacob. *Balanced Deflation, Inflation, or More Depression.* Minneapolis: University of Minnesota Press, 1933.

———. *The Long View and the Short: Studies in Economic Theory and Policy.* New York: Free Press, 1958.

Visano, Brenda Spotton. *Financial Crises: Socio-economic Causes and Institutional Context.* New York and London: Routledge, 2006.

Volcker, Paul A. *The Rediscovery of the Business Cycle.* New York: Free Press, 1978.

———. *The Triumph of Central Banking?* Washington, DC: Per Jacobsson Foundation, 1990.

Von Neumann, John. *John von Neumann, Selected Letters,* ed. Miklós Rédei. Providence, RI: American Mathematical Society, 2005.

Von Neumann, John, and Oskar Morgenstern. *Theory of Games and Economic Behavior.* Princeton, NJ: Princeton University Press, 2007.

Wagener, Hans-Jürgen. *Economic Thought in Communist and Post-Communist Europe.* New York: Routledge, 1998.

Weil, David N. *Economic Growth.* Boston: Addison-Wesley, 2005.

Weintraub, E. Roy. *How Economics Became a Mathematical Science.* Durham, NC: Duke University Press, 2002.

Wells, Wyatt. *Economist in an Uncertain World: Arthur F. Burns and the Federal Reserve, 1970–1978.* New York: Columbia University Press, 1994.

White, Lawrence H. *A Theory of Monetary Institutions.* New York: Wiley-Blackwell, 1999.

White, Lawrence J. *The S&L Debacle: Public Policy Lessons for Bank and Thrift Regulation.* New York: Oxford University Press, 1991.

Wicker, Elmus. *Banking Panics of the Gilded Age.* New York: Cambridge University Press, 2000.

———. *The Banking Panics of the Great Depression.* 2nd ed. New York: Cambridge University Press, 2000.

Wigmore, Barrie A. *The Crash and Its Aftermath: A History of Securities Markets in the United States, 1929–1933.* Westport, CT: Greenwood, 1985.

Williams, Andrea D., ed. *The Essential Galbraith.* Boston: Houghton Mifflin, 2001.

Wilson, Scott. *Remade in China: Foreign Investors and Institutional Change in China.* New York: Oxford University Press, 2009.

Wolfson, Martin H. *Financial Crisis: Understanding the Postwar U.S. Experience.* Armonk, NY: M.E. Sharpe, 1986.

Wong, Stanley. *Foundations of Paul Samuelson's Revealed Preference Theory.* New York: Routledge, 2009.

Wood, Christopher. *The Bubble Economy: Japan's Extraordinary Boom of the '80s and the Dramatic Bust of the '90s.* New York: Atlantic Monthly, 1992.

Woodward, Bob. *Maestro: Greenspan's Fed and the American Boom.* New York: Simon & Schuster, 2001.

Wray, L. Randall. *Understanding Modern Money: The Key to Full Employment and Price Stability.* Northampton, MA: Edward Elgar, 2003.

Wright, Russell. *Chronology of the Stock Market.* Jefferson, NC: McFarland, 2002.

Yarbrough, Beth V., and Robert M. Yarbrough. *The World Economy: Trade and Finance.* Mason, OH: South-Western, 2006.

Yonay, Yuval P. *The Struggle over the Soul of Economics: Institutionalist and Neoclassical Economists in America Between the Wars.* Princeton, NJ: Princeton University Press, 1998.

Young, Warren. *Harrod and His Trade Cycle Group.* New York: New York University Press, 1989.

Zahariadis, Nikolaos. *State Subsidies in the Global Economy.* New York: Palgrave Macmillan, 2008.

Zamagni, Stefano, and Ernesto Screpanti. *An Outline of the History of Economic Thought.* New York: Oxford University Press, 1993.

Zandi, Mark. *Financial Shock: A 360° Look at the Subprime Mortgage Implosion, and How to Avoid the Next Financial Crisis.* Upper Saddle River, NJ: FT Press, 2009.

Zarnowitz, Victor. *Business Cycles: Theory, History, Indicators, and Forecasting.* Chicago: University of Chicago Press, 1992.

Zmirak, John. *Wilhelm Röpke: Swiss Localist, Global Economist.* Wilmington, DE: ISI Books, 2001.

Web Sites

Association of Southeast Asian Nations (ASEAN) Web site: www.aseansec.org.

Basel Committee on Banking Supervision Web site: www.bis.org/bcbs.

Conference Board Web site: www.conference-board.org.

Congressional Budget Office Web site: www.cbo.gov.

Consumers International Web site: www.consumers-international.org.

Council of Economic Advisers Web site: www.whitehouse.gov/administration/eop/cea.

Department of Housing and Urban Development Web site: www.hud.gov.

Dow Jones Indices Web site: www.djaverages.com.

Emerging Markets Monitor Web site: www.emergingmarketsmonitor.com.

European Central Bank Web site: www.ecb.int.

Executive Office of the President home page Web site: www.whitehouse.gov/administration/eop/.

Fannie Mae Web site: www.fanniemae.com.

FDIC Web site: www.fdic.gov.

Federal Housing Administration Web site: www.fha.com.

Federal Housing Finance Agency Web site: www.fhfa.gov.

Federal Housing Finance Board Web site: www.fhfb.gov.

Federal Reserve System Web site: www.federalreserve.gov.

Freddie Mac Web site: www.freddiemac.com.

Government Accountability Office Web site: www.gao.gov.

Government National Mortgage Association (GinnieMae) Web site: www.ginniemae.gov.

International Monetary Fund Web site: www.imf.org.

International Organization of Securities Commissions Web site: www.iosco.org.

Morgan Stanley Web site: www.morganstanley.com.

Mortgage Bankers Association Web site: www.mortgagebankers.org.

NASDAQ Web site: www.nasdaq.com.

National Venture Capital Association Web site: www.nvca.org.

New York Stock Exchange Web site: www.nyse.com.

Office of Federal Housing Enterprise Oversight Web site: www.ofheo.gov.

Office of Thrift Supervision Web site: www.ots.treas.gov.

Securities and Exchange Commission Web site: www.sec.gov.

Securities Industry and Financial Markets Association Web site: www.sifma.org.

Standard & Poor's Web site: www.standardandpoors.com.

Statistics Canada Web site: www.statcan.gc.gov.

Treasury Direct Web site: www.treasurydirect.gov.

U.S. Bureau of Labor Statistics Web site: www.bls.gov.

U.S. Department of Labor. "Wages" Web site: www.dol.gov/dol/topic/wages.

U.S. Department of the Treasury Web site: www.treasury.gov.

World Bank Web site: www.worldbank.org.

Index

Note: Page numbers in italic indicate illustrations; "t" indicates tables.